SATAN'S POWER

SATAN'S POWER

A Deviant Psychotherapy Cult

William Sims Bainbridge

University of California Press

Berkeley · Los Angeles · London

University of California Press
Berkeley and Los Angeles, California

University of California Press, Ltd.
London, England

ISBN 0-520-03546-1
Library of Congress Catalog Card Number: 77-80466
Printed in the United States of America

1 2 3 4 5 6 7 8 9

CONTENTS

ACKNOWLEDGMENTS

The advice and moral support of many colleagues contributed greatly to this research project. Without their constant interest and friendly criticism, I might not have been able to maintain my sanity and sociological perspective throughout my career in a very deviant world. Some were so brave as to accompany me on visits to the Power cult, while others, equally valorous, explored my manuscript to suggest ways it might be improved. I especially want to thank Grant Barnes, Alex Blumenstiel, Hedy Bookin, Barbara Cosgrove, Carol Fisler, Kathryn Garnhart, Cyndee Keen, John Lofland, George Oberhofer, George Psathas, Lee Rainwater, Marilyn Schwartz, Rodney Stark, Robert Wuthnow, and several anonymous reviewers.

I treasure the friendships I developed within the Power cult, and wish I could acknowledge by true name those astonishing Powerites who helped me most.

STATEMENT

To protect the privacy of the members of the cults I studied, I have given them all pseudonyms. I also invented the names Technianity, The Power, and The Establishment. In choosing new names for these people and groups I tried to convey the general style of the colorful names they adopted for themselves, while assuring their anonymity. Every other detail reported in this book is fact, either observed by me or told me by people I trust. Only the names are fictitious.

ONE

Rumors of Satan

IF A MAN ASKS: WHAT IS THE POWER? SAY TO HIM. It is
the End, the Final Ending of the world of men. It is the
agent of the End, the instrument of the End and the
inexorable Power of the End.

—*If A Man Asks*, Power scripture

This book is an analytic ethnography, a psycho-history of a Satanic cult. A
journalist might want to write on this subject because he could exploit
public interest in the bizarre. But why should a sociologist care? Surely
Satanic cults are rare and unimportant. There is some question if any really
exist at all. Sometimes, of course, we can learn about social life by inspect-
ing a tiny, unusual part of it. Durkheim discovered society behind the
solitude of suicide. If a real Satanic cult did exist, perhaps we could learn
from its rejection of society's virtues something new about society and about
virtue.

The Power was a Satanic cult, but it was other things as well. It began as a
psychotherapy movement and evolved into a religious community. What
separates psychotherapy from religion, and what happens at their common
border? The Power was born among normal young adults in the English
monied classes who fled London to live on a Mexican beach, then wandered
the streets of Europe and America begging. How can a cohesive deviant
group emerge from a diffuse network of conventional people? The Power
began with a few simple assumptions about the nature of the human personality and evolved a complex culture of Gods, symbols, rituals, songs, and
social customs. What are the ways that abundant new culture can be
created? The Power followed Satan but also pursued every other God and
spirit that promised a way out of the human condition. What are the ways
people seek to transcend the lives given them, and what are the results of
each kind of attempt? Satan, the God beneath contempt and beyond belief,
was an expression of The Power's will to escape the inhibitions of society. In
its erratic quest, the cult explored the margins of conventionality and
sojourned in more than one area of deviance.

I

CONFLICTING REPORTS

Colorful, bizarre, even terrifying, The Power called forth interest as well as antagonism from those who encountered it in the late 1960s. The cult's striking public performance evoked a variety of metaphors from reporters. Some journalists saw only the most superficial characteristics: "They wear dark space-suits with red Satanic emblems sewn on the chests and are usually accompanied by German-Shepherd dogs." Others pretended to see far beneath the surface and called the cult "Satan worshippers" and "mind-benders." One reporter visited the cult and was surprised to discover that Powerites were not really fiends from Hell. "What I found was no secret cult of drug-taking Devil worshippers, but one of the most curious, and curiously attractive, of all the unorthodox religions in America." Another reporter was impressed by the mysterious ambiguity surrounding The Power. "They have been charged with devil worship, rumored to perform ritual murder, accused of drinking dog's blood. While their church services and hierarchy would make a pope proud, their symbols and secrets are a gossip's playground."

The Power came to national attention in 1970 and 1971, when journalists publicly charged that it was ultimately responsible for the infamous Tate-LaBianca murders committed by Charles Manson and his followers. Without any good evidence, they wrote that Manson had been a member of The Power and indoctrinated in Satanism by it. The prosecutor in the Manson case said a direct connection with The Power could not be proved, but he felt the ideologies and structures of The Manson Family and The Power were so similar that some connection was quite likely. One journalist reported that The Power was extremely deviant sexually. He explained its success with converts as the natural result of this deviance:

The Power, as did Manson, employs sexual excesses as a means by which to shake loose any influence society may still hold over the initiates. Both groups practice communal living and indiscriminate sexual relations among members. . . . Savage and indiscriminate sex is forced on the entrants into the cult not as a means of religious communion but as a means of purging the initiates of any residue of Grey Forces [conventionality] that might be latent in them. Sex is a means of cutting members off from the outside and subjecting them to the will of the group, or the wills of the group leaders.

My years studying The Power convinced me that the specific claims of wickedness made by some outsiders were false, but that a quasi-sociological hypothesis hidden behind these stories was correct. I found no actual connection between Manson's murders and The Power. "Savage and indiscriminate sex" was not forced on new recruits. The Power was, however, a closed social universe created and maintained by intensive emotional interaction between participants. In this it resembles the Manson Family or any other small sect or deviant subculture embodied in a specific social group. Power-ites often spoke of "sexual energy" as the glue that held them together, referring not to orgiastic group experiences but simply to intense bonds of positive feeling that tied members together in a strong, closed social net-work.

Powerites enjoyed projecting a wild image. Their black uniforms and red emblems excited cult members as much as they worried the general public. In its own imagination The Power was a Satanic cult. ["Black is the color of the Bottomless Void to which the human race is doomed by its insistence upon a GODless compromise of living death. So Black we shall wear in mourning for the doom mankind has brought upon itself." Announcing themselves with such lurid rhetoric, the Beings of The Power stalked Europe and America in the late 1960s and early 1970s, dressed in sinister black uniforms with flowing cloaks, accompanied by huge Alsatian hounds and plagued by the vilest rumors, bearing on their chests the sign of the Devil, the red Mendes Goat badge. "And upon the Black we shall wear Red for the blood that man has shed amongst his fellow men. We shall wear Red for the blood of CHRIST that man has shed and still sheds to his own damnation. And we shall wear Red for the rivers of blood that shall be shed in the Latter Days, for man has taken blood and blood shall he give in recompense. And we shall wear Red for the Fires of Hell where the Lord SATAN shall execute the Final Judgement of the world."]

An outsider observing a Sabbath Assembly would have had few doubts that this was a real Satanic cult. Through the haze of heavy incense he would have seen swastika-like symbols carved in a wooden altar. The amber light of flickering candle flames was lost in the black uniforms of cult members but infused faces with the appearance of harsh strength. The outsider would have heard alien chants and terrifying proclamations. He might have been intimidated by the haughty tone of the officiating priests. Figure 1 shows a Sacrifist and Evangelist from the Power's Sabbath Assembly, dressed in their sacerdotal robes, standing in front of the painted face of Satan that dominated the ritual room. But of course first impressions are often wrong. The Power was easy to misunderstand because it was complex and richly metaphoric. Founded by young adults of the English middle class, it drew on occult and countercultural traditions to create a vivid lifestyle reminis-cent of a theatrical performance or a particularly innovative primitive tribe. Powerites wore many colorful uniforms and emblems, enacted dramatic

Figure 1. Powerite priests dressed for the Sabbath Assembly, standing in front of the Mendes Goat, symbol of Satan. The Sacrifist on the left and Evangelist on the right wear colorful tabards over their black gowns and carry red and black books of scripture

rituals, composed touching songs and chants, conducted intense public demonstrations, traveled over a range of seven thousand miles, and planted communes in several cities. Organized as a hierarchical secret society, The Power put neophytes through a series of occult therapeutic exercises called Telepathy Developing Circles, Progresses, Sessions, Powerplays, Mediumistics, and Enactments. Through scripture and seminars it instructed them in a large corpus of doctrine.

The Power was a Satanic cult, but *Satan* had a very special meaning for Powerites that no outsider could easily grasp. The complicated Power theology identified four Gods: Lucifer, Jehovah, Christ, and Satan. Lucifer, male God of the air, represents sensousness, liberality, and intellect. Jehovah, female God of the earth, represents austerity, authoritarianism, and emotion. The cult believed that cosmic forces were working for the Union as if in marriage of Lucifer and Jehovah. Christ, male God of the waters, gave himself in love for the unification of all beings and the resolution of conflict. Satan, female God of fire, reserved herself in hatred to achieve the separation of all beings and the propagation of conflict. The cult claimed that it was the terrestrial manifestation of the coming Unity of Christ and Satan, a force moving to achieve the end of the world in service of Satanic destruction so that a Christian Golden Age might dawn.

RESEARCH METHODOLOGY

The evidence on which this book rests was collected intermittently over a period of nearly six years through a variety of ethnographic methods. I first encountered Powerites in Boston near the end of 1970, when I was just completing a six months' study of another cult which I will call Technianity. At first I planned to investigate The Power only briefly, along with other groups, and develop a comprehensive theory of culture-creation through comparative analysis. Consequently, I began my research following the classical anthropological approach exemplified by Malinowski's work. Although I allowed myself to be initiated into the cult, I did not become a core participant but developed the status of friendly associate, an unobtrusive observer of Power rituals and interviewer of native informants. Although I felt my main task was documentation of the official culture of the group, I kept a detailed diary of field observations that included many reports of member interactions, problematic disruptions, and other revealing incidents.

I observed the Boston chapter of The Power consistently throughout 1971, then switched to relatively infrequent contact for the next three years. My time was monopolized by graduate study and by a research project about spaceflight. I was not free to devote much time to The Power. This limitation turned out to be a blessing in disguise. Because I was unable to devote my full time to research on the cult, my observations were stretched out over a long span of time, and I was able to witness many changes in group society and culture. Over this period of less intense contact, I documented changes in the rituals, shifts in cult policy, and also was able to increase my collection of documents and descriptions of relatively rare events such as weddings. In 1974, I became aware that The Power was suffering a great upheaval, although I had become so busy with other work that I could not observe the chaos and cataclysms firsthand. This limitation also turned out to be an advantage, because I was left free to establish good equal relations with all fragments of the cult after it split asunder. Had I been on the scene at the time of the great schism, I might have been identified with one faction rather than another, and my objectivity would have been compromised.

I reestablished contact with the two main fragments of the broken Power at the end of 1974. A Harvard freshman, George Oberhofer, came to my office in late September, looking for advice concerning a possible field research project he might undertake. I suggested he check out a group of dissident Powerites in the Boston area, and put him in touch with them. He proceeded to study this mini-cult at its house in Waltham, Massachusetts, and subsequently wrote two excellent term papers about them. In December, I joined George in his research on this splinter group and began intensive field investigations that continued for six months. Without the stimulus of George's project, I might never have returned to my Power research. But once I had become very active once more, I saw that I had the opportunity to complete a truly rich ethnographic social history.

Many of the Powerites I had come to know well in 1971 were then setting up a new cult headquarters in New York City, so I began visiting them as well. In 1975, I made excursions to see the groups in Chicago and Toronto. Edward de Forest, original founder and charismatic figure of The Power, had come to Boston late in 1974, a victim of the great schism, and over a period of six months I came to know him quite well. Ethnographer Rosalie Wax has commented that of all the factors that contribute to good field research, "no technique or talent is quite so valuable as luck."[1] My own experience supports her observation. I was extremely fortunate throughout my Power research. Threatened disasters never materialized; several times, as Edward himself said, I happened on the scene just as something revealing was happening. The schism that tore the cult in 1974 was a great advantage for my research, although a sad misfortune for members. The breakup not only produced much interesting material in itself, but also made possible many rich interviews and the collection of hundreds of pages of previously secret documents. The Power was a closed secret society that kept members in the dark until years after they joined, so without the schism it would have been far too expensive of my time and spirit to penetrate to the heart of the cult. Of course, it is common for groups like the Power to suffer fragmentation, and it is common for them to expel their charismatic leaders, so my luck consisted merely in being at the right place at the right time.

In 1975, researching the Boston dissidents, I had to take a much more participating role than before. I helped the group beg for food, did many errands with my car, and lived part-time in the Chapter House, sleeping on the floor or a couch. Conscious of the necessity of preserving my intellectual independence, I nonetheless felt it was justified to perform whatever tasks were given me. Therefore I participated in the rituals, playing the role of

[1] Rosalie Wax, *Doing Fieldwork* (Chicago: University of Chicago Press, 1971), p. 115.

priest in the Sabbaths, Telepathy Developing Circles, Meditations, and even three Baptisms. After being asked to do so, I also conducted doctrinal seminars for the cult; it was not necessary that I believe the doctrine, but rather that I understand it and be able to communicate it. Edward de Forest included me in a committee working to develop a formal correspondence course based on his Teachings. These tasks gave me the opportunity to test my understanding of Power culture in the most direct way, by demonstrating cultic competence.

The most important tool of data collection was of course my lengthy field diary. In the early months of my research I was a detached observer, forced to write my observations down a few hours after the fact, and therefore forced to memorize the rituals, chants, and interactions as best I could. It was actually rather easy to document the cult's official practices this way, because each ritual or therapy exercise would be repeated many times, permitting me to refine my descriptions until they were just right. By the end of my research I also had the benefit of the cult's own training and possessed copies of all the "ritual formats," documents written for Power priests delineating each step in each ritual. As time went on, there came to be more and more occasions when it was appropriate for me to take notes while actually in the field. Although my status with the group was ambiguous in the beginning, after the first year or so members were quite content to see me as both a sociologist and a friend. At the end, Powerites saw me as the historian of their cult.

Photography proved to be a very useful tool. The Power was an extremely visual cult, quite literally a colorful cult. I began in 1971 by taking pictures of Powerites on the streets, then gave copies of color prints to some of the cult members in them. The results convinced the leaders of the Boston Chapter to employ me to do photography work on a regular basis. The Power used my pictures in television appearances, in its magazines, on photo-identification cards for inner members, and for a variety of private purposes. Throughout the last half of 1971, I was able to document not only the clothing, physical setting, and work activities of the cult, but also some rituals and informal behavior. The photography allowed me to develop a relationship of happy reciprocity with the group, giving it useful services in return for sociological data.

Tape recordings proved invaluable. I made tapes of about two dozen rituals, including several Sabbaths, a Telepathy Developing Circle, an Evening Assembly, a Powerplay, midnight meetings, and even a marriage ceremony. The cult was happy to sell me recordings of about thirty of its radio programs to add to the half dozen I had taped off the air. In 1974 and 1975, my able research assistant George Oberhofer conducted recorded interviews with most members of the dissident Boston group. Subsequently, from March 1975 through September 1976, I used a tape recorder in interviewing cult members in Boston, New York, and Chicago. Many of the direct quotations in this book were taken from transcripts of these recordings.

Field research in The Power gave me many opportunities to collect cult artifacts. In this respect my project followed anthropological rather than sociological traditions. My collection includes many badges and other physical symbols of Power membership and rank: rings, crosses, other jewelry, Satanic emblems, priests' badges, and even a cultic belt buckle. I also obtained a hooded cloak and a priest's ritual tabard that were made by Powerites, two paintings of the Lord Satan, and a complete set of ritual furniture, including two carved priests' chairs and a circular altar with fire and water stands.

Over the years I was able to amass a large collection of Power literature, comprising every magazine and book that was publicly available, and also all the doctrinal scripture available to most inner members and many of the cult's administrative documents. My priest's Missal counts as both artifact and literature because it has an elegant black binding imprinted in red with the Power symbol. Although I constantly refer to cult scripture, administrative documents, and some correspondence in this book, I have not wasted the printer's time peppering my pages with footnotes. At the moment, essentially none of the Power material is publicly available, and we do not know what form it might take if it ever did achieve publication. With the thought that another scholar might undertake research on The Power at some time in the future, I have preserved copies of all the literature, but I see no point in giving the reader several hundred citations he cannot use.

Reports by journalists and a few term papers by college students provided some additional information, but the published sources on The Power are few and superficial. I drew upon a large corpus of published material on Technianity, the older cult from which The Power was in part derived. Although I give the names of students whose papers I cite, I have avoided footnoting the handful of newspaper articles and book chapters that mention The Power. To do so would be to reveal the acutal names of the cult itself and several of its members.

THEORETICAL ORIENTATION

This book is an analytical ethnography. It is neither a comparative study nor a theoretical treatise. However, it is informed by ideas from many sources and is concerned with the building of theory. The ethnographic task of this book leaves little room for the intensive comparative analysis that some readers might wish to see. My bibliography gives some hint of the wide range of social phenomena I see as basically similar to The Power. I have cited standard sociological theory only when it seemed necessary to explain and interpret the history of The Power. But it should be clear that I feel the social forces and structural principles I observed in this tiny, deviant cult are quite common in society and are found in settings and institutions of many kinds.

My original research aim, to discover ways that novel culture is socially generated, is partly achieved in this book. Because The Power turned out to be so interesting in its own right, I have concentrated on the one cult here, and plan to expand my cultural analysis in future projects of a comparative nature. Here I do show the basic processes by which Power culture was derived from Technianity and from the experiences of core Powerites, and describe the cultural transformations effected by The Establishment when it sought to break with the old Power.

After my first contacts with The Power, I developed a second theoretical interest. The Power appeared to be the only *polytheistic* group available for me to study. The Gods Lucifer, Jehovah, Christ, and Satan represented alternate moral systems, competing models of the ideal person, and even different intellectual conceptions of the world. How could a social group maintain mundane authority in the face of such celestial conflict? To what extent did the theology actually support multiple social and phenomenological realities? More generally, what happens when radically different ideologies attempt to co-exist within the same organization? The Power looked like a combination of medieval-authoritarian and modern-liberal values, and I wondered whether such a hybrid could possibly be viable.

These two theoretical interests immediately point to the body of theory that was most important for my project: the indigenous theory of The Power itself. Of course I was interested in the group's beliefs as an ethnographer. But beyond that, the ideology of The Power is a collection of alternate social theories. By and large, the occult is more of a deviant social science than it is a deviant description of the physical universe. The Power drew its inspiration not only from pseudosocial sciences like Technianity, but also from standard sources. The cult's Teacher, Edward de Forest, was influenced by classical psychoanalysis, for example, although it must be admitted he never studied the subject in a formal way. He accepted Freud's idea of the subconscious, Adler's goal theory, and Jung's notion of the collective unconscious, but acknowledges, "I've read hardly anything of these things. It's just what I pick up, what I hear people talk about, or what occasionally I see in some book that I happen to pick up in a bookshop and flip through." So the ideologies of cults may in part be loose extensions of standard social-scientific thinking as well as deviant alternatives to it. Sometimes a cult may independently invent a system of thought that is accepted within some branch of social science. As we will see, The Power developed a structuralist analytic perspective very similar to that of anthropologist Claude Lévi-Strauss; Powerites used this perspective not only to create their own ideology but also to interpret the mythological systems of other groups. Beyond their similarities with and connections to standard social science, the beliefs of The Power provide a valuable source of theory because they were developed through the living experience of the members. Just as I do not accept all the theories of my sociological colleagues, I am not a believer in The Power's ideological system. But it was an important source of theories and hypotheses.

My approach to sociological theory is thoroughly eclectic, with its main emphasis on the social-psychological level. While not a disciple of any particular psychoanalytic school, I am convinced that depth psychology analysis of individual persons is valid and valuable. Analysis of the microstructure of social relations is also important. In particular, I am interested both in understanding the positive social bond and in analyzing the strategic interaction of individuals seeking benefits from each other within intimate social settings. The nature and history of The Power render macro-sociological analysis less useful. I do not view The Power primarily as the product of the times and society in which it emerged, but of micro-social processes that take place to some extent in all ages and all societies.

Because of my social-psychological emphasis I have not attempted to follow the rich traditions of standard sociology of religion. I use terms like "cult," "sect," and "church" quite loosely because I want The Power to be defined by its own characteristics, not by the ideal-typical characteristics of a theoretical category to which we might assign it. It will be clear to anyone knowledgeable in the sociology of religion that many of the qualities of The Power are shared by other "religious" groups. But they are also common today in many other kinds of voluntary organizations, especially psychotherapy and communal groups. I happen to believe that it is most fruitful to step back from the traditions of the sociology of religion and look at the phenomena afresh simply as *social* phenomena to be interpreted and explained in terms of very general principles.[2] However, one specific theoreti-

---

[2] William Sims Bainbridge, book review of *God's Blueprints* by John McKelvie Whitworth, *American Journal of Sociology* 81:6 (May 1976): 1555–1556.

cal model from the sociology of religion has stimulated and guided my thinking from the very beginning of my research: the model of "conversion to a deviant perspective" proposed in 1965 by John Lofland and Rodney Stark.[3]

This model was developed on ethnographic data the two collected inside the first branch to reach America of the Korean messiah Sun Myung Moon's Unification Church. A single middle-aged woman had been sent over to launch the church in the states, and a small group of converts had clustered around her. Today the church is quite successful, but its growth was probably the result of a second importation attempt. Consequently, while the Lofland-Stark model is intended to apply to a wide range of phenomena, it was developed using data from a group that may not be entirely typical. Although The Power may not be typical of contemporary religious communities either, it is sufficiently different from The Unification Church to provide a valuable comparison.

The Lofland-Stark model is eclectic, and although it is said to be "based on a 'value-added' conception," [4] it may be interpreted best as a collection of factors that facilitate conversion, rather than as a rigid causal sequence. This model can be adapted to describe the original formation of a deviant subculture, as well as the later recruitment of new members. It states:

For conversion it is necessary that a person:
1. experience enduring, acutely felt tensions;
2. within a religious, problem-solving perspective;
3. which lead to defining himself as a religious seeker;
4. encountering the cult at a turning point in his life;
5. wherein an affective bond to adherents is formed (or pre-exists);
6. where extra-cult attachments are low or neutralized;
7. and where, to become a "deployable agent," exposure to intensive interaction is accomplished.[5]

By "deployable agent," Lofland and Stark mean a committed member who will do as he is told and may be used to recruit more converts. The life histories they give of converts make it abundantly clear that by "tensions" they mean serious life problems caused in most cases by personal inadequacy. Lofland says that points 1 to 3 describe a predisposition to join and may be considered as *background factors*, or what are classically called predisposing factors. Points 4 to 7 he calls *situational factors*.

[3] John Lofland, *Doomsday Cult*, (Englewood Cliffs, N.J.: Prentice-Hall, 1966). John Lofland and Rodney Stark, "Becoming a World-Saver: A Theory of Conversion to a Deviant Perspective," *American Sociological Review* 30:6 (1965): 862–875.

[4] Lofland and Stark, "Becoming A World-Saver," p. 863. Neil J. Smelser, *Theory of Collective Behavior* (New York: Free Press, 1962).

[5] Lofland, *Doomsday Cult*, p. 8.

My interviews with early converts to The Power indicated that point number 3, *religious seekership*, was unimportant for this middle-class cult. Few of the original Powerites said anything that indicated they were actively seeking a specifically religious solution to life problems at the time they converted. The fourth item, *turning point*, is a bit ambiguous. Although some Powerites said they were at loose ends, others did not. Looking backward, they saw their conversion as *constituting* a turning point, so perhaps this item is tautological or poorly articulated. In itself, the idea may not explain anything not already explained by other elements in the Lofland-Stark model. It can be interpreted either as a subjective feeling held by a person that some life decision is necessary, or as an objective description of a time when a person's social relations and institutional commitments are temporarily quite weak and he is open to new involvements.

Rather than accept the model as a rigid system, I extracted from it three fundamental themes useful in forming the basis of an analysis of The Power. They are:

1. Pre-existing, acutely felt tensions (point 1)
2. Problem-solving perspective (point 2)
3. Evolving structure of personal relationships (points 5–7)

All three will be discussed at appropriate places in this book. Each is a reasonable hypothesis and a good conceptual tool. But it is the third that explains best the origin of The Power. The key to a proper sociological understanding is analysis of the evolving structure of social relations among members and between members and prospective converts. I am not the only sociologist who would prefer to separate the Lofland-Stark model into its elements and test each one against the others. An associate of Lofland and Stark, Travis Hirschi, has outlined three "fundamental perspectives on delinquency and deviant behavior." Each one is meant to describe several popular sociological theories, yet each describes only part of the Lofland-Stark model. Hirschi summarizes the tenets of the three perspectives:

According to *strain* or motivational theories, legitimate desires that conformity cannot satisfy force a person into deviance. According to *control* or bond theories, a person is free to commit delinquent acts because his ties to the conventional order have somehow been broken. According to *cultural deviance* theories, the deviant conforms to a set of standards not accepted by a larger or more powerful society.[6]

The "tension" assumed as a pre-condition in the Lofland-Stark model represents *strain* motivating a person to take radical action. The implication in many statements of strain theory, certainly the feeling conveyed by

[6] Travis Hirschi, *Causes of Delinquency*, (Berkeley: University of California Press, 1969), p. 3.

Lofland and Stark, is that the "tension" or "strain" that motivates deviant behavior must be unusual, must represent deprivation in comparison to the person's reference group. But is it true that only people beset by extreme life problems or suffering from something like psychopathology join deviant movements? Stark has presented very convincing evidence that psycho-pathology and religious commitment are not connected, at least for members of relatively conventional religious groups.[7] There is also good evidence that members of some deviant religious communities show average or better than average mental health.[8] Robert Ward Wilson's recent review of the social-psychological literature on conversion produced no simple con-clusions, unless it is that we cannot say much of anything about the types of personality most likely to experience religious conversion.[9] An important theme of this book is an exploration of the connection, if any, between membership in a deviant cult and the experience of "enduring, acutely felt tensions."

A religious problem-solving perspective, presumably acquired in child-hood as part of the culture in which the person was socialized, represents *cultural deviance*, at least from the perspective of many irreligious social scientists. The cultural strands analyzed in this book are many and complex. The Power can be analyzed as the result of contact and interpene-tration of different cultural traditions, for example as the marriage of Angli-canism and Psychoanalysis. But I argue that for the most part culture has its base in social realities. It can influence social reality, acting as the memory and imagination of the social organism, but ultimately arises from social life and is its reflection, not its cause.

The remaining elements of the Lofland-Stark model focus on the social bond. A person at a "turning point" when attachments to people in the conventional order "are low or neutralized" is free of *control*, and therefore open to new commitments. I will present the hypothesis that the key factor in cult formation and conversion is the development by any number of processes of social structure of a certain shape. Because I think the proper structural conditions may themselves have many different causes, I do not believe facile, all-encompassing explanations of cults and their features are possible. The more precise and universally correct a "theory of cults" becomes, the closer it is to being a mere definition.

[7] Rodney Stark, "Psychopathology and Religious Commitment," *Review of Religious Research* 12:3 (1971): 165–176.

[8] Joseph W. Eaton and Robert J. Weil, *Culture and Mental Disorders* (Glencoe, Illinois: Free Press, 1955). Benjamin Zablocki, *The Joyful Community* (Baltimore: Penguin, 1971).

[9] Robert Ward Wilson, "A Social-Psychological Study of Religious Experience with Special Emphasis on Christian Conversion" (unpublished doctoral dissertation, University of Florida, 1976).

I define *cult* as *a culturally innovative cohesive group oriented to supernatural concerns.* Cults have existed in many ages of history, and at many times they have been an accepted variant or even the preferred form of religious society. My data suggest that a cult can arise without the necessity of either strain or cultural deviance. Therefore a theory of cults need not be a theory of deviance. But although times and standards are changing, cults are deviant at the moment from the standpoints of most people. Until they are so numerous as to define acceptable variance, if not conventionality itself, cults will be implicated in many kinds of social deviance in ways that conventional churches may not be. And, in a sense, my definition of a cult suggests a quality of deviance: in that a cult is innovative, it is deviant with respect to the past; in that it is cohesive, it is deviant with respect to outsiders; and in that it is oriented to the supernatural, it is deviant with respect to everyday concerns. The complex interplay between deviance and conventionality in the formation and persistence of a cult is a major theme of this book.

The Power was deviant, but it cannot be understood merely through theories of deviance nor from a narrow social problems perspective. In analyzing the formation of cults we have to bring to bear everything we know about cultural and social differentiation. To understand the life and customs of a cult we must use all the intellectual tools of social science developed for understanding human society. In short, we must realize that *cult is culture writ small.*

AN OUTLINE

The structure of this book is dictated by my historical, ethnographic, and theoretical purposes. Following this introduction, Chapters Two through Five recount the history of The Power from its birth in 1963 to its height just before the schism of 1974. The historical survey first describes the emergence of the cult as a deviant subculture born from conventional middle-class English society through the mechanism of a pseudo-psycho-therapy group. Next, it follows the Powerites to a wild beach on the Yucatan peninsula and shows the steps through which the group came to be a church. Then, the story follows the erratic wanderings of Satan's Horde all over Europe and North America on their quest for a door out of this world, and examines the paradoxical period in which they reversed course and tried to gain acceptance in the world as an established and progressively more conventional church.

The next three chapters describe The Power at its height, when six branches of the church were founded in North America, the culture was most perfectly developed, and the unusual lifestyle blossomed. These chapters describe Power life, the procedure of joining and the communal existence of members, the Gods, symbols, and chief rituals, and the variety of deviant psychotherapy practices followed by the cult.

The historical narrative resumes in Chapter Nine with The Great Separation, the schism in which the nominal leader of the cult was expelled and the cult's organization disappeared in the formation of The Establishment Church of the Apocalypse. There follows the rocky tale of the second Power created by the exiled charismatic leader and a band of dissidents who clustered around him. The book concludes with a retrospective view and the recognition of Satan's triumph over Her own creatures.

Image and analysis alternate and intermingle throughout this book. At times I decided to let my analysis lie implicit in descriptive passages, at others I wrote separate analytical sections. The Power was extremely complex, created by highly intelligent, thoroughly educated young men and women. I cannot describe it quickly, but some kind of introduction is necessary. Let us begin with a vignette taken from my own experience.

A SABBATH IN THE WOODS

We had to get out of the city. The sun was setting, and it was nearly time for our Sabbath Assembly, the most sacred hour of a Powerite's week. Providence, Rhode Island, was not in fact a place of providence, and gave us no freedom to shout the praises of Jehovah, Lucifer, Christ, and Satan. We drove north along the river in our Champion camper, seven of us searching for a secluded place.

We had just come from The Rubicon, a second-floor, scruffy, anti-drug youth hangout, where we had flashed our capes and spoken of the Unity of Christ and Satan. An Italian guy in a checked shirt had liked the idea of Satan and made us explain why we wore not only silver crosses but also red and black badges showing the head of the Prince of Darkness, half goat and half man.

"I think it's wild," he said, "because I agree with the whole idea. I'm not so sure I feel it's necessary to have symbols, but I do agree with the concept, very much so. I recognize that there's a lot of crap in me. A lot of bullshit. I'm fucked-up in a lot of ways. All my life, eighteen and a half years, I spent pushing that down, saying 'If I think about these things, and I feel these things, they make me unique.' You know what I'm saying? I mean *nobody* ever felt like a homosexual before! Or *nobody* ever fucked their male cousin in the ass! You know what I'm saying? Or maybe the way I treated my mother, or my parents, the little screw-up things I did against them. All these things, I kind-of stuffed them down."

He had gone on at length about the intensity with which he used to despise himself. Even now, the Christ and Satan within him were not entirely reconciled. "I mean, I'm screwy. I'm crazy. I'm a little perverted." Then we realized he was not really responding to us, to the message of The Power, but was giving a testimonial for The Rubicon, explaining how much comfort and release he had been given. These were among the products The Power was selling, but without the deviant religious packaging of our polytheistic cult. He continued his spiel. "I sat down with a guy and I was talking with him about some of these things, and he said, 'Yeah. I feel thé same way.' I says, 'Oh, shit!' 'Wait a minute,' I says, 'what are you talking about?' And he got into it, and he explained how everyone feels these things at some times and acts this way and that way. And at first I said maybe it's just him and me. I got into it, and holy shit! It was like three hundred pounds of cement off my back!"

We nodded and told him The Power had also lifted many burdens. We were glad his were lighter through the realization that everyone is dominated by the Power of Satan at one time or another. "With Satan there is no right or wrong, no success or failure. There is simply what is. Satan demands nothing." We took our leave from The Rubicon. "As it is. . . ." we gave The Power's passwords, ". . . so be it."

We had to get out of the city. After seven o'clock, Saturday, October 23, 1971, we were driving north out of Providence, hurrying to find a setting for a makeshift Alpha. Then, on the left, there were trees at the other side of a meadow. It was some kind of park. We suddenly realized we didn't have a single candle! Sister Eve and Sister Roxana ran down the road to a line of houses, ringing doorbells looking for someone willing to donate a half dozen candles for "a religious ceremony." Sister Ishtar turned the pages of our Sabbath Assembly Book, choosing hymns and pointing them out to Brother Thomas, who would be Music Officer. We needed a bowl of water, to symbolize the life-giving power of Christ, and a bowl of fire, to symbolize the purifying power of Satan.

Christ's water was easy enough—a plastic cereal bowl filled from the camper's sink. Satan's fire was a problem. Brother Mark struggled to make an oil lamp out of a shoe polish can. Brother Eros looked on with his always vaguely interested, always vaguely friendly expression, and agreed that the shoe polish can had promise. Sister Ishtar was convinced it would never work. Eve and Roxana climbed back into our van. They had candles! Wonderfully red Satanic candles. Mark punched a hole in the top of the can, and inserted a torn bit of shoe polishing cloth for a wick. He poured vegetable oil into the can and struck a match to give Satan's fire a trial run. It burned perfectly, a steady, bright flame.

The sky was dark now. We crossed the field and went into the woods a short distance along a narrow path. There was a little clearing ahead, just large enough for us to form a tight circle. We arranged everything where it belonged and sat on the dry leaves. Brother Mark placed himself at one end of the circle, and Sister Ishtar sat opposite him. They were both of Prophet rank, senior to the rest of us. He would be the Sacrifist in the ceremony, she the Evangelist. We lit the shoe polish lamp and opened our Assembly books. Eros lit candles and gave them to us to hold or stick into the soft earth. The wind threatened to blow out the flames, so we sat close together and spread our capes on each other's shoulders. We began the first chant, a proper chant to sing outdoors at night beneath the Heavens:

> Contact reaching to the stars
> Through the Spirit of the Christ;
> Knowledge of the Universe,
> He is the way to life.

Brother Mark began the Declaration. "The Final Reckoning."

Sister Ishtar responded. "An End and a New Beginning."

Mark continued. "And for this purpose Christ and Satan joined."

Ishtar answered him. "The Lamb and the Goat."

"Pure Love, descended from the pinnacle of Heaven, united with pure Hatred raised from the depths of Hell."

"Repayment of the debt."

"Fulfillment of the promise."

"All conflicts are resolved."

"An End and a New Beginning."

"The End of Hell and the Beginning of Heaven."

"The End of Darkness and the Beginning of Light."

"The End of War and the Beginning of Peace."

"The End of Hatred and the Beginning of Love."

"The End is now. The New Beginning is to come."

Brother Thomas announced the first hymn, "And the Clarion Calls." We sang joyously of the joining of the Gods and the birth of new life. "Beauty and power in the light of the sun, now that the Gods are One. We have the gift of love through the Gods. And the battle is won!"

Eros turned the pages of one of our magazines and read by the glow of a dancing candle flame. "Brethren, the Relevance is taken from *The Power on Death*." It was a passage about Lucifer, the quiet God of sensuous love, opponent in The Conflict of the Mind to the harsh, aggressive Jehovah.

"Lucifer is the God of Rebirth and Immortality; have faith—in yourself, in your undying spirit, in your future, most of all in your immortality. This is what matters: that in the end, you are infinite; in GOD you are infinite.

"For you, there is no death without rebirth. Death is the gate to life. And no man passes through the gate, but he reaches the other side.

"Before death is birth, and after death is rebirth. In your death you will be reborn." While Eros read, Thomas played a quiet melody on his guitar. "As it is. . . ." Eros concluded. We responded, ". . . so be it." Thomas plucked a strong, harmonious chord on his instrument to simulate a stroke on the big brass gong we used back at the Boston Chapter House.

Mark, Eve, and Thomas recited The Convocation of the Gods, explaining who the Gods were and how they were coming together, playing their roles in the End. We sang the hymn "Rise Up, Rise Up," then meditated for a while "on the purpose of our lives in service to Christ and the Gods." Mark read The Prophecy of the End, describing in horrendous language the coming apocalypse. After each terrifying phrase we chanted, "And we shall conquer fear with love!" There was more recitation, then we sang again:

> Cleanse us in the Water of Life,
> Purify our Souls in Your Fire,
> Holy Father, Holy Mother,
> Christ and Satan, Unity and Love,
> God and Goddess, Salvation to our GOD.

Sister Ishtar rose to her feet to begin the evangelical Revelation. "Brethren!" She looked down at each of us, an expression of pride and comradeship on her face. "There aren't many religious groups, or any kind of group really, that would consider this a religious ceremony, or be able to sit out in the woods with a can of shoe wax as a fire and scrappy pieces of paper as religious articles. But we are. And the reason we are is because we don't need the materialistic things to bring the presence of the Gods and the Beings to us. While we were invocating the Gods, a leaf fell down right in the middle of us, which was in a way a message of them telling us, 'We're here.' "

She had seen how often we looked around us in the dark, expecting to be disturbed, chased by police or interrupted by strangers. She assured us, "There are no physical beings here, but there are thousands and thousands of Beings and Superbeings which are gathered here right now. Because they can feel our presence. They can feel our worship."

Ishtar spoke of the great purpose each of us has, however much it may be hidden beneath the triviality of each mundane day. "We each have a particular relationship to one another in terms of the Hierarchy, and in terms of the Game." The Sabbath was one way of validating the Gods and reasserting our sense of purpose. "We're given energy and spurts of energy at particular times during the day to fulfill particular kinds of functions. Ten minutes ago we were all exhausted. And now we're all out here completely filled with energy, because there's a service that we have to give to the Gods. And They're all here."

"This is a very special trip," she told us. "It's the first one of its kind. We're making history." It is the first evangelical tour of Southern New England in the camper which was just brought up from the New Orleans Chapter. I am the first person of lowly Initiate rank to go on a Boston Power expedition. It will be the most documented trip, because I am taking photographs for the *Love* issue of our magazine, and Roxana is taking notes for an article to go around them. But for the seven participants, two Prophets, one IP Messenger, three OP Messengers, and one Initiate, it is an historical trip because it places their lives within a meaningful historical context, within the Latter Days leading to the Final Judgement. We make History by our every act. "Without The Power, we wouldn't be able to do this. We'd be nothing. And with The Power we're able to know that we belong and that we have a purpose in life."

Ishtar turned toward me. "And now, all those Initiates who would like to rededicate their lives in service of Christ and the Three Great Gods of the Universe, come forward now and kneel before me."

I knelt and bowed my head, gripped by emotion and by paradox. In my own mind I rededicated myself to the research project which has now produced this book. Ironically, I now feel that in a sense that was the same as dedicating myself to The Power and to the Great Gods. All six of the others, Mark, Ishtar, Eve, Thomas, Eros, and Roxana, have remained together in a Church, but the Church is no longer itself. Two and a half years later, these people expelled their charismatic leader, Edward de Forest, expelled the Gods Lucifer, Christ, and Satan, leaving only rigid, narrow, old Jehovah. They rejected the living essence of the cult by discarding the dynamic name *Power* for the static name *Establishment*. In 1975, after that grey revolution, Ishtar would use her "telepathic powers" in a Psychic Workshop to discover that my chief secret virtue was "Loyalty." She did not know what that meant. In the woods, in 1971, she stood over me and said, "In the Name of the Lord Christ, and in the Name of the Lord Satan, I accept you as Initiate of The Power—Church of Armageddon. As it is."

I replied, "So be it."

We sang two more hymns, ending with the phrase, "The evils of the world of men are perishing, Satan's Hordes consume them. Out of the ashes of the old shall arise the beginnings of a New Age." "Brethren," said Roxana, "the Assembly is now ended. As it is. . . ." We responded together, "So be it." We rose and walked along the forest path. Power means change. That Sabbath in the woods captured the living Power as it was at that instant. It was never the same.

We had to return to The Rubicon to hold a Midnight Meditation for the troubled teenagers there. We were about to drive off when we saw a young man and young woman walking hand-in-hand beside the road. They stopped near the place we had held our Assembly, and knelt, facing the spot, with bowed heads. Had they seen our service? Had they sensed the magic we had drawn to earth? They meditated for a moment, then went on their way.

TWO

A Social Implosion

> But when all is brought together, when space and time
> no longer channel all existence into a chaos of tiny pieces
> divorced by the dimensions from each other, but instead
> feed back the splinters, concentrate them outside the
> separating limits of dimensional existence, so that all
> may become one, having one nature, one substance, one
> being, one orientation, one power, one truth, one
> knowledge, one awareness . . . then we can say . . .
> "GOD IS."
>
> —*God Is*, Power scripture

The Power is not a thing but a force, an unfolding, a mode of evolution. Sister Samantha told me, "It's been said the only thing that's absolutely definite about us is change." Looking back on the changes over a dozen years of his membership in the cult, Father Moses said, "The whole evolution was a continuous revelation experience." Not only was it different at different times, but each Powerite experienced his own Power. To Edward de Forest, the cult's Teacher, The Power is the projection of his own mind's subconscious processes, linked magically to the cosmic processes of universal history. To other Powerites, it is the collective adventure they have shared in their quest for an unnamable goal. In the beginning, it was the personal, private relationship between Edward de Forest Jones and Kitty McDougal. For a dozen years they worked as partners in love and partners in building a movement. They shared high intelligence and an interest in uncovering the secret nature and hidden powers of the mind. In every other way they were exact opposites. They discovered Gods in each other and invented a world in their imagination.

EDWARD AND KITTY

Edward de Forest Jones was born in Shanghai, China, October 8, 1935, the son of an engineer and the grandson of a barrister and of a vicar. Before he was a year old, Edward's mother returned with him to England. He says, "My upbringing was fairly conventional middle-class English, reasonably happy and uneventful." After the Second World War, his father became

managing director of a time recorder company, "built the company up from
virtually nothing when he took it over . . . to a thriving enterprise when he
sold out a few years before his retirement." Edward's family was large and
extended. In addition to an older sister and two younger brothers, he
enjoyed the proximity of many relatives, a number of them fairly well
connected. One great uncle was an earl. Another served in Parliament for a
decade at the turn of the century. One was an unsuccessful inventor, devis-
ing a horse race game, a tennis ball practice set, and an air raid turret
shelter, among other things that did not sell. Uncle Prim, who was
wounded at the capture of Delville Wood in 1916, is a haughty and proper
gentleman. The family seems thoroughly respectable, hovering just at the
bottom of the English upper class. This impression is given not only by
Edward himself, but by the reports of those who know his parents, and in
the pages of a family genealogy printed by grandfather Reverend Albert
Jones. Edward's sister Audrey married and settled in Canada to run a riding
academy. All three of the brothers wound up professional members of cults.
The youngest, Arthur, joined Edward in The Power, and is now called
Father Remus. The other brother, Harold, was at last report a leader of the
California Technianity organization.

Edward received a strict Christian training at an exclusive private school.
He was offered a slot at a leading university to study toward an engineering
degree, but, unsure in motivation, he decided to satisfy his military obliga-
tion before continuing his schooling. In 1954, he began training for the
elite *Lifeguards* display cavalry unit, but then transferred to the more active
15th–19th King's Royal Hussars. For six months he was stationed with the
hussars in Malaya, where the British were successfully fighting Communist
insurgents. He says the hussars, like the Lifeguards, were too "twee," that
is, too affected. A transfer brought him back to England and lodged him
first in a unit made up of men who shared the single characteristic of being
misfits. He ended his service in 1958 as transport officer in a transport unit
stationed in Wareham, Dorsett.

Edward reckons that his time in the cavalry was excellent training and
experience. There he developed aristocratic poise and a dignified bearing,
great assets for the charismatic leader of a cult. At discharge from the
military he was entitled to only a single month of educational benefits,
which he invested in an art course. He then spent three years studying at an
architectural institute. He completed the training necessary for his Inter-
mediate Certificate, but did not go the full five years to get an architectural
license. Edward learned basic principles of design, useful not only for
designing cult symbols, but also transferable in a more abstract way to the
designing of doctrinal structures.

Edward vividly described his struggle with sexual inhibitions given him by his prudish Anglican training. He says it wrongly convinced him that religion and sex were incompatible. His first marriage, bland and uninspiring, did not last, and he says very little about it. I am told he fathered two children, but I know nothing about them. In 1962 he was ready for a change.

Kitty McDougal's background was in most respects the exact opposite of Edward's. She was the illegitimate daughter of Kate McDougal, a Scottish woman. Her father, also a Scot, left Kate before Kitty was born. Kitty was raised not by her mother, but by a succession of relatives. Perhaps I should say she was not raised by anyone, but simply grew up on her own. She was poorly treated as a child and learned quickly how to take care of herself. Kitty boasts that she came from the wretched Gorbals section of Glasgow, and claims she never had a single day of formal education. The only person who ever gave her love in those years was an older man who died of exposure sleeping off a drunk behind a warehouse. He had vainly wrapped himself in newspapers against the cold.

Kitty apparently learned well the skill of giving men what they wanted at her price, and rose to become the favored companion of prominent Londoners. She was a keen observer of other persons' feelings, and used her insight to control them for both her protection and her gain. A famous actor and a world-renowned comedian were among her series of male friends, and at one time she was going to marry a famous prizefighter. She was maintained well by her London friends, kept in furs and comfort by their generosity.

Kitty's lifestyle was not, however, one of great security. She had many friends and admirers, but there was only one certainty ahead—as she aged, her successes would be gained with greater and greater difficulty. There was no obvious resting point. She had no legitimate career and had experienced a long series of temporary intimate relationships. If she were to find security while still maintaining the excitement to which she was accustomed, she would have to strike out in a new direction. She was a demanding and emotionally volatile person. Relatively indifferent to the sufferings of humans in war, she became furious at any mistreatment of animals. It is said she once smashed a television set because it was showing pictures of a bullfight. Perhaps she identified with the powerless, abused creature fighting gallantly in a hopeless struggle. In 1962, she also was ready for a change.

Two kinds of personal characteristics of Edward and Kitty deserve analysis, two areas of personal qualities that guided them in the creation of The Power and made success possible: *skills and needs*.

First, they possessed skills and native abilities that when combined made them an extremely effective team. Both had high native intelligence. Their minds had been educated in opposite and complementary directions. Edward had learned to write elegantly in school, to project an aristocratic bearing in the military, and to design logical structures in his architectural studies. Kitty had learned the effective exploitation of other persons' emotional needs, based on deep understanding of each individual; her power was sufficient to make some individuals thoroughly dependent on her. Edward was trained in those skills necessary to make him the doctrinal Teacher of the cult and its charismatic leader, while Kitty could provide the personal analysis and intense emotional commitment required to bind and control the first ranks of members.

Second, they were driven by intense, complementary needs that guided their actions and resulted in a highly creative synthesis. Edward had been unsure of himself and of his future for a long time, suffering acutely in a struggle to cast off the sexual inhibition that had dominated his upbringing. Kitty's life had always been chaotic and devoid of stable focus. Because the kinds of tension they experienced were nearly opposite, the solutions they sought were in opposite directions. Edward, depressed and dependent, wanted someone to intervene in his life to repair it. He wanted to explore his own feelings, escape from his inhibition, and receive Love. Kitty, anxious and aggressive, wanted absolute control over other people so they would serve her, yet never betray her. She wanted to develop her already strong personality, bend people perfectly to her will, and achieve Power. Having experienced repression, Edward sought liberation. Having experienced disorganization, Kitty sought control.

In Lofland's terminology, Edward and Kitty had opposite problem-solving perspectives. One might construct many typologies of these perspectives. Lofland suggests that our society primarily offers members a choice of three "alternate perspectives, or rhetorics, that specify the nature and sources of problems and offer some program for their resolution," the psychiatric, the political, and the religious.[1] These three types are only distinct, I believe, because each is connected to a different standard societal institution. The Power was created apart from any other church, political party, or medical institution. It was both religious and psychotherapeutic. If we define *problem-solving perspective* broadly as constituting any cluster of major assumptions about how human problems can be solved, rather than identifying it with one or another standard societal institution, then the orientations of Edward and Kitty are opposite but complementary perspec-

---

[1] John Lofland, *Doomsday Cult.* (Englewood Cliffs, N.J.: Prentice-Hall, 1966), pp. 41–42.

tives. His was a *liberation perspective*; hers was a *control perspective*. The two could fit together in the same way that a masochist and a sadist can achieve a complementary relationship; to some extent each provided what the other wanted.

These opposing tendencies equally guided The Power in its development, at times conflicting, at times cooperating. When the theology was in its most developed state, Kitty's control orientation was expressed in the personality of the aggressive, female God Jehovah; Edward's liberation orientation was expressed in the personality of the passive, male God Lucifer. We will discuss the Great Gods of the Universe later, but it is important to realize from the start that the beliefs of The Power were projections of the personalities of its founders.

Their needs and their perspectives on how to satisfy them derived from their individual life experiences. But these experiences in turn derived from their social origins. Edward came from the respectable, repressed middle class. Kitty came from the despised, chaotic underclass that lurks beneath the stable working class. Using language slightly different from mine to describe the strata of society, John Howard has written on the Hippie movement of the 1960s, a type of deviant people who tended to find The Power attractive. Howard thought he saw consistent differences between the classes in their attitudes toward drugs and therapy groups. He said there is a "common middle-class belief in the need to 'break out' " of a confining culture. "The socialization experience of middle-class children probably gives them the sense of a 'divided self,' the sense that there is an inner self which is more joyous, more buoyant, freer, and more innocent than the controlled, proper, achieving outer self."[2] This desire to break out, to liberate the inner self in all its narcissistic glory, was important for most early members of The Power, but not Kitty. Howard believes that other social classes typically have other needs.

It is not clear that lower-class people feel this bifurcation, this schizoid burden. Indeed, middle- and lower-class people appear to have opposite problems. Whereas middle-class people exert themselves to facilitate impulse expression, lower-class people strive for impulse control. Whereas the middle class strives to be less "proper," lower-class people strive for propriety. Encounter groups encouraged people to touch each other; group members were encouraged to get outside themselves, experience others in sensate ways which violate middle-class conceptions of personal boundaries. It is not clear that lower-class people feel constrained in the same way.

Middle-class people, then, spend a good deal of time, money, and energy seek-

[2] John R. Howard, *The Cutting Edge* (Philadelphia: Lippincott, 1974), p. 188.

ing therapies, experiences, or substances which will enable them to break out. Lower-class people use drugs, but without the elaborate ideology which attends middle-class use. In addition, they use drugs for a different reason. Whereas middle-class people want to break out of lives experienced as too confining, lower-class people seek to forget lives experienced as too harsh and painful.[3]

Anthropologist Anthony F. C. Wallace has framed a similar general hypothesis about which kinds of therapy will be emphasized in cultures experiencing different social conditions:

In a highly organized sociocultural system, the psychotherapeutic needs of individuals will tend to center in catharsis (the expression of suppressed or repressed wishes in a socially nondisturbing ritual situation); and . . . in a relatively poorly organized system, the psychotherapeutic needs will tend to center in control (the development of a coherent image of self-and-world and the repression of incongruent motives and beliefs).[4]

Many sociological studies of psychiatric health care delivery support the idea that the higher social classes seek, if not liberation, at least warm, personal expression in therapy, while the lower classes seek means to establish quick and firm control over their lives.[5] It is possible that this class difference is not a necessary one, the result either of accidental historical circumstances or the imposition of an unjust system by the dominant classes. In any case, Howard's and Wallace's observations apply well to the people who created The Power, and to those who came later to become members. The issue of liberation-versus-control was one of the most powerful forces in the history of the cult, and is a major theme of this book.

ALFRED ADLER

Both Edward and Kitty independently became interested in the work of psychoanalyst Alfred Adler, most particularly in his extremely simple theory of human goals. Edward described it as a theory of *compulsive goals*, saying Adler assumed each person "was in pursuit of something, and he wasn't speaking of the conscious aims and ambitions that we all have, but

[3] Ibid., p. 189.

[4] Anthony F. C. Wallace, "The Institutionalization of Cathartic and Control Strategies in Iroquois Religious Psychotherapy," in *Culture and Mental Health*, ed. Marvin K. Opler (New York: Macmillan, 1959), p. 94.

[5] August B. Hollingshead and Frederick Redlich, *Social Class and Mental Illness* (New York: Wiley, 1958). Stanley T. Michael, "Social Class and Psychiatric Treatment," *Journal of Psychiatric Research* 5 (1967): 243–254. Van Buren O. Hammett, "A Consideration of Psychoanalysis in Relation to Psychiatry Generally, Circa 1965," *American Journal of Psychiatry* 122 (July 1965): 42–54.

the unconscious driving forces that really motivate our actions. This both Kitty and I were in agreement with. And we also agreed with Adler that bringing these unconscious goals to consciousness could relieve the tensions, the pressures, the conflicts, the problems, and the sense of failure to which every human being is subject."

Adler said many things; Edward and Kitty took some of his ideas and rejected others, apparently according to the emotional response each idea elicited from them. They liked the theory that each individual lives according to a specific set of principles that can be identified, agreeing with Adler that "the psychic mechanism pursues a definite aim according to a definite interpretation of the world, and along the lines of an ideal behavior pattern. . . ."[6] Edward's goal was unconditional love and nurturance; Kitty's was unlimited power and security. In the theory, each person had a hierarchy of goals built on top of the basic one because of failure to satisfy the basic goal. For example, we might conjecture that Kitty's basic goal was security, and because she assumed that people could not be trusted, she believed security could only be achieved through power. So power became her manifest goal, serving the deeper goal of security.

Adler says that each individual builds a world-view or cosmic picture, to match his primary goal. It could be described in Lofland's terms as a problem-solving perspective, but, Adler feels, is really broader than this, coloring all the person's perceptions:

The ever-present goal which determines all our activity influences also the choice, intensity, and activity of those particular psychic faculties which serve to give shape and meaning to the cosmic picture. This explains the fact that each of us experiences a very specific segment of life, or of a particular event, or indeed, of the entire world in which we live. Each of us values only that which is appropriate to his goal. A real understanding of the behavior of any human being is impossible without a clear comprehension of the secret goal which he is pursuing; nor can we evaluate every aspect of his behavior until we know that his whole activity has been influenced by this goal.[7]

Adler had been the first of Freud's major disciples to break away from the master psychoanalyst, and Philip Rieff, an admirer of Freud, has complained that Adler oversimplified, looking for quick solutions and abandoning scientific analysis for magical commitment:

Adler's passion for finding what he called a "guiding line," a master doctrine, was the precise opposite of what Freud had trained himself to achieve: to tolerate

---

[6] Alfred Adler, *Understanding Human Nature* (Greenwich, Connecticut: Fawcett, 1954), p. 47.
[7] Ibid., p. 49.

uncertainty and always entertain multiple analytic perspectives until, in the cruel competition of ideas, some few survived.[8]

For Reiff, Freud's critical, stoical approach was the most noble. He condemns schismatics like Adler for pressing "commitment therapies" on their clients:

Both Adler and Jung sought in psychoanalysis a total theory, to which a patient could commit himself wholly. But all such therapies of commitment belong to the religious category of cure: that of souls. More modestly, Freud sought to give men that power of insight which would increase their power to choose; but, he had no intention of telling them what to choose. . . . Adler and Jung sought, each in his own way, a *cure*, while Freud, knowing there was no cure, in the classical sense of a generalizable conversion experience, sought an increase in human power without reference to any of the established ideals.[9]

Reiff is a passionate supporter of Freud, and may exaggerate Freud's virtues while correctly distinguishing the two ideal types of therapy. The direction he says Freud took may lead to Science. The direction Adler took certainly leads to Religion. Several social scientists have suggested, however, that psychotherapeutic cure is indistinguishable from religious cure.[10] Both may be vain hopes that often encourage unrealistic expectations. J. A. C. Brown has written that there were several reasons why Adler's brand of psychoanalysis might appeal to people, including the optimistic impression he conveyed that

treatment was a relatively simple matter which could be conducted on the basis of friendly chats with one's analyst who would point out the style of life with its fictive goals and give some practical advice for a more sensible future strategy.[11]

Although inspired by Adler's writing, Edward and Kitty did not become patients of an Adlerian analyst. Certainly, few people have social connections to such a professional; there aren't many in the world. But there is another barrier. One of the great costs of participating in psychoanalysis,

---

[8] Philip Rieff, *The Triumph of the Therapeutic* (New York: Harper and Row, 1968), p. 95.

[9] Ibid., p. 87.

[10] Jerome D. Frank, *Persuasion and Healing* (New York: Schocken, 1961). John G. Kennedy, "Nubian Zar Ceremonies as Psychotherapy," *Human Organization* 26:4 (Winter 1967): 185–194. Wolfgang Lederer, "Primitive Psychotherapy," *Psychiatry* 22 (August 1959): 255–265. Lloyd H. Rogler and August B. Hollingshead, "The Puerto Rican Spiritualist as a Psychiatrist," *American Journal of Sociology* 67:1 (July 1961): 17–21. Kilton Stewart, "Dream Theory in Malaya," in *Altered States of Consciousness*, ed. Charles T. Tart (New York: Wiley, 1969), pp. 159–167. William Sargant, *Battle for the Mind* (New York: Harper and Row, 1959). Ari Kiev, ed., *Magic, Faith and Healing* (New York: Free Press, 1964). Richard F. Larson, "The Clergyman's Role in the Therapeutic Process: Disagreement between Clergymen and Psychiatrists," *Psychiatry* 31 (1968): 250–263. Peter Roger Breggin, "Psychotherapy as Applied Ethics," *Psychiatry* 34 (February 1971): 59–74.

[11] J. A. C. Brown, *Freud and the Post-Freudians* (Baltimore: Penguin, 1967), p. 40.

aside from the monetary expense, has been the expense to self-esteem. One must accept the role of *patient*, admit that one suffers from *neurosis*, and bear the stigma of *mental illness*. In recent years, several therapies have appeared that do not demand this sacrifice of honor. Technianity is one.

TECHNIANITY

Quite independently, Edward and Kitty discovered the deviant brand of magical psychoanalysis we are here calling Technianity. Invented by Gordon Rogers, an American science fiction writer, and announced to the world in a 1950 science fiction magazine, Technianity had grown into a thriving "technological religion" with world headquarters in England by the early 1960s. Edward told me how he made contact. "I first heard about Technianity from a young man who came to stay in my father's house for a while in 1960—or thereabouts. My brother Harold was in a very rough state at the time. My parents were worried about him, were willing to try anything, and packed him off to Technianity, where he got back on his feet and found a purpose in life.

"My own interest was aroused by the fact that here seemed to be a way of helping people to get out of a state of intense confusion and dissatisfaction. A workable form of therapy, no less. My first wife was in such a state, and I'd not been able to get her out of it. (Her state was nowhere near as bad as Harold's.) So I went there to find out what it was all about.

"I took a course (I can't remember how much it cost), and became a therapist within fourteen weeks. I didn't pay very much attention to the theory. Most of it was science fiction. But I liked the practical applications, the stress on communication between people and on helping people to discover their inner blocks and motivations in a systematic way."

The founders of The Power met at this time. "Kitty was already on the therapist's course part-time when I joined it. We had little contact to begin with, but later discovered that our interests coincided at many points and so did our assessment of Technianity." They were most impressed by the simple, easily learned techniques that seemed effective in uncovering the unconscious goals postulated by Adler's theory.

The basic purpose of Technianity therapy is the achievement of what Rogers calls "an ultimate personal state of unlimited potential." Although there are today many organizations like Technianity, several of them derived from it, I shall not use the correct name for this ideal state, because to do so would reveal the correct identity of the group. I shall call it *super*, the super-normal level of functioning aspired to by all members of Technianity. The optimum individual is *the Super*. Not only does a Super suffer from no psychosis, neurosis, compulsions, repressions, psychosomatic ills, or common colds, but he also enjoys being "high above the current norm" in intelligence. He "pursues existence with vigor and satisfaction." A Super "has complete recall of everything which has ever happened to him or anything he has ever studied. He does mental computations, such as those of chess, for example, which a normal would do in half an hour, in ten or fifteen seconds." Technianity is designed to turn an average person into a superman. The Super "is to a current normal individual as the current normal is to the severely insane." At least so Rogers claimed. Actually, in the early 1960s there was not a single client of Technianity who had yet attained the state of super. It was an ideal condition devoutly to be desired.

Technianity offers two basic routes toward super. In the more passive, a person becomes simply a client, submitting to the therapy as he might in psychoanalysis. In the more active, he enrolls in a series of courses to become a Technianity practitioner, receiving therapy from fellow students while learning how to give it. Both Kitty and Edward chose the latter route. Thus they completely avoided being put in the low status of neurotic psychiatric patient, but were elevated quickly to the apparent status of mental health professional.

In the most basic practice therapy sessions, they would sit on opposite sides of a small square table with a little electrical device called an E-Meter (electrometer) between them. Edward would hold two electrodes connected by wires to the E-Meter. Some machines had fancy, chrome-plated, cylindrical electrodes, but most that I have seen (like the one I own) use emptied tomato juice cans. A tiny electrical current is passed through the body of the client, and the meter measures changes in his electrical resistance. Kitty would ask Edward questions, and he would respond. As his emotional state varied, so would the sweatiness of his palms, and thus also the electrical resistance measured by the E-Meter and indicated by a moving needle. Kitty would pay close attention to the reactions, writing down responses and asking new questions to follow up on the most interesting ones. All the time she would turn various knobs on the E-Meter, adjusting the sensitivity and returning the needle to its center position.

Supposedly, the meter guides the therapeutic interaction and verifies answers. It helps uncover the client's subconscious feelings, memories, and assumptions. It is a simple, inaccurate, but psychologically powerful lie detector. It forced Edward to disclose his thoughts and feelings to Kitty. Participants in Technianity have no choice but to accept such E-Meter sessions and render themselves psychologically naked before their therapist. In 1961, Rogers wrote, "There is no known way to help anyone without using a meter. The person who says the meter is not a precision instrument is either unfamiliar with one or has something to hide. A therapist's questions can be off. The meter never is."

For Edward there were at least two major consequences of the 14-week course. First, he found such mental excavations extremely interesting and his work with clients and other students abundantly rewarding. Second, his many hours in practice with Kitty as his therapist bound him to her in a most powerful fashion. Looking back, he analyzed it in Freudian terms, commenting that a *transference* had taken place, making her the center of his life for the next decade. He also described it in more popular language. In their sessions together, Edward fell deeply in love with Kitty.

They worked for the London Technianity organization as Certified Therapists for six weeks after graduating from the course. Then they left Technianity and soon established their own therapy business. Technianity was far too authoritarian for their tastes. Its doctrinal literature and procedural formats described in lavish and oppressive detail everything they were to believe or do. Several aspects of this obsessiveness rankled.

They doubted the perfection of Technianity's doctrines and methods. Edward says he felt most of Rogers' writings were unsubstantiated speculations. He heard the man speak at the Technianity College and had to listen to many tape-recorded lectures in the course. Edward says, "some of them were entertaining; there was a lot of jargon and a lot of science fiction." He felt Technianity claimed too much. He believed Rogers could not really produce Supers and was therefore forced to invent a string of excuses to explain why Supers were not in evidence. He told me about one such excuse employed when he was in the group. This was the idea of "missed withholds," a therapy error that Rogers said was blocking real progress. *Withholds* were related to *overt acts*, or *overts*. In Technianity jargon, an *overt* is a "harmful or contra-survival act." In practice an overt is the same thing as a sin. People feel ashamed of the overts they have committed. In a 1960 speech, Rogers described them. "The thing which you are suppressing and mustn't tell somebody must have been an overt act. See that? That's what an overt act is. An overt act is that thing which a person feels he better not do again." All such acts ever performed by the client were supposed to come out in therapy. The therapist asks the client a long series of questions concerning a list of relevant people and objects, and the E-Meter ferrets out the overts. "For the meter reacts on any person or thing on whom the *subject* has committed *overt acts*!" This is reasonable. The client will feel guilty about his past behavior toward someone, will experience anxiety when the person's name is mentioned, and the E-Meter will register the sweat produced by that anxiety. But sometimes, Rogers felt, the client would conceal an overt nonetheless. An "undisclosed contra-survival act," or hidden overt, is called a *withhold*. If therapy fails to disclose one, it is called a *missed withhold*. So long as the client was blocked by missed withholds, he could not fully participate in the process of therapy and would bog down in his progress. Although this theory is actually rather reasonable, Edward came to see it as a mere excuse papering over the real truth—that Supers were not being produced.

Because they doubted Rogers and because they were intelligent, exploring individuals, Kitty and Edward chafed at the rigid system of therapy demanded by their superiors. One of Rogers' favorite slogans, simultaneously a boast and a demand, is "100% Standard Tech!" This means, Technianity's spiritual technology is to be followed exactly, without the slightest variation. Kitty was especially anxious to experiment in the sessions she ran, changing the questions slightly or departing from the established order of procedures. Edward says he was less inventive than she at first, but both of them wanted the freedom to try out their own ideas. They did not want to be mere robots in Rogers' science fiction world.

The doubt and constraint they felt in Technianity became focused when Kitty discovered to her immense anger that the session rooms were bugged. She accused her superiors of listening in on her sessions through hidden microphones. If they were in fact doing this, it was to make sure she and other therapists performed correctly and gave their clients 100% Standard Tech. There had been no complaints about her or Edward. Both of them were considered excellent therapists. They felt the bugging was an invasion of their privacy which neither of them could accept. They left Technianity, according to Edward parting amicably with the Technianity organization.

COMPULSIONS ANALYSIS

Founders of new cults almost always serve some kind of apprenticeship beforehand, learning skills that will be useful later on. Often they serve as lieutenants to the leaders of other cults before going into business for themselves. The word *business* is the right one. It is appropriate to view the founding of a new cult as an entrepreneurial act, on the same order as the founding of any new small business. If the cult succeeds, its founders will become rich in both material wealth and honor. For those in the cult business, there is nothing crazy about founding one.

Kitty and Edward did a little more exploring before setting up The Power. For a short while they exchanged ideas with a group of four amateur psychological experimenters bankrolled by a lawyer who hoped the "Fearsome Foursome" would achieve a spiritual breakthrough that he could share. They, too, were using E-Meters and hunting for subconscious goals. Edward says this "lawyer friend of Kitty's was helping them to set up their own consulting business as therapists, and the precise structure of the original Power therapy was his idea."

Soon, Kitty and Edward established themselves under the name *Compulsions Analysis* and began looking for clients. They found that their talents combined were much more effective than they would have been separated. "Kitty was the real drive in the situation," Edward says, "I was the intellect. She had the certainty, I had the answers. She had the eye for an opening, I had the means to navigate it. She knew the move to make, I knew how to make it. Without her, I'd have been too uncertain to plunge ahead; without me she'd have been too ill-equipped to plunge ahead. But between us we had the essential elements, and in no time at all we were in business."

Like Technianity, Compulsions Analysis did not present itself primarily as a paramedical means for transforming disabled mentally ill patients into functioning members of society. Edward explained its orientation to a reporter in late 1965. "Our aim is to make people become aware of themselves, and so more responsible to themselves and to other people. We are not so concerned with healing the mentally sick as are the more orthodox psychoanalysts. We want to help people fulfill themselves." Unlike Technianity, however, Compulsions Analysis did not promise infinite benefits. Once Edward and I discussed mystical groups that try to reach beyond this life into an occult realm on the other side of existence. He said, "We are not offering super-powers but a means that people can live on this side more effectively." It is important to realize, however, that Compulsions Analysis and The Power never set any limit to what might be achieved. Psychiatry sets normal functioning as its limit as well as its goal. For Kitty and Edward's movement, the sky was the limit.

Their first client was an old boyfriend of Kitty's whose real purpose was to get back into her favor. When he saw that he had no chance with her, he dropped out. The next two clients were good friends of Edward's. They had good, ordinary English names, but I will call them Pius and Elijah from the start, because these are the cultic names I have assigned them as leaders of the later Power.

Compulsions Analysis recruited clients through Edward's friendship network. Kitty's lively but jaded and chaotic network did not contribute. Pius and Elijah knew each other, but Edward feels he was closer to them than they were to each other. They were very different men with different styles and different friends of their own. Edward says, "They were my friends. And somewhere they knew I had the answers. And after them came *their* friends. A whole group of them, male and female, eager to discover what they had discovered."

Like Edward, Pius and Elijah were students of architecture, so it was not surprising that they quickly brought in two other architects, Bathsheba and Siegfried. The five were already somewhat close together and were quick to mobilize their energies as a group. Elijah recalls, "Edward and I were very close for some time. Pius and I were very close. Siegfried and I went to India together, and Morocco, so we were very close." They had already conspired on one rather rebellious project. The architectural school they attended put out a magazine, *Polygon*. Elijah says, "We decided to take it over. Two days away from publishing, we took it over and rewrote it. We worked solidly for about fifty-two hours." They were not even members of the *Polygon* staff. "We just took it over." The issue they produced "really represented for the first time a psycho-humanist approach to architecture, as opposed to a design-aesthetic approach." The rebellious future Powerites wanted their architectural profession to grow in new directions. Elijah delighted in designing buildings that could not be seen, mirror buildings. Like many energetic young people, they did not want to submerge their creativity in the drab monotony of the commonplace. If there were a practical way of achieving a superhuman style of life and work, they would seize it. If we were offered such an opportunity at the right points of our lives, perhaps all of us would. Compulsions Analysis seemed like their best chance.

Edward and Kitty were the only trained therapists, so there was a limit on the number of people that could be gathered in by Compulsions Analysis. Some of their analytic hours were wasted on people just passing through, people who did not like the therapy or did not like the therapists. They began training their associates, and over the period of about a year, developed a large clientele of people involved in various degrees.

They charged clients three guineas per fifty-five minute session. Often the sessions were sold in blocks of six. There was no limit to the number a person might receive. One disgruntled woman reported getting 300 sessions before she quit, while the angry father of two satisfied customers gave up after 60. The early sessions were E-Meter therapy interactions, but once a handful of clients had assembled, Compulsions Analysis organized group meetings at which several exercises adapted from similar Technianity meetings were practiced. They offered a Communications Course patterned on the one given at Technianity centers.

Whatever good the therapy sessions may have been as personal exploration, they functioned to give people an opportunity in which they might develop powerful bonds with Edward and Kitty, bonds like the transference relationship between them. The participants in the Communications Course practiced psychological exercises with each other, like the ones I will describe in Chapter Eight. Thus, clients could build intense personal relationships with each other. Some knew each other already, while others were strangers. They were already members of the same extended social network, and as their interactions continued, the network became more highly interconnected and evolved into a group.

All the people who later formed the core of The Power community entered therapy in the two and a half years from the middle of 1963 to the beginning of 1966. It is impossible at this late date to determine what personal characteristics might have distinguished those who joined from those who did not. Most were effective middle-class young adults. Some were experiencing greater *tension* in their lives than others. I doubt that any were mentally ill. Perhaps only one or two exhibited the "enduring, acutely felt tensions" predicted by Lofland and Stark. Based on interviews I had with them, I will describe how seven came to join: Isis, Juliet, Abraham, Paul, Moses, Cain, and David.

EARLY RECRUITS

Isis

Isis was a student at an English art college where she met Adam, a young man who had been studying to be a concert pianist. His older brother was Siegfried, a close friend of Elijah, who was an intimate friend of Edward. Isis was drawn into Compulsions Analysis through this long chain of strong social ties. Edward brought in Elijah, who brought in Siegfried, who brought in Adam, who brought in Isis. She had no particularly intense life problems. "Nothing dramatic was happening at that point in my life. I wasn't going through a vast trauma, or anything like that. I was at a crossroads, really, in terms of a career. Would I do teaching? Which I didn't really look forward to with a great deal of pleasure, 'cause . . . with the qualifications I had it would have meant teaching art in grade school. It really didn't excite me terribly. Or should I go on and do further training in order to qualify for a different kind of teaching position? Or should I take up painting? It was a period of indecision. But nothing deep or wrenching."

When she came into contact with the group, it was indeed "a kind of psychotherapy," perhaps one might call it an "encounter group." For Isis "it was quite a profound experience of self-discovery." She had no contact with other groups or techniques where she could feel emotions as profoundly within a symbolic context that seemed to describe vividly her thoughts and desires. "I had no contact, or very little, with any kind of psychotherapy. I mean, I don't think I would have known at that point what a psychoanalyst was. It just wasn't in my background. My background was the arts. I had read a bit, as a child. I'd been an avid reader in the public library, and I had got out books on weird things like metaphysics and Freud and Bertrand Russell and Jung, and couldn't make head nor tail of it." She used to read with a dictionary, trying to make sense of the unfamiliar words, attracted by something but not yet gripped. When she encountered Compulsions Analysis, she was amazed "that such a thing existed." Her first few sessions had a tremendous impact. She saw herself and her emotions in an entirely new light. "The big thing was knowing that there was an unconscious mind." The therapy "answered so many of the almost unasked questions that I had. And that was how it was. It was quite: *Good Heavens*! It was really almost like a revelation to me, and opened up for me a whole area of exploration and discovery. And I decided, after contact with the group for a short time . . . *not* to pursue a teaching career in art but to study there, with that group, and become a part of it, become a worker. At that stage we weren't a community. I simply wanted to do that kind of work, which was helping people to uncover what was going on deep down inside that was maybe causing problems." The aspect of Compulsions Analysis that Isis said was most important was the intensity of social interaction. "It wasn't something I was used to at all, and could use quite a lot of." She says that few people in England at that time were involved in such experiences of self-discovery and sharing such intense, intimate feelings. For Isis and the others, Compulsions Analysis "was quite radical and new."

Juliet

Juliet met the group in the early days after she had already begun a career as an actress. "I had done a lot of repertory." English repertory theater is a bit like summer stock in America, except that it goes on all the time. "At that time I was doing radio, the BBC. I subsequently then did a play in the West End and television and this sort of thing." Juliet denies she had any problems in her work. "I was having a successful career . . . was becoming better known. So far as that was concerned it was very good. But I wasn't totally satisfied. I was very happy to entertain a lot of people at one go. I was not particularly happy with the way I related on a personal level. The idea of a conventional marriage to a doctor, or lawyer, a psychiatrist, a whatever, which is what my background would have supposed would happen. Something like that and the raising of a family in a conventional setting absolutely—for some reason, I don't know why—just appalled me! I could not imagine that kind of existence as being too fulfilling."

Juliet knew Bathsheba, one of the original group, and Cain, who came in a little later. Although she had no prior interest in developing her inner self, she went along to a meeting to see what was going on. "The thing that struck me was the degree of intensity at which the work was being done. The kind of questions the people were asking, and not only asking themselves but asking one another. The degree of intense *personalizing* that went on, which I was unaccustomed to. One didn't ask those kinds of questions!" Juliet laughs when she recalls how unconventional the intimacy and openness were. "The absolute commitment to truth about self, and ownership of the answers. Like owning, '*I* feel this. *I* do X,' or whatever. Discovering that people didn't fall apart. I didn't fall apart. In fact, it made me feel a lot stronger, and it made other people feel stronger too. I thought that it would end up with people not being able to speak to one another at all. In fact, it had the opposite effect." Juliet laughs again to remember how "fascinating"—indeed, "more than fascinating"—the experience of sharing such psychological intimacy had been.

There were group sessions as well as the individual therapy sessions with Edward and Kitty. Which did she feel were most striking or most successful? "I thought, to begin with, that it was the individual ones, because I like attention. I felt I was getting a lot of attention. But, in fact, more happened in the group situations than happened in the one-to-one situations."

She came to a decision point. Should she give up her acting career and throw body and soul into Compulsions Analysis? The safe thing would be to stick to her career and keep the therapy for a hobby. "As my friends kept telling me, 'Things are really opening up for you. Why do you want to give up a career which is now beginning to completely open up for you and give you promises of films?' I said, 'Because I know what it's going to be like from here on in. Even though I don't know the exact jobs, I know where it's going to go.' I had a whole vision of what my life would be like if I followed that career, and I suddenly felt there was no challenge. I thought, *Oh, I see.* And from that point I lost interest [in acting] and became much more interested and fascinated" by Compulsions Analysis. It was "like I was interested in knowing the answer to questions, and I didn't even really know the questions. But I knew that it was more challenging than what I had been doing previously. There was a certain amount of fear in that decision, but that was part of the challenge."

Abraham

Abraham joined the group in January 1966. He had known some people who were already members for a number of years. He knew Pius well and had shared an apartment with Elijah for an extended period. Abraham had many friends outside Compulsions Analysis, and was successful in his work.

He was a management consultant, had already worked eight years for the same company, and "was considered one of the bright young people who would go far." There was nothing pathological about his life, and yet he was not entirely happy. Perhaps, if we were honest with ourselves, we would have to admit we are all somewhat dissatisfied with our lives, but for most of us there never comes a moment when we see a glimpse of something better, a way out of a grey life into a vivid existence full of excitement and triumph. Abraham was an effective, normal member of the middle class. He could be attracted away from his conventional lifestyle only by the convincing promise of a route to supernormal existence.

Abraham says, however, there were two factors that disposed him to join the group. First, he had found adulthood disappointing and disillusioning. In childhood he had hoped for a great and exciting life, but when he grew up he "found a fantastic discrepancy between what I expected of life and what actually transpired. I think one has to be dedicated to keeping a degree of excitement and interest and stimulation and constant development." But in his conventional career, as in most, that excitement was lacking. His contacts with Compulsions Analysis suggested that a splendid life could be enjoyed within it. "I remember very specifically my first reactions in going to my first meeting of all the people, which was one of an absolute whirlwind of energy, stimulation, intensity! Dynamic! All of the things you'd wish. Extraordinarily intense! It happened purely on the basis of the intense involvement of people, which was something that was completely new and nice."

Second, Abraham says, "I'd always had the feeling that I was a special person who was *intended* to do special things in their life and to rise beyond what I would call a normal life." It bothered him that he was caught in an ordinary life. "Obviously I equate normality with something less than exciting." At first he participated in the therapy exercises in the hope that they would give him greater effectiveness in his job and his outside personal life. But he began to feel that his unique personal identity flourished when he was within the group. "I don't think I ever said to myself, 'Oh, here is a situation where I *can* be special.' But it felt like I was employing some talents that I had" in a special way. Over the years, Abraham's involvement in the group has permitted him to feel special, both in the intensely personal social life of the group, and in flamboyant public presentations.

Abraham describes his decision to join the group and abandon his earlier lifestyle in terms of investment, risk, and return on investment. "The idea of moving into a community was not something I did very easily. I had my own place and my own situation, friends, job. That was one of the investments." The group put no pressure on him to join. "When I was having problems whether I was going to be coming into the community or not, I was told, 'Well, whatever you want to do. You make up your own mind.' Nobody was making *any* attempt to get me involved." But he became totally involved. His hours inside the group were more gratifying than his hours outside it. Compulsions Analysis offered the possibility of greater gain but at greater risk. In the end, he left his job and moved in to live with other future Powerites. The people where he worked thought he was "quite insane to leave," but then they had not experimented with Compulsions Analysis and found it exhilarating.

Paul

Paul is a man of charm and ability who left science for the cult not because of failure, but because the cult gave much greater personal and social gratification than laboratory research work. His actual conversion involved some temporary strain and a tortured personal reevaluation, but was highly situational rather than the result of any longstanding problems. Like Abraham, Paul came to feel that conventional life alternatives, however good, were inferior to the unconventional alternative, Compulsions Analysis.

Paul grew up in Australia and did well in college. He earned a B.A. in Chemical Engineering from one university, and a Master's degree in Chemical Engineering Science from another. In 1965, he and his Master's thesis advisor submitted two technical articles for publication, based on Paul's research. Both were published in scientific journals. Like most successful student theses, the project was neither radical nor particularly creative, but a solid example of careful journeyman science. Paul's work did not give evidence yet of scientific genius, but a successful scientific career was definitely open to him.

Rather than complete his Ph.D. in Melbourne, a very practical course because he could do it in a short time, Paul decided to accept a studentship at London University. He says he did this "mainly because I wanted to see Europe." He had no friends in London and did not quickly make friends at the university. In Australia he had been surrounded by people close to him, but now he was isolated from social support. His previous academic work had been closely supervised, not only in the technical sense that the details of his work were closely monitored, but also in the social sense that his attitudes were supported by those of others.

Paul had looked forward with such anticipation to London University that it was a bitter discovery to find that he "didn't like it at all when I got there . . . found the work extremely tedious and completely lost concentration on it there." Scientifically, he should have found the work very rewarding. "I did Biochemistry in the same department with people who had

made real breakthroughs in Biochemistry. And I was very excited about
genetics research at that time. They were first discovering the DNA mole-
cule, and the RNA was very recent, and I was drawn towards that area. But
I couldn't take the Biochemistry at all! The tedium of Biochemical Engineering sterilization procedures and all that sort of thing drove me crazy.
My mind was working much faster, but my concentration span was shorter
by that time."

Despite the gloom spreading from the tedium of his work, there were
bright points because "I got off to Europe and the British Isles as much as
possible." He filled his senses with exciting but unconnected impressions of
the world outside the Laboratory. "I found most things quite unsatisfying
at that time." He had "a number of hobbies" but lacked the vital feeling
that his life had a stable core.

The friends Paul made in London were not scientists but architects. One,
Hal Dale, had some contacts with Compulsions Analysis. He told Paul
about the group and suggested he attend one of the public meetings. On
impulse one evening, Paul dropped in. "It was just like walking into an
alternate universe! It seemed to be so lively, so interesting, and so challenging. And people's faces were so alive! The questions that were being asked,
and the answers that were being given were so much on what I really
wanted."

One night, several meetings later, Paul was riding home on his motor
scooter with Hal, when Hal asked, "Are you thinking of joining?" Paul
liked the occasional meetings, but was he ready to commit himself further?
Paul replied, "Oh, I can't. I'm doing a Ph.D. at London University." Hal
asked, "Would it matter to you if you didn't get your Ph.D.?" Paul
remembers "it was just an incredibly placed question in that moment of
time. It was a very odd thing. Nobody had ever asked me a question like
that before." He realized that his degree did matter to him, but he was not
sure how or why. His course seemed compulsively aimed at the degree,
rather than being the result of free, conscious choice. "I was on a compulsive
pattern where I didn't even stop to think. It was a fantastically freeing
question." As he thought it over more, he realized that in a very real way his
spirit had died. "My life was a closed cycle. I *was* going to get a Ph.D. in
Chemical Engineering, therefore I would become a Chemical Engineer, and
therefore I would join an industry, and therefore I would get married, and
therefore and therefore to the grave. Which was a totally compulsive path!
That [realization] opened up the possibilities infinitely, you know? Because
if it didn't matter to me, I could do any number of things. And I determined that very night to resign, to resign my Ph.D.

"I felt so incredible, like I'd never felt for years. Chills up and down my spine. I felt completely euphoric. I couldn't sleep. I was so excited about not getting a Ph.D., I felt more alive than I'd felt in years. And the next morning I went in and resigned, and the euphoria lasted for months. I never looked back, and I never once wished I got a Ph.D." His fellow graduate students were not happy with Paul's decision. "They all thought I was crazy. They'd all gotten used to the rather dead, academic student that I was. That was the only recourse for them, really, to assume that I was crazy. That way they could rationalize it and still accommodate their own work. Because If I'd truly had a revelation, and in fact the best course for me would have been not to get a Ph.D., that would have involved them having to review what *they* were into."

The cultural relativity of norms for the expression of joy is shown in a study by Sandifer and others in which British and American psychiatrists were shown sound films of mental patients and asked to list their symptoms.[12] The British were much more likely than the Americans to list symptoms "that overshot the mark," symptoms of too much activity, too much elation, according to English standards. The American doctors were more likely to see depression in the same patients. The national standards for the expression of joy were quite different. Paul's joyful excitement may have been entirely healthy, yet it violated the standards of those around him. So when Paul began exhibiting euphoria to his fellow students, they took it as a clear symptom of serious mental derangement.

For example, there was the famous cartwheels incident. This was a story of happiness that so violated the standard norms that it became a legend among outsiders who knew about the cult. "I remember that we used to go out to lunch at the cafeteria, any number of the research students, a fairly routine deal. But this time I was feeling particularly good, and did a series of cartwheels down Galloway Street. They really couldn't accommodate this!" The other students continued walking soberly to lunch, but the acrobatics "must have really shocked them, because some months—even years—later I was selling Power magazines somewhere in central London and somebody looked at the magazine and said, 'Oh, yes, I know about this organization. A friend of mine knew someone who joined it, and he used to do cartwheels down Galloway Street!' "

In a series of capricious moves, Paul rearranged his personal life, living for a short time in an apartment with Elijah and Abraham, then following

[12] Myron G. Sandifer, et. al., "Similarities and Differences in Patient Evaluation by U.S. and U.K. Psychiatrists," *American Journal of Psychiatry* 126:2 (August 1969):206–212.

these two men when they joined a larger group of Edward's clients. "One of my big problems in life before was making decisions. I always found it hard to make decisions, and I'd drive myself crazy trying to think of what I should do. But I lost that problem as soon as I joined up with the group. I felt the last decision I made was to join, and I've never really had a problem with decision-making since then." What did the initial impulse to visit Compulsions Analysis for the first time feel like? It was a "total experience where I felt that in a sense the decision was made for me, that it wasn't actually a decision I made. It was like something was taking control of me. Anyway, I was propelled through the street and went to that meeting. I got dressed very quickly and ran through the streets of London to get to the meeting on time. Hop in the elevator, out of the door, open a door, and there they all were." Was Paul driven by a powerful subconscious desire, or by the will of God? Powerites say they are the same thing.

Moses and Cain

Two of the earliest recruits, Moses and Cain, were consciously dissatisfied with the course of their lives, investigated Compulsions Analysis as a possible solution, and grew quickly to become leading figures in the cult. Neither had close ties with the original members.

Moses was a student at Oxford University, concentrating in Politics, Philosophy, and Economics. He found little joy in his studies or in the turmoil of student life. "I couldn't relate to what everybody was getting terribly worked up about. I could see the time at Oxford was leading nowhere, leading just into more education." Somebody he met at Oxford had a friend who was attending meetings at Compulsions Analysis. "It was a very tenuous connection," but enough to give him the idea of attending a meeting himself. His first visit was striking, but despite his articulateness, he finds it hard to describe. "There wasn't anything about it itself so much as the people. Walking into the room. Pius was there. Siegfried was there. Mother Isis. Maybe one or two others." There was an "inexplicable sense that we belonged together working towards *whatever*." Moses believes each person there had a special feeling: "There is somewhere I have to go. There is something I have to do." Something extraordinary, something not possible in the context of the lives they had been leading.

Cain was the most disturbed of the first permanent recruits. Edward says Cain was depressed to the point of suicide. By his talents, Cain was a superior man, but he was also an unhappy one. "For about as long as I can remember, I've had the feeling of watching, looking, wanting something, occasionally touching something, usually losing it." He experienced this longing "often quite acutely, usually with a sense of despair, because I felt I couldn't touch or hold or reach, and I felt very unworthy." He was employed as an accountant, successful but unhappy in his work. Dissatisfied with his own life, he contemplated the courses of his friends' lives and found them dreary. "I could see that in my terms they were *dying*." They were "marrying and settling down and being very good citizens," but the life was draining out of them. "I could see compromise and defeat, or defeat in the form of compromise, entering into their lives. And that they were ceasing to aspire in terms that were meaningful to me. I wasn't particularly interested in becoming director of a company or top of the civil service. It didn't hold my attention, that kind of thing." The firm of accountants for which Cain worked offered him a partnership and a big boost in salary. Instead of accepting, he resigned from the company and began to look in new directions. He was accepted at Harvard Business School, where he thought he might improve his prospects from good to excellent, but he never went. An old friend put him in touch with Compulsions Analysis and its "interesting bunch of people." It was just the prospect he was looking for.

David

David was the only original Powerite from a working-class background. He grew up in Paisley, a textile town near Glasgow, Scotland. His mother worked in a thread mill and was able to invest in seven years of piano lessons for David when he was a boy. At 14 he flunked his music theory exam for the third time, and the piano lessons stopped. His next interest was soccer. He hoped to become a professional player. A little later he also became interested in rock bands and other kinds of popular music. At the end of his teens he saw that his soccer was coming to nothing. Some of his friends began to make money at it, but no soccer scout ever recruited David to a professional team. That left performing popular music as the only apparent chance to escape the drudgery of factory work. "I worked in a factory for four years," he recalls with little pleasure. "Rubber. Making vacuum brake pipes on a train. It was only a way of making money. The faster you did it the more money you made."

At the age of twenty he joined a semi-professional band. After playing together for a while around Glasgow, the group of five men decided to quit their regular jobs and try their luck in the big city, London. They called themselves "The Pinnacle," but in London took a new name, "The Silhouette." They hung on in London for nearly a year, playing wherever they could get a gig, and cutting a few single records. They clung to their hopes. A new record was scheduled to come out at the beginning of 1966, so when David went home to Scotland for the Christmas holidays, he was dejected but not yet desperate. "And who should walk into my house in Scotland but Edward de Forest. He was a friend of a friend of mine. I was given a card for The Power, 14 Wigmore Street, London. Put it in my pocket."

David had no interest at all in deep questions about the human psyche and had drifted away from the Catholic religious training of his childhood. When his band's failure became more acute and hope ran out, he had no thought of seeking any kind of "therapy" to improve his condition. He needed a job. "This was a very rough time for me." A painful time. He did not want to return to the rubber hose factory. But what else could he do? "I remember walking around, thinking *Well, where to next?* Needing help, needing support . . . money." Money was the main thing. He remembered the card in his wallet that Edward had given him. Edward had seemed prosperous, and what little he had heard about his group suggested there was money to be found there. "It was mainly money and a little curiosity" that brought him to visit the group on one of its open evenings.

He found "lots of nice people" and a "very nice atmosphere. Father Pius, I remember, answered the door, and he was very charming. There was an air of success, and a good feeling." Edward invited David to return the next day and bring the entire band with him. On his second visit, David saw a good chance he could make some money off the group. "The band that I was playing with was invited to join and write music for The Power. We were offered to be put on a wage, fifteen pounds a week, which was very nice for us." It was more than they had been earning. On that basis David joined. He discovered other reasons for staying, and was, as it happened, the only member of his band to continue with the cult until the present day.

THE POWER EMERGES

Compulsions Analysis evolved from a therapy service into a social group. Edward and Kitty settled into their roles as cult leaders. There came a time when participants realized they were a group, something above and beyond the original therapy. They began inventing new words, new symbols to express the emerging reality. Although Kitty has often been described as the strongest personality in the group, she did not become its charismatic figure. Rather, she gave that role to Edward and withdrew from public sight to exert her influence through more hidden means. Kitty felt Edward's name was not grand enough. He should change it. *Edward Jones* was the name of an ordinary person. His middle name, *de Forest*, had more class. It pointed to a glorious ancestral past. Legend has it that Sylvester de Forest came to England with William the Conqueror in the grand year of 1066. Knightly forebears included Sir Roger de Forreest (1273–1343), his son Sir

William, and Sir Gerard de Forreest (1318–1396). A Marmaduke Forest
was knighted in 1603. Edward received this heritage through his paternal
grandmother. At Kitty's insistence, Edward dropped the plebeian name
Jones and became *Edward de Forest*. Among cult members he was often
called *The Teacher*. Kitty, now Mrs. de Forest, was called *The Oracle*.

Compulsions Analysis needed a new name, too. Various alternatives were
suggested, but no one idea received enough support to get adopted. Eventually, the group merely capitalized a common word they had been using to
describe their therapy, and this became the evocative name of the cult. Of
course, the word was not *power*, but it had some of the same connotations.
The Power is a good name, and it might just as well have been the real one.

Members of The Power were Powerites. A couple of years later, the group
began staging theatrical presentations called Powerplays. The uniforms
worn in later years were called P-Gear (Power Gear). Automobiles and
campers were P-Cars. Soon after Compulsions Analysis became The Power,
the E-Meter used in the sessions was renamed the P-Scope.

In 1965, or possibly even earlier, Edward began writing Power literature
of two kinds. He composed many bulletins giving instructions for performing the different therapy exercises. Eventually there were hundreds of different bulletins, some written by Pius or Cain, giving authoritative instructions for carrying out each ritual, each activity, and each aspect of church
work. Edward also began composing the first pieces of semi-religious scripture, *The Logics*. These are short dissertations on the human personality that
provided theoretical background for the actual therapy procedures. No
other member of the group could write scripture the way Edward could.
Cain and Moses tried, but their productions were markedly inferior.

The group also needed a symbol. One day several of them were sitting
around a table, sketching various symbols and looking for one that was
eye-catching and expressed something about The Power. Sibyl invented the
winner: four thick lines that came together something like a Nazi swastika.
They outlined the letter P for Power, seen from four different directions.
This was very symbolic, since The Power was a coming together of contrast-
ing people from different directions for a common purpose. The symbol is
shown in Chapter Seven.

Finally, The Power needed a headquarters, something better than the
Wigmore Street apartment they had been using, a place large enough for
public activities. They took a lease on a large stone house at 2 Balfour Place,
in London's fashionable Mayfair district. They put a big version of the new
symbol on the door and began moving in around the beginning of 1966. At
first, Abraham says, "We didn't conceive of people moving into it and it
becoming a community. It was just that various people would live there,

and that would be the center of operations. But that began to change in
character very rapidly. January, February, March. We began to feel that
what we should do is live as a community, create a community, because
there already was one in terms of our interests. We were all interested in the
same things, so we would all live together."

ANALYSIS

Many factors made The Power what it was, but two related sociological
phenomena explain its origin and the recruitment of new members. First,
people who participated in Compulsions Analysis saw it as a rational and
initially low-risk step that might lead to increased personal effectiveness
and satisfaction. Second, the structure of social relations was transformed
because of the new standard of intimacy set by the therapy procedure itself.
An originally extended social network collapsed into a closed, cohesive
group. We can call the first phenomenon *optimization*, the second, *implosion*.

Optimization

Lofland and Stark tell us, "For conversion it is necessary that a person . . .
experience enduring, acutely felt tensions." [13] They needed a concept about
the motivation of people who found and join strange cults. The converts to
the group they studied were unsuccessful people suffering various chronic
life problems. They were so incompetent in presenting their own doctrines
that Lofland had to rewrite their literature for them, and Stark was pressed
into service as the voice of the cult in tape-recorded lectures. The life stories
of these folk, published by Lofland and Stark, depict them as chronically
miserable, maladjusted, untalented people. Clearly they did suffer "enduring, acutely felt tensions." They could not be more different from my
Powerites, most of whom were quite able and seemed reasonably successful
in their careers.

How does Lofland define his *tension?* "This tension is best characterized as
a felt discrepancy between some imaginary, ideal state of affairs and the
circumstances in which they actually saw themselves." [14] If we look back at
the life stories of founding Powerites I have just told, we do see evidence of
tension, so defined. At least when people decided to give up their old lives
in favor of The Power, it seems they had become dissatisfied with their
ordinary careers and reached for a more ideal state. In a 1976 doctrinal

---

[13] John Lofland, *Doomsday Cult*, p. 7. John Lofland and Rodney Stark, "Becoming a
World-Saver: A Theory of Conversion to a Deviant Perspective," *American Sociological
Review* 30:6 (1965):862–875.

[14] Lofland, *Doomsday Cult*, p. 34.

lecture, Father Cain, who had been the most intensely disturbed of the original group, pointed to a felt discrepancy such as that predicted by Lofland. But Cain said all people feel it, not just a few pathological types. "The only lack is the lack of Love. If there was lots of Love, I think problems wouldn't exist. I'm saying that from the point of view of assuming that everybody feels there are problems, there are difficulties. There is a gap between what we want to be and what we actually are. There is a gap between the reality as it is right now and the ideal out there in the future as we would like it to be." Cain said we all want to receive more love and give more love than is possible in conventional society. The Power was a grand attempt to approach the ideal life which would be drenched with love.

Lofland's definition of tension does not really describe the pathological tension his converts suffered, but the normal tension required to motivate any organism. It explains absolutely nothing about cults per se that it does not explain about everything. Social psychological literature is rich with theories and studies indicating that people (and animals) tend to act so as to maximize their rewards. The first of George Homans' famous Five Propositions states: "For all actions taken by persons, the more often a particular action of a person is rewarded, the more likely the person is to perform that action." [15] The related Third Proposition makes a similar point: "The more valuable to a person is the result of his action, the more likely he is to perform the action." [16] These axioms concern normal action, not pathological behavior.

Joining a deviant cult may often be perfectly reasonable behavior. If the Powerites had left their ordinary, successful lives to become movie stars or U.S. Senators, we would hardly feel their behavior demanded an explanation. It would be obvious to us that they had improved their situations, and we would not immediately assume that the lives they left had to be unattractive. We might all want to be movie stars or Senators. Therefore we are quick to agree that a fairly happy person might leave a cozy and familiar occupation for the advancement such splendid careers would offer. But when a person leaves a conventional life to join a crazy cult, we tend to feel that a special explanation is required.

Why are we so foolish? I can think of two reasons. First, we judge the Powerites' actions from our own position, hindered by our own prejudices and lacking the evidence they had in deciding The Power was a positive alternative. Second, The Power developed its own norms and values, a counterculture we do not share. When the Powerites grew close together,

[15] George C. Homans, *Social Behavior: Its Elementary Forms* (New York: Harcourt Brace Jovanovich, 1974), p. 16.
[16] Ibid., p. 25.

they pulled away from us to form their own society, thereby opening a gulf of mutual deviance between their group and ours. The first point is a statement about *optimization*, the second about *implosion*.

We have to remember that people choose alternatives according to their own momentary estimations of the payoffs, not according to what the real payoffs are going to be or according to the views of outsiders not caught up in the situation. People will do what they think is best for them, not what we might imagine they ought to do. My interviews with founders of The Power suggests that seven factors made future Powerites more likely than other people to place their bets on the side of the cult.

1. The ideologies of the artistic training many members had received were congruent with that of The Power. There were five architects, a couple of musicians, an artist, a research scientist, and an actress in the original group. In these fields creativity is said to be a prime value. Unfortunately, the actual opportunities for creativity are strictly limited. Architects and industrial engineers may believe they are creative artists, but most of them are simple workers employed to do completely mundane jobs. Technological gurus like Victor Papanek and Buckminster Fuller urge designers to fulfill a revolutionary, utopian role in society.[17] In The Power, people were able to realize these goals and values better than in their original occupations, even though the socialization to the role of creator had taken place in the conventional institutions. Elijah told me the work he and the others performed building The Power was a natural extension of their architectural training. "It's a very architectural thing, building up a [group like The Power]. I call it religious engineering."

2. The founders of the cult were isolated from social control, from social forces that would have inhibited their cult involvements. All had left the homes of their parents. Some had recently lost social ties with outsiders, Paul by leaving Australia, Moses by leaving college, Cain by leaving his job. The others counted many fellow Powerites among their friends. None was deeply involved in a conventional religious organization. Apparently, none was involved in any conventional psychiatric treatment. None had been trained in academic psychology, which might have inhibited participation. Resistance from friends and co-workers only came when people were already deeply involved in the cult, because initial experiences with it in no way interfered with the maintenance of conventional jobs or friendships. In short, the future Powerites were all free to experiment with the cult.

3. Compulsions Analysis offered something *new*, an alternative that was

[17] Victor Papanek, *Design for the Real World* (New York: Bantam, 1973). R. Buckminster Fuller, *Utopia or Oblivion* (New York: Bantam, 1969); *Operating Manual for Spaceship Earth* (New York: Pocket Books, 1970); and *I Seem to Be a Verb* (New York: Bantam, 1970).

plausible because it had not ever been discredited. In the history of therapy and self-improvement techniques, we see many examples of new ideas that gain tremendous support for a while, then are rejected just as vigorously when their limitations become manifest.[18] This phenomenon encourages the emergence of fashion cycles. The newest idea has the least evidence against it, so at first it triumphs over the tired ideas of the past that have already been found wanting. People who commit their lives to a new fad, perhaps by becoming professionals in it, may promote it until the ends of their lives. Today, many well-educated middle-class people encounter a pseudo-therapy cult and exclaim, "Oh, not another one of *those*! I've seen so many others, and they're all bunk!" Future Powerites could not react this way. Psuedo-therapies were so new in their social circles that they had not yet been discredited.

4. The founders of The Power were all young adults, at that time in life when adventure and risk are most normal, when idealism and hope can be high, and when a person's talent and energy can make it most possible to act decisively.[19] The 1960s were the decade of youth, in which radical students, young rock stars, and colorful hippies amplified the usual vitality and adventuresome character of young people.

5. Several, but by no means all, of the future Powerites joined at a period in their lives when some kind of decision was necessary anyway. Lofland and Stark would say they were at turning points. Cain was consciously searching for a radical change. Isis had to decide whether to take a job or continue with her schooling. Moses didn't know what he wanted to do. The Power was not the only game in town, but it looked like a good bet to these three partly because they were ready to bet on something new, rather than hang on where they were. The others also needed to be convinced that betting was in order.

6. People were able to sample Compulsions Analysis and The Power at little risk before committing themselves. They could try it out, decide whether they liked the therapy, and develop friendships in the group. Much of the literature on religious conversion emphasizes the striking, sudden, emotional transformation of people who join almost instantaneously.[20]

[18] David J. Rothman, *The Discovery of the Asylum* (Boston: Little, Brown, 1971). George Rosen, *Madness in Society* (New York: Harper and Row, 1969). Michel Foucault, *Madness and Civilization* (New York: New American Library, 1971). Robert Darnton, *Mesmerism and the End of the Enlightenment in France* (New York: Schocken, 1970).

[19] Erik H. Erikson, *Identity, Youth and Crisis* (New York: Norton, 1968). Karl Mannheim, "The Sociological Problem of Generations," in *Studies in Social Movements*, ed. Barry McLaughlan (New York: Free Press, 1969), pp. 352–369. Erik H. Erikson, ed., *The Challenge of Youth* (Garden City, New York: Doubleday, 1965).

[20] William Sargant, *Battle for the Mind*.

This cult allowed newcomers to take their time. At each step in a ladder of increasing commitment, the risk and immediate cost were low.

7. The people who did join report they found the experience extremely satisfying. They saw direct evidence that the claims of the cult were sub-stantiated. Paul, for example, *saw* his compulsions just as Compulsions Analysis said he might. To the extent that people did find participation rewarding, they could anticipate that continued and even greater participa-tion would be still more satisfying. While the therapy claimed objective benefits of personal improvement, I think the real rewards were social. But these social rewards looked like the improved personal effectiveness that was promised.

The most important returns from high-status conventional occupations are social in nature. Conventional status symbols happen, not surprisingly, to be expensive and rather remote from direct social interaction. Costly houses and exalted titles convey symbolic status but are often difficult to transform into the direct respect and appreciation given by close friends. Who has the greater feeling of personal power, the bureaucrat who shuffles thousands of lives with his administrative papers, or the cult leader who has intimate control over one or two individuals? In The Power, members could experience immediate social benefits—*immediate* not only in the sense of *instantaneous*, but also in the sense of *direct*, that is, *not mediated* by any complex chain of cultural symbols or social institutions. Sociation is the stuff of society. We want the constant, warm attention of other human beings. In "alienated" complex societies we must take much of our social gratification second-hand, displacing or sublimating our needs for love and stimulation onto abstract social constructions. In sharing intensive, posi-tive social interactions of a kind unusual in English society at the time, Powerites could achieve their desired social gratification without the neces-sity of laboring toward distant, indirect satisfactions in conventional insti-tutions. Therefore, the experience of participating in The Power could con-vince them, at least over the short run, that the cult was in fact a better alternative than the conventional ones open to them.

Those who have remained with the cult from the beginning right up until the present time tell me they did in fact maximize their satisfactions by betting on The Power. The cult shifted course many times, sometimes in radical ways, in continual *optimization* of its perceived chances of reward.

Social Implosion

The Power emerged from Compulsions Analysis, a pseudo-therapy. In Chapter Eight we will examine the specific therapy exercises used by The Power and see that all function to build unusually intense, intimate bonds between participants. We have already seen that Edward used the technical language of psychoanalysis to say that his therapy sessions with Kitty caused him to develop a *transference relationship* with her that lasted a dozen years. In pure psychoanalytic theory, this would mean that Edward had displaced powerful feelings onto Kitty that had their origins in his childhood relationships with his parents. Psychoanalysis may be mistaken. But it is certain that for him, and for other participants in Compulsions Analysis for whom the therapy was effective, an overwhelming involvement developed with the therapist, a relationship of such intense dependency that it over-powered other relationships in the person's life. Because every therapist in Technianity and Compulsions Analysis was also a patient to some other therapist, the sessions created intense, interlocking bonds of transference and countertransference. The basic therapy interaction forces the disclosure of the patient's inner feelings and builds a powerful if asymmetrical inti-macy between the two participants. The tie between them can become the dominant social reality for the patient, and the therapist develops a number of rather strong ties to his several clients.

John Lofland, Mark Granovetter, and many other sociologists stress the importance of a "pre-existing friendship net" in the growth of a brand new cult or other kind of movement.[21] Essentially all of the early recruits were members of Edward's own friendship network or contacted Edward through a chain of social relationships. As Siegfried says, "It was all friends of friends." Compulsions Analysis recruited outward through this network until Edward and Kitty had as many clients as they could handle.

As soon as there were many clients, this fragment of a network began to develop into a cohesive group. Clients began interacting more frequently with each other. Group therapy sessions were set up in which they shared intimate feelings. Compulsions Analysis provided participants a supremely rewarding, exciting, vivid social life. It established a new norm for the quality of social interaction. Consequently, social ties between members strengthened markedly, while the network was becoming more thoroughly interconnected. The rudiments of a group culture evolved. Several of the members I interviewed spoke of coming to feel that only other participants understood them completely, and said it grew more and more difficult to communicate with friends who were not participants. At the same time that ties were strengthening with other participants, ties with nonparticipants weakened. What I call a *social implosion* took place.

In a *social implosion*, part of an extended social network collapses as social

---

[21] Lofland, *Doomsday Cult*; Mark Granovetter, "The Strength of Weak Ties," *American Journal of Sociology* 78:6 (1973): 1360–1380.

ties within it strengthen and, reciprocally, those to persons outside it
weaken. It is a step by step process. I suppose that social implosions may be
set off by more than one kind of circumstance. In this case, the introduction
of a new element of culture, a "therapy" technique that increased the
intimacy of relations around a point in the network, triggered the implosion.

The key factor was the sessions with Kitty and Edward. They did not
quickly train other therapists from among the recuits; had they done so, this
new culture might have spread widely in English society rather than producing an implosion. Although we are not in a position to quantify the
parameters of the social situation, the implosion required that the growth of
intimacy among participants proceed in some measure more rapidly than
the growth of the group through recruitment.

Kitty and Edward did train a couple of their closest lieutenants to do
some of the therapy routines. But at the same time, new routines were being
constantly invented, and participants' schedules increased to take advantage of the new processes. Thus the invention of new techniques counter-
acted the tendency of training to aid diffusion. Siegfried, for example,
"worked in the morning as an architect, and in the afternoon as a therapist.
In the evening we would have courses in communication, sensitivity development." The density of social relations increased faster near the center of
the network than the wave front of participation could expand.

For a certain distance out along the ties of Edward's network, Compulsions Analysis was strengthening ties in the direction of Edward and Kitty.
This distance was a function of the amount of time its therapists could give
divided by the amount of time required each week by a deeply involved
client. Beyond that distance, ties began to weaken. The social fabric tore
along the periphery at this social distance. People quit their jobs and let
friendships lapse with people further out along the network. They moved in
together, all living as one small society at Balfour Place. They developed a
consciousness of creating and joining a group. They invented a name and a
symbol for it.

The phenomenon of social implosion may be very common, and many
examples have undoubtedly been reported in the sociological literature,
though not analyzed in exactly the same way. Quarantelli and Wenger have
reported on a Ouija board cult that apparently experienced a short-term social implosion. This is another example of an implosion that followed the
introduction of a social mechanism that increased the intensity of social
relations among participants, in this case the use of a Ouija board supposedly to communicate with spirits but actually to share powerful emotional experiences and intimate communication. The cult developed among eight

female students at a large university after a particularly intense Ouija board session. Afterwards they met regularly at midnight to work the board:

The more the cult members participated in using the Ouija board, the more they were seen and saw themselves and their behavior as different. Negative reactions expressed by outsiders intensified this process. Cult members became increasingly secretive so as to protect their activities and themselves from "nonbelievers." This had the dual effect of increasing the separation between participants and nonparticipants and of bringing the participants even closer together in sharing something exclusive.[22]

This social implosion was only temporary; it did not produce a permanent group that could successfully maintain its integrity for a long period. Members' participation in the Ouija board cult rested upon their attendance at the university. The cult dissolved when two members left the university, another left the dormitory they had been residents in, and the informal leader lost interest.

A social implosion can be reversed at any point if relationships within the group lose their special quality or members begin having especially rewarding contacts with outsiders. An implosion is most likely to become permanent if the initial phase of actual implosion is immediately followed by a period marked by an absence of involvements with attractive outsiders or enticing career alternatives. The social implosion that created The Power became permanent after the entire cult packed up, abandoned London, and went to live on an isolated Mexican beach.

At a place caled Xtul in the Yucatan Peninsula, geographically separated from the society in which it had emerged, The Power took its social implosion to the logically extreme conclusion: the generation of a thoroughgoing alternate society which described itself in religious terms. In this chapter we have seen how The Power came into being as a deviant psychotherapy group. In the next we will see how it evolved into a religious cult.

[22] E. L. Quarantelli and Dennis Wenger: "A Voice from the Thirteenth Century: The Characteristics and Conditions for the Emergence of a Ouija Board Cult," in *Deviance: Action, Reaction, Interaction*, ed. Frank R. Scarpitti and Paul T. McFarlane (Reading, Mass.: Addison-Wesley, 1975), pp. 143–157.

THREE

God at Xtul

We traveled on into Mexico
And on through Yucatan
And in a ruin on the Maya coast
We found our promised land.

Xtul, you simplify our lives
Xtul, you clarify our love
　　for our GOD.
　　　　　　　　—A Power Song

The Power became an "Army of God upon earth," a deviant religious group following the four Great Gods of the Universe, over a period of two years, from late 1965 through late 1967. Originally a therapy cult, it evolved into a religious sect and finally became legally incorporated as a church. Six factors combined to produce this social and conceptual shift. First, although many of the Powerites considered themselves agnostic, all had received some religious training, so religious concepts and language were available to them, and they were able to use the general religious culture of England as an interpretive structure through which to understand themselves and their experiences. Second, the Adlerian analysis of personal goals was open-ended in design, encouraging participants to discover magical desires within their psyches, wishes that could not be accommodated inside conventional, mundane reality. Third, the effect of the social implosion was to incorporate the individual people in a social personality, perceiving the presence of a group mind that they felt existed quite apart from their own personalities, and which they identified as God. Fourth, the events and emotions of those years seemed to confirm their religious assumptions and provide ever deeper glimpses of divine intervention in their lives. Fifth, the claim that God provided guidance and made demands was a kind of excuse made by members, and especially by the leaders, for acting impulsively, for avoiding responsibility to any human law or to the welfare of followers. Sixth, the religious label was used strategically, to control the response of the general public. These six factors operated in various combinations at different times. At the end of the chapter we will suggest what their unifying principle might be.

BEFORE DEPARTURE

Some Powerites say their group became religious before it visited Mexico, others say the change happened in a ruined plantation on the Yucatan coast. The date each assigns to this transformation depends, I think, on when each individual's consciousness changed. The term *religious* refers not to a well-marked objective reality, but to a particular consciousness, to a particular interpretation of social reality. Abraham had a religious orientation almost from the beginning. For Juliet, the word "*religion* had so many negative connotations" that "presentation of ourselves as a religious group was not readily acceptable" until her feelings changed "simply as the reality of God became much more of a personal experience."

By late 1965, many Powerites had recognized that their concerns went beyond the strictly psychological to include religious feelings and desires. Edward explained to a newspaper reporter how this had happened. "The Power started off purely as psychotherapy. But the more we worked with our clients, the more we realized we were closer to a religious approach. Nearly everyone kept coming up with their religious goals—with their own concept of God."

As another reporter noted about the same time, The Power was becoming "increasingly religious and introverted." This is a good observation, because the early development of religiosity in The Power came from two parallel changes going on that could both be described as introversion: (1) as Edward said, individuals were discovering and admitting their secret magical desires in the therapy sessions; and (2) the group was becoming intensely cohesive and all-encompassing. The first was individual introspection, the second, social implosion.

Siegfried's view agrees with mine. He notes that The Power began as a group of normal people who encouraged each other to aspire to the supernormal, and as a result became a religious cult. The "initial stage was more psychotherapeutic than it was religious. But we were not people with problems. We were normal people ourselves, and so were our friends. We had good jobs. We had reasonable situations. I was an architect. I had also written a number of stories, a couple of which had been published, and I'd been commissioned to do a mural. So I wasn't a failure in worldly terms. We weren't struggling, or in the hands of psychiatrists. We were essentially looking for something *more* than society was apparently capable of delivering. We were looking for greater fulfillment than we could see stretching ahead of us" in the careers society provided.

"We essentially *researched*, both using ourselves and the people who came to us for help, and reached, about the middle of 1965, a recognition that

underneath everything (in every person who we helped or in our own
research on ourselves) we came to what we would call a basic religious reality
. . . a sense of religious purpose, or a sense of purpose in life." Siegfried was
raised Catholic but was agnostic at that time. His religious background
made it possible for him to define the end result of his own therapy as a
religious consciousness. But his experiences in therapy really were *supernatural*, if by "supernatural" we mean phenomena beyond the normal ability
to understand and describe. "We recognized that essentially we were talking about religion in the broadest sense, so in our public presentation we
began to become more religious and talk about God and religion more than
we had up to that point."

Mother Isis believes the emergence of The Power's community facilitated
the development of a religious conception. When people were still living
apart, "we had very private things, private realities, private thoughts."
Once they were sharing many intimate hours together, private thoughts
and feelings "started coming out. And we all found that there was a thread
in common, and that was that somewhere deep inside there was a very
strong belief in God. It quite amazed me as much as the preliminary
discovery of the unconscious mind." Her comment is apt. The religious
discovery was both an *extension* and a *reversal* of the discovery of the subconscious. As an expression of personal desires that had been repressed by society's disdain for them and were now liberated by the developing subculture's tolerance, religiousness was a product of the subconscious. But the
new religion was also the product of a superconscious mind, the cognitive
and emotional currents that began to flow in the group, around and beyond
the individuals that constituted it.

The intimacy produced by the implosion stimulated mystical feelings.
Individuals lost a sense of independence. Decisions were often made subliminally in group meditation sessions. Individuals contributed fragments of
feelings and ideas to the social decision-making process, and no one could
readily distinguish his own feelings and ideas from those of the others.
Ideas, feelings, and decisions were therefore perceived as coming out of
the blue from an obscure, uncanny, occult source. The appearance of occult
and pseudo-telepathic subjective events in psychoanalysis has been documented,[1] and similar phenomena are common in Technianity. People who
know each other extremely well respond to the nuances in each other's behavior, coming to know things that have not been said and predicting

[1] George Devereux, ed., *Psychoanalysis and the Occult* (New York: International Universities Press, 1953). Nandor Fodor, *Freud, Jung, and Occultism* (New Hyde Park, New York:
University Books, 1971). Philip Seitz, "ESP-Like Experiences in a Psychoanalyst: A Possible Psychological Mechanism," *Psychoanalysis and Contemporary Science* 4 (1975): 189–209.

behavior without conscious analysis. Of course, I do not believe that real telepathy or clairvoyance take place. But people do communicate without knowing how they do it, and do anticipate each other's behavior without the slightest conscious idea what information they used. However much the outsider might disbelieve, for the participant these experiences can be very convincing evidence of the supernatural.

And the same therapy that produced these uncanny phenomena also stimulated a will to believe. In psychoanalytic language, one might say that patients in any intensive analytic therapy *regress*. Whether or not we want to conceptualize this as a return to the habits of childhood, or merely a transformation that resembles such a return, does not matter. The patients lose some of the veneer of maturity and begin admitting their autarchic, magical, infantile desires. As they mutually liberated themselves from any external control over the expression of fantasies, Powerites came to express completely unlimited desires, oceanic feelings, longings for absolute power and absolute dependence. These wishes could not be accommodated within ordinary reality. They are the kind of thing banished from polite society, even though all people might feel them. I believe we will see why this is true when we examine the later history of the cult.

If my analysis is correct, then it ought to be very easy for psychotherapy groups to become quasi-religious cults. Why doesn't this happen often? Why don't psychoanalysis and its more recent descendents follow the same pattern? First of all, the fact is they often do, perhaps when therapists forsake Freud's skeptical *analytic* approach and adopt commitment therapies.[2] Second, the medical metaphor used by psychiatrists and others trained thoroughly in university settings both defines the goals of therapy narrowly and identifies the patient's mystical sensations as symptomatic of his neurosis. Third, after his didactic analysis, the therapist is not commonly expected to receive intensive therapy himself and will, therefore, remain relatively unmoved by patients' religious urges. From a different perspective, we can say that the tendency of a psychotherapy to evolve into a full-blown religious cult is inhibited if the therapist keeps himself aloof from the intense experience of his patients, and is stimulated if the therapist enters completely into the experience himself, accepting alongside the patient the role of suppliant and permitting his own consciousness to be transformed by intense social intercourse. A therapy is most likely to remain pedestrian if its administration is securely locked into a standard medical institution, and is most likely to become a cult if it is practiced independently of any restraining institution of conventional society.

[2] Philip Reiff, *The Triumph of the Therapeutic* (New York: Harper and Row, 1968).

THE DEPARTURE

Almost as soon as the Powerites had moved into Balfour Place, they were talking about leaving London altogether. Relations between members and their old outsider friends were now rather painful. Abraham, Paul, and Juliet were serious when they said their friends thought they were crazy to give up normal lives for membership in a deviant cult. They made several attempts to tell London how wonderful The Power was. Abraham recalls they often gave public presentations. "One of my first evenings out was to go with a group of people speaking up at Oxford. And we went there and created quite a stir. I didn't feel it was fantastically effective! We were talking too much above people's heads, or too wide of where they were at. A lot of what we were doing was shaping our own identity, and you only get that from being different to somebody else, so already there was a strong situation to have a conflict. Maybe one makes a few converts, but basically what you're doing is creating an argument and a conflict." I am not aware of a single convert made at those public presentations. Apparently the Powerites would harangue their audiences mercilessly.

Juliet believes this breakdown in communication was at the heart of the decision to leave London. "My own recollection was the feeling of not being understood. It was a feeling of having found something very important and discovering that there was no understanding from other people. We couldn't communicate it basically. It was noncommunicable at that point. . . . Certainly in terms of my friends, there was nonunderstanding on both sides. I couldn't explain what I was doing . . . what made me want to do it. . . . And they couldn't understand, because I couldn't explain it. . . . It was like having a germ of a feeling, a sense of something which was definitely not being confirmed in that environment. It was at odds with, and therefore noncommunicable." The social reality of The Power was at odds with the social reality of London, so the perceptions and values conflicted as well. Edward de Forest told me the group left London because the city was "a miasma." *Miasma* means a noxious influence or atmosphere. Contact with outsiders had become unpleasant. By 1965, the first aggressive newspaper reporters had begun invading the cult, writing extremely unfriendly stories expressing scorn and disapproval.

Abraham says, "I wasn't surprised when we began talking about moving away from London. The concept of creating our own community, a self-supporting community, where we were away from the distractions and the effort of convincing somebody" was very attractive. "So the idea of moving away from London everybody thought was a great idea."

Isis says the decision to leave London was a step forward in the attempt to become a cohesive group. "We still weren't much of a community. We'd just started living that kind of a lifestyle, i.e., a lot of people in one very large building. We didn't have much contact with each other. Everybody had their own room; maybe two people were in a room. I don't even think we had meals together at that point. We may have just started. It was still very isolated. And so we didn't have the same kind of group feeling that we've since developed—on decisions, and knowing exactly what things were going on—that kind of feeling. I remember for myself the decision to go to Nassau, and then later to go to Xtul, was based on a feeling of 'It would be nice to create something a bit more cohesive.' Because there was a lot of isolation at that point. And there didn't seem to be anything within that situation that we could work with, living in the middle of London."

Siegfried says the only clear feeling was "to get away from *civilization* and to see what we really wanted to do. We weren't really sure. We didn't know whether we were packing our bags for good, maybe never coming back to civilization as we knew it, or whether we were going away for a period of time." Where would they go? The Power rejected the all-too-modest standards of conventional life and reached out for the ideal. Edward says they decided to search for "a tropical island paradise." Abraham puts it this way: "We thought 'We'll get an island. We'll get some land. We'll get an island, and we'll become self-sufficient and self-supporting.' "

In May 1966, Siegfried was sent out to look for a suitable tropical island. He went to Nassau in the Bahamas and began shopping around "for an island where we could set up a self-contained community." The Powerites pooled their resources, contributing everything they had to a central fund. According to one report, Siegfried himself contributed more than 10,000 English pounds from his inheritance. After a few weeks, he found some property that looked suitable, a small, uninhabited island in the Bahamas that was for sale.

On June 23, 1966, the core group of Powerites, numbering about thirty, left London by ship bound for Nassau. With them went six German shepherd dogs. In mid-July, a reporter for a London newspaper interviewed Siegfried, who admitted, "Our plans are fluid." The Power rented a large colonial house for everyone to live in. Group therapy sessions continued, and many participants had the conscious desire to grow closer to each other. The house was so big, however, that individuals retained some privacy. Compared to later years, Isis says, "It was a time when we didn't have a lot of contact," and "We still were strangers to each other in many ways."

Nassau was not a megalopolis like London, but it was a city, and the house was right in the middle of it. Most Powerites took jobs, wandering off in different directions during the day, leaving the house almost empty.

There were many distractions. Isis says, "We still had a lot of attention outwards, in a sense, because we were working. People were going out in the morning, working in an office, then coming back at night. So we were very much connected to *the world* and the ways of the world." Siegfried, for example, worked in his old profession of architecture. He took a job with the city and helped to design a police station.

They stayed in Nassau for about three months. They never bought the island. Nassau had been intended merely as a way station, and it was time to move on. Siegfried recalls the next decision vividly. "One night we sat down in the garden of the house, by the swimming pool, and we had a Meditation. This was something we'd developed over the years, the idea of meditation. We hadn't started out with that, but by going into a gradually more religious lifestyle, obviously meditation was a part of it that had grown up. We meditated on where we should go next from the Bahamas, what the next move was. And it came down to either we would go to Mexico City, or we would go to Caracas. Both of them were about equidistant, as I remember, from Nassau. And we decided on Mexico City. It seemed to have the more positive projections. And so, quite shortly after that we ended our jobs, we ended our lease on the building, and we took off with our savings for Mexico City." They stayed there for only a few days before wandering on. "And again, very much following signs and portents given to us in meditation, we traveled south in a rather rickety old bus that eventually took us up to Sisal, which was a little coastal village where they used to make hemp until nylon came in."

XTUL

Near Merida, the largest town in the state of Yucatan, lies the little fishing village of Sisal. The group of about thirty Powerites arrived there in early September 1966. Elijah found a fishing cottage they could rent. There were coconuts hanging from the trees, and the Mayan Indian villagers let some members come along on their daily fishing expeditions into the Gulf, so there was enough to eat.

About a week after they arrived in Sisal, they held another Meditation. Power meditations are not like Transcendental Meditation or any similar brands. There is no mantra or other standard stimulus upon which the meditator fixes his attention. Rather, the Meditation leader suggests a fresh topic each time. The participants close their eyes and let images and feelings about the concept drift through their minds. After a little while, the Meditation is over, and they describe what they saw, sharing their sensations with each other. Thus, Power meditation is directed group fantasy, free association to a common stimulus, an exploration of the collective subconscious of participants. This time, as always, they sat on the ground in a circle, joined hands, and closed their eyes. "What should we do? Where should we go?"

Images came. The Meditation ended. They opened their eyes and described what they had seen. Siegfried says, "It was like putting a jigsaw puzzle together. Everybody had a bit of a vision, and also indications of what we would see along the way" to our destination. "I saw some ruins . . . a long wall, very white. . . ." "Near the sea, but you can't see the sea." "Very green, like an oasis." "Lots of little lights in the sky." Juliet predicted an explicit sign, "We'll see the man with the stick and the dog."

"How do we get there?" they asked themselves. "Start walking in the morning."

"What direction?" Since the coast ran east and west, the choice was narrowed to these two directions. The nearly unanimous response was "East." Only one member, the daughter of a world-famous scholar and architect, said "West."

They did not sleep that night. About eight o'clock the next morning they began walking east, singing enthusiastically. After a couple of hours, their spirits sagged. They trudged along, searching in vain for the realization of their fantasies. It was terribly hot. Endless walking. Late in the afternoon they turned a corner and saw, to their happy amazement, exactly the sign Juliet had predicted—a man with a stick and a dog!

The thirty ran madly past him. Here was their destination! Here indeed was a cluster of half-ruined buildings surrounded by coconut palms, a place they could stay, a place the real Power could come into existence.

It was called Xtul (pronounced sh-tool), a Mayan word they thought mean *terminus*, marking the end of a journey. From Xtul onward, a couple of special Power words would always be spelled with "X" to indicate an initial "sh" sound. Both of the words appear to derive originally from Yiddish or German slang, but to be in use in London circles and merely adapted for Powerite use. One is *Xpiel* (spiel), meaning the flow of words from a therapist or patient in one of the group's sessions. The other is *Xtumm* (stumm). This is an important concept, defined in the notes to a series of essays Edward wrote at Xtul, the *Xtul Dialogues*:

To xtumm (pronounced "Shtoom"; oo as in "good") is to "kill," either physically, spiritually, or mentally, depending on the context. The extent of the "death" can vary. For example: to xtumm someone could mean simply to silence him, to knock him senseless, or to destroy him completely. Also atmospheres can be xtummed, conversations can be xtummed, contact between people can be xtummed, etc. In the present context, a "xtummer" refers to one who kills contacts and atmospheres on a spiritual level, with heavy deadening projections and attitudes.

Xtul was the opposite of xtumm. Xtul, the endpoint of the spiritual voyage of the last three years, was a turning point in the history of The Power. They came to Xtul a group of thirty individuals tied together by their involvement in a deviant psychotherapy process. They left Xtul slightly reduced in numbers but members of a cohesive community and founders of The Power Church.

Physically, Xtul was an abandoned coconut plantation, but in the mythology of The Power it was the Land of Oz, a magical place worthy of legend and song. Years later, many Powerites who joined after Xtul would still think of it as their magical beginning.

> Come to Xtul, cries the voice of angels in the wind.
> Come to Xtul, where the wonders of this world begin.
> For you the glory of Xtul!
> For you the glory of Xtul!

The Xtul mythology was very poetic. Was Xtul really an exact substantiation of the meditation image? Was a man with a stick and a dog a true sign or a coincidence? And the magic name? A year later, when Sister Ruth joined The Power, she told Father Abraham she doubted that *Xtul* meant *terminus*. Ruth had a Master's degree in Anthropology and had spent a year in Mexico studying Mayan linguistics. She thought *Xtul* was one word in a phrase the Indians used to name the plantation, the entire name meaning "Place of the little she-rabbit." Abraham agreed the Indians used a whole phrase with *Xtul* just a part, but wanted to stick with the official definition even after Ruth's professor from the University of Chicago supported her theory. In a Power magazine five years later, Abraham stresses the magical-poetic feeling of Xtul:

We had found Xtul by taking a jump of faith. We had found Xtul by a miracle. And the place was miraculous: we knew that we had been guided to it. Some of the Mayan Indians at the nearby village, Chuburna Puerto, told us they had been waiting for us.

The Powerites took possession of Xtul by the simple act of living in it. There were three principal buildings. Nearest the sea was a large wooden house with a tile roof, relatively intact. Inland from it was the biggest building, a roofless and overgrown stone structure that came to be known as "The Monastery." A smaller stone building in similar condition was a short distance to the east.

At the village, about a mile's walk down a dusty road, they met a fellow named Balthazar who was supposed to look after the ruined plantation for the owner who lived in faraway Mexico City. With some trepidation, the Powerites wrote a letter to the owner, explaining how they had found Xtul and offering to pay a small rent for the right to stay there. The owner agreed in a letter which commented, "Thank you for your distinguished letter. I understand completely that you were led to my property by 'voices.' There is, however, one thing that slightly worries me. What if the voices tell you not to pay the rent?"

They slept on straw mats and in hammocks. Isis recalls, "The weather was so fine that many of us chose to sleep outdoors. I did myself." Only on the rare nights when it rained did everyone cram together in the imperfect shelter of the old house. There was no running water, of course, and the water in the well was saline. No problem! They had a bona fide hydraulic engineer, Paul, expert in fluid dynamics. He rigged up a system of bamboo pipes. Expeditions went out daily to get good drinking water and other necessities from the village.

There were coconuts to eat, but as Isis told me, "Coconuts get awfully boring after a while, Bill, I can assure you." Bathsheba started a vegetable garden. The fishing was good. And then there were the prickly pears, many of them, growing wild. they are not *pears*, exactly, but an edible cactus, with hair-like little spines. Isis explains, "Unless you clean off the fruit very well, you'll get them stuck in your tongue. . . . I got quite scared of them after a while. I wouldn't touch them, because I hated this feeling [of getting the prickers in my tongue]. It was awful." Everyone warned everyone else to be careful and be sure to cut away all the spines before eating. But again and again, some poor fool would impulsively bite into one that still had a few prickles. It was almost impossible to remove the spines from one's own tongue. Somebody else had to do the job. Often, a little group of victims would gather, sticking out their tongues piteously. One of the women would operate on them with a pair of eyebrow tweezers. There was one solution to the prickly pear problem that both produced safe food and allowed Powerites to exact vengeance on the nasty fruit: they squashed the cactus into prickly pear jam.

Most members of the group did "an enormous amount of physical work," Isis says, "building, repair work, because the place wasn't in good condition when we took it." They spent a lot of time clearing out The Monastery, and made such useful items as a log table and sleeping mats woven of palm fronds. One fellow succeeded in making a functional musical instrument out of a gourd and accompanied Brother David who began composing songs. Few of the members were used to hard physical labor. It was a good body-building experience.

Individual P-Scope sessions and even the group therapy sessions had temporarily given way to much more fluid, more religious activities: Meditations, Vigils, prayer, fasting, much discussing and dreaming. As an anonymous Powerite wrote later in one of the cult's magazines, "Without really realizing it, we were developing our own civilization in Xtul. Much of the theology, religious observance, and day-to-day community ethos and lifestyle came through intense discussing and enactment. And through simply observing what worked—and what didn't."

Isis speaks for the entire group when she recalls the two most important lessons she learned at Xtul. First, she discovered that many of the modern conveniences she had taken for granted in London were not really necessary for a comfortable life. Electricity, flush toilets, and supermarkets are not in fact vital necessities. This insight, learned on a deep emotional level through living at Xtul, is parallel to one of the major doctrines of The Power: Our lives are distorted, impoverished, imprisoned by "human agreements." These are assumptions, like Paul's compulsion to become a chemical engineer, false beliefs that some specific thing, goal, or behavior is absolutely necessary for our survival. In the original therapy sessions, Powerites hunted for these human agreements in order to uproot them and liberate themselves. At Xtul, the same process occurred through day-to-day life in this new environment. In later years, The Power chanted this discovery that turning away from the compulsions of the mind toward a magical destiny, abandoning civilization for something transcendental, was the best course:

> Freedom from the human game,
> Freedom from the mind;
> In service of the Purpose
> Lies freedom for the soul.

Isis' second lesson is the mirror image of the first, the discovery of the bountiful miracle that is Nature. "I can remember having strong feelings about sleeping on the beach at night, looking up at the sky . . . feelings of space and dimension and size and scope and wonderment—something I really hadn't been into before. And just feeling and acknowledging the Higher Presence, really." She describes her experience of Nature as intensely *spiritual*, the rapturous psychological opposite of that Human miasma that was London.

On his weekly radio show, six years later, Father Paul expressed his wonderful feelings about the animals that shared the ruined plantation with them: There were "iguanas, like prehistoric monsters in miniature. They would lie in the sun all day. And then when our dogs got near them, they would look around, and with their legs out sideways they would run off as fast as they could, and get up a tree before the dogs could get to them.

"We had wild horses as well, grey and white and black and tan, grazing, nomadic, and free. And pelicans would fly overhead in formation, going who knows where on some migration. We also had snakes, some big ones something like a boa. We had vipers in the water and coral snakes, pink and writhing in the grass. Scorpions—very scary—but nobody ever got hurt, fortunately. Jumping spiders as well, and fish, lots of fish. They used to jump around while we swam in the waters of the Gulf.

"Beautiful place! One day I remember the birds danced outside the window while we watched them. It was a real magic. A place called Xtul in Mexico." On another broadcast, he said, "When we lived in Mexico, way back at the early days of the church, we lived very close to the earth. And we had a rule of only using local materials when we were doing things, building things. And we made our roofs out of thatch, walls out of rocks and limestone. We ate corn and beans like the Mayans around us. And somehow the countryside and the colors seemed much more vivid. And we were much more conscious of animals and plants and birds and insects than we are in the cities."

This romanticizing of Nature included the local Mayan Indians. In later magazine articles about Xtul, Abraham reported a number of occult speculations about the superiority of Mayan civilization as though they were authenticated facts. The Mayans were said to be descendants of the Chaldeans who brought the pyramid with them when they migrated across the Atlantic. Their great wisdom is demonstrated by their invention of the zero and the related concept of illusion or nothingness called *maya*. Of course, *maya* is actually a Hindu concept, and only sounds related to the Mayans. From this jumble of pseudo-historical free association, Powerites concluded that "the Mayas had developed a super-religious civilization and a super-detached concept of reality."

Along with a new consciousness of the world came new personal identities. Several members of the group assumed bold new names during their sojourn at Xtul. David, one of them, explained how the names were chosen. "It just kind-of happened. We drew them out of a hat!" He laughs. "It felt right at the time. We were very much into an Old Testament, Biblical time." The earliest names all came from the Old Testament. "We were thinking about who" in the Bible each of us resembled, and only half-seriously decided, "He looks like an Abraham; he looks like a Moses, and he looks like a David." Some members did not take new names until several months later. For example, Isis adopted this ancient Egyptian name a whole year later. This practice of adopting a Sacred Name later became a standard step in becoming a member of the cult.

Father Paul told a reporter years later that he had gotten "completely absorbed" in the identity of St. Stephen. The events at Xtul, both psychological and physical, convinced him he was being swept away by powers much greater than his own will. "I thought of all the ways I could escape my fate. But I could see the time when I was meant to die." Paul told me he experienced many visions—auditory hallucinations—in which voices predicted everything that was going to happen to him. At Xtul, the reporter says, Paul "felt worthless. He felt that he had nothing to contribute to the group." Paul may indeed have felt somewhat cut off from the group, coming from a scientific rather than an artistic background. Edward de Forest once exclaimed to me that he never understood what Paul had in common with the others. At Xtul, feeling worthless and identifying himself with St. Stephen, Paul felt he should duplicate his saint's martyrdom by stoning. "I went through how it would feel. I could see stones hitting my body. I felt the dizziness: felt the stones hit my head." He proclaimed to the group, "I'm completely unworthy, but I can give my life." The others were quite surprised to discover how isolated Paul felt, and quickly assured him there was no need to die.

HURRICANE!

A week before the end of September, Mr. Macmillan, the British Consul stationed in Merida, paid a surprise visit to Xtul. He drove over to warn the Powerites that Inez, a great hurricane, was headed directly toward Yucatan. "You must move away," he said. "Come and stay with me in Merida. The hurricane will sweep you away. There will be 200 mph winds. A great wall of sea will come in and sweep you to kingdom come." The group gathered and discussed their situation for a few minutes. Their resolve was clear. They thanked Macmillan for his concern, but said they had decided to stay. Consul Macmillan abandoned the Powerites to their fate.

They immediately started getting ready for Inez. For safety's sake they removed the tiles from the roof of the wooden house. Swept off by the hurricane winds, they could be as dangerous as cannon balls. They decided to build a shelter inside the roofless Monastery, taking advantage of its eighteen inch thick masonry walls. The five architects held a technical conference. They agreed that the best site would be on the inside face of the thick north wall, on the sea end of the building but best shielded against waves. Quickly they constructed a large lean-to using old doors, stone blocks, beams, and pieces of burlap and canvas to plug gaps against the expected wind and rain.

The sky turned dark and the wind rose. Palm trees bent and the air filled with blown missiles, coconuts, and branches. The sea chewed away at the shore, in some places eating as much as thirty yards of land. An entire section of the wooden house was crushed, and its pieces scattered. Weeks later, the official count of people killed by Inez reached 293, and could easily have included all the members of The Power. Looking out from the fragile shelter of their lean-to, they saw the solid walls of The Monastery sway, then lurch "like so much plastic foam." Their strongest protection became their greatest danger. The heavy south wall collapsed inward! Had they built their shelter there, many would have been crushed. They ran terrified out into the storm.

They huddled under blankets, drenched by the rain and chilled by the wind. Flying branches lashed them. They sang songs to boost their miserable spirits. Hurricane Inez ravaged Xtul for two whole days. It was a time of agony but also of a fascinating psychedelic consciousness. The air was so dark it was often impossible to know if it were day or night. The interplay of internal psychological turmoil and external meteorological chaos made it seem they were in the grip of transcendent, cosmic forces. The wrath of God! Daemonic powers, black magic. A falling limb almost crushed one of the men. He could not believe his escape was a meaningless, chance event. It was a meaningful moment, in which he was the center of a cosmic struggle.

Inez passed, and the weather began to clear. Everyone was safe. The beach was littered with junk, some of it interesting fare for beachcombing. A fishing boat from the nearby town of Vera Cruz had washed ashore. The Powerites helped the fishermen secure it and shared some of the catch. Three Powerites walked to Chuburna Puerto for food. After their return, most of the group went to the village to offer help in repairing the damaged houses. They divided into four or five groups and energetically set to work, earning the gratitude of the villagers, who rewarded them with thanks and food. Nobody in the village had been seriously injured, so despite the devastation, rebuilding was a time of joy and festivity. David sang some of the first Power songs he had composed. Paul danced with the mayor's daughter. Several joined in a rousing song popularized by the Beatles rock quartet. The Powerites remember Xtul in poetic terms. One began chopping up a fallen coconut tree, when "the axe-head cut into a hive of tiny black stingless Mexican bees. Most of them had deserted the nest. With a little finger I tasted the honey on the blade of the axe. It was sweet, so fresh and with a wonderful subtle flavor of coconut."

The cult shared in the disaster relief sent by the Red Cross and the U.S. and Mexican governments. They were given tortilla mix and black beans and some building supplies. The villagers gave them roast ducks in thanks for their help. They began putting Xtul back together.

The hurricane and its aftermath heightened the social processes and spiritual development that were in progress. They had experienced both sides of the God of Nature: His benevolence and His wrath. Later they explained, "Xtul was the place where we met God face to face. It was the experience that led to the establishment of The Church. In terms of commitment, it was the point of no return where each one of us, plucked by fate out of a workaday world, found that we had a God-vocation."

A few members lost commitment, while the majority gained. Both were given religious interpretations. One week, Paul says, two or three people "were deciding the pressure at Xtul was too much for them, and they were leaving." When each person actually left, a large limb fell from one of the trees. "We would sit around under the tree, talking. And there was appearing some stress. People decided they would like to leave, and a branch fell on each occasion. That's rather dramatic! The sort of thing a passerby would not notice, or would attribute to coincidence. But when you were actually involved on the scene, it was a very poignant moment."

Edward began writing the *Xtul Dialogues*, writings that only real insiders would be allowed to read in later years, composed in the form of eight conversations between a student and his teacher. Edward *writes* his teachings, yet he says he merely *channels* them. He stores up ideas, impressions, phrases, perhaps taken from the conversation and experiences of the entire core group of The Power. Then, in long, intense bouts of lightning writing, he spills doctrine out onto the page. I have photocopies of many pages of his handwritten first drafts in my collection, as well as the final typed draft, and it is clear he does a significant amount of editing and some rewriting, but the basic draft is produced very rapidly. Edward wrote several short pieces while living with me in 1975, so I am familiar with his work habits. He is aware that he composes the literature, but still speaks of it as *recorded* or *channeled* from some Higher Source. In theory he is only the medium through which it expressed itself. Edward has not clarified whether this Higher Source was God, in the traditional sense of the word, or the collective mind of The Power, or his own personality. Powerites dispute the degree to which Edward, their Teacher, composed the writings on his own or as the mouthpiece for the entire group.

One of the most striking features of the mature Power theology was the doctrine of the Great Gods of the Universe, Jehovah, Lucifer, Satan, and Christ. The only God specifically identified by name at Xtul was Jehovah, God of strength, wrath, and Nature. The second *Xtul Dialogue* discusses the connection between the psychological level of perception and the higher consciousness a man can have of God. It begins with a question:

1. Is there more than one universe?
> Yes. On various levels there are many universes, but they are all only part of the One True Universe, which exists on all levels. That is to say, there are many Gods, but only One True GOD who embodies all of them.
2. Is each God, then, a universe?
> Or an aspect of a universe. Jehovah, for example, is the Knowledge of the Physical Universe.

As we will explain in a later chapter, the Gods were projections of different human personality types, discovered among the original Powerites. This passage written at Xtul is the first scriptural hint of their emergence, and the theory of the Gods did not reach a developed form until two years later.

Official church stories of Xtul do not mention the last disaster that struck, a calamity made by men, not gods. Sir Edgar Clayton, father of a nineteen-year-old girl in the cult, conspired with two other parents whose Powerite children were just twenty. They sent a solicitor from London to Xtul to drag the three youngsters home. Under the law, they were still minors, subject to parental control. The solicitor arrived at Xtul accompanied by an official of the British Embassy and an immigration official of the Mexican government. The three were told they would be deported unless they went along with the solicitor willingly. In the third week of November, they arrived in London. Sir Edgar immediately took his daughter away on a French holiday.

The solicitor told London newspaper reporters he had found twenty-two Powerites at Xtul, fifteen men and seven women. All were wearing casual and tattered clothing except Kitty, who "was wearing a bikini and silver-painted fingernails. She seemed to be treated like a kind of high priestess by the others. They acted like her slaves." His impression of their lifestyle was unfavorable. "They were living like hermits, dressed in rags and many without shoes. The men wore beards and the girls were working like peasants, growing, or trying to grow, vegetables to eat." Xtul offended his strict sense of propriety.

The three officials carted away the three young Powerites. The remaining group sat right down, discussed the crisis, and held a Meditation. They decided quickly that most of them should return to London for a while, both to rescue the three that had been taken, and to prevent the abduction of the two remaining under-age members. Adam, Siegfried's brother, one of the captives, was indeed ultimately rescued and grew to be one of the leading figures in the cult. About eight Powerites stayed behind to hold the fort. The cult still intended to make Xtul its long-term headquarters. One member humorously told a reporter, "We have nothing to hide, and we all plan to return to Mexico. We just decided, suddenly, to come home for Christmas." Three of the eight remaining at Xtul left a bit later, and the last five did not vacate the plantation until a year after they arrived. Isis recalls the last months with special joy. She gave birth to her first child, a son, in Mexico, and talks about returning some day to visit that "very special place," Xtul.

BACK TO CIVILIZATION

Despite the troubles with the authorities, the return to London was triumphant. The Powerites had gained a feeling of immense strength at Xtul. Juliet says, "I remember coming back to England with a sense of invulnerability and power that, so help me, I never had experienced in my life." Where did the feeling originate? What was it like? "I was convinced that it came from God. It was a bit like feeling like Superwoman!" She laughed. "Which was a very nice feeling . . . invulnerable. . . . The idea of not having ready food, the idea of having your house burnt down, the idea of not having *anything* on the physical level was no longer a threat." At Xtul, "God" had provided. "This was a fantastic strength. I no longer needed to put my faith in the insurance companies. I was very happy to sell my life insurance without a single qualm, which I did."

Xtul had the same effect on Siegfried. "When I went back to London three months later, I really realized at that point how invulnerable I had personally become to the pressures and problems that in normal life one is totally vulnerable to. In so many ways those didn't matter anymore." Xtul gave not only a sense of security, but also a special pride, a sense of self-worth. "What came out of that was a recognition, to put it in religious terminology, that God had a mission for us in the world. That we weren't meant to be an isolated community for the rest of our days. That our experiences in Xtul and the time leading up to Xtul we were in fact meant to take out to the world. We were meant to relay those experiences, particularly since all of us had a real feeling of close contact with God. . . . That God does care, that God does love us."

Back in London, Siegfried says, "We started off with quite a bang! We started off by opening a coffee house" in the old Balfour Place headquarters,

which was still on lease to them. They were active "running courses, having
lectures and services. We also started publishing a magazine." The first
issue was titled *The Common Market* and criticized Britain's projected entry
into the European Economic Community. "There is a prophecy in the Book
of Revelation that talks about the Ten-Headed Beast, and many interpreters
of prophecy do relate this to the EEC. One of these ten heads is England,
and it's not a very nice prophecy!" They interviewed a few members of the
House of Commons for this inaugural issue, then gave copies to every
member of Commons. The topic of the issue was an entirely perverse choice
for the cult, newly returned from Paradise, but this irrationality set the
pattern for many future Power public relations.

A great deal of work was invested in the invention of many aspects of the
"church." Rituals were invented step by step. The therapy exercises were
expanded and further codified. Powerites began wearing black uniforms
and constructed unusual church decorations for Balfour Place. A church
rhetoric developed.

It seemed natural to express the communal experience of the group in
religious terms. Mother Ruth says that, so far as she is concerned, The
Power is really "a community" but called itself a church because that was
the nearest thing that outsiders could understand. Abraham looks at it the
other way around. "The thing about a community is that there has to be
commitment and involvement. It's a way of living." But it is a special way
of living that seeks a high quality of life for all members, therefore demanding a high level of performance from them. "And so, you see, that automatically puts you into a religious, spiritual sort of space, because there's
nothing else which is going to produce that kind of commitment. It's
impossible [without a religious orientation]. We live in very unspiritual
days, and I think you see the result in people. They're unhappy because they
don't have that core or that perspective on what they're doing." So the
religious conception of The Power is a way both of calling forth from each
member the greatest possible commitment and of giving him the most
powerful hope.

This new religion elevated Edward to the status of prophet. Despite his
passive temperament, Edward de Forest was the man for this important job.
His physical presence and manners radiate dignity. A slim man, over six
feet tall, his leonine features and sandy mane project strength. His regal
bearing was the outcome of his elite cavalry training, and his intelligence
was refined in his private school education. Edward once told me he had
briefly belonged to Mensa, the social club for underemployed intelligence,
and had scored 163 on the I.Q. entrance test. More a philosophical than a
benevolent man, he was happier composing doctrine than sharing the

problems of his followers. He says it was Kitty's idea that he withdraw from public encounters and play the role of charismatic leader from a distance. But this haughty, imperial detachment suited Edward. His dramatic photograph and thundering scriptures became key elements in the Power presentation, while Edward the man withdrew from sight into private mystery.

CHURCH STATUS

In April 1967, Edward, Kitty, Cain, and Kitty's mother left London on a grand tour. From this time on, the pair of top leaders would usually be separated from the rank and file. Calling themselves The Omega (pronounced OH-muh-guh), Edward and Kitty would travel independently, live outside the church chapters, and rule from afar.

The Omega went first to Greece, Edward recalls, "We arrived in Athens the day before the Military took over." That means they landed in Greece April 20, 1967, the day before George Papadopoulos and a clique of military officers seized power. "There were tanks in the streets and all kinds of things" that the Omega found exciting and impressive. They stayed for several days in Piraeus, the ancient port of Athens.

"Then we went to Israel" Edward says, "and that must have been in May, because we left Israel the day the war broke out." Israel triumphed in the famous Six Day War, June 5 through June 10, 1967. This must have pleased Kitty a great deal, because she was an admirer of Israel and of both the ancient and modern Jews, although not Jewish herself. As their boat pulled away from the Israeli shore, they heard booming noises that sounded like gunfire, but did not know a war was on until a few hours later.

When Edward recounts his trips to Greece and Israel, he hints that perhaps it was not chance that they arrived in Greece just as a coup began and left Israel at the start of a war. Those conflicts seemed to have a connection with The Power. They were signs that the cult was at the center of History, headed in the right direction. They were signs that repressive "civilization" was crashing down to make room for something new.

They sailed to Turkey, where they stayed as tourists near Izmir. Here Edward began to write the first sections of a work called *The Tide of the End*, an apocalyptic condemnation of the world, an analysis of the human condition, and a prophecy of the coming Millennium. It is the most emotional and poetic of his writings, yet also contains many of the most important intellectual concepts of Power doctrine. It continues on a higher literary and philosophical plane the basic ideas of Compulsions Analysis but adds the social and religious experience of the early Power. It continues the search for ways of overcoming ordinary human limitations, and as a natural extension of this, expresses the social gulf and antagonism that had developed around The Power as a result of the social implosion. The first phrase of the first book of *The Tide of the End* proclaims: "Humanity is doomed!"

Written from October 1967 to May 1971, *The Tide of the End* is a collection of thirteen short books in seven "phases." One of the books, *Christ Came*, may have been written by Kitty. It is the shortest, only a single page long, and not very intelligently written. Cain and Moses also wrote books of the type collected in *The Tide of the End*. Moses actually wrote his . . . *And There Was Darkness* soon after leaving Xtul, in February 1967, before Edward began writing in the same spirit but with greater skill. The book by Moses reflects his Jewish background and is a book in praise of Jehovah. Cain's book is dated November 1967, and rejoices *For Christ is Come*. Neither of these is particularly radical theologically, and it was Edward's work that led The Power in surprising directions. While *The Tide of the End* speaks in religious language, it is at heart a book about psychotherapy. It presents Edward's theory of self-transformation through psychological analysis, using metaphor and flowery rhetoric. The introduction to *As It Is*, the first of the thirteen books, expresses the theme of the entire work:

A man cannot change his way of life by changing his clothes nor by speaking out with a different voice. To change basically, permanently and meaningfully he must reach down into himself and pluck himself out by the roots. . . .

As IT IS is written for those who want to break away from the futile human pattern of seeing reality as it is not and thereby living a lie, to abandon the anaesthetic of ignorance and suppression within which man cocoons himself and to embrace the intensity of reality—as it is.

The mixture of psychotherapeutic and millenarian sentiments in the following passage from *As It Is* is typical of the broad sweep of Edward's writing during this period:

1.16 So we must break our links, sever our ties; plumb the depths of our unconsciousness, and cut the bonds with which we've bound ourselves.
2.1 And there is not much time. The distant rumblings that are heralds of the End have become a mighty roar closing in about us, piercing our eardrums and causing the very Earth to quake beneath our feet; so that very soon even the blindest, numbest, most oblivious of us will no longer be able to shut out the sound of it.
2.2 By then the whole world will be stricken by the sound of its own approaching doom. Every man will gaze in horror at his fellow man, and see his own fear reflected back to him.
2.3 And by then we must be free—if we are ever to be free. By then the bonds

that bound us must be broken, and we must stand above the terror of the End, aloof, detached, a part of something new.

2.4 For with every end there is a new beginning, and if we are not of the End, then we shall be of the New Beginning.

Like wealthy tourists, The Omega took ship from Izmir and jaunted across the Mediterranean, stopping briefly in Chios, Athens again, Naples, and Madeira. They crossed the Atlantic and spent a few days in Miami, Florida. They came to rest in New Orleans at the end of August or beginning of September. A group of Powerites came from London to meet them in New Orleans with the idea of going on to Xtul. But New Orleans seemed such a favorable city, and its citizens gave such gratifyingly great attention to The Power, that The Omega decided to stay. The last five people still holding the fort at Xtul were called up to New Orleans, and the coconut plantation was abandoned. It fell back into ruin, and all the effort invested in fixing up the place was forgotten. The Power opened a New Orleans Chapter.

Siegfried says, "We went to New Orleans very much in an expansionary mood. We weren't precisely sure what form the expansion would take, but we had a good model in how Balfour Place was operating." Was the cult interested in gaining new members? "We were keen on recruiting, although we weren't proselytizing. We were doing it by example. People would come into the aura and say, 'Well, I like this! I want to be part of this!' "

Lilith was one of those who joined. New Orleans was her home. She says The Power brought great excitement to the streets. "The entire city knew that they had come to town, because they were so obvious. They really made an impact on New Orleans." The Powerites' physical appearance was striking. In 1967, respectable men shaved their faces and wore their hair short. Flamboyant dress, long hair, and beards were then foreign to the conservative style followed by middle-class people. Only the strangest people, alien ethnic groups, unruly poor bums, and the hippies that had just emerged in California looked anything like The Power. The cult adopted a rule in Mexico that no member should trim hair or beard. Several of the men are rather tall, so with hair down past their shoulders and chest-length beards they had a frightening appearance.

Over their black shirts and black trousers the Powerites wore astonishing purple capes. Circular, they came down to the knee and were crowned by small standing collars. Lilith believes the effect was too startling even for some members of the cult. The capes "were so flamboyant that I think a lot of people in the organization who were extremely conservative didn't want to wear them." The Powerites marched around the city in groups, accompanied by their large German shepherd dogs. When any member opened his mouth to talk with a local resident, extraordinary English accents came out. The Power rented a large house, offered coffee and activities, and drew in crowds of visitors. Lilith says, "They used to just pack that house out, daily. Just hundreds of people pouring through that place. It was amazing, really amazing!"

The black- and purple-garbed Powerites walked the streets asking passersby for contributions to the "church." This activity came to be the major source of money to support The Power. New members were no longer of such a high social class that they brought in fortunes with them, and admission fees for Power activities were modest. Because the cult was traveling, and because it had turned in a more religious direction, therapy sessions were no longer practical, either as recruitment devices or as a major source of income. The street soliciting later came to be called "the street ministry," in which Powerites gave "contact" and other spiritual benefits to civilians who reciprocated by giving money. Powerites engaged in the street ministry were said to be *donating*. The people of the city were not *donating* to the church, in this terminology, rather The Power was *donating* to them. The practice of donating served to keep Powerites busy and advertise the church to tens of thousands, as well as being the major source of income.

To legitimate the street begging and the public activities at the Chapter House, the cult became incorporated under the laws of Louisiana in the city of New Orleans. Its official name was *The Power—Church of Armageddon*. Later there were incorporations in London and Toronto, but the original church charter was filed in New Orleans in 1967. This legal step was an important advance in the direction of respectability, institutionalization, and the attainment of conventional church status.

Still, as Lilith explained, The Power "was not rooted" or "establishment-oriented" as it later became. Little interested in becoming just one more standard denomination, The Power was much more concerned with "the basics," she said, with "the End of the world, detaching from the establishment, being a group unto ourselves. And simply the mission was to pick up other Powerites. It was not to convert large masses of people. It was not to fill up the ranks with large numbers. It was not to become a part of the establishment. It was simply looking for people who were Powerites."

The fourth verse of the seventh chapter of The Book of Revelation suggests that precisely 144,000 human souls will survive the End in glory. The Omega suspected this meant there were 144,000 natural Powerites scattered throughout the world. To the extent that the cult had a mission to the world, it was mainly to present itself publicly so those people who were already Powerites without realizing it could come forward and join. As we have already seen, many who joined had an instant shock of recognition when they encountered the cult. This was true throughout the entire history of the group. Lilith recalls, "When I met them I knew: *Right, well, this is it!*"

A half dozen people joined in New Orleans. The cult set up a "crash seminar" to teach Power doctrine and transform the newcomers into members. The literature used in these classes was limited to the *Xtul Dialogues* and some of *The Logics*.

A system of membership ranks was quickly devised. The newcomers were called *Messengers*. They were also described as *Outside Powerites*, or OPs, and it was assumed at first that they would never be able to join the inner core of The Power because they had not shared the Xtul experience. Over the next few months, however, several of the new Messengers rose to positions of higher rank. The designation Outside Powerite was used from then on to describe members who had not yet been admitted to the heart of Power society. The people who had been at Xtul, and others later admitted to their intimate circle, were called *Inside Powerites*, or IPs. When the ranks were invented, the people who had been at Xtul were divided into four groups, according to influence and ability. Edward and Kitty already constituted The Omega, the highest stratum of Power society. Their leading lieutenants were called *Masters*, in charge of day-to-day decision-making. Less exalted, but still influential, were the *Priests*, and below them were the *Prophets*. So there were now five ranks, as follows:

Omega　　　Master　　　Priest　　　Prophet　　　Messenger

The development of another important custom was completed at this time—the practice of taking *Sacred Names*. As we noted earlier, some Powerites had adopted biblical names at Xtul. In New Orleans, new names were handed out to all members. Kitty selected many of the new names. Now that The Power conceived of itself as a church, it decided to adopt the Catholic monastic practice of calling leaders *Mother* or *Father* and other members *Sister* or *Brother*. Priests and Masters now held names like Father Cain and Mother Isis, while Messengers and Prophets had names like Brother Herod and Sister Lilith. This new custom stressed not only the religious definition of the group, but also the close, family-like relations that now bound members together.

THE RELIGIOUS IMAGE

From the abandonment of the name Compulsions Analysis to the incorporation as The Power—Church of Armageddon, from late 1965 through late 1967, the cult evolved from a psychotherapy service into a religious group. At the beginning of this chapter we suggested six factors that operated to accomplish this transformation and bring about the adoption of the religious label. Now we will review them, seeing how they apply to the evidence given in this chapter, and developing a clearer perspective for understanding the further evidence in later chapters.

1. The language of religion was available to Powerites as a system of interpretation through which they could attempt to understand and communicate the things that were happening to them. None of the original members was well educated in any social or behavioral science. When I first introduced myself to Edward de Forest and said I was a sociologist, he asked me to explain the difference between sociology and psychology. While some members had read books on psychoanalysis, the language of Freud's system was not well suited to all their purposes, because it assumed that their unusual hopes and desires were pathological. At Xtul, Powerites found the Bible a good source of comparisons and ideas to interpret their own situation. Many of them named the new self-conceptions they developed after characters in the Bible.

2. We have seen that the original Powerites were very conscious of the fact that the personal goals that emerged in their Adlerian therapy sessions were not goals that conventional society encouraged. The magical desires they expressed in these sessions, and which were encouraged by other members, could only be realized outside the context of normal life.

3. In group therapy, and in the group living situation that developed, members lost the feeling of independence, lost ego boundaries, and gained the feeling of incorporation in a larger being. This group mind operated most obviously in the group Meditations, but was a social fact at all times. With its experience of implosion and concern for unity, the cult tended at first to define the group consensus as divine guidance. In later chapters we will see that the fact of group divisions and competing personalities generated a theology of several Gods.

4. The hypothesis that God existed and intervened in The Power seemed confirmed by a number of experiences the cult had in this period. The discovery of Xtul, the bounty of Nature at Xtul, the wrathful hurricane, and the Greek and Israeli military actions were taken as signs demonstrating the presence of God.

5. We have begun to see how intuitively and impulsively The Omega ruled. Edward and Kitty took off on their expensive Mediterranean junket supported by the rank and file. We will see in the future many examples of ways in which they exploited followers economically under the justification of doing God's work and of mediating between the cult and God. Furthermore, the practice of following *signs and portents*, a method of making decisions that will become clearer later on, is a way of holding power without taking responsibility. Often these signs are practical exigencies, but equally often they are nothing more than the personal whims of the leaders.

6. By the end of 1967 in New Orleans, The Power had discovered that it could use the *label* of religious group to control to some extent the response of the public. The incorporation as a church not only made it legal for members to beg on the streets and supported their claim that people ought to give them money, but also freed them from the problem of income taxes.

We can look at these six as stages in the adoption of a label. First, the label was available, already invented and given powerful connotations by the larger society. The second step was the discovery that the label served individual psychological purposes, permitting and expressing personal desires and fantasies. The third step was the development of a social reality which was most easily understood by participants in religious terms. In the fourth step, the Powerites confronted the physical environment of which human life is but a part, and found that they needed the concept of God to explain the astonishing universe around them. The fifth step was a strategic use of the religious conceptualization to shape the group's power structure and social relations within it. The sixth step took that strategy to a larger field, and sought to control public behavior toward the group through use of the religious label.

This logical progression of steps expresses a continuity of principles, each built on the one before it. But there is also a single unifying principle behind this sequence: the nature of the religious label itself.

In his classic discussion of the meaning of religion, Emile Durkheim argues that the most important thing we must understand is the conceptual distinction between *the sacred* and *the profane*. He says, "the sacred and the profane have always and everywhere been conceived by the human mind as two distinct classes, as two worlds between which there is nothing in common." [3] "The two worlds are not only conceived of as separate, but as even

---

[3] Emile Durkheim, *The Elementary Forms of the Religious Life* (New York: Free Press, 1965), p. 54.

hostile and jealous rivals of each other."[4] Durkheim then explains the concept of religion:

The real characteristic of religious phenomena is that they always suppose a bipartite division of the whole universe, known and knowable, into two classes which embrace all that exists, but which radically exclude each other. Sacred things are those which the interdictions protect and isolate; profane things, those to which these interdictions are applied and which must remain at a distance from the first. Religious beliefs are the representations which express the nature of sacred things and the relations which they sustain, either with each other or with profane things.[5]

The Power became religious because it sought to rise above ordinary life and escape the bonds of conventional society. *The Human Game* that Powerites attempted to escape was *the profane world.* In his book *Humanity Is the Devil*, written in May 1968, Edward explained that the greatest profanity is not Satan, but Humanity, the ordinary conduct of human life. Durkheim argues that the sacred has a single source, but I believe it does not. The sacred is a label for all those human dreams which cannot find fulfillment within conventional life. Religion is a hope and a demand: a hope that rapturous fantasies will be realized; a demand that others respect those fantasies.

In a way, the terms *sacred* and *religious* refer to a variety of *social deviance* —thoughts, behaviors, and social claims that violate everyday principles, yet are held to be legitimate. The relationship between the sacred and the profane is the same as that between the deviant and the normal, except that society accepts the sacred and rejects crasser forms of deviance. The Power was able to beg on the streets despite laws against begging, because their activity was defined as religious, and therefore not really begging. A religious statement is not a lie merely because it is arbitrary and unsupported by fact. Religious beliefs are not madness, although they sound like madness. Religious ritual is not absurd clowning, no matter how silly the clothing and the gestures might seem outside a church. Priests are not swindlers or madmen, *by definition.*

Religion is a fantasy of profundity, the assertion of glory without accomplishment, the claim of membership in a powerful community that cannot be seen. Religion differs from art and humor because these admit that they are fantasies, while religion is the dream that claims it is real. Religion differs from crime and insanity in that society tolerates it. Because religion is simply legitimate deviance that is taken seriously, the word can cover many phenomena of quite varied origins. It is a label that came easily to mind to

[4] Ibid., p. 55.   [5] Ibid., p. 56.

describe The Power. The therapy group started by Edward and Kitty did not really *become* a religion. Rather, after it had grown socially alienated and sufficiently deviant, its members symbolically dealt with that deviance by *adopting the religious label*. The Power was a religion because it had fled the normal world into a form of preposterously arrogant deviance, yet wanted to be received warmly. The Power was a religion because it was gloriously good deviance.

FOUR

In Search of the Miraculous

My soul has wandered through many lands,
I've seen the times of old;
I feel the New World growing stronger,
I feel new strength,
New life unfold.
                    —Power hymn: *Rise up, Rise Up*

The founders of The Power created their cult to achieve unlimited goals of personal satisfaction and effectiveness. During the social implosion and at Xtul they received ample "proof" that their collective gamble was paying off. After Xtul they continued to recruit new members, convincing them to join the cult's odyssey, but were extremely unclear in their plans for the future. How could the promise of The Power be fulfilled? The cult was faced with a vague but intense crisis. Powerites felt they were approaching their transcendent goal but could not quite reach it. As fast as they rushed toward it, it retreated. The result was an erratic, chaotic quest in search of the miraculous.

NEW RECRUITS

The 144,000 Powerites the cult hoped to collect were not only supposed to be marked with the seal of God, but also to be the best people according to many of the standards of the world. All millenarian sects assert that their members are somehow superior to nonmembers, but The Power was in fact originally staffed by good, talented people. They were elitist in conventional terms, as well as presumptuous in their unconventionality. The Power encouraged aspirants for membership who happened to have talent and education, and discouraged the riffraff majority of ordinary religious seekers and deadbeats who mistakenly wandered in the door. The aristocrat of millenarian sects, The Power recruited people of worth in the years 1967–1971.

We might ask what kinds of excellent people were running loose in society in those years, sufficiently unattached from conventional institutions to be recruited to new movements and deviant groups such as The Power. The answer has three related parts. 1) Young people from solid middle- and even upper-class families who had been touched by the powerful youth-drug-counterculture of the late 1960s and did not value conventional careers highly enough to pursue them with vigor. Like the original Powerites, these people were attracted by visions of escaping mundane inhibitions and achieving a vastly superior lifestyle. 2) College students halfway into a career who stalled in their progress, often simply because they discovered they did not enjoy the particular field they were getting into and were given no quick route to a happier conventional alternative. 3) Young people who had just lost many of their intimate social ties, either through a divorce or other family disruption or merely because they had gone wandering in search of their fortunes. Several were temporarily weak in social attachments merely because they had just completed a geographical move—for example, going away from home to attend school.

Although some individuals who fit one or more of these descriptions might also be suffering from personal pathology (neurosis, tension, strain . . . whatever), there was no necessity for them to be troubled. The Power was not interested in troubled people. For example, Father Herod told me he was not suffering any kind of emotional distress or personal trouble when he joined in New Orleans in 1967. Herod was a native of Mississippi. He liked his home but at the end of his teens felt a desire to go out into the world. He went to New Orleans, the big city, with the excuse that he was going to attend art school. He entered the school in 1966, and wasted six months halfheartedly attending art classes and loafing. Art school did not inspire him. He was looking for an enjoyable cosmopolitan life, and art was just one plausible alternative to check out. He considered other options but found none particularly attractive. When the Power appeared on the scene, and looked really exciting, he joined. In retrospect, he thinks the real reason he left Mississippi was in order to join The Power, guided by an intuitive impulse or by benevolent fates.

Brother Mark encountered The Power while on vacation in New Orleans and did not formally join until the cult reached New York, a few months later. His case is more complex than that of Herod, and shows a measure of personal distress, but no long-term pathology. Mark had attended Auburn College and New York University, majoring in physics, with some interest in electrical engineering. But he found the program less than inspiring and had some difficulty keeping up with the reading. "After three years I decided I didn't want to complete it, but I had spent all this money which I felt responsible to my family for. And so I thought I would work with them, and try to make up some of the expense." So Mark went to work in his father's real estate business, unhappy in his job and wishing he could find a way out, a way to something grander. "I had feelings of responsibility around my family. My father was a semi-invalid, was becoming more and more dependent on me. The whole thing was a setup—a perfect guilt situation. So I had resolved earlier that I would have to enter some kind of religious life. I didn't know what kind. . . . I was involved in Eastern religions, and Yoga, but no particular religious orientation one way or the other.

"Anyway, I was on vacation, and I was traveling around with a friend, and I met somebody who said, 'Go to this address. There are some interesting things happening there.' And I said, 'Ah! They'll be glad to see *me*!' And when I went there I was completely amazed. I didn't agree with things, intellectually, but it was an immediate emotional rapport and attachment that fixed on me. . . . The People. The lifestyle. The degree of commitment. Just the feeling around the place. It was purely an emotional attachment and attraction. A feeling of rightness about the whole thing. And a feeling of wanting to be with these people . . . a kind of magic."

SAN FRANCISCO

In New Orleans, The Power completed its evolution from therapy group to religious movement. That clarified things but solved nothing. Where would the cult go? What would it do? Which road led to heaven? A traditional activity of religious movements is the founding of new pioneer churches. More than a year earlier, even before the group left London to go to Xtul, Father Cain had "a vision . . . about a new group in San Francisco." It was a very precise image. "I saw it as a miniduplicate of what we had in London, with me playing a central role in the thing, and new people joining, in San Francisco. That was what I saw, and that was what happened." Cain left New Orleans in December 1967 to found his dream chapter.

He arrived in San Francisco at an interesting time. Hippies and radicals abounded. Cain immediately visited the area's colleges and universities to give talks and meet young people. San Francisco State was in an uproar with "Black Power hitting the campus really big, and there were lots of riots." At Berkeley and at other centers of youth activity, Cain made contact with many potential converts. Father Moses came up from New Orleans to join Cain, and they rented a house for use as a public chapter.

"We were located very close to the Haight-Ashbury district," Cain recalls. This was "right at the crest and beginnings of decline of the Flower
Power bit." He felt Haight was a "totally undisciplined environment. I
think people who went to it didn't have the self-discipline to hold either
themselves or the whole situation together. And it disintegrated rapidly
and rather disastrously, and became rather ugly." The flamboyant public
presentation of The Power was attractive to many members of the youth
culture, so the Chapter House became a popular hangout. Cain and Moses
set up a coffee house where people could drop in and socialize. They held
Sabbath Assemblies each week in an *Alpha* ritual room, and conducted
Telepathy Developing Circles.

An introductory doctrinal course, the First Progress, was offered to
those interested in joining, and another crash advanced Progress (seminar) was set up for a few young people of particular interest and attractiveness. About a half-dozen achieved full membership in the cult, including later leaders Amaranth, Israel, and Orpheus. More than eight
years later, Cain told me he still feels a special personal relationship with
those he recruited in San Francisco. "We got to know each other very
well. The bond has strengthened over the years."

In February 1968, The Omega decided to move again, and closed
down the New Orleans Chapter. They had been staying in the United
States on three-month visitor visas, and their time had long since run out.
Not ready to leave America, they decided to avoid the authorities by
keeping on the move. The entire group went to join Cain and Moses in San
Francisco for a brief time. Then everybody moved down to Los Angeles.

Los Angeles was where the cult recruited Brother Pan, a young Japa-
nese-American. His story is a good example to illustrate the recruitment
style of the cult in those years. Pan had been living with his parents and
attending college, when rising dissatisfaction with his social relations
and growing interest in the flourishing youth counterculture inspired
him to explore new lifestyles. He felt that he and his old friends were
caught in lives that lacked "immediacy . . . communication . . . contact." Utopian ideas were in the air. Pan had a vision "of being in a
group environment." Through a friend of a friend, he learned about a
large house inhabited by a variety of young people, strangers into alien
things, a place where he might find a better way of living. "When the
flower children were in blossom, I saw a potential for this ideal to become
a reality." He moved into the house, and almost immediately (and coin-
cidentally) many of the young people moved out. He discovered he didn't
like the drug scene. "It was leading nowhere. As you know, the flower
movement wilted." Pan longed for a "special group, a very dynamic,

cohesive group that had a sense of purpose, direction, drive, and dedication."

One day Pan was sitting in his room when a couple of his housemates burst in and exclaimed, "Eight-foot priests from London have come in! In robes!" It was The Power. They had made contact with the owner of the house, who agreed to let them stay in return for several hours of work a week maintaining his other properties. In a few days, all the non-Powerites except Pan left, "to pick strawberries in Lancaster." He was now living in the midst of thirty members of The Power. They set up a semi-private chapter in the house and began holding their rituals and classes.

Pan was invited to attend the Sabbath Assembly. At that time, the ceremony included a moment near the end when any newcomers were invited to "come forward" and join. The Evangelist completed his "Revelation" sermon and called for Pan to rise. "Well, what happened was, my feet came forward. My feet got up and started coming forward. Either I would fall back on my head, or I had to follow my feet! I followed my feet. I didn't have any alternative." Pan was now a member of a group just like the one he had dreamed of. In May, the Los Angeles Chapter closed down, and the whole lot went on to New York, where yet another temporary chapter was opened in Greenwich Village.

I believe the main pressure behind this constant migration was the American immigration authorities, who had not given the British Powerites permission to settle in the U.S. According to one story, the departure from California was caused by hostile members of Technianity who called the authorities and reported the address where the cult was staying. One Powerite told me the group left California because, like many mystical young folk at the time, they believed the state would soon be devastated by earthquakes. I rather think "bad vibrations" of a more social variety than earthquakes were at fault.

One of those who joined in New York was Sister Ruth, a young anthropologist. She had enjoyed her graduate studies at the University of Chicago, but not the academic life, with its departmental politics and status games. She had been in Mexico at the same time Xtul was occupied by the cult, but had never visited it. From two young women who were in contact with the cult, she received a couple of Power magazines secondhand: the *Common Market* issue, and the one titled *Freedom of Expression* with rock superstar Mick Jagger on the cover. Her doctoral project was on Mayan linguistics, and she found field research disappointingly boring. Nothing was happening in the village she lived in. Twice she took vacations from the field, returning to the States.

Ruth visited a friend at Tulane University in New Orleans. While there, she visited the Power Chapter House a couple of times. She "was completely fascinated, bug-eyed!" Ruth "tended to discount the theology. I was mostly interested in the people." She returned to Yucatan. During the year, her attitude toward conventional American society became progressively more negative. Like many others, she was a fan of liberal politician Bobby Kennedy. His assassination in June disheartened her. Nixon's speech accepting the Republican presidential nomination disturbed Ruth. She saw a dark future ahead for America. She visited her family in New York and ran into The Power again at its Greenwich Village location. "The feeling was of a community that was actually going somewhere and actually had something to offer in terms of a lifestyle." Because she believed America was a sinking ship, she was happy to climb aboard The Power.

Ruth has her own interesting theory. "The thing about anthropologists is that basically all of them don't like their own society very much. If they did, they wouldn't be anthropologists. What they're actually trying to do is get out of ordinary American society anyway. They usually find a field area that they like, and they're usually very happy when they're in their field area. And they're a bit miserable when they're at home! And that goes for archaeologists as well. They have a wonderful time in the field, wherever they've decided they want to be, and are totally miserable in the office, writing."

She believes most anthropologists share this characteristic. "They have a strong sense of alienation from our society." Consequently, they seek to escape, at least periodically, to a better society. The only problem for each was to find an alternative society that pleased him. For some anthropologists the alternative society is that of the Mayan Indians.[1] But Ruth found the Mayans terribly boring. She was a believer in cultural evolution. If you go from America to Bali, you are going "down the scale" toward less advanced, less exciting styles of life. Ruth even felt that her visits to Europe were steps "down the scale." She didn't like backward people and wanted to find a society that was a step up from America, a modern or even futuristic tribe. "The Power was *up* from ordinary American society." She believed every anthropologist was looking for his tribe. The Power was hers. Ruth once asked me to carry a message back to one of her former professors. It was a simple bit of news, "I went native."

Power culture constantly grew and changed. The purple capes of the costumes were discarded, partly because some members were embarrassed to

---

[1] Evon Z. Vogt, *The Zinacantecos of Mexico: A Modern Maya Way of Life* (New York: Holt, Rinehart and Winston, 1970).

wear them, partly because the supply ran out. In New Orleans, Powerites had worn only one religious symbol, a silver cross. In New York, they added black triangular emblems embroidered with red, humanoid goats' heads. This *Badge of Mendes* indicated the acceptance of the power of Satan. Step by step throughout 1968 a theology solidified, identifying three equal parts of God, Lucifer–Jehovah–Satan.

MUNICH

In March or April 1968, soon after the New Orleans Chapter had closed, while the main group was traveling in California, Abraham and Siegfried flew from the London Chapter to Munich, Germany, to set up a little branch there. Sister Gretel, one of the new recruits, was sent from America to join them, because she spoke German fluently. Abraham knew the language well, while Siegfried spoke it very little. They "were very interested in the political situation because it was a time of considerable unrest," Siegfried said. England was still brooding over membership in the Common Market, so the English Powerites had a certain nationalistic interest in checking out the Germans to see what kind of partners they would make. The Power was in search of *intensity*, so the Nazi mystique attracted them. They wanted to learn "how Hitler could have happened to a country" and whether similar forces were still at work.

The tiny Munich Chapter immediately made contact with both German political extremes, the leftist student SDS movement, and the pseudo-Nazi NPD political party. "Both extremes," Siegfried says, "were very active." The SDS staged marches through the streets of Munich to protest the Vietnam War. "One time a lot of SDS people lay down on the tram tracks in Munich, which held up a lot of people. It was a very politically stupid time for them to do it. It was four o'clock in the afternoon, when everybody was going home. Now, if they'd done it when everybody was going to work, it would have been a different matter. Of course, the SDS are not into getting up at seven or eight in the morning!" The three Powerites traveled to Nuremberg, scene of Hitler's greatest public displays, and to Koburg, to view right-wing NPD rallies. They met Adolf von Thadden, leader of the party, and found him "a very impressive man," a "dignified . . . big, rather florid man" with "quite a lot of charisma."

Siegfried remembers one grand incident that illustrated the complex relationship between the cult and the political extremes. It expressed exactly the image the cult wanted to present and exactly the reception it sought. Abraham, Siegfried, and Gretel decided to visit a right-wing rally that was being protested by a mob of left-wingers. They marched toward the meeting hall dressed in their all-black uniforms with flowing capes, two huge beards and three heads of long hair clearly visible. The SDS saw them coming and "thought we were left-wing. We weren't left-wing, although we had a number of elements about us that people could have mistaken for left-wing. They saw us go into this rally, and they thought this was terrific! Obviously we were going in to disrupt it. So they cheered and clapped. Great performance! Lot of people. And we went into this hall where they were having the rally. It was all very orderly. All regimented. And we were dressed in our gear, in uniform, black at that time. We walked down the center of the aisle looking for a seat, and everybody started cheering! And waving! Of course because we were in uniform we looked like right-wing!" Power doctrine had already begun to emphasize the idea that the extremes of human experience and expression were superior to mundane blandness, and that the extremes could be reconciled without dilution within the cult. The Power display at the rally was a "sort of transcendence of this absurd situation."

The Powerites supported themselves in Munich by selling their English-language magazines on Leopoldstrasse, asking for donations and finding people who would put them up temporarily in their homes. They lived off the curiosity and benevolence of the Germans. In return they put on quite a show. In addition to their street performance, they carried on in cafes, and even once in a bar. After getting the proprietor's permission, they would sing Power songs for the bemused customers and act out dramatic little skits depicting various elements of the evolving cult doctrine.

Abraham, Siegfried, and Gretel gave a particularly memorable impromptu performance in the Englische Garten park. At one point, the park ground rises in a low hill topped by a cupola or bandstand. In good weather there were always many Munich citizens sitting about on the grass, relaxing and chatting. The three costumed Powerites stormed up the knoll, unannouced, with only a vague idea what they might do. Their colorful act "was a kind of demonstration of the various aspects of God, through chanting, music, enactments." Three aspects of God, three archetypes, were dramatized: Jehovah, Lucifer, and Satan. "People didn't know *what* we were doing," Siegfried remarks. "We were giving this performance, but they didn't know what it was. They thought it was terribly funny. Those crazy English people, what are they doing! Afterwards they all clapped and pelted us with coins. So it was all in good fun, but it was really a crazy situation!"

As is usual for The Power, it was a time of extreme ups and downs. Apparently relations within the tiny Chapter, consisting of two men and one woman, were not entirely harmonious. Things got so bad that Gretel dropped permanently out of The Power. "Not surprising," Edward de Forest told me. "That was a carve-up situation."

Around July 1968, two or three more members were sent to Munich, so the expanded group decided it was time to rent their own apartment and establish the beginnings of a real Chapter. None of the literature was ever translated into German, and the cult's impact on Germany was slight. But this tiny Munich Chapter, which only lasted six months, served as a stable starting point for the extensive wanderings in Europe that began later that year.

AIMED FOR LONDON

The New York Chapter was really the staging area for return to England. The group in Greenwich Village was busy collecting enough money to ship everyone across the Atlantic, and sent the few untrained newcomers over first, as finances permitted. Mark went over in June 1968, with another new American member. The small London Chapter not only started training them immediately in doctrine, but also thrust them without delay onto the streets as instantaneous spokesmen for The Power. The day after he arrived in London, Mark was spreading the cult's antivivisectionist opinions from a soap box at Hyde Park Corner.

Kitty had always been intensely antivivisectionist. As we mentioned, she once smashed a television set because it was showing pictures of a bull-fight. Edward shared her feeling that experimentation on animals was evil, but he was less outraged in his opposition than she. Directly inspired by her, he wrote an antivivisectionist tract in May 1968, *The Ultimate Sin*, later published by the church in book form. But when Mark first spoke at Hyde Park Corner, surrounded by hecklers and competing soapboxers, he had no script for his tirades. "*The Ultimate Sin* hadn't been published then, and we were all just talking about our own realities on vivisection." They felt the carving up of living animals was "rejection of God's creation, rejection of God, hostility towards God and enacting that hostility on God's creation. You're not going to get anything but death out of utilization of death. If you employ death in the procedure, that's going to be inextricably entwined in the results. So you're going to apparently do something beneficial, but you're also going to do something destructive and detrimental, which was borne out by the effects of drugs and dependence on drugs and symptomatic medicine." That's the sort of thing Mark would say to the crowd.

Three or four Powerites would troop over to Hyde Park every Sunday, and take a stand by their soap box. Actually they used a milk crate that they dragged with them, but it functioned as a soap box. They would form a little line, and the first Powerite would step up on the box and begin haranguing the passersby. When he ran out of steam, he would cede the box to the next in line, who would take over and launch into his spiel. They would go on in turn like this for several hours. The last London issue of the cult's magazine has a picture spread on the inside front cover showing two views of Power soapboxers speaking to a large crowd. One of the pictures is clearly faked. The audience has been augmented by the splicing in of two sections of other photographs. The Power wanted to believe it had a tremendous impact on people.

"You had to bellow out as loud as you can to attract attention," Mark recalls. "It's really exciting. It's not something that you can look forward to, but it really has an element of life and energy to it. It gets you through a lot of feelings of vulnerability and what you can and cannot do . . . dealing with hecklers and that kind of thing. There were some of these people who would just go there every week to heckle, and they have elephant voices that sound like *Baarrrrooooooommmm!*, these big, bull-moose things. They disagree with absolutely everything, even if it's the thing they just said."

In September, about two dozen Powerites, including most of the new American recruits, were put aboard a modest ocean liner named The Waterman, bound for London. Edward and three others stayed on in New York for a short while. When I asked him why the group was sent over, he first replied as if everything had been part of a clear, voluntary plan. "We had an idea of just focusing all our attention in London, and spreading throughout Europe from there." Lilith recalls that "We were not exactly a smash hit in New York." As an afterthought, Edward admitted the British members knew they had to get out of the States and wanted to take the new Americans with them. "You see, originally we had appalling immigration problems, 'cause we had no money at all. We were all trying to be immigrated, but we just had this 'church' which had no prospects at all, and no money, so we couldn't get our immigration. This was right back at the very beginning, and which is why eventually we just left the country and went back to Europe." But the cult interpreted the problem as something grander than a mere bureaucratic hassle. They saw it as a divine message, a sign or a portent. "That was another *sign*, because we couldn't stay any longer." The American Powerites were, as Lilith says, "a pretty motley crew" and in no position to carry on a New York Chapter by themselves. The only well-established center was in London. She says, "The idea really was to try and get us into London, I suppose, and consolidate us more, train us more."

When The Waterman arrived at London, the British immigration authorities came aboard ship to check those passengers who wanted to get off.

Most of the two dozen Powerites were not English citizens, and few of them had any money, so they were refused entry. None had work permits, any clear means of support while in England, nor return tickets to justify defining them as tourists. So they were rejected. Edward explained, "So that meant the whole lot simply stayed on the boat! Apparently the Immigration people were thoroughly unpleasant."

Pan, one of the rejected Americans, could see the officials' point. The English Home Office doubted that the tiny London Chapter could support so many Americans and had not been given any kind of warning that they were coming. Siegfried thinks "the main reason was that there were just too many Americans. We were comparatively unknown as a religious order, of course, at the time. And it wasn't like fifteen Catholic priests were trying to get in. It's not too surprising they turned them back! What we did after that, and it was stupid of us not to do it beforehand, was we went to the Foreign Office in England and set it up. We gave them all the evidence they needed that these people would not become burdens on the state and public wards. But it never occurred to us in our naiveté at the time that they couldn't just walk in."

It is quite possible there was another reason the group was turned away by British authorities. At this very same time, the British Government was barring the entry of noncitizens who wanted to study and receive therapy at the Technianity College. Early in 1967, the House of Commons debated the alleged dangers of Technianity, and a government policy aimed at discouraging the growing cult was developed in 1968. Newspapers from the summer of 1968 contain a number of reports concerning people turned back at London airport or otherwise refused entry. One chartered flight intended to take 180 Americans to the Technianity College was canceled. The connection between The Power and Technianity was well known in London, and it is quite possible the Powerites were seen as just one more Technianity group.

Mother Sibyl was in charge of the party on The Waterman and had to deal with the situation. There were few options, and the one they took was the most passive. The two dozen of them simply stayed on the ship and continued on to its ultimate destination, Rotterdam. They did not stay there long, as Lilith reports. "We went to Amsterdam, where accommodation had been arranged for us in this great big old loft in an abandoned school. We all lived there with about thirteen German shepherds."

There was, of course, a tiny chapter in Munich. In their brief German travels, Siegfried and Abraham had found it possible to get along without jobs or money. Would it be possible to maintain the two dozen stranded Powerites in Germany this way? Much of the responsibility for a solution fell on this little band in Germany. The immigration problem "was a bit of a shock for everybody," Siegfried says. "So we had to do some fast thinking in Germany. Father Abraham and Mother Cybele, who had by that time joined us, set off first of all to Hannover and then subsequently to Hamburg to try and establish some kind of accommodation for the people who were coming in." They founded a temporary center in Hamburg, and the groups in Amsterdam and Munich converged there.

MATTHEW TEN

Back in New York, Edward and his associates frantically discussed the challenge thrown before them by the British authorities. *The Book of Matthew*, Edward's personal favorite among the books of the Bible, provided inspiration. On the first of October 1968, Edward wrote a letter to all Powerites, setting their current difficulties in the optimistic context of the New Testament. Titled BI-6 (*Brethren Information* letter number six), it sought to explain everything in the best possible light:

1.1 In Matthew Chapter 10, Christ instructs his disciples, before sending them out in pairs to go from city to city preaching the Word.

1.2 The instructions he gave apply now, possibly even more precisely than they did then.

1.3 We have talked for some time about Powerites going out in pairs preaching the message of the End, and it looks as though we shall very soon be ready for just this kind of operation. And Matthew Chapter 10 supplies the blue-print for it.

The following sections of B1-6 are a commentary on Matthew 10 written by Father Cain from notes of his discussions with Edward. Cain explains the relevant passages and gives specific instructions for the conduct of traveling Powerite pairs. For example, verses nine and ten of Matthew 10 say, "Provide neither gold, nor silver, nor brass in your purses, Nor scrip for your journey, neither two coats, neither shoes, nor yet staves: for the workman is worthy of his meat." Cain and Edward commented on this passage, translating it into instructions for their followers:

6.3 Take no money. For the individual Powerite has no need of it for himself. For our physical needs will be met by those to whom we give spiritually. If we are doing our job properly, then we are "worthy of our meat," and our physical requirements will be taken care of.

6.4 This does not mean that The Power has no requirement for money, nor that a Powerite should refuse to accept money. Quite the contrary; he accepts the money, making it clear to the person from whom he received it that it will be devoted to the purposes of The Power, and not to his own needs. And immediately he passes the money up the hierarchy, thus making his own contribution upwards in physical form.

6.5 In fact we go with no physical possessions at all, beyond the bare minimum of clothing. We have nothing to give downwards on a physical level, no hand-outs for the hungry or the poor, no bowls of soup, no Welfare payments. Our job is to channel spiritual sustenance and to take spiritual responsibility for those beneath us in the hierarchy; not to take physical responsibility for them, nor to look after their physical needs.

This passage shows clearly how traditional scripture was bent to serve the practical problems of the cult leadership, and how new doctrine could be generated in response to a problem. The theology grew out of social relations and sought to control those relations symbolically. A practical solution required more than philosophizing and exhortation; it required a practical test. Two of the new Americans, Nathaniel and Herod, were sent to Frankfurt on a trial run. "It was a bit like Noah's Ark," Siegfried recalls. Nathaniel and Herod were the doves that left the ship in search for dry land. "We sent two out to see whether the flood had subsided and they would come back." It had. They did.

Under the circumstances, the invocation of Matthew 10 was a brilliant maneuver. It transformed a disaster into an opportunity, a grievous mistake into a creative inspiration. It denied that the leadership had failed, and reasserted their dominance over the rank and file. The large group in Hamburg was split up in pairs and sent out into Germany, instructed to follow Matthew 10 and spread the Word. Of course, the chief purpose of this plan was to have some place to put the Powerites, activity to keep them busy, and a way of supporting them without money or much work from the leaders.

There were other functions the Matthew 10 episode served, unintended but important. For those who stuck with the cult through this trying period, Matthew 10 was great experience in dealing with large numbers of strangers and in maintaining themselves without help in a strange environment. It was also an initiation rite and commitment mechanism. Those who made it through this time were firmly bound to the cult. Relationships between them were deepened through the shared struggle and adventure. For those who had not been at Xtul, it was the defining experience, a personal watershed.

The pairs headed in all directions. Siegfried and Abraham visited Wuppertal, Frankfurt, Heidelberg, and Stuttgart. In the last of these cities they rendezvoused with a number of others. A party of four headed back to London by way of Paris. Siegfried recalls the French capital fondly. "Had a wonderful time in Paris. It was late fall, and it was beautiful. People were so receptive to us. We were selling so many magazines we didn't know what to do with ourselves. We really had a terrific time."

Mother Sibyl picked the pairs and aimed them at their first destinations, but, as Lilith says, "Once they were sent, basically, we were all *really* under our own steam. I mean it was literally following the whole Matthew 10 thing. When I arrived in Düsseldorf, the first thing we did was donate accommodations, donate food, and start donating money. And that's basically all we spent our time doing, was donating money, donating accommodations, and donating food."

Brother Pan joked that the treks were a tourist's nightmare: "How to see Germany on minus five cents a day!" Lilith described the trips to me in detail. "We went out in pairs, and we relied completely on the people that we met to feed us and house us and to give us funds to keep the church going. If a city was not being hospitable, if you could not find accommodations, or if you got stopped by the police for donating, well then the idea was that you didn't persist in that city, but like in Matthew 10 you shook the dust of it off your sandals and carried on to another city. And it was all done through hitchhiking as well. We hitched from city to city. And many of us had dogs with us. Adam and I had two dogs. We had Satan and Beelzebub.

"We were on the streets chronically, just walking all the time. Things would happen. Like in Düsseldorf we had a really bad stretch and we couldn't get any accommodation and for some reason that I can't remember now we didn't leave the city. We stayed there about five days. We had to sit up at night in a German bar, a students' bar, without sleeping." She and Adam suffered through those days together, without any support from the cult's leadership. "You would have incredible hardships! First of all, it was freezing cold and we were not very well dressed for a German winter. And you would have lean periods where you would not be getting fed very well, or your accommodation would be very bad, like just sleeping on a bare floor with a blanket or something. Not being able to get a bath because the places you were staying in didn't have baths, or they only had cold water."

Lilith remembers the times of good fortune with great pleasure. "It was quite a miraculous period, you know, being in Germany, not being able to speak German. Being put up by strange people who very often couldn't speak English. But in some sort of way you would be able to get it across to them that you needed a place to stay. And some people being unbelievably good to us. Really generous, kind. Things like: going into restaurants with the dogs and just having the chefs come out of the kitchen and feed the dogs with all kinds of bones, and people from the tables coming over with food for the dogs. Extraordinary personal things: people being really open and generous, and willing to give whatever it was that they could give."

Matthew 10 was a guide for activity at the London Chapter as well as among the Powerites in Germany. Brother Mark says he traveled all over England and Scotland, perhaps not from Land's End to John o' Groats, but at least from Plymouth to Aberdeen. Like the Powerites in Germany, they went out in pairs and lived off the charity of strangers while spreading their message and advertising the cult. Mark recalls it well.

"Sometimes you'd get taken into nightclubs, given front-row tables, and you'd get a whole show and revue and big steak dinner. You'd go up to the manager and say, 'We're traveling for a church, doing work of our church, et cetera, et cetera. Can you provide a meal for us, and help us on our way with our work?' And some people would say, 'No, no.' And other people would say, 'Sure, come on in; these two gentlemen are ministers in a church.' Introduce us to the maître d', and have us sit down—waiters running all around—the whole schmeer. And other times we'd find ourselves ending up with little or nothing, depending on how well we had done our work."

Here again Mark expresses the Power ideology, the blanket explanation for variations in response that makes everything seem meaningful, moral, and uncontaminated by blind chance. Good work would be rewarded by God through the agency of human generosity. "The reward was very clear and very precise and very immediate. Sometimes we'd find an accommodation in a hotel. We'd go to a hotel and ask if they had a room for us. You'd leave your shoes outside the door, and they'd get polished. And they'd wake you up in the morning with tea and toast in the room, and then you'd go down and have breakfast. That was on one side of it. And the other side of it was shivering in a heatless flat, curling up under a rug trying to keep warm. So there was every extreme.

"There were levels and levels of significance to everything. It was like God was intervening very precisely, saying, 'You deserve *this*; you don't deserve *that*. Suffer for a while. You've suffered enough. Here's your reward.' I remember one night being totally frustrated, on the verge of tears, stuck out in Glasgow, pouring rain, nobody on the street, with no place to stay, huddled in a doorway. Seeing one person come out of the train station, seeing one person go running across the street. Last chance! We had given up, completely. This guy was the sweetest! Like an angel. Took us in, fed us, in his house. He and a friend had an apartment. Fed us, invited us back. His friend gave us Judo massages."

Abraham says, "There was an extraordinary quality" to the Matthew 10 trips. "You went where you went to. There was no concept of how long it was going to take to get there. And every person you met had a significance." It was an entirely different experience from conventional traveling. There was a sense of great purpose, but no sense of plan. Abraham agrees, "It was a very magical time."

HUNTING FOR HEADQUARTERS

In mid-October, The Omega left New York and landed in Bremerhaven, Germany. Powerites gathered for a big meeting with Edward and Kitty. A large contingent came from nearby Hamburg, and a few were sent from London. Then The Omega went directly down to Oberammergau, intending to find a place to set up a Power Center in southern Germany. The nearest large city was Munich, where there was now a small cult Chapter, and Oberammergau was a place of beautiful scenery and religious spirit that could give The Omega both pleasure and inspiration. Indeed, it always seems that the travels of The Omega were intended to give pleasure to Edward and Kitty, but were explained as giving inspiration. Perhaps pleasure and inspiration were identical in their minds. The street-begging rank-and-file members were expected to support The Omega in its search for both. A euphoric tourist book about Oberammergau describes the arrival of the comfortable visitor:

At once you feel transported into another world, a world which seems dream-like and fantastic. Longhaired men in white shirts and embroidered braces, with steel-strong limbs showing in knitted hose beneath their leather breeches, hoist your heavy suitcases on their shoulders as if they were matchboxes and stride ahead, leading you on to your lodging, which quite probably will be in a private house, possibly a real chalet dating back two or three centuries.[2]

Such must have been the arrival of The Omega, though the entry of lower-status members into Oberammergau was far more humble. Edward and Kitty were drawn to this religious tourist city by its romantic mystique, a quality of mood they wanted for their own cult. In 1632 and 1633, like many another village, Oberammergau had been ravaged by the plague. Always a particularly religious community, the people of Oberammergau sought a religious solution to the disaster that had befallen them. The town council resolved to give one year in ten to the Lord by presenting a magnificent Passion Play in which all citizens would take part. The plague departed, but the play remained. It transformed this modest mountain town into a world-famous religious center.

From Oberammergau, The Omega sent messages to many of the pairs and groups scattered throughout Germany to join them for a while in this

[2] Elisabethe Corathiel, *Oberammergau and Its Passion Play* (Westminster, Maryland: Newman Press, 1960), p. 102.

spiritually uplifting, mountain-ringed village. Communication was very uncertain, since many of the Powerites were constantly on the move. Although the people in the field sent a daily letter to London and to The Omega now in the south, letters to the wanderers often had to chase them from city to city. Having no sacred places of its own, The Power borrowed Oberammergau to provide a rich spiritual environment for a convocation of its members. The cult often tried to gain spiritual strength from the holy shrine or magical symbol of some more successful church or movement.

After a few days, most of the Powerites who had come down from Northern Germany were sent back, dispersing to follow Matthew 10 once more. The Omega was busy looking for the Power Center. Edward recalls with some amusement that they were hoping to find a suitable place for free. "In fact, we wanted to get someone to donate a Schloss to us." Siegfried and Abraham were sent out on a Schloss quest, searching in Austria as well as Germany. For a while they were negotiating with a Bavarian countess who appeared to have an extra castle. But it never materialized. An Austrian doctor offered his large house. "But it was horrible," Edward says. "I mean it was the most ghastly, depressing place you've ever been into! So we passed that up. We were very grateful, but we passed it up."

The most fabulous location considered for the Power Center was one of Nazi field marshal Herman Goering's homes, Veldenstein Castle near Nuremberg. It was for sale. The Omega inspected photographs provided by a real estate agent and dispatched Siegfried to look Veldenstein over. Veldenstein was a complex of square-walled buildings dominated by a high observation tower, nestled in tall trees and overlooking a landscape of fields and forested hills. A romantic dream, Veldenstein would have been an intensely inspiring site for the Power Center. Just what the cult was looking for, another injection of magic to match Xtul, a physical terminus to their search for the miraculous. The fact that it had belonged to the decadent Luftwaffe leader was a strong point in its favor. Edward was impressed that "This is where he used to have his weird performances." Veldenstein must have stored up very powerful vibrations, a black magical aura of fantastic intensity.

Actually, Veldenstein had been the boyhood home of Hermann Goering, while his chief adult residence was Karinhall in northern Germany. He loved the castle and had developed a taste for feudal glory during the years his family lived there.[3] Veldenstein had been the scene of "weird performances" by Hermann's mother, however, since the castle really belonged to her lover rather than her husband. Father Goering must have experienced

[3] Erich Gritzbach, *Hermann Goering: The Man and His Work* (London: Hurst and Blackett, 1939), pp. 148–149; see the photograph of Veldenstein preceding page 129.

great disgrace living off the generosity of his wife's boyfriend, an emotion
that may have been shared by Hermann as well.[4]

Siegfried inspected Veldenstein and reported that the buildings themselves were not overwhelming, "nice, but very domestic in scale." He liked
it. "It was a magnificent location. They kept falcons there, but they were
just regular people." Except for the high watchtower, it did not seem like a
castle at all. The walls were not castellated, and there were no turrets. The
beauty "was much more the way it was landscaped than the actual buildings." Unfortunately, The Power was unable to come up with enough cash
and had to continue its search for a Center.

In its romantic, erratic way, the cult followed *the signs* from place to
place, from project to project. What does that mean? Edward explains.
"We were seriously looking for a Center, but we didn't find one. So then we
thought, okay . . . we got various signs."

"Signs?" I asked.

"Signs. Which told us to go further south."

"What kind of signs?"

Edward explained that a sign was a possibly divine message about what
The Power was supposed to do. For example, two dozen members "got on a
boat and they went to London, and the Immigration wouldn't let them into
London. The boat was going to Amsterdam anyway, so that's a *sign*. Now
that is a kind of completely choiceless sign—literally they had no choice.
Sometimes you get things like that where the line of least resistance takes
you to a particular point. And when you fight it and resist it and try to do
the thing that you originally were setting out to do, you still move in that
direction. And that's a sign. Like if you're trying to do something, and
everything's blocking it, everything's stopping it, but then something sort-
of opens up *here* that indicates *this* is where you at least can go or can do,
that's a sign. So, you see, the signs were against finding a place in Germany,
'cause we just didn't find a place."

The signs indicated that the Power Center might be found in Italy.
"Well, if you go to Italy," someone said, "you'll find that there are huge
monasteries which are completely unused. And people will either sell them
to you for almost nothing, or will rent them to you for almost nothing."
Two of the senior men set out for Italy to survey the possibilities. They
traveled all over, receiving their food, transportation, and lodging as gifts
from the people they met. They were very pleasantly surprised by the highly positive reception given them by Catholic priests. Unlike English clergy,
these men claimed to find much merit in Power theology. Edward says,

[4] Roger Manvell and Heinrich Fraenkel, *Goering* (New York: Simon and Schuster, 1962),
p. 23.

"It was the most open reception that we'd ever found within established churches."

The Powerites hunting through Italy sent back photographs and drawings of several places they had found. But there was something wrong with each of them. Some were for sale at impossible prices. Some were already half occupied by a Catholic order. It seemed inappropriate to share a monastery with a rival creed. Now the signs pointed in the direction of Sicily, where The Omega heard there might be large establishments going for tiny rents or unused monasteries that could be had for a song.

At the same time, there was another sign. A few Powerites became interested in Aleister Crowley, a cult leader and magician who had set up his group in the early 1920s at Cefalú on the north coast of Sicily. There were many similarities between The Power and Crowley's cult, such as their common attempt to transform members into intense personalities sharing mystical consciousness-expanding exercises in a surreal utopian community.[5]

Crowley's maxims bear some similarity to Power principles. Edward de Forest begins his personal letters with "As it is . . ." and ends them with ". . . so be it." Crowley sandwiched his written communications between two rather more ornate maxims: "Do what thou wilt shall be the whole of the law" and "Love is the law, love under will." Crowley's principle of *Thelema*, an intellectual support for his magical practices, included an idea shared by Technianity, and I think privately applied by Edward de Forest to himself: "In particular, each individual is conceived as the center of his own universe, his essential nature determining his relations with similar beings and his proper course of action."[6]

Crowley wrote that he chose Cefalú in Sicily as the site for his Abbey of Thelema because the repeated casting of *I Ching* fortunes gave no other favorable response but that for Cefalú. I have seen Edward cast *I Chings* at a time of crisis, looking for hints of the future. The Power's belief in signs and portents similarly indicates the use of magic to make decisions, presumably to avoid painful responsibility and the threat of personal failure. Lured by Crowley's reputation and the idea that his abandoned Abbey of Thelema might be an ideal headquarters, The Omega left Oberammergau for Cefalú.

Kitty and Edward stayed in a small hotel set in an orange grove. Beautiful but primitive. The majority of the hotel's guests were rats, and the place was absolutely filthy. Powerites fanned out in search for a headquarters building near Cefalú, with little success. One possibility, a castle-like

[5] John Symonds, *The Magic of Aleister Crowley* (London: Muller, 1958).

[6] Aleister Crowley, *The Confessions of Aleister Crowley*, ed. John Symonds and Kenneth Grant (New York: Hill and Wang, 1969), p. 796.

monastery, was not suitable because the owner wanted to lend them only the worst part. The Omega moved to nearby Palermo to check out an incredible bright-red hotel on a rock promontory overlooking the sea. Exciting, but too expensive. This was a bleak and depressing time. Edward says Palermo was "the bottom end of the universe." A Power Center had not materialized, "and by then also we were going through a lot of very heavy spiritual enactments," squabbles, tantrums, and scenes of desperation. "We reckoned that we'd hit the bottom end of everything in Palermo." Powerites were scattered all over Germany, trying to survive through begging. The Omega was exhausted by several months of struggling to lead its followers and groping to follow the signs. They had not found a door out of the world; they had not found a higher plane of existence. But Christmas was coming. There was a small group of members in Rome, so The Omega decided that everyone except the few in London should converge for Christmas in the holy city.

ROME

Even more than Oberammergau, Rome was a rejuvenating experience. The few Powerites already there had parked themselves in a large rooming house run by an accommodating landlord who didn't demand much rent. The Omega arrived and found a big, splendid apartment. It belonged to the Italian Ambassador to Finland, who had left to serve his country in that northern land. The apartment covered an entire floor of a large building and had a huge terrace on the roof. Marble floors, filigree furniture, and the roof garden made it a deliciously elegant place to celebrate Christmas. All the Matthew 10 wanderers were called down from Germany.

The apartment bulged with Powerites over the holidays, so in January another place was rented to hold the overflow and act as a regular Power Chapter House. For three or four months they maintained an actual open Chapter in Rome, people settled in, and Edward had a chance to write several pieces of scripture based on their recent experiences. He composed five of the "Letters from the Omega to All Brethren," BIs eight through twelve. *The Adversary*, BI-8, was an important developmental step in the evolution of the theology. It began, "Literally Satan means the Adversary," but goes on to explain that Satan, the divine personality, is no longer our adversary. Instead, the pettiness within us has taken over that role. BI-8 continues a line of thought Edward began in earlier pieces, *The Two Pole Universe* and *Humanity Is the Devil*, a dualistic conception of the moral universe in which the opposite poles are antagonistic, but neither is evil. Several leading Powerites told me the key doctrinal concept of The Unity of

Christ and Satan emerged during the stay in Rome. The group already recognized three Gods (or aspects of God) and accepted the teachings of Christ despite the gulf between the traditional Christian system and their own. Acceptance of Satan, announced through the wearing of a Satanic symbol adopted in New York, was now reconciled through the new doctrine. The group was beset by conflict and tugged by contrary influences. Edward attempted to solve these real problems symbolically through a new theory of reconciliation, a doctrine that Christ and Satan could transcend the differences between them and join together, without either losing His character. As an idea it was received very enthusiastically by the group, but the real test could only come in its effect on actual events. The logic of the doctrine was simple; it took Christ's ancient teaching one step beyond good and evil.

> CHRIST said: Love your enemies.
> CHRIST'S Enemy was SATAN and SATAN'S Enemy was CHRIST.
> Through Love enmity is destroyed.
> Through Love saint and sinner destroy the
>   enmity between them.
> Through Love CHRIST and SATAN have destroyed their
>   enmity and come together for the End;
> CHRIST to Judge, SATAN to execute the Judgement.
> The Judgement is WISDOM; the execution of the
>   Judgement is LOVE.

The other BIs spoke rather directly about the problems the cult had been suffering. BI-9 explained the confusion that had gripped them for months. It both promised and urged the dawn of a new day in a new Eden. "As we move out of humanity and into the Garden, via enactment after weird enactment, a change seems indicated in our attitudes to one another within The Power." Edward explained that enactments had social value. "If a Powerite pulls something, falls flat on his or her face, that is a sign for all of us, not just for that Powerite." The concept of *enactment* defines evil and strife out of existence. A Powerite could not misbehave, because everything had a spiritual meaning. Someone who displayed anger was said to be *enacting anger* or *manifesting anger* or *channeling anger*, bringing the Platonic ideal Anger to public awareness, performing a necessary spiritual service for the others, rather than simply choosing to be bad. "There are Powerites whose function it is to carry the burdens for all of us, to channel the agonies that all of us bring upon ourselves, to manifest the errors and wrongness which all of us bring into existence."

These pieces of scripture assert that nothing happens without good reason in The Power, that each event, even each untoward behavior, is a positive step forward in the realization of the collective dream. The doctrine may have reassured followers and leaders alike, rendering everything apparently meaningful and denying there was any cause for anxiety or alarm. It seems also to be an attempt by The Omega to assert charismatic infallibility.

PARIS

The brief trip by four members to Paris in 1968 had been so successful that the cult decided to launch a more permanent Paris Chapter. In the spring of 1969, the Rome Chapter was closed down, and all the people there went to Paris or London. The Paris group stayed for a while in a small suburb, then moved outside the city to a tiny village named St. Vrain, a few miles from the market town of Arpajon. Siegfried recalls, "We used to go into Paris pretty well every day." They held meetings and sold Power literature. There were "enormous numbers of tourists, so even if the French didn't want to buy it because it was in English, there were lots of Americans and English who would buy it." I know of two members who met and joined the cult in Paris, both expatriate Americans. Apparently the cultural barrier discouraged French citizens from developing the kind of ties with Powerites necessary for them to be recruited. Another barrier was geographical distance. The Paris Chapter was *open*, in the sense that nonmembers could attend activities, but as Edward commented, "The fact that it was out of the city meant that it wasn't too open." It did not have complete facilities, such as a coffee house, and attracted few visitors.

St. Vrain was an ideal place for the group to live, however, because of the calm, pastoral mood of the area. They got their milk from a farm next-door, Siegfried says. "It was a beautiful place that we lived in. It was quite cheap, because it was out in the country. It was an old manor house—stone and timber, great beams. Even the depths of winter were beautiful."

LONDON

The Omega reestablished its headquarters in London, and the majority of the members moved into Balfour Place, the grand stone building the cult had leased since late 1965. The immigration difficulties had been solved, and the cult retreated temporarily into its old home. When the London Chapter filled up with the returning English Powerites and the new Americans, they experimented with novel customs. Brother Ariel reports that the cult was a "matriarchy" for a time. Kitty was described as The Oracle who inspired The Teacher, and she was therefore at least symbolically superior to Edward or their lieutenants. Ariel says, "In the hierarchical structure, the females were higher than the men." It was unwise for a man to argue with one of the Power women, because she might pull rank on him. When the high-status Inside Powerites would descend the great staircase, making a formal entry to some gathering, they went in order of rank, from highest to lowest, but "the lowest woman would go before the highest man." Edward explained, "There was a period around 1968/1969 when the emotional side of The Power generated a heavy and intense female chauvinist bias, which I suppose was an understandable reaction against the human norm. But it didn't last too long before the balance was redressed and we returned to a state of assumed equality. But that period did prompt me to write a lot about the male-female relationship, which was no doubt part of its purpose." As usual, Edward assumes the *purpose* of events was to have some perhaps divinely inspired effect on *him*. Everything happens to teach him something, which he can then teach to others. He is the intellect of the world.

Two Balfour Place was an ideal headquarters for the London Chapter, situated in a good section of the city, not far from several big tourist attractions and some very expensive stores. The building was dark stone and brick. The door carried a huge black version of the original Power symbol, like a swastika spiderweb. Newcomers usually visited the coffee house first, a dark room called Guess Who's Cavern. The *Who* in question was Satan. The Cavern was on two levels, a main floor and a gallery reached by a winding stair. Constructed of heavy beams and boards, the gallery looked like a gigantic box kite. Three globes hanging from the ceiling provided dim red illumination, supplemented only in spots by the flickering light of candles on the tables. Among the decorations were Goya prints—witchcraft and monster scenes. Upstairs, three dragons were painted in red on the black wall. A large collection of popular records played continually on the phonograph.

The menu was extensive, offering Power concoctions and exotic dishes. In addition to cokes, hot chocolate, and many kinds of milk shake, the drinks included such nonalcoholic delights as watercress, tomato, and carrot juice elixir. There were Ogmars, "Which the Angels will tell you is a Milk Potion which can be made with Honey, Almonds, Cinnamon, Eggs, or Bananas." Sandwiches, rice dishes, soups, and several complete dinners were available. Among the poetic names given the dishes were Seventh Heaven, Cloud Nine, Epicure, and Devilled Supreme.

Brother Ariel says there was a tendency for newcomers to sit on the gallery, looking down on the main floor of the Cavern. "People who sat downstairs were people that knew The Power and felt comfortable about it." Upstairs, strangers were able to sit back, uncontaminated by the strange so-

ciety beneath them. The Powerites did not got out of their way to produce
an atmosphere congenial for everyone. "At no time was the Cavern comfortable to alien influences. If you were Grey Force [conventional] or unsympa-
thetic, there was just: 'Who are you? Forget it! We're not even going to
talk to you.' If your questions were at all implying that The Power might be
wrong, it was like: 'Forget it! There's no point in us talking.' If you were
the least bit interested, though, they became very friendly."

The Chapter held Sabbath Assemblies and Chant Sessions, but they were
not open to the general public. Only inside members and those specially invited attended. Activities like the Telepathy Developing Circle, Midnight
Meditations, and the Powerplay were open to the public. There were three
levels of classes for neophytes: First Progress, Second Progress, and Third
Progress. These were held in the chief ritual room, the Alpha, and in other
meeting rooms. Most rooms were whitewalled, decorated with paintings
by members, many with fireplaces. Most inside members lived in the upper
stories of this large building, but by the end of the 1960s, Edward, Kitty,
and occasional lieutenants lived in a nice apartment elsewhere in London.

The Power became an important, if anomalous, part of the London occult
scene. Françoise Strachan's 1970 catalogue, *The Aquarian Guide to Occult,
Mystical, Religious, Magical London and Around*, lists about 200 strange
groups, such as The Bardic and Druid Order, The Ghost Club, The Hermetic Brotherhood of Light, The Order of Melchizedek, The Order of the
Pyramid and the Sphinx, The Pagan Movement, and The Power. Strachan
invited each to submit a self-description. Some described themselves at
length, but The Power merely asked a question and gave its address. "And
at the judgement shall you show yourself a servant of the un-God, con-
demned to endless alienation from all truth or shall you show yourself a servant of the Gods, raised up and reborn into the New Age?—The Power,
Balfour Place, Mayfair, London W.1."

A FAILURE OF MIRACLES

The Power sought in vain for a door out of this world. At Xtul it attempted
to leave conventional society altogether and claims it found magic and a
God. But the cult did not find an exit at Xtul, merely an experience. The
weeks at Xtul were like looking out a sealed window and glimpsing a heav-
enly vista; the door had to be found somewhere else, somewhere near, but
where! In its wanderings the cult hunted for a spiritual breakthrough, a
magical headquarters better than Xtul, and new ideas that would explain
everything and give instructions on how to achieve everything.

In its wanderings it skirted the edge of the world, finding no exit and discovering that it could not escape the demands or benefits of conventional society. Everywhere they went there were troublesome immigration officials. They wanted a castle or monastery for their headquarters, and at first refused to accept the implications of the fact that such a structure must have been built by members of conventional society. Nobody was prepared to donate an ideal Schloss, and it would take a lot of money to buy one. The source of money that fitted best with the wandering lifestyle, and which could be handled by low-status members without bothering The Omega about the problem of income, was street begging. Contrary to the ideology, God did not provide—people provided. In the following chapter we will see important consequences of this fact.

Those recruited in this period were socially detached middle-class young adults. But they were not pathological individuals. There are many reasons why a young middle-class person might be temporarily without strong attachments. Not inferiority, but a normal desire for superiority and membership in a grand social enterprise motivated converts. Not belief in the doctrine, but positive relationships with the Original Powerites defined membership and was the essence of conversion.

The first important factor for recruitment to The Power was simply that the person NOT be intensely committed to something else, that is, NOT bound firmly through strong social ties to people outside the group. Social isolation might produce tension in many people, and social isolation might be the result of prior life difficulties, but there is no necessary connection between personal problems and temporary social isolation. It was the structure of social relations around an individual that predisposed him to membership, not his psychic state. While the cult was on its migrations, bonds with newcomers had to be formed quickly. Because people poor in outside relations were free to form new ties quickly, social isolation was of supreme importance for conversion in this migration period, although it had been of no importance in the beginning, when the original members had been torn out of an extended friendship network by social implosion, and it became less important later.

The second important factor was that the newcomer and members of the cult had to find each other personally attractive. It was necessary that a newcomer develop ties that were not only strong but reciprocal. The Power was selective in letting new people in. Composed of talented, intelligent people and created through a process that laid great emphasis on personal intimacy, The Power rejected any prospective member unless old members liked the individual very much. By 1970, only one non-Caucasian, Brother Pan, had been permanently admitted to inner membership, and later only one other, a woman of half American and half Pacific descent, became an inner member. Thus the group tended to recruit people who were like themselves through the development of friendships and intimate relationships.

These years saw the height of the youth counterculture, and many recruits to the cult had been deeply involved in it. But it would be a great mistake to explain The Power as merely an extension of the cultural upheaval of the sixties. Its true genealogy goes back quite far, through Technianity and Adler to the Rosicrucian and Psychoanalytic movements of the turn of the century. Many new cults have arisen in each recent decade, more often the result of microsocial conditions than of any general cultural changes. In the late sixties there were large numbers of unattached young people ready to join something, but there are always far more potential recruits in the world than a cult like The Power can readily incorporate. Cult policy more than anything else would determine who joined and how the group evolved.

FIVE

Paradise Misplaced

> Now is the time for a change. Now is the time to weight
> the balance on Lucifer's side. . . . Lucifer gives to those
> who ask of Him, but those who demand of Him, even
> when He meets their demands and gives, do not find His
> presence in the gift. They find only disillusionment.
> —BI-19, BI-22 Power Scriptures

In early 1970, at Lilith's suggestion but in accord with what many felt, Edward de Forest announced the end of The Old Game in The Power and the beginning of The New Game. The first seven years of the cult, a period of exploration, suffering mixed with exaltation, and angry alienation from conventional society, were described as Jehovah's Game. Edward's book *The Gods and Their People* explains that Jehovah is the harsh, intolerant aspect of God:

Of His people He demands all. He demands their life blood; and He inflicts upon them every dismal failure and deprivation in order to test the extent of their loyalty to Him. No easy pleasure-filled life for the Jehovian; his is the harsh road of expiation, the road of stringent self-sacrifice.

For to JEHOVAH, success in human terms, pleasure and satisfaction by the standards of humanity, are snares that lure a being from the straight and narrow path of purity and self-denial. They are the traps that can cause a being to turn from his God and worship life as man knows life; the transitory shallow habitation of a human form.

In Edward's theology, Lucifer was the precise opposite of Jehovah, a conflicting standard and therefore the symbol of a radical change for the cult. The New Game was to be Lucifer's game. Lucifer "urges us to enjoy life to the full, to value success in human terms." Lucifer was quite different from Satan; only the propaganda of Lucifer's opponent, Jehovah, caused people to misidentify Lucifer with Satan. The Power had exhausted itself in its program to curse the world and escape it. Beginning in 1969, it discovered that life was much more comfortable in established Chapters. In 1970, the cult turned away from Jehovah toward Lucifer. "His is the scented road of sweet and unpretentious luxury. But also it is the road of action, of pursuit, of movement; it is a road of exploitation, of making full use of all that is."

EXODUS FROM ENGLAND

At the beginning of 1970, the leaders of the cult decided to launch a second
invasion of America. The American ministers collected in 1967 and 1968,
and now thoroughly integrated into the group, provided the personnel
necessary for a mission to the States. The immigration authorities could not
expel them, so The Power could plan the establishment of permanent
American Chapters. The first American visit had been very successful, Siegfried recalls. "We had had an enormously positive and exciting response in
the United States the first time we were here. It's in a sense much freer,
more open than Europe." Cain remembers the feelings behind the decision
to come again to the States. "There was the sense that America was the place
of the future, that it was there that things were happening, that we could
make a significant contribution."

    In February or March 1970, Father Cain sailed to New York with Sister
Lilith and Ed Smith, two U.S. Powerites. Smith ran out on Cain immediately, and Lilith was privately contemplating leaving the cult, so Cain's
companions were not the best choices. Cain and Lilith had a list of people in
New York who might help them. She says, "We arrived with our dogs,
Satan and Seth, and we called up some of the names we had on this list, and
we got put up for the night. And basically did the same thing we did in
Germany—finding different people to stay with, donating on the streets,
generally testing out the water, seeing what things were like. We traveled
around. We came to Boston. We visited Woodstock. We went back to
New York again. Decided Boston felt like the right place." They began
negotiations to rent a house on Inman Street in Cambridge, right across
the Charles River from Boston. But they were not quite ready to move in.
Cain and Lilith rented a car and set out to explore America further.

    They went to New Orleans, where Lilith's family lived, then crossed to
Los Angeles. Cain says they were "on a general scouting expedition to see
where it felt like the right place to be, initially." Lilith abandoned Cain in
Los Angeles and flew to San Francisco where she had friends. Cain, now all
alone, returned to Boston. Because the main chapter was still in London, it
made sense to establish the first American chapter on the East Coast, to
keep traveling distances to a minimum. Cain says another consideration
was "what was happening in Boston at the time, which was quite exciting.
There were a lot of very stimulating people there. Very alive atmosphere
around the place. It felt like a good place to be. And the response to us felt
very nice." Sister Amaranth, an American, and British members Moses,
Adam, and Bathsheba soon joined him. Amaranth's family happened to
live in Boston, "which was a temporary asset in the situation, in that they
were able to help us in the physical sense."

The Chapter House that Cain rented at 29 Inman Street was a typical central Cambridge residence. The location was very convenient, halfway between Harvard and M.I.T., only a couple of blocks from the Central Square subway station. The building was attached to 31 Inman Street, and the two structures shared front stairs. A reporter described the brand new Boston Chapter in mid-1970:

Fairly attractive house in Cambridge with three floors and a cellar. Everything is spotlessly clean. Besides a coffee shop, the cellar has a kitchen completed by the members, as well as a small workshop where some of them make handcrafted silver earrings, beads, necklaces, and rings. All lovely and I was tempted to buy some. . . . The coffee shop had benches, wooden tables, and little lights with red shades. On the wall were murals in reds, whites, and gold, depicting a large dragon and an angel and several childlike figures.

The coffee house was called The Cavern. In the late 1960s a great number of youth-oriented coffee houses had sprung up around the country, many supported as a social service by conventional churches. There were several in Cambridge when The Cavern opened, so it had to compete with more lavish hangouts at the same time that it benefited from the popularity of such places. Brother Ariel told me the murals were the work of Brother Herod, Father Adam, and others, "all done in oranges and blacks and silver tin foils put on, very nicely done." One mural showed the Four Horsemen of the Apocalypse, another St. George slaying the dragon. A crowned female figure astride the moon. A figure of Death. Most were scenes out of the Book of Revelation. Ariel's favorite was "the Whore of Babylon on the seven-headed beast. That was quite exciting!"

The first floor had two main rooms. One, which outsiders never saw, was an L-shaped space at the back, the office and sleeping quarters of the Master in charge. The large front room was set up as the Alpha, the main ritual room of the chapter. Here Sabbath Assemblies were held for members and invited guests, and at least three activities were held for the general public: Telepathy Developing Circles, Powerplays, and Midnight Meditations.

The second and third floors were reserved for inner members. The second floor had a bathroom, two large bedrooms, and a tiny little room where therapy sessions were held. Ariel commented that even two years later this former Session Room "had a really burnt-out feeling to it that nobody could get rid of." It was said that the many intense sessions held there had spoiled the aura of the room. "Whether that's true or not, I don't know," Ariel said. "But it always did have a very dead atmosphere." There were four rooms on the top floor, including one reserved for meditation. Ariel says the Meditation Room was always kept neat and "was the most peaceful room in the house."

In the fall of 1970, the Boston Chapter rented another house in Cambridge, a good-sized wooden structure on Concord Avenue which had at one time belonged to Harvard University. A new Cavern was set up in its basement, and the first floor dining-room/living-room area of the house was transformed into the Alpha ritual room. The high-status members of the chapter lived on the second and third floors. The original Chapter House on Inman Street became a communal residence for new Messengers.

Once the Boston Chapter was a going concern, a second group of pioneers opened a Chapter in Chicago, at the beginning of the summer. In June, Edward and Kitty came to the U.S., landing in Florida. They considered starting a Miami Chapter but did not act on this idea for nearly two years. Possibly inspired by a famous movie starring Humphrey Bogart, Edward G. Robinson, and Lauren Bacall, they bought an expensive house in Key Largo, south of the city. By the time they moved in, sometime in September, The Omega had completely withdrawn from everyday Power society. Even some Messengers who joined in 1970 have never met Kitty, and the general public was seldom even told where The Omega lived at any moment.

At the end of the year, Father Moses went from Florida to New Orleans to found a new chapter there. Personnel were sent down from the growing Boston and Chicago chapters to staff it. About this time the Paris Chapter was closed down. In an unpublished paper, social psychologist Lee Lawrence has reported some of the changes she observed in The Power near the end of 1970:

On December 6, the Cambridge members were told of some changes in the hierarchy which promise to have far-reaching effects for the group's future. From London came the news that there was to be a rank of Disciple, effectively creating a lay following within the church. The main reasons for the changed structure are unclear: perhaps more members were needed for spreading the doctrines; perhaps many people had expressed a wish to join but not to devote their lives to the cause; perhaps an influx of people was needed to get greater financial support for the activities of the group.

Disciple rank was said to be equal in status to that of Messenger. Disciples could wear cult uniforms around the chapter and while on cult business. Like Messengers, they were called Brothers and Sisters of the church. They did not give up their outside attachments, however. From their conventional outside jobs, they were supposed to tithe, to give one tenth of their incomes to The Power. After a few months, some Disciples at each chapter gathered to form their own communes, living in imitation of Messengers. Although Lawrence reports Disciple rank was created by the central organization in London, it was never adopted there, and the weight of cult activity had shifted to the United States. Lawrence reported on another change that marked evolution toward a more open church society:

As part of the general loosening of the hierarchy, actual entrance into the church was made easier for all. Formerly a person had to declare his intent to become an Acolyte, work for three weeks at the chapter house, and be invited by the group into their Sabbath Assembly to officially *become* an Acolyte. The stage of Initiate involved about 19 hours per week of training for eight to nine weeks; now, although the length of time is the same, the training has apparently been lightened. The opening of the Assembly to the public is indicative of the new focus on more widespread proselytizing and the de-emphasis of the need to have total commitment to the group.

Sister Eve told me that the first open Assembly had been a thrashing success. *Eleven* people came forward to become Acolytes. "I was flipped out!" she said. In the first weeks of 1971, I observed an average of slightly more than two individuals come forward each week to become Acolytes, and about one a week become an Initiate. The format of the Sabbath Assembly was changed to make it more educational for newcomers. Sections were added incorporating a few of the basic doctrinal statements and explaining such mysteries as the Gods and the coming Apocalypse.

About this time, the rank of Priest was renamed Superior. Messengers were divided into two levels, OP (Outside Powerite) Messengers, the newest ones who all lived in "the Messenger flat," and IP (Inside Powerite) Messengers who lived with The Hierarchy (high-status members) in the Chapter House. Within each rank there were distinctions of seniority, and each chapter was run by a High Master, assisted sometimes by Provisional Masters. Thus in 1971 the system of ranks took on its fully developed form, the pattern followed throughout the years of the cult's greatest size. From the newcomer at the bottom to the Omega at the top, the system was as shown in Table 1.

The next new chapter was established in Toronto. Like many other steps in the development of The Power, this was the response to a practical problem, but interpreted in somewhat magical terms. At the end of 1970, after the New Orleans Chapter was in business, Edward says his younger brother Remus "went to Toronto because there was a problem with his immigration. You see, this is another *sign*. He had to get out of the country, and the only place he could go to without going back to England was to Canada. So we said, 'That's a sign. Go to Toronto and open a chapter.' So he did."

Toronto was a very useful place to put Powerites who had legal trouble in the States. At this time many young men had gone to Canada to escape military service during the Vietnam War, many inspired by strong antiwar sentiments, others by more selfish motives. Only one of the American

Table 1: **The System of Ranks, 1971–1974**

Rank	Category	Person is called
The Omega	none	Edward or Kitty
Master	Inside Powerite	Father- or Mother-
Superior	Inside Powerite	Father- or Mother-
Prophet	Inside Powerite	Brother- or Sister-
IP Messenger	Inside Powerite	Brother- or Sister-
OP Messenger	Outside Powerite	Brother- or Sister-
Disciple	Outside Powerite	Brother- or Sister-
Initiate	Outside Powerite	by his ordinary name
Acolyte	Outside Powerite	by his ordinary name
(visitor "GP")	General Public	by his ordinary name

members of the cult, Brother Herod, had any serious draft problems. Father Siegfried says, "We were continually fighting to get him conscientious objector status with the draft board, and they were very very unwilling to play ball. So we simply sent him to Canada so he wouldn't have a hassle with it. We successfully negotiated with the draft board for a number of our people." The Power argued that its young men were not only conscientious objectors to the slaughter of war, but also *ministers* of a church who should be exempt for that reason as well. Only in Herod's case did a draft board reject this argument for any length of time. "We were simply not going to send one of our top people away to a senseless war. And if necessary we were going to keep him in Canada until they came to their senses, which they did, eventually."

Early in 1971, the London Chapter was closed down. With the Toronto Chapter and effective procedures for getting British Powerites admitted to the United States for unlimited periods, there was no practical need to maintain an English branch. With the majority of the members in North America, the London Chapter became geographically isolated from the new center of the cult. A reporter for *The Harvard Crimson* wrote about London:

Following a series of ineffectual lawsuits against them, the Powerites lost a suit filed against their operation of a basement coffee house in violation of city zoning laws. This lost suit was taken as a sign that the Church should leave London, and the London chapter was closed. But the Boston Powerites expect the London chapter to be reopened some day.

Father Siegfried says the London Chapter had been dwindling for a year anyway, simply because "we were continually taking people out of it" to create the new American chapters. "The overall reception we got was so much stronger, so much more positive on the American side of the Atlantic, that it was our instinct really to pull people out of London. England was very much into a decline at the time. We felt the work would be much better, much more productive" in the United States and Canada. The problem with the zoning laws "was something that we really didn't bother to fight very much." It was "the final sign that we needed." The cult could have fought the issue, "but none of us really wanted to stay there. There was nothing to fight for."

The Omega temporarily left its Key Largo home in May 1971, and moved to Toronto, possibly because of short-term immigration difficulties. As the church became more established, one by one the English "ministers" could apply for resident alien status and work toward citizenship. The more like a conventional religious organization the cult looked, the easier it was to achieve this. Immigration was one of a whole series of practical factors pushing The Power back toward conventionality. In the second half of 1972, chapters were established in New York City and Miami, bringing the total to six. It is interesting that the New Orleans, Chicago, and New York chapters were ultimately situated right in the middle of high-class entertainment districts. New York eventually became the church headquarters.

NEW RECRUITS

With the establishment of fixed church chapters in 1970 and 1971, the cult's ability to collect people ready to make useful contributions declined. Some of those recruited in 1970 and 1971 were people of moderate talent, little creativity, and marked tendencies toward dependence on strong parent-figures. These people made decent members, willing to do the tough and unrewarding street begging, and were therefore valuable to the original Powerites. But after each chapter became established, its coffee house filled up with useless, talentless, pathological, problematic riffraff. Some of these people succeeded in achieving membership for a time, only to cause trouble and drop out again. In Chapter Ten we will learn more about these people, but here I will describe eight men and women who were admitted to Messenger status between 1970 and 1974. These eight people were at the top end of the scale attracted to the cult in these years: Norma, Goliath, Moira, Lot, Noah, Roxana, Clementine, and Samantha. Three characteristics describe them in varying degrees. Some, like Norma and Goliath, had recently suffered traumatic experiences and a collapse in their careers. Others, like Moira, Lot, Noah, Roxana, and Clementine, might be described as *dependent personalities*, possibly "immature" but certainly looking for strong guidance and a lifestyle in which they did not have to act as independent individuals. Seen from another perspective, many of them had always lived in "institutions" that encouraged dependence, and after leaving one set of all-encompassing institutions, they adopted The Power as a substitute for the lives they had known. A third characteristic might be described as the professional motivation behind joining. Roxana, Clementine, and Samantha had been professionally trained in occupations very similar to the work of The Power and entered it as a fulfilling job as well as a lifestyle.

Norma

Sister Norma once theorized, "A lot of people used The Power as a psychiatrist. Everybody who's come into The Power has just had some horrendous problem that happened just before, and The Power gave them the security to solve the problem." This theory fits Norma and some of her cohort but does not fit many of the people who joined earlier. Of course, Norma never heard the stories of most members of the earlier generations, because they, as higher-status members than she, tried to cloak themselves in an air of mystery.

In 1971, Norma was wandering around, footloose, uncommitted. She went to Schenectady, New York, where she was supposed to meet some friends and go across country with them. They failed to show up, and she was left without definite plans. Friends she was staying with wanted her to meet a young man who happened to be dying of cancer. "I didn't want to get mixed up with that!" she says. She wound up meeting him anyway. Norma was making a little money as a singer; the guy with cancer played the guitar for her at a gig. The day after, she moved in with him. It was "the most perfect relationship I have ever had." Not only were they extremely well suited for each other, but his very special problem elevated the relationship above the ordinary. His parents accepted her, and when she was not alone with him, she was with his whole family. Even after he entered the hospital for the last time, she lived in his apartment and spent a considerable amount of time visiting him or his family. She met him in November 1971; he died the following March.

His parents immediately sent Norma back to her parents' home in Boston. Her feelings were intense and disorganized. Norma felt "cheated by God" and "looney." She lived with a couple of men for a while, then alone, held a job for a bit, then joined The Power. "The Power was the only place I could turn to. Nobody else understood what I'd gone through." Norma describes the cult in its own jargon: "I thought they had more reality around emotions and around people and their feelings than other people I knew. I just felt more comfortable there." *To have reality around* means to be deeply moved by, to feel that something is powerfully real, or merely to believe in. The Power was built on unusually intense social relationships, and Norma had just been stripped away from such a tie with another person. For a while, her contact with other Powerites took the place of that relationship. Norma left the cult a year after becoming a Messenger.

Goliath

Son of a working-class Boston family, Goliath was on his way toward a career as a carpenter or cabinetmaker when drugs and the promise of excitement lured him out to California where he joined the Iron Cross motorcycle gang. Over the four years that I knew Goliath, he always looked the part of a biker, defiantly overgrown with hair, intense but unchanging expression on his lumpy face, a rolling walk that suggested suppressed violence. The only features of his appearance that didn't fit the motorcycle ogre image was his short stature and light build.

As we sat in the Power coffee house in 1971, sharing my glass of cider and my brownie, getting acquainted, Goliath told me about the three men he had killed in California. One was battered out of this life in a fight. A second was accidentally pushed downstairs to a broken neck. The third was a Hell's Angel whom Goliath scrubbed out on the road—forced him off into a fatal crash while they were on their motorcycles. When interviewed by *The New York Times*, Goliath told the same story and added that he "used to ride across the country robbing gas stations." I checked around and discovered that Goliath had told other people he had only seriously damaged the three men in these incidents, not killed them. The stories conveyed the kind of image Goliath wanted to project, whether they were true or not.

The friends of the Hell's Angel sought revenge and ran Goliath off the road in return. He suffered cracked ribs and other injuries, the most serious of which was shattered eyesight. I do not know for a fact how Goliath came to lose much of his vision, but the thick glasses he wears indicate his eyes are indeed in bad shape.

Another possibly apocryphal story Goliath told me symbolizes perfectly the state of his life. He drove his car into Boston and parked it in a lot near the Prudential Center. Some friends lived nearby, and he spent several hours with them, smoking marijuana and getting very high on LSD. It was one or two in the morning. Goliath wandered back to his car, got in, and turned on his engine. He let out the parking brake, stepped on the gas, and began driving away. Amazing! The colors and phantoms of his drug trip made the night very exciting. He drove and drove. Remarkable! Boston's buildings seemed to move ever so slowly. In fact, they did not seem to move at all. After a few minutes, when he realized that the Prudential Center had not moved an inch across his window, Goliath turned off the engine, set the brake, and got out of his car. Surprise! Somebody had jacked the car up onto metal milk delivery baskets and run away with all four wheels and tires.

That was the story of his life. Nothing seemed to work. He never got anywhere. Goliath wistfully told me the only things keeping him from resuming apprenticeship in cabinetmaking were his ruined eyesight and the fact that he had fallen out of the good graces of the local union. Goliath was a Messenger for only a short time, dropped back to Disciple rank, then lost contact with the cult altogether. In the winter of 1974–1975, I saw him sick and unemployed on the streets.

Moira

Sister Moira is a very thin young woman, apparently half-crippled by some childhood illness. She grew up in Toronto and was working in an office in that city when she first encountered The Power about 1971. She was hurrying home from work one day, rushing to meet some appointment, when she saw Powerites selling magazines. "The person I met on the street impressed me a great deal. She seemed to hold within her all the qualities I aspired to. She was very dedicated, very energetic, very enthusiastic, open. She responded to people. She wasn't just a salesman. She was someone who cared about me." The Powerite's name was Sister Helena, a fact which impressed Moira deeply because she had dreamed about this beautiful name for years.

The next day, Moira went looking for Helena on the street after work. At their second meeting she felt "willing to do anything. She [Helena] said, 'Can you help us?' I was willing to take on whatever it was, just on the strength of my feelings for this person. I think I almost knew I was going to join when I first met her. My feeling was that I wanted to be a part of whatever she was doing. It looked good, and it felt good, and I could see that it had a very good effect on her. All the people that I met at the center at that time impressed me in the same way, and the more I went around, the more convinced I was." She worked at the Power chapter for about a year before becoming a Messenger. "I suddenly realized that everything that had any kind of meaning for me was there. The times when I wasn't there were just faded images; none of it had any kind of color or enthusiasm. And the color—the atmosphere—was at The Power."

Lot and Noah

Brother Lot joined the cult in 1970. He told me he had always lived in "institutions" and needed the security and direction of an organized life. His family was the first institution that provided this, then school, then college. After three years at Iowa State, he "crashed," began using drugs, was arrested, and was sent to prison. When he got out of this institution, he came to Boston and was considering taking courses in psychology at Boston University, but joined The Power instead. He told me his perspective on membership. "For us crazy people, we like to stay in the house!" He looked up at the buildings of Boston University that stood around us as we talked. He dismissed them with a sweeping gesture and a laugh. "We can't operate here!"

Noah was the son of a middle-class Connecticut family. Before reaching the age of sixteen, he left his parents and what he saw as an intolerable, disintegrating family situation, abandoned high school, and went to Boston where his sister and her husband were studying at Harvard. He held odd jobs such as short-order cooking, successfully secured an apartment, and began to make friends. It was quite a challenge for a young man not particularly wise in the ways of the world. Like many other unattached young people in the Cambridge area, he was attracted to the Power coffee house and began to spend a good deal of time around the chapter. He said it offered "a very homey feeling . . . very nice close-knit feeling." Although he was able to fend for himself in Boston, his life separated from his antagonistic parents and busy sister "was a little depressing and lonely." In a Sabbath Assembly "around Christmas time" in 1972, he came forward at the designated moment to become an Acolyte. Because of his youth, he was not permitted to become a Messenger until October 1973. At the end of the year, he was transferred to the fresh New York Chapter, founded by Father Cain and Mother Amaranth. There, in the overpowering metropolis, his only continuing social relationships were with Powerites. They were his family.

Roxana and Clementine

Among the most energetic but thoroughly dependent recruits who joined in the early 1970s were Sisters Roxana and Clementine. Roxana, a young woman of very sweet disposition, told me early in 1971 how wonderful she felt it would be if she could find someone to share happiness with, someone upon whom she could be completely dependent. A little later she became a Messenger, dependent upon the entire cult but contributing much to it. Both Roxana and Clementine had been student nuns in the Catholic Church. In a Power magazine article, Roxana complained about the strictness of her Catholic training. "All attention was focused on the ascetic and mortification of the flesh," in her order. "If we had time to talk, we had to have at least three people there—a measure, we learned later, to guard against homosexuality, among other things. You had to make sure that you never sat next to one person at recreation too much. It got the work done, but in terms of having a friendship it was very impersonal." The Power was a religious community, therefore a familiar environment for Roxana and Clementine. But it was different. Although it controlled personal relationships, it encouraged them. Sexuality was not repressed. Speaking for herself, Sister Clementine explained what she felt was the most common reason priests or nuns left the Catholic Church: "the rule of celibacy." In her view, these defectors from the convent, herself included, "want to experience life on a sexual level, but you can't be a sexual person as a nun or priest; they knew that if they want to express themselves in this sort of way, they simply have to move out." She and Roxana had moved out of Catholicism into what for them was a similar kind of religious community.

Samantha

Sister Samantha was the first new member to join in Chicago in 1970. After graduating from high school, she got a job with a small theatrical company, doing odd work and occasionally playing small bit parts in the productions. Her ambition was to be an actress, but aware of the uncertainty of an acting career, she cautiously planned to take whatever secure job she could find associated with the drama. She and some friends were wandering through one of the entertainment sections of Chicago, one evening, when they happened to come near the third-floor apartment where The Power had just set up operations. Someone had given them a handout, stating the address and inviting them to visit. On impulse, Samantha dragged her friends into the dark, candle-lit front room of the Power apartment, which was an informal coffee house. Samantha happened to be wearing her work clothes. Her theater was a theater-in-the-round, so the people who changed the sets between scenes had to operate in full view of the audience. Consequently they wore black clothing to be nearly invisible. So when Samantha entered the Power den, she was dressed all in black, wearing out of sentiment her Christian cross. She was astonished to meet her first Powerite, who was also dressed in black, wearing a cross!

At first, Samantha was drawn in by a sense of mystery, but was repelled by the idea of religion. That first night she found herself dragged along to an open meeting. "I fell madly in love with a couple of the people there immediately." Already she considered becoming a member. "I didn't even know what it was, and I was talking about joining it!" Over the next few weeks it became her habit to visit frequently. "I still didn't know what they believed. I was attracted to the people more than anything else." Her "strongest involvement to start with was the people," and not just any kind of people, but the most interesting, attractive, high-ranked members. She says she had a real advantage meeting the group as early as she did, when the best members of the cult were running the coffee house and open to her friendship. Later on, newcomers were forced to make contact through cult members and Cavern denizens of far less attractiveness. Samantha loved the drama of the original Power. Just as the cult was a sexy monastery for Roxana and Clementine, it was a real-life theater for Samantha. Here she would be encouraged to put on a show for many audiences, every day, and to be the center of many exciting scenes.

THE MANSON DISASTER

In August 1969, Charles Manson led his ragtag "dune buggy attack battalion" in the murders of actress Sharon Tate and six other persons. The California police arrested Manson in November, and very soon a rumor began that Manson's sinister group was an offshoot of The Power. A Los Angeles radio station telephoned the London Chapter of The Power asking if the rumor were true. When Cain and Lilith were scouting out the American territory early in 1970, they were both worried and attracted by the idea that Manson was a schismatic Powerite. Manson was one of the reasons the pair drove out to Los Angeles. Lilith says, "I got a real wild idea in my head and decided we should go off to California and check out Charles Manson and what was happening out there. 'Cause we had just been pointed out as being involved in these strange ritual murders." I asked her if there were any real connection between Manson and The Power. "None. None whatsoever!" Had he ever come to a meeting? "No. No one of us had ever met him, heard of him. None of us recognized him when we saw pictures of him. If he had any contact with us—which he may have done, he may have spoken to someone on the streets who was selling magazines—it would have been a very brief contact which whoever it was didn't even remember. And I have the feeling that he never actually spoke to any of us." This is exactly the response I got from other knowledgeable Powerites.

The Manson murders were a public relations disaster for the widespread youth counterculture of the late 1960s. Many Americans were quick to believe that Manson accurately represented the counterculture. A counterculture reporter recalls reading the news reports about the murders with a friend. They agreed "We are in trouble." They knew they and other harmless deviants would suffer guilt by association in the public mind. "Neither of us rushed out to shave and get a haircut, of course, but when, a few months later, long-haired, bearded Charles Manson (ballyhooed throughout the press as the leader of a tribe of "hippies") was arrested for the crime, I began to wish I had. For a time it seemed as though every freak in the country was on trial, as the media made no attempt to distinguish between the drug-crazed, hairy beast called Manson and every other drug-crazed, hairy beast walking around."

Vincent Bugliosi, prosecutor in the Manson case, could never quite decide what kind of link there was between the Manson Family and The Power. Certainly, he never attempted to bring any Powerite to court. Bugliosi notes several parallels between the Manson Family and The Power, and says, "They are enough to convince me, at least, that even if Manson himself may never have been a member of The Power, he borrowed heavily from the satanic cult." Bugliosi conjectured at length:

I'm inclined to think that Manson's contact with the group probably occurred in San Francisco in 1967, as indicated, at a time when his philosophy was still being formulated. I believe there was at least some contact, in view of the many parallels between Manson's teachings and those of The Power as revealed in their literature.

Both preached an imminent, violent Armageddon, in which all but the chosen few would be destroyed. Both found the basis for this in the Book of Revelation. Both conceived that the motorcycle gangs, such as Hell's Angels, would be the troops of the last days. And both actively sought to solicit them to their side.

In 1971, Father Adam, then head of the Boston Chapter, admitted his feeling to a newspaper reporter. "Manson had obviously got hold of some of our ideas from somewhere and had taken and distorted them in a particular way. It is unfortunate. If we had had the opportunity to speak to him, we could have avoided that series of very brutal killings." I rather think Father Adam had been swept along by the press reports, just as many other readers were. The ideas common to The Power and Manson's group are not all that unique. Other "satanic" cults existed, most notably Anton Szandor La-Vey's *Church of Satan* that has lurked and performed in San Francisco for years.[1] Surely the Book of Revelation is available for anyone ready to open a Bible. To the extent that both groups were socially isolated, introverted, millenarian cults that arose in Christian nations at the time of the youth counterculture, we would expect them to have some of the same characteristics, even if they differed absolutely in their practices concerning violence. But some of the more bombastic, rhetorical passages in Power literature do sound like Mansonian proclamations. *The Gods on War*, completed by Edward in August 1967, announces, "The final march of doom has begun. The earth is prepared for the ultimate devastation. The mighty engines of WAR are all aligned and brought together for the End. The scene is set." This stormy book, packed with pictures of war, contains three long essays attributed to the Gods Jehovah, Lucifer, and Satan. In each, one of the Gods

[1] Randall H. Alfred, "The Church of Satan," in *The New Religious Consciousness*, ed. Charles Y. Glock and Robert N. Bellah (Berkeley: University of California Press, 1976), pp. 180–202.

expresses His orientation toward war. Each essay is really a character study of one of the Gods. The book assumes that destruction is coming, that the world has entered into the Latter Days, and seeks to take rhetorical advantage of all the powerful images of war provided by press coverage of recent conflicts. In a passage most Mansonian in mood, the Lord Satan advises the reader to participate fully in the holocaust:

Release the Fiend that lies dormant within you, for he is strong and ruthless, and his power is far beyond the bounds of human frailty.

Come forth in your savage might, rampant with the lust of battle, tense and quivering with the urge to strike, to smash, to split asunder all that seek to detain you. And cast your eye upon the land before you. Choose what road of slaughter and violation you will follow. Then stride out upon the land and amongst the people.

Rape with the crushing force of your virility; kill with the devastating precision of your sword arm; maim with the ruthless ingenuity of your pitiless cruelty; destroy with the overpowering fury of your bestial strength; lay waste with the all-encompassing majesty of your power. . . .

For the world can be yours, and the blood of men can be yours to spill as you please. And you can have your pleasure of the world through violence and the wielding of the sword. And your lust can stride upon the face of the land, taking whatever it desires, and discarding the empty husks when you've sucked them dry.

This is pure rhetoric, bombast meant to arouse the emotions and make The Power look intense, formidable, unusual. No real Powerite I knew ever made the mistake of thinking these words were commandments that required action. Father Adam once told a reporter, "Very satanic members find it difficult to fit into the church. They cannot live as Inside Powerites." The cult did attract some violent young men, but they seldom stayed with it for long and almost never became inner members.

Stung but interested by the alleged tie to Manson, The Power sent two leading members out to California, where they spoke with Bugliosi and Manson. They told the prosecutor they were innocent but apparently did not completely convince him. Manson was not helpful to the cult's cause. During the murder trial, Bugliosi asked him if he knew Edward Jones, also called Edward de Forest. Manson said he did not know de Forest but claimed he did know Jones: "You're looking at him." Another time he said, "Jones and I are one and the same." This was pure mystification.

The *Death* issue of the Power magazine, which came out in 1971, did not help the cult's image. News reporters noted it contained a brief article by Charles Manson, "written especially for The Power." Manson describes death as "Total awareness, closing the circle, bringing the soul to now. Ceasing to be, to become a world within yourself. Locked in your own totalness." Calling death "peace from this world's madness and paradise in my own self," he identifies it with isolation from the world, from outer reality, an isolation created by his own madness and developed through the social autarchy of his cult. Death—the ultimate in social implosion.

Other rumors circulated, linking The Power to heinous, inexplicable events. For the last few years, reports of *animal mutilations* have come from several sections of the country. Cattle or wild animals are found cut to pieces, their carcasses lying ripped on hillsides, far away from human settlements. Rumors about these mutilations have spread and evolved, an interesting example of collective behavior and the collective development of myth.

Some reporters spread the tale that a sinister satanic cult called The Xtul Group was responsible for all these animal mutilations. Of course, the Xtul Group is meant to be The Power. It was not in fact responsible. From its very beginning, the cult has been antivivisectionist.

The last straw was an assault on The Power by Ed Sanders, former leader of *The Fugs* (a rock band) and literary light of the counterculture. At the end of 1971, he published a series of magazine articles, and then a book, about the Manson murders. He devoted an entire chapter to The Power, saying it was an important "sleazo input which warped the mind of Charles Manson." Sanders called Powerites "hooded snuffoids," and described the cult as "The black-caped, black-garbed, death-worshiping Power Church." He said it was "an English occult society dedicated to observing and aiding the end of the world by stirring up murder, violence and chaos, and dedicated to the proposition that they, the Power, shall survive the gore as the chosen people." His chapter on the cult was a stew of information, misinformation, and hate.

In quick response to Sanders' attack, The Power went to court, lodging a libel suit for $1,500,000 against the book and another one for $1,250,000 against the magazine article. The book publisher, E. P. Dutton, said "The book was carefully checked by our attorneys and speaks for itself." A public relations lady hired by The Power pointed to "false and defamatory material" published by Sanders, "statements that Powerites were linked with the Manson family prior to the murder of Sharon Tate and that a Power member opened the kitchen door to Sirhan Sirhan shortly before he murdered Senator Robert F. Kennedy." She also accused Sanders of claiming The Power enjoyed "eulogizing Hitler, sacrificing humans and animals and then drinking their blood, sex orgies, kidnapping, and loving dope."

In public statements, cult leaders tried to convince reporters that this horrendous smorgasbord of disgusting satanic delights was fantasy. Father Adam asserted, "We don't have orgies; we don't practice cannibalism; we don't sacrifice animals; we don't drink blood; we don't practice magic rituals or put curses on people or say the Lord's Prayer backwards." But the story was impossible to stop. *The New York Times* described the reception that Powerites often received on the streets. " 'Are you devil worshippers?' ask the very curious. Others, less curious than angry, make rude remarks." At this time almost all the income of the cult was derived from the street begging. The Power was struggling to project the most bland, appealing, innocent religious image so that people would be inclined to contribute to their "church." Sanders' publicity about Manson threatened financial disaster and endangered the very economic survival of The Power.

The Power's trouble extended to the Toronto Chapter. The cult had received $23,049 from the Ottawa government under the Local Initiatives Programme. This money was to be given to young people hired through the church to do social service work. The group contends that all the money was properly spent and that church money went into the projects as well. In March 1972, a newspaper, *The Toronto Sun*, attacked the program by denouncing the "Satanists" who had run off with public money. Prime Minister Trudeau was drawn into the controversy on a radio talk show. As The Power tells the story, all ended well, with an outpouring of friendly statements from civic leaders and knowledgeable reporters drowning the negative "Satanist" comments.

Sanders' publishers decided to settle the libel case out of court. The book company undoubtedly wanted to sell thousands of copies and was anxious to come to a fast settlement. In a press release issued March 8, 1972, Dutton said, "A close examination has revealed that statements in the book about The Power Church, including those attributing any connection between The Power and the activities of Charles Manson, accused and convicted murderer, have not been substantiated." Dutton agreed to remove all references to the cult from future editions and to join with it in announcing a cooperative end to the lawsuit. Writing in an open letter as the spokesman for The Power, Father Adam said, "We are satisfied that the actions being taken by Dutton, the publishers of the book, and Ed Sanders, the author, constitute suitable vindication of the Church." On the third of April, a parallel settlement was announced with the editors of the magazine that had printed Sanders' articles. They were able to get out from under the suit against them by publishing excerpts from the press release issued by Dutton. The cult got no money from either publisher. In a meek attempt to assert its new, clean image, the cult inserted the following self-description in the press release: "The Power is a religious organization devoted to spreading the work of Christ."

The cult also sued the English publisher of Sanders' book, and there the outcome was quite different. The case actually went to court, and a verdict was rendered in March 1974. The Power lost! Their case against Sanders and the English publisher was dismissed, and the cult was ordered to pay court costs. Of course, this does not mean that Sanders' statements about The Power were true.

The Power was not responsible for Manson, but the controversy had a tremendous impact on the cult. Already committed to making peace with conventional society, already completely dependent on the good will of conventional society for its economic life, The Power was spurred to even greater attempts to clean up its image and downplay the Satanic aspect of its doctrines. St. Peter denied Christ and suffered for it; The Power would deny Satan and also suffer. To escape the dark halo of Satan, it would compulsively overfulfill the demands of Christ. To gain public support, it would first hide, then later abandon some of its most precious symbols and concepts, leaving a gnawing cultural void. Without Satan, what would distinguish The Power from all other religions?

CLEANING UP THE IMAGE

To wash away the Manson stigma, and as part of a general adaptation to its economic relationship with conventional society, The Power made a number of changes in its image. The first one I saw was a new uniform that began replacing black P-Gear in the spring of 1971. The *blacks* were replaced by *greys*, homemade light-grey uniforms, cute instead of menacing. The new suits had jumper fronts with pockets, flared trousers, and were made of light material suitable for summer wear. In really hot weather, street donators wore short-sleeve grey shirts, but in cold weather they put on the old black cloaks for warmth. The big old Mendes Badges were retired in favor of tiny plastic triangles, black with silk-screened goats, to be worn on the lapels. Christ's silver cross was tacked at the collar. Perhaps because they were homemade, or perhaps because of the appallingly drab color, the grey uniforms made the women look dowdy and the men silly. They looked like stewardesses from a third-rate airline. Figure 2 shows the old uniform; Figure 3 shows the new.

The uniform change was a shock to inner members. For years Powerites had inveighed against the Grey Forces of conventional society. The symbolic character John Grey was an object of derision. John Grey, archconformist, follows the path of "hypocrisy, mediocrity, blasphemy." The black uniforms had been a projection of the cult's longing for intensity, for an impressive image that would make people take notice. Now the greys seemed to indicate a conscious search for blandness, a perfidious acceptance of "hypocrisy, mediocrity, blasphemy." The theological explanation for the change was the notion of The New Game, a shift from the angry Jehovi-

Figure 2. A Powerite dressed in the black uniform, early 1971, with the Cross of Christ and the Goat of Satan on his chest

an Period of the cult's first seven years to a happier Luciferian Period for the second seven years.

Brother Ariel says the grey change may have made sense to The Omega, "but it made no sense on the ground level" of Messengers. Only the respect Messengers felt for the cult hierarchy kept them from exclaiming, "Hey! Isn't this a basic policy mistake?" The leaders candidly told us the grey was meant to improve the public image. The Chapter Houses and Caverns were likewise transformed. The striking, colorful paintings that had lavishly decorated public rooms were put in storage, and such bland decorations as rya rugs and paintings of children's balloons were hung in their stead. The walls were repainted in light tones.

At the end of 1971, there was a second change in clothing styles and color. After discovering that the grey clothing was unattractive, the leadership ordered a switch to blue. First tried out as uniforms for the cult's rock bands, the new medium blue clothing was a hit. Much more dignified than the grey, it was still friendly in mood and had some of the impact of the black. Much of the blue clothing was produced for The Power by a company that specialized in making theatrical costumes. The new suits were quite

Figure 3. Powerite woman and man dressed in the new grey uniforms, Summer 1971, posing in front of the Christian cross in the assembly room

stylish and usually fitted well. Wardrobes now showed a greater range of variety. The most formal attire is shown in Figure 4.

In a Canadian newspaper interview, Edward de Forest admitted that the stylish conventional suit he was wearing was intended to project a new image. "He feels that, particularly in America, the Satanist rumors are more likely to be believed if they look like down-and-out sack cloth and ashes prophets. Also, many prominent people they need to reassure will simply not walk into a Power chapter, as they are free to do. 'We have to have an image those kind of people will respond to,' he said."

Sometime early in 1972, Father Paul and Sister Amaranth were guests on a radio show broadcast by Boston's NBC affiliate, WBZ. The show went well, so the station invited the pair to return the following week and do a program of their own. As Paul said on a show three years later, Power radio "just got rolling from there. We did some rock interviews on the Boston Common in the summer of '72, and we interviewed Blood, Sweat and Tears, Chicago, Dr. John, The Beach Boys, a lot of big names. And the show got better and better." The station run by Boston University gave

Paul a second show, so by the fall of 1972, The Power was on Boston air twice a week. The NBC show began to be picked up by other stations, until about two dozen were carrying it. The cult received the air time for free, and most of the production costs were borne by the stations. The show never brought in any significant number of recruits, but it was a successful step toward public acceptance.

In order to be accepted by the public as a legitimate *church*, worthy of financial support, The Power was forced to engage in a good deal of social service work. Powerite theory suggested that people ought to support the cult for two reasons: 1) because The Power was actively engaged in important research into the nature of human existence, and 2) because The Power mediated between mankind and the Great Gods of the Universe. But no outsiders believed the premises upon which these two justifications were built. Consequently, the cult was forced to move quite far away from its own basic assumptions and toward the public view that churches should be supported for the social service work they perform. Three other functions were served by the cult's programs. Edward and some other leaders who

Figure 4. A Powerite wedding couple in their formal blue robes, posing in front of a new symbol, the Unity Cross

were dedicated to the service of Christ (rather than one of the other Gods) believed it was their duty to extend love and help to the world's unfortunates. Also, the social service work gave Messengers a break from their street begging, the opportunity to put on a show for appreciative audiences, and a source of some feeling of personal worth. Finally, the social work was a poor but not entirely barren technique for the recruitment of new members.

In the fall of 1971, The Power first turned its attention to social work. When the first donators were working the Boston streets, they often found it expedient to present themselves as a drug rehabilitation program. This bordered on fantasy. The only clients this "program" served were a few already cured members of the cult. The only method of treatment, neither particularly effective nor attractive to the public, was the conversion of a drug user into a dedicated cultist. The first social programs I saw were two in-house giveaways. I helped set up The Free Store in the Boston Chapter. It consisted of a cellar room just off the coffee house area at the foot of the entrance stairs. We painted the walls satanic red and installed shelves and a rack for clothing hangers. The church had collected a good deal of second-hand clothing, which they then presented to any poor person who wanted to take some. Those who came in hungry from the streets were offered a free meal, usually big sausages, potatoes or dumplings, and cabbage. For a while The Power had permitted runaways and others to "crash" for the night, but this was discontinued because of police pressure against harboring underage fugitives. The Cavern coffee house did however serve as a kind of loose youth placement service, on an informal basis. Those with no place to stay could meet more stable coffee house denizens and make arrangements to move in with them.

In Toronto and New Orleans, the free food program expanded until quite a number of derelicts were being fed each day, usually male alcoholics and other older bums. In Boston, the project served only some young counter-culture wanderers. After a few weeks of the free food program, a large plastic sign was hung on the Cavern wall asking those who took clothing or food to make some kind of contribution to the chapter, in labor if they had no money. This request was not really an attempt to get valuable compensation for the food and clothing. Rather, it tried to initiate a relationship of reciprocity between the cult and recipients of its charity. This could be the first step in a series of escalating exchanges leading to full membership.

Messengers of the cult were sent out on missions of mercy. In Boston and New York, the cult developed continuing relationships with hospitals for the mentally retarded. Once, a number of the inmates were taken to see a play. Often, Power musicians went to entertain the inmates. They also frequently visited homes for the aged, and prison visits were also attempted. From mid-1972 onward, these services were featured in the cult's monthly magazine, sold on the streets. The cover of the February 1973 issue shows a deadbeat geezer being feted in "The Free Kitchen." Retardates and Powerites mingle on the covers of several editions. A prison visit was publicized in May 1973, and a day with the senile in June. Writing under her pre-Power name in the June issue, Mother Ruth announces "The Quiet Revolution," the shift decided upon in the annual Masters' conference at the end of 1971 to put great emphasis on social service. The credit for getting the volunteer programs off to a big start was given to Father Siegfried, Master in charge of "Expansion." There is no doubt that The Power did feed, comfort, and entertain literally thousands of unfortunate persons in its social service work. The administrators of several of the institutions served by the cult were happy to give enthusiastic testimonials. But one Powerite called the social work "our credibility program" intended to legitimate church status.

The cult still lacked a major resource before it could become a real church: it had no congregations to speak of. If we count Messengers and above as clergy, and those below this rank who regularly attended activities as laity, then the clergy/laity ratio was 1:1 or even worse. Disciples and Initiates provided only a small fraction of the income required to support the inner members. Some religious communes find an economic base other than contributions. The Oneida Community made silverware and animal traps.[2] The Bruderhof manufactures toys.[3] Twin Oaks attempted to sell rope hammocks.[4] Technianity provides expensive psychotherapy. In its implosion and wanderings, The Power lost its therapy business and was actually in a bad position to launch new therapy services. The competition was stiff in American cities because there were so many therapists with academic or medical credentials and established referral networks. The street people and other members of the counterculture attracted to The Power by its colorful image and recruited through the coffee house were neither interested in nor able to afford serious psychotherapy. Finally, the cult's culture was now so religious in its symbolism that, so far as I can tell, leaders never considered returning to psychotherapy as a source of income and new recruits. Compulsions Analysis was a thing of the past. In their

[2] Maren Lockwood Carden, *Oneida: Utopian Community to Modern Corporation* (Baltimore: Johns Hopkins, 1969).

[3] Benjamin Zablocki, *The Joyful Community* (Baltimore: Penguin, 1971).

[4] Rosabeth Moss Kanter, *Commitment and Community* (Cambridge: Harvard University Press, 1972), pp. 19–20. I myself was one of the few early customers to buy one of this commune's hammocks.

own development, leaders of the cult felt very distant from psychotherapy by 1971. This situation was extremely unfortunate for the cult. A psychotherapy business might have served superior people like the original founders, people of wealth and talent, an ideal congregation. Failing to return to this successful strategy, The Power tried to adapt to the status of church.

INTO THE FAITH HEALING BUSINESS

In June 1972, The Omega traveled from Toronto to Vancouver on the west coast, on a long tour that was partly a vacation, partly another hunt for a splendid Power headquarters, and partly a research voyage for the establishment of healing services. On most legs of the journey, Kitty and Edward went by commercial airliner, while Lilith (who had returned to the cult) and Moloch drove The Omega's Pontiac Grand Safari station wagon with all the luggage and the dogs. The Omega enjoyed traveling in style, supported by the street-begging Messengers who struggled to follow and serve it.

Edward says, "Vancouver didn't come across as the kind of place we had any wish to open a chapter in at all." They looked at houses in the Canadian city, and Edward composed more doctrines concerning the Gods. The Omega discussed religious healing at length. BI-26, written back in 1970, says that "however it is done, and on whatever level it manifests, the basis of all our healing is the same; the lifting of guilt." This extreme statement may be appropriate for a psychotherapy concerned with resolving the emotional conflicts of its patients. But now The Power conceived of the lifting of guilt as a practical means for healing physical illness, tumors as well as psychosomatic ills. Edward says, "Christ made no differentiation between healing and the forgiveness of sins." This is religious healing.

The Omega had heard of Kathryn Kuhlman, the famous American faith healer, and took the claims of her powers very seriously. They talked about her, as Lilith recalls, in "just hours and hours of discussion about 'What is this thing? Where does it come from? It must have a physical basis.' Discussing how faith healers heal, physically, when these things happen. What they feel like afterwards. What the person being healed physically feels when it happens." They heard that Kuhlman was coming to Seattle, a short drive south, and decided to attend her public meeting and then go down to California "to receive for The Power the healing power."

There was some risk for Kitty and Edward reentering the United States, because their immigration difficulties were not quite solved, but they made it across the border without difficulty and from then on were free of problems of this sort. The Omega took seats in the Seattle auditorium where

Kuhlman was to speak, but Lilith was left outside by mistake, forced to sit on the grass and listen to the event over the loudspeakers set up for the overflow crowd.

Kathryn Kuhlman began to speak. Lilith recalls, "It was rather dull, to tell the truth, and I was feeling very disappointed. She sounded very strange. She had a very strange inflection, very odd way of talking. But what she was saying was very boring." Many minutes passed. "And then a very strange thing happened. She said, 'I feel the presence of the Holy Spirit.' And at the time she said that, it had been completely calm, totally clear sky. A sudden wind came up! Tiny drops of rain and a gigantic rainbow out of nowhere appeared over the auditorium. I WAS ABSOLUTELY STAGGERED! And right after that, she started saying, 'Someone is being healed in the back row on the left. I can feel your ear opening up.' And she started calling out the healings. What she does is she spiels, she just talks, she talks, she talks. She just says whatever comes. And then all of a sudden it starts coming through. She starts picking up on people in the audience being healed, and that's it. She doesn't spiel anymore. It's all concentrated on, 'I feel someone being cured of blindness. I feel someone being cured of spinal disease.' "

Edward says the keynote of her miracle service is drama. "Her performance is stupendous; apparently spontaneous, but in fact highly—and brilliantly—calculated over twenty-odd years of trial and error and hard work of finding out what is the best method for HER to channel the power that comes through her. She is magnetic and hypnotic, and looks quite off her head a good deal of the time! And her effects? The blind see, the deaf hear, and the lame walk. She channels a power that heals goiters, cures cancers, and can bring the dying back to life. A spectacular Satanic performance, backed to the hilt by Lucifer, and showing us something of what is possible when these two work in unison."

After Kuhlman's performance, The Omega went down to California, looking for a splendid mansion to buy for itself with church money. Near Santa Barbara, in Montecito, they found what Edward calls "the most beautiful house you've ever seen." A widow owned it. The very day The Power was all set to buy it, she remarried and decided to keep the house. "Anyway," Edward says, "it was a sign. Obviously we weren't meant to have that house."

They drove to Los Angeles, in the terrible heat of early September, and checked out houses along the way. The signs were against all the houses. The car's air conditioning broke down: a clear sign they were headed in the wrong direction.

Los Angeles happened to be the next stop on Kathryn Kuhlman's itiner-

ary. "We knew she was going to appear that night," Lilith recalls. "And lo
and behold, we drove directly past her, standing on a corner outside of a
shop, obviously waiting to be picked up by someone, dressed in regular,
ordinary street clothes, her face all screwed up against the sun. She had the
whole projection and look about her of somebody who was very crazy. I
yelled, 'Look! Look! It's Kathryn Kuhlman!' We drove past her and the
bloody air conditioner started working. 'Look! She healed the air conditioner! Wow!' "

The Omega found a possible Chapter House in Los Angeles, but it was
too expensive. Then they heard about a fantastic Bicentennial House that
had been built by real estate speculators as the showpiece for a development
called Diamond Bar. It was for sale, so The Omega went to inspect it. Edward was very impressed. He wanted to live in The American Bicentennial
House. "It was a fortress on top of a hill. It was Spanish style, but modern,
built with enormous twenty-five foot windows that went two stories, with
huge battered walls and columns." When people finally built homes on the
lots that surrounded the hill, it would be like a "castle with the villagers all
living round about." The price was a mere $100,000, or thereabouts, while
the real value must have been closer to $300,000. The cult made arrange-
ments to buy. But at the last moment, the deal fell through. "It was just
whipped out from under our noses. So obviously that wasn't supposed to be
the place."

The Omega flew to Florida and reoccupied its house in Key Largo. They
continued to work on the development of faith healing. They visited local
faith healers in the Miami area and invented new rituals that would incorporate healing into group activities. Around the various chapters, sensitive individuals such as Brother Herod, Mother Juliet, and Sister Hannah discovered they possessed healing gifts. One of the new pieces of ritual was a
healing invocation used to channel the power of the Gods through the congregation who spoke the following words, "Jehovah, Lucifer, Satan,
Christ, in Your Names and by Your Grace let the burdens of sickness and
negativity be lifted from (name of sick person), and let the blessings of good
health and positivity be his." The Friday and Saturday Midnight Meditations had been relaxing therapy sessions for participants, but now they were
changed to make them magical-religious rituals to channel the healing
power of the Gods to distant suffering loved ones.

The Omega focused its attention on its own pleasures as well as the
healing of the halt, the lame, and the blind. Another series of trips finally
secured a new secret home for Edward and Kitty, an expensive house hidden
away in Westchester County, near the Connecticut border and within an
hour's drive of the New York Chapter. Although the purchase of this new

home might be denounced as an act of cynical exploitation of the Messengers who ultimately earned the money for it, Edward explained his love of luxury theologically. When he and Kitty took greater material rewards for themselves, God would give greater rewards to all followers. "If we moved up the scale of property—like if we moved out of one level of quality house into a higher level of quality house—everybody moved up. Like they'd get out of ditches into P-Cars, while we got out of rat-ridden holes into slightly classier" places like the $70,000 home in Key Largo. "But we always had to make the first move." And one proof of this proposition was the "fact" that The Omega could get homes cheap. The Key Largo place had been worth $150,000, because somebody had once offered this sum for it. So The Omega believed, "We've got to make the move into a better house, and then everybody can move into better chapters. And if we want a really big, magnificent headquarters, then we've got to get a better house." The Omega moved into the Westchester house, and the cult began negotiations for a $900,000 headquarters building in New York City.

Mt. Chi, as the secret home of The Omega was called, was a nice place nestled between forested hills and overlooking a lake. Rank and file members of The Power, the Outside Powerites who paid for it, were not told of its existence. Some Messengers began noticing that certain Masters would disappear from sight for weeks at a time, not being present in any of the six chapters. Where were they? For a while the Messengers privately postulated the existence of a Great Chapter up in the Sky where the missing leaders must be. Of course they were at Mt. Chi. Other trusted members served The Omega in its new home. Lilith was the housekeeper and Brother Luther the cook. Messengers finally learned about Mt. Chi by chance. One of them was working the streets in New York, one day, and happened to stop a member of the public who happened to have done some renovating work on Mt. Chi. So the basic secret was out. Even today, most church members do not know the address of The Omega's hideaway.

The development of healing practices and the purchase of a new and more splendid home for The Omega suggest how the transformation of a new public image was linked to the desire to improve the cult's economic situation for the benefit of the leaders. Another sign was the evolution of the magazines sold by street donators. From 1969 through 1972, the magazines changed from vivid, psychedelic explosions of color and bombast into bland, pale pleas for love and support from conventional society. The *Fear* issue of the big, early magazine was filled with powerful, even disgusting images. The pages dripped purple, red, and silver ink in a surrealistic burst of horror. The next issue, on Death, was more sedate, and the *Love* issue which followed was friendly and gentle.

In the spring of 1972, the cult came out with a new magazine, *The Pow-erites*, an eight-page black-and-white photo-essay publication that cost lit-tle to produce. All the layout work was done by Power artists in their own studio. I myself took eighteen photographs that were published in these magazines, and several other cult photographers documented the blandest aspects of cult life and the superficialities of social work programs. The monthly *Powerites* had at least three commercial functions. First, as a kind of illustrated church newsletter, it projected an image of the cult as a work-ing church, with many ongoing programs worthy of public support. Sec-ond, it was much cheaper than other Power publications and could be used to extract donations of twenty-five cents to a dollar from passersby unwill-ing to buy an expensive book. Third, because it was a monthly, *The Power-ites* could be used to achieve repeat business, sold month after month to the same customers. Twenty-seven issues of *The Powerites* ultimately appeared under this title.

LOWER SATANIC MANIFESTATIONS

The new emphasis on magical and religious healing of the body and soul was a natural response to the problems of the cult's new clientele. Many were sick in mind and body. Many were poor, stupid, or undisciplined. There were many peripheral members of the church who wanted admission to the inner core of cult society but were refused entry. One common type was called Lower Satanic Manifestations, or LSMs. These people were dis-ruptive individuals attracted by the satanic rhetoric of the cult but unable to accept the authoritarian discipline imposed by the hierarchy. Most of them were economically unproductive and had almost nothing to contrib-ute to the church. But the cult's rhetoric made it difficult for the Masters to reject the LSMs entirely, so a continuing, gnawing crisis plagued Power chapters. What to do with these people?

Let me give some examples. Ron Forbes was an aggressive social outcast. He possessed very high intelligence, but he used every neuron in his brain to devise ways of being obnoxious. I could give many examples of Ron's habit of insulting everyone around him, but his language was so fiendishly offensive that any direct quotations would be unpleasant. In his own way, Ron was a comic genius, and many Powerites found his behavior amusing. But nobody wanted to live with him. Rejected from Messenger status in the fall of 1971, Ron took on the airs of a Messenger anyway. He told me he actually went before a judge and had his name legally changed to Brother Sodom. He began producing his own scripture, heading his documents

The Power—Church of Armageddon, and signing them *Sodom* in imitation of Edward's style. Sodom document number two is particularly poignant. It is about sex. Women found Sodom repulsive, and his chief sexual gratification was assaulting people of both sexes with very personal dirty jokes. Sodom wrote, "Mankind has turned sex into a vile perversion. What used to be a God-given and beautiful gift, is now ugly and obscene. It is with great contempt that I see what humanity has done to this gift." Writing from his heart he admitted, "the overall picture is bleak and filled with despair." Another Sodom scripture, written in Boston the day after Christmas, 1971, urges service to Satan. "The gates of Hell are opened and the jaws of death are quick to take up those who falter from the path of Satan. Fiends already released from the pit stalk the earth, to destroy those who will follow them. For the fiends are Satan's slaves and help him reap his harvest of death." Not surprisingly, The Power refused to accept Ron's writings as bona fide scripture.

Another case was Julio Famagusta. More delicate than Ron Forbes, Julio made up for his lesser native obnoxiousness by laziness, failure to bathe, and by constant assertion of his superiority over everybody else. A lowly OP in June or July 1973, he came to feel there was a lack of unity in the Boston Chapter. Ishtar, Adam, and Paul "were on a power trip," he said. Julio invented his own ritual, called *The Hour of Unity*, and urged other OPs to join him in performing it as a cure for the lack of unity they felt. Some of them actually carried out the ritual a couple of times in the chapter's OP Room. Then the three leaders of the chapter, still on their "power trip," squelched Julio's Hour of Unity. Of course his ritual was a symbolic grab for power. If he could get others to perform his ritual, he would acquire status over them. The ritual itself, similar to a Telepathy Developing Circle or Midnight Meditation, was innocuous. His independent introduction of the ritual, however, was obnoxious, especially because he never made any other, more positive contributions.

Sister Norma recalls the kind of trouble LSMs could cause. One evening she was in charge of the Cavern coffee house. That meant, at least in theory, that she was to handle emotions on every level in the Cavern, keeping order no matter what the threat. One of the male LSMs was drunk and belligerent. He commanded her to turn the record player up. She said the music wouldn't go any louder. He demanded. He ranted, threatened, and started a fist fight with the parent of a Messenger!

I saw many disruptions by persons obviously mentally ill. A man dominated a seminar with utterly unintelligible hebephrenic monologues. A paranoid lady rushed around the coffee house accusing people of trying to kill her and striking them. A retarded boy mistook a Priest's sermon for a personal discussion with him, and killed the ritual mood by replying at length to everything the Priest said.

Many LSMs achieved Disciple rank and swaggered around in their P-Gear uniforms, contributing little for all the trouble they caused. Disciple rank was supposed to be equal in status to that of Messenger, and the LSM Disciples took every opportunity to remind everyone of this theory. But Disciples really were inferior in status. An administrative document of June 28, 1973 explains the differences. It says, "A vital requirement for Messenger and therefore of course IP status is a basically high level of practical responsibility in terms of self-discipline and self-control, and a high degree of detachment from any personal problems." The LSMs did not qualify. Other unproductive types took Disciple status and wanted to be Messengers, for example depressives. Soon Disciple rank became a residual status, collecting "all those who are not suitable for the Messenger line." The rank had been originally invented for normal people with too many outside commitments to want to become Messengers, successful people who could contribute significantly. But Edward proclaimed, "No one is refused Baptism as a Disciple, as long as he has fulfilled the simple practical requirements." As Disciple rank filled up with disruptive and inferior people, they drove out and away any person of quality who might otherwise want to join.

Sometimes the LSMs were good for a laugh. Brother Ariel remembers one of the more bizarre figures lurking around the Boston Chapter, Hermann, "a little thin man, very short, blond crew cut, who wore black glasses, very neatly dressed with Nazi insignias. He was a real Nazi fanatic." Ariel fancifully wondered if Hermann were really a CIA agent planted to check out The Power. "He knew the Nazi sort of approach would fascinate us, and it certainly did. So we invited him to lunch." Hermann proceeded to explain his theory of History to the bemused Powerites. Agents of the Jewish, Bolshevik Conspiracy, of which The Power was part, had changed into wolves. "The real people were sheep, and of course the wolves would eat the real people. But out of the ranks of the real people were to arise werewolves who were like the Nazis, who would devour the wolves. They were reformed sheep . . . supersheep." Ariel and a couple of other Messengers were responsible for staging a weekly show in the dramatic Powerplay activity, and decided Hermann's crazy theory would be an ideal subject for one of their productions. That week they put on an elaborate play, complete with masks and costumes. The story was "about a sheep getting killed, and a werewolf." Ariel says, "It was the first time we used my Death Mask, which has no expression, and it got some shudders. So it was a successful play." Hermann gave a solo standing ovation. The players made "ba-ba-ba" sheep noises throughout the skit, and this effect became a private joke. In later weeks, when a show was sagging, one of the actors would say "ba-ba-ba" and the audience would laugh heartily.

Disciple rank progressively declined, even to the point that LSMs were complaining that their status was debased by the super-inferior late recruits. There was one revealing incident in which the Boston Chapter experienced a minor Disciple revolt. At this time, three-time "murderer" and bike monster Brother Goliath had flunked out of Messenger status and was a leader of the LSM Disciple mob. He and the other LSMs complained bitterly when they found out that an Initiate named Willie was scheduled for Disciple Baptism. Ariel recalls, "If Willie was going to be made a Disciple, they wanted to turn their crosses in. Willie is the extremely retarded newsboy that used to come around and slobber on all the girls. Up until we started having mentally retarded visitors to the coffee house, people like Goliath were considered the worst LSMs. Here the worst LSMs—the EX-worst LSMs—were complaining that Willie was being made a Disciple, and they were saying the Disciple line was being cheapened!"

THE JANUARY BLUE SALE

The lower membership ranks were gradually debased throughout 1972–1973, leading to a climax at the beginning of 1974. At the end of 1972, a new status was invented, that of Field Disciple. Really equivalent to Initiate rank, it was intended to exploit in some way the interested people Powerites met on their trips around the country, people who wanted to join but did not live near a chapter. The Power wanted more people and more money. In an administrative bulletin of September 19, 1973, Edward sought to whip up more energy among his followers, to raise them to greater exertions and achieve the success that was eluding the cult. "The aim in any Chapter is the maximum ACTIVITY both in and around the Chapter and Sphere. For that, people are required. WITHOUT people there can be no activity; but equally, without activity the people will not be attracted." He gave several lists of projects that might be undertaken by the chapters, and areas where more energy might be invested. "If a project fails, embark on another. If one succeeds, stay with it and expand it."

The demands placed on the Messengers increased terribly. They were expected to put in ever longer hours on the streets, pulling in new members and great amounts of money. For the first time, money quotas were set. A Messenger could not come home until he had collected his quota for the day. The January 1974 issue of *The Powerites* proclaimed that its circulation "more than TRIPLED in 1973," a clear sign of increased donating activity.

In at least one chapter, the leaders decided to quit spending any money on food for members, and served meals using food donated to the church. Morale dropped precipitously.

The central leadership was not yet ready to change course, and did not abandon its obsessive, dysfunctional approach until after the major crisis which came to a head in March 1974. The last struggles of the old Power culminated in an unrealistic attempt to expand membership. In an explosive couple of weeks, later known derisively as *The January Blue Sale*, the number of Messengers was suddenly increased in the futile hope that a greater work force could be made to collect the desired money and overcome all obstacles to success.

Before April 1973, an Initiate would be baptized Messenger whenever he was completely ready, in many cases enjoying a special ceremony conducted just for him. Beginning in May of that year, Baptisms were held only once every three months, for Disciples as well as Messengers. This new system rationalized the practice at the cost of impersonality. Baptism had become a bureaucratic event rather than the intimate acceptance of a newly beloved person into central cult society. The first Messenger Baptism of 1974 was scheduled for January 19th.

Anxiously casting about for solutions to its problems, the cult's leadership decided that each of the six church chapters should baptize at least six new Messengers at the January 1974 ceremony. There was a growing tendency for individuals to drop out of Messenger status, IPs as well as OPs, and it had become difficult to keep the chapters staffed, let alone build them and get the cult moving again. The old requirement that a neophyte must spend six weeks "on Messenger line" or "on dedication," living the life of a Messenger and proving his worth, was abandoned. This further demoralized the people who were already Messengers and had achieved their status at great effort. Ariel says, "It was just said that anybody can become a Messenger that wanted to. We thought it was because they needed the money" that The Omega took such a drastic step. "People on the whole felt badly about it." Each chapter succeeded in producing exactly six new Messengers in January. How many were of true Messenger material? "Toward the end, none at all." Sister Claire told me the Masters practically scoured the coffee houses looking for people willing to be baptized. Ariel recalls a moment when he had to give Father Nathaniel the message that Stinky, one of the Cavern LSMs, wanted to see him. Nathaniel rolled his eyes and exclaimed, "Wonder what he wants! To become a Messenger?" All the worst people wanted to be Messengers. Now they could be.

The thirty-six new Messengers were almost without exception people of the crudest sort, unable or unwilling to make the kind of contribution expected of them. It would have been disastrous if they had remained Messengers for long, because as a class they constituted thirty percent of the inner membership. Within a very few days almost every one had dropped out.

Melvin Potts was one of the thirty-six. An affable but extremely erratic fellow, he had contributed a good deal of work as a Disciple and had lived with others in a Disciple House commune. Nonetheless, he had a tendency to get into fights, had a serious medical problem, and had very poor body coordination. Melvin was marginal Power material, neither a total loss, nor particularly talented. He describes what happened. "The standards dropped. The requirements dropped. At the same point, the morale inside and outside dropped. I was what was called the Blue Streak Messenger of January. There was a quickie one-week baptism where they threw on a bunch of people. Not one person lasted. Most of them were out in one week or two weeks afterward. A big cut-down in morale for the inside people, because they had spent months and months of being trained to go on, and these people didn't have two seconds of training. They were thrown into a uniform and told to go out on the street and donate." Vertical communication had broken down. The followers didn't know what was going on, and the leaders paid no attention to the feelings of the Messengers. "I know how I felt doing it!" Melvin says. "All of a sudden I was out there donating, for ten hours, with quotas to make, and a certain amount of money to bring in." He was quickly disillusioned and quickly left.

ANALYSIS

Exhausted by its fruitless quest, The Power took root in 1970. Not having found glory outside conventional society, it would seek glory and comfort as well inside the normal world. Edward and Kitty settled in a secret mansion, and their followers began the normal jobs of making money, raising children, gaining status in the community, and setting up a stable church institution. In 1973, the last real therapy sessions for insiders were dropped. The intensity of social relations had long since hit a ceiling, so the therapy sessions no longer had much appeal. The growth in cult membership leveled off by 1973, making upward mobility inside the cult almost impossible.

When the chapters were being set up in 1970 and 1971, there was an influx of originally middle-class college dropouts. These people were suffering "acutely felt tensions," as the Lofland-Stark model of conversion would predict, but they also fitted the pattern of earlier middle-class recruits in that by dropping out of college they had lost social ties. Those who were successful in gaining full membership in The Power were suffering temporary dislocation rather than chronic failure. Given a stable life within the cult, they were able to recover their balance and enjoy cure from their brief bout with "tension." It is entirely possible that many of them would have resumed normal, reasonably successful lives in secular society had they not been incorporated into the cult.

After 1971, about the only people who attempted to join Power chapters were unattractive, unsuccessful individuals: displaced high school children, violent motorcycle gang members, underclass exconvicts, irredeemable drug dropouts and alcoholics, and mentally ill or retarded persons. Without intending to, The Power was being forced into the role of social service organization, feeding and entertaining a large number of people who were not eligible to join. In the name of Christ, Edward demanded that these people be brought into the cult. In the name of economy, Kitty and the Masters of the Church struggled to contain the problems created by the new and inferior clientele.

The main source of money for The Power became the street donating. In Germany during the Matthew 10 period, Powerites supported themselves directly through this technique, but from 1970 onward they paid all money to the Treasurer or High Master of their chapters. The emphasis was on making a lot of money to finance growing chapter expenses, to support The Omega in style, and make expansion possible. Street donating became the major activity in a Messenger's life. It paid the bills and was also the first step in recruitment. People met on the streets would be invited back to the local Cavern coffee house. Here newcomers had a chance to get to know Powerites and form social bonds with them. Whenever a public ritual or activity was held, all the people in the coffee house were invited to attend.

Although this recruitment technique successfully brought in many new people, it was dysfunctional in that it recruited mainly very inferior members. The Cavern became a hangout for runaways, unemployed unskilled young adults, and mentally ill individuals. Coffee house society was its own social environment and by 1971 had become rather unappealing to talented, attractive people of the type that had originally founded The Power. To join, newcomers had to form strong reciprocal ties with members, but the coffee house recruitment procedure forced high-quality newcomers to associate primarily with scruffy coffee house denizens whom they were unlikely to find attractive. I saw many valuable individuals visit the cult once or twice, then never return, so the problem was not that the supply of potential recruits had suddenly disappeared, but that the recruiting process was no longer working.

One of the greatest problems for cult leaders is how to keep followers busy at tasks that will not require much investment in money or the leaders' time. Many activities that look from the outside like pure recruitment work are really intended as busywork for low-status followers. Their effectiveness in bringing in new recruits is secondary. For example, middle-rank Power-ites spent much of their time visiting nearby cities, going into public insti-tutions for the aged and retarded, and standing on street corners chatting with people who had nothing better to do. The coffee house recruitment procedure was dysfunctional in that it tended to attract low-quality new-comers, but was functional in that it gave members a variety of relaxed social tasks to perform. The whole setup permitted Powerites to put on exciting performances for admiring audiences. But to rejoice in their supe-riority over their audiences, members had to put up with inferior audiences. Function and dysfunction were inextricably joined.

Thus, while each of the steps taken by The Power can be explained in terms of its history and purposes, a tremendous contradiction developed in its structure and means of survival. In the next three chapters we will de-scribe the culture of The Power at its height, before we turn to the cata-clysm that followed.

SIX

Power Society

What is The Power for you?
What can The Power give to you?
What can you give to The Power?
—Questions asked of a
candidate for Messenger baptism

Outsiders often believed that all Powerites partook of a rabidly deviant lifestyle. But this was not the case. Middle-ranked members did not enjoy unusual license, nor even the conventional freedoms, but dwelt within a fairly rigid and demanding system of rules designed to exploit them for the sake of the cult's leadership. In this chapter, I describe Powerite life as I observed it in the years 1971–1973, when the cult was at its numerical height and the culture was most developed. The structure of the narrative is simple; we scan Powerite life upward through the hierarchy of ranks and across the main issues of communal existence. The underlying theme is the way the system exploited and controlled middle-ranked members through the actual provision of gratifications and the promise of greater gratifications to come. I describe many Power customs, beginning with an overview of the scale of the cult and ending with a discussion of the economic structure. The ordinary details of everyday life were not left to chance, but arranged by the leaders to give them the greatest power at the least cost.

THE SCALE OF THE CULT

Power chapters were never particularly large. The absence of a well-developed congregation kept participation in mass activities rather modest, but the relative size of the committed "clergy" ensured the vitality of each branch. I attempted to count the number of people present at cult gatherings over a three-month period, January 23, 1971 through April 24, 1971. The biggest weekly activity, the Saturday evening Sabbath Assembly, tended to draw between 60 and 75 people, including almost everyone of Messenger rank or above. At nine Sabbaths where I was able to count the numbers of new Acolytes and Initiates, 26 people were acolyted (an average of 2.9 a week) and 14 were initiated (an average of 1.6 a week). Extrapolating these figures, we can estimate that the Boston Chapter took in 150 new Acolytes and 75 new Initiates a year. This 2:1 ratio really indicates a 50% dropout rate after people "came forward" to join the cult, because the rank of Initiate was in every way superior to that of Acolyte, carrying no special burdens and some advantages. Nobody who stayed with the cult for long would fail to be initiated. For a while, a weekly Initiates' Meeting was held every Sunday, drawing ten or fifteen people each time. The number of truly active Initiates seldom rose above two dozen.

The Friday Telepathy Developing Circle tended to draw between 30 and 40 persons at the Boston Chapter in 1971, including eight or ten Messengers. The OP Progresses, the seminar and group therapy sessions, open to Initiates, Disciples, and OP Messengers, seemed to draw 20 to 30 persons each time. The total number of different persons who attended a Progress at least once in April 1971 was exactly 50. This suggests the total number of active Boston Powerites was around 75.

In October and November 1971, I was asked to photograph all members of Disciple rank and above so that photo identification cards could be made. These cards would be used to convince police and other officials that donators and members performing other public functions were authentic and deserved toleration. My photography work enabled me to complete an accurate census, as shown in Table 2.

For the nine adult IPs, the sex ratio is very close to 50–50, as it is for the total of 37 adult members. I counted the Powerites of Messenger rank and above named in the issues of *The Powerites* magazine, 1972–1974, and arrived at a total of 92, exactly 46 males and 46 females. Edward tells me there was no conscious effort to keep the numbers of males and females equal. Presumably if sexual attraction was one of the forces bringing in new

Table 2: **The Boston Chapter, November 1971**

Rank	Males	Females	Total
Masters	1	1	2
Priests	1	0	1
Prophets	1	3	4
IP Messengers	1	1	2
Children	4	2	6
OP Messengers	3	7	10
Disciples	12	6	18
Total =	23	20	43

members, one might expect the ratio to approach equality, because a surplus of one sex would tend to recruit members of the opposite sex until an approximate balance was achieved.

In 1971, there were two big chapters, Boston and Chicago, the dwindling London group, and two small chapters in New Orleans and Toronto. From the 75 members in Boston we can estimate that there were around 200 or 250 members of all ranks, altogether. The booklet *Fax 'n Figgers*, put out by the cult in early 1972, states, "As of December 1971, at a conservative estimate, the number of Powerites stood around the 100,000 mark, and is growing rapidly every day." What could this 100,000 figure mean? I estimate that less than 10,000 people could have visited coffee houses. I therefore suspect that 100,000 is a rough estimate of the total number of people who ever contributed to a donator on the streets, casual benefactors who could hardly be called members. True formal membership required a person to experience a series of initiation ceremonies intended to transform him into a Messenger of the cult.

MESSENGERS

A person became an Acolyte by responding to the Evangelist's call near the end of the Sabbath Assembly. After his emotional sermon, the Evangelist would call "upon all who wish to belong to the Army of GOD and to dedicate their lives to the service of the Lord Christ and the Three Great Gods of the Universe, and who have not already been received into the Church, to come forward and kneel before me." If any did come forward and kneel, the Evangelist would stand over them, make the sign of the cross with his outstretched arms, and say, "In the Name of The Lord Christ and in the Name of the Lord Satan, I accept you as Acolytes of the Church of Armageddon." Later, in a private meeting, the new Acolyte would learn from The Guardian of Acolytes that he had just taken a "first step within the hierarchy of The Power" and had made "a gesture of commitment." The status of Acolyte was really of no significance, and each newcomer was urged to become an Initiate as soon as possible, perhaps in as short a time as one week.

When I was initiated in 1971, the procedure involved attending two First Progress classes, meditation on Christ and Satan, twenty-four hours of fasting, and a public ritual. In the middle of a Sabbath Assembly, Isolde and I knelt before the Sacrifist, received our Initiate's crosses, and proclaimed our desire "to serve the Lord Christ and the Lord Satan." We were anointed with water (Christ) and fire (Satan). What was my function as an Initiate? The ritual formula explained I was to "play my part in Their joining together for the Final Judgement of humanity and the ending of the world of men." In fact, Initiates had very few functions. Chiefly, they filled up the coffee house and the rituals, while some of them were recruited to become Messengers.

It was not easy to become a Messenger, except in the time of the infamous January Blue Sale. For six weeks before baptism, a candidate had to "go on dedication" or "Messenger line," following the rules required of Messengers to prove he could accept the discipline. In many cases, a promising Initiate was allowed to move into the OP Messenger Flat, the commune on Inman Street. If all went well, a baptism was scheduled. The ceremony was held privately in the Chapter House. Because the ritual was closed to people below Messenger rank, the candidate would not know what to expect, never having seen somebody else receive baptism. Sometimes the noise of a Messenger Baptism could be heard in the Cavern—the beat of drums and loud voices—and wild rumors spread about the horrendous things that happened to the victim being baptized. A candidate for baptism might be told he would be branded with a hot iron, or informed he might share in a cult orgy immediately afterwards. Of course, both the branding and the orgy were pure fantasy.

The ceremony was bland but did have the power to evoke strong feelings in the candidate because he was the focus of the entire group's attention and gripped by a sense of mystery produced by the secrecy in which the baptism was held. Like all Power "Consecration Ceremonies," the Messenger Baptism was presided over by a Sacrifist, who anointed the candidate with fire and water. In the midst of the ritual, the new member was given his Sacred Name. Late in the history of the cult, people chose their own Sacred Names or suggested three from which the Master of the chapter would pick one. But earlier, the names were chosen by Kitty or some other leader and not told to the candidate until he had been proclaimed a "Messenger of the Unity of the Lord Christ and the Lord Satan." So when the Sacrifist said, "Henceforth you will be known by the Sacred Name ———, which means ———," the candidate was gripped by great excitement. Who will I be?

A new Sacred Name marked a new identity for the person. Sister Roxana was deeply impressed by her baptism. "The fact of getting your name, and having just like this incredible whole revelation of your inner identity, having that crystallized by your name!" Roxana says, "I like to think of myself as my name." She has studied the mythological significance of her name, and feels Roxana "was such an incredible woman." Sister Eve says her name means Living One, and "I know that's me inside." I often heard brand-new Messengers talk excitedly about their Sacred Names, and watched them attempt to grow into their names, to fulfill the significance of their names.

Powerites used their Sacred Names in public as well as in church settings. Their secular names (Grey Names) were only used in legal documents, on driver's licenses and identification cards, and in financial transactions. A number of members I knew over the years changed their Sacred Names. If someone dropped out and then returned, he would receive a completely new Sacred Name upon rebaptism. Often Powerites wore out their names, came to feel they no longer expressed the right personality, and requested new ones. I have used a single fictitious name for each person in this book to avoid confusing the reader, but names really changed fairly often. Sister Amaranth had three different names, Isolde four, and Lilith five!

As soon as the new Messengers had received his Sacred Name, he would join the senior Messenger in reciting a Dedication:

We are the Messengers of the Second Coming of the Lord Christ, who comes to reabsorb all evil from the world of men. And we are the Messengers of the Redemption of the Lord Satan, who comes to release the power of love into the world of men. We bring the Message of the Unity of these two Great Beings who once were enemies, but who now are joined together in an unbreakable bond of Unity. We are the Messengers of the Unity. As it is . . . So be it.

The new Messenger would now move into the Messenger Flat, if he had not already done so. In theory, the resident Messengers would vote whether to accept each newcomer, and a single negative vote would count as a veto. But in fact, new Messengers were always admitted. The twelve months each OP Messenger had to live outside the core of Power society were a kind of probation period. At the end he would become an IP if he had not dropped out or been expelled first. By placing the OP Messengers in their own commune, the IPs could insulate them, control them, yet still escape responsibility for them. A general but unstated principle of Power leadership was that the leaders wanted control but would not accept responsibility over the followers.

OP Messengers without their own resources would be given a modest allowance for living expenses. In 1973, when six or seven were living in the flat, its running expenses were around $150 a week. Any Disciple or Initiate living with the Messengers on a trial basis was expected to pay his own way. Messengers were permitted to keep any money sent them by their families, and some were able to afford big record collections, extensive libraries, wardrobes of clothing, and decorations for their rooms. The largest bedrooms held two to four people, and sometimes as many as fifteen crowded into the house. Even the Head of House, a senior Messenger who acted as liaison officer with the IPs and who had a luxurious L-shaped room on the first floor complete with refrigerator, was often required to have a roommate. In many respects, the lifestyle resembled that of a group of college students sharing an apartment.

The only real meal of the week at Inman Street was Sunday dinner, when everybody came together for a feast. This might mean chicken, but not really fancy dishes such as the pork roast I once bought for the IPs' Sunday dinner. At other times, individuals ate when they felt like it, fixing their own food in the downstairs kitchen. There was no house cook. Ariel says the kind of food usually available included "hamburger, a couple of cheeses, eggs, always bread, peanut butter, jams, sometimes fruit." In addition to conventional food and goodies like the ice cream Messengers often bought with their allowances, they consumed great quantities of vitamin tablets and other dietary supplements. In October 1971, they were required to follow the schedule below, swallowing 29 items daily:

Morning: 1 multivitamin, 1 kelp tablet, 4 brewer's yeast, 1 halibut or cod liver oil, 3 bone meal, 4 liver pills, 1 dolomite, 1 organic iron (female), and 3 almonds. *Evening:* 2 lecithin tablets, 2 wheat germ oil, 4 vitamin C, 2 vitamin E.

These pills were bought in bulk at a local health-food store. In addition to supplementing the Messengers' diet, they served two social functions. First, they extended the IPs' control over Messengers' daily routines, symbolically underscoring the IPs' superiority. Second, they extended parental nurturance, stating in effect that the IPs cared about the Messengers and were looking over them.

Aside from the above-average consumption of vitamins, I saw no evidence of any unusual attitude toward medical care among Powerites. Some religious groups are reluctant to turn to physicians with their physical problems. The Power cult, however, regularly allocated some of its income for "medical and dental treatment and care" and for P-Beauty ("cosmetic surgery, etc."). When Sister Ishtar spilled stinging perfume in her eyes, she was rushed to the emergency room of a nearby hospital without hesitation.

The Messenger Flat on Inman Street was much like any American home. The downstairs Cavern coffee house had been converted into a comfortable living room. There was a large wooden dining table, benches, chairs, sofas, a television set, and a stereo record player. The downstairs also had a bathroom with shower. Members of Messenger rank and above were usually extremely clean people. They did not need to urge each other to bathe. The women used makeup. The men frequently splashed on aromatic potions. Deodorants were in use.

At regular Sunday house meetings, one of the chief pieces of business was allocating work assignments to Messengers. Brother Ariel recalls some of the specific house tasks given individuals on a regular basis: "Hallways and stairways, the Cavern, the kitchen, the front hall, the Alpha, the Meditation Room, garbage, laundry, the upkeep of the house, the boiler room. People were given good jobs and bad jobs, and some jobs counted extra. Everybody tried to have them as even as possible. Laundry was traditionally given to the lowest hierarchical member of the house. More senior Messengers had responsibilities like upkeep of the real Alpha on Concord Avenue, or upkeep of the coffee house." Among the specific posts were some with formal titles: Maintenance Officer, Economy Officer, Timing Officer, and Mail Officer. The Timing Officer was unpopular; it was his job to wake everyone up in the morning.

The Inman Street ritual room, the Alpha, was closed to the public. There OP Messengers held their Morning and Evening Assemblies. Members took turns playing Sacrifist for these twenty-minute rituals. One section of these brief Assemblies was the Seal of Identification, which enacted the Messengers' unity with each other symbolically through their connection with the Gods. It would begin with a "round" of the circle of participants, in which each would say his name: "I Brother Eros . . ." "I Sister Roxana . . ." "I Sister Eve . . ." "I Brother Thomas . . ." And then the group would follow the Sacrifist in reciting: ". . . do identify myself with Christ, our Lord of Truth, who is the Unity of GOD; with Jehovah, our Lord of the Universe, who is the Power of GOD; with Lucifer, our Lord of the New Age, who is the Light of GOD; with Satan, our Lord of the End, who is the Love of GOD." Finally, the same words would be chanted to a rather sweet melody.

FESTIVITY

Brother Ariel says, "Inman Street was quite a lot of fun." When I asked for an example, he described a moment of great festivity: "We had a very large collection of records that was left over from many, many different people. And we put on this Greek music that got everybody up dancing around, wearing pots on our heads, and playing things together . . . screaming, yelling, hollering."

Powerites often had fun, even when times were rough. Looking back through the hundreds of photographs I took, I see many pictures of fun. A shot of Eve, Roxana, and Ishtar dancing. Eve chewing on the ace of spades in a card game. Four Messengers and two Prophets climbing up the equestrian statue of General Burnside in a public park. Semisexual horsing around: Thomas crushing Eve; Mark bouncing Ishtar on his lap. Once Eve and Eros found a trapdoor on the lawn of a state Capitol, probably repair access to pipes. They pretended it led to Hell, scrambled inside, and pulled the door down over them. With a shout they threw it open and leaped out. They were Satan's Hordes rising to ravage the earth!

The playful spirit of The Power was expressed in members' attitudes toward the cult's doctrine. They frequently exhibited what I call *belief distance*, by analogy with Erving Goffman's concept of *role distance*.[1] When a person broadcasts more or less subtly that he is larger than the role he plays at the moment, he exhibits role distance. When a person similarly broadcasts that he is not rigidly bound by his belief system, he exhibits belief distance. It is as if the person were saying, "I do not really believe these things; I am merely playing the role of believer when it suits me." Both kinds of distance can be communicated through humor, especially self-irony. One of my photos shows Father Paul, second in command of the Boston Chapter, mocking meditation in a silly pose for my camera. He holds his hands pointed upward as if in prayer. His eyes are closed. He has made a fishmouth by sucking in his cheeks. Powerites frequently joked about the Great Gods of the Universe, about various aspects of doctrine, and about each other.

To a great extent, the cultists did not *believe* their tenets in the conventional sense. For them, the Power culture was not a series of statements about a real, external world. Rather it was a collection of attractive and powerful symbols through which they could express themselves. The Power was a kind of living theater. A waking dream, a fantasy that made no apologies to reality, The Power enjoyed playing with itself. It was simultaneously real and fictitious, not a lie but a work of art. In the nineteenth century, Richard Wagner tried to create total works of art in his operas, unions of all forms of artistic creation in one.[2] He only half succeeded. The true *total work of art* would be an artistically created human community with a distinctive lifestyle and culture. *The Power is a total work of art.*

From the perspective of sociological role analysis, following Goffman's dramaturgical model for example, it might be said that the true total work of art is the individual human personality. My greatest act of creation is to create myself. This is what Powerites tried to do. From the moment of receiving his new Sacred Name, each Messenger cultivated a distinctive personality. They wanted to be superheroes. They delighted in the similarity between themselves and the superheroes portrayed in Marvel Comics. On

[1] Erving Goffman, *Encounters* (Indianapolis: Bobbs-Merrill, 1961), pp. 83–152, especially p. 108.

[2] Ernest Newman, *Wagner as Man and Artist* (New York: Random House, 1924).

several occasions I observed members reading such comic books as *Thor*, *The Avengers*, or *Spiderman*. They often discussed the exploits of these surrealistic beings with great seriousness. While outsiders might read *Time* or *Newsweek* to catch up on the news of the conventional world, Powerites read Marvel Comics to keep up-to-date on the news of the magical world. In fact, The Power counted among its closest friends the creator of Marvel Comics, published Marvel panels in its magazines, and was inspired by the comic heroes.

One day I snapped a picture of Brother Thomas reading *The Avengers*. He lunged at me growling like The Hulk. One time I tagged along with him when he ducked into a greeting card shop. He wanted a card to send home to his parents and shouted in joy when he found exactly the right one. It showed the Marvel Comic hero Thor, striding forward with his magic hammer raised to strike. The caption was, "The answer at last!" How apt. Thomas hoped The Power was an answer for him, a way he could become a transcendent heroic being, rising far above normal life to dwell with the Gods.

On donating trips, during visits to hospitals, and in guest lectures to school and college classes, cult members tried to act out heroic parts, presenting themselves as Marvel characters in cloaks, caped crusaders endowed with magic powers. The Messengers wanted to be superheroes but did not accept challenges in an independent spirit. Quite the contrary. They were extremely dependent upon the guidance of the Masters. On every trip, one senior person was in immediate command. Groups that were away from the chapter for long, kept in touch by telephone with the Masters back home. If the game of superhero was a childish fantasy, then Messengers lived it as children, under the close supervision of their parents, the Superiors and Masters. This may seem paradoxical, because I have also said that Inman Street was not supervised. Outside its safe walls, the Messengers practically begged for guidance.

Both the festivity and drama of the cult were reinforced by the extensive use of music. Songs, hymns, chants, and popular recordings were very important elements in its culture. As in other areas, the cult's approach was rampantly eclectic. Some Power tunes imitated familiar music, others were directly lifted from a popular source. For example, the tune to *The Hymn of Repentance* was taken from the traditional Scottish anthem *Scots Wha Hae*. Every Tuesday evening, the chapters held Chant Sessions, enjoyable singing hours that prepared the congregation for that week's Sabbath hymns. Three of the chapters had their own rock music bands that played in public as well as at private cult functions. I traveled with one band when it played southern New England coffee houses. I photographed them at a Boston TV studio. I watched them arouse the college boys in Harvard Square as Sister Eve belted out songs and Sister Chryse danced.

The favorite music of the group was usually the kind of rock and folk music popular in the youth culture around 1970. One typical record collection included The Beatles, The Band, Johnny Cash, The Who, John Mayall, Crosby Stills Nash and Young, The Grateful Dead, The Jefferson Airplane, Jethro Tull, Tom Rush, and Joni Mitchell. Edward de Forest's personal record collection was considerably more intellectual: Bach, Telemann, Albinoni, Tartini, Pergolesi, Vivaldi, Scarlatti, Beethoven, and Mozart. Although some Power hymns had a Gregorian quality, most of the original music by members was closer to the folk-rock tradition.

The most festive hour of the week was called Knees-Up, a private, informal dance held in The Cavern after Saturday's Midnight Meditation. All the Disciple OPs were invited, and it was their chance to socialize on a fairly equal basis with the higher-ranked members of the chapter. After the peaceful Meditation, the Initiates and members of the general public would slowly take their leave. There was always a line in the kitchen—people waiting to use the bathroom—and a scramble to collect overcoats. The Knees-Up would not begin until all the outsiders had left.

Some of the men would clear the Cavern floor for dancing, dragging chairs, tables, and cushions out of the way. The Messenger in charge of the coffee house would select a few phonograph records. The IPs disappeared upstairs to change into civilian clothes. Sister Cher says the entrance of Brother Ariel was always a high point of the evening. He would appear wearing something startling, splendid, elegant, then begin a slow solo dance at the bottom of the stairs. Everyone who came in would get a good view of his performance.

About 1:00 A.M., the dancing would be on in earnest. Knees-Up was like a high school prom. Many of the girls stood around the sides of the room waiting for the guys to ask them to dance. For many, Knees-Up was a ritual. They would always dance one or two times with a list of special partners, reaffirming an otherwise unmarked relationship with each person. Messenger Brother Anthony and Disciple Sister Cher Lennan would always have a slow dance together, even though they hardly spoke to each other for the rest of the week. Fast dances would alternate with slow ones. The last dance was so fast that everybody worked himself into a frenzy, leaping and spinning into exhaustion.

Then it was time for the OPs to leave, the Messengers to Inman Street and the Disciples to various destinations. The IPs stood on the stairs, in the OP Room and in the kitchen near the back door, to say goodbye. People with feelings of special closeness would always kiss and hug, but often a near stranger would rush up and give an unsuspecting OP an exuberant embrace. The OP Messengers had two miles to walk; sometimes Disciples gave them a lift in their cars. The Boston subways were not running at 2:30 when the walkers reached Harvard Square, so there were always a few Disciples who had to hitch rides to get home.

With Knees-Up happening on a weekly basis, and with so many group rituals and therapy sessions, The Power probably did not need many annual holidays. Only Christmas and Foundation Day were celebrated. The Christmas Eve Assembly was open to all Brethren of the chapter, and involved a meditation on "The New Beginning" as well as some carol singing. The theological justification for celebrating the birth of Jesus was a bit weak. In theory, Edward de Forest (and possibly many others) might represent the Christ Spirit as fully as did Jesus. The Powerite purist would say: Jesus was not the Christ, rather Jesus was one of many men who channeled the spirit of Christ. Edward's birthday, October 8, was not a time of public celebration. Christmas was a concession to the Christian sentimentality of most members, a substitute for a visit home, and a taste of Saturnalia. After the public ritual, the Chapter House was vacated by those below Messenger rank, and the rest would proceed to get roaring drunk.

Foundation Day, June 13, sometimes called Founders Day, commemorated the traditional date in 1963 when the cult was founded. It had a public side and a private side. The day would be spent at the beach, OPs and IPs frolicking together on the sand. Afterward, the Messengers and IPs would repair to the Chapter House to demolish a vast store of booze that had been laid in.

LOSS OF AUTONOMY

While making tremendous demands on the Messengers and Prophets, the leaders sought to maintain control without taking responsibility. If a Messenger failed, it was his own fault. On the philosophical plane, the cult's doctrine simultaneously asserted that each person has complete responsibility for everything that ever happens to him, yet is without choice, living a God-determined life. These paradoxes fitted a religious notion of authority. Messengers never knew what was coming next, yet had to live in faith and acceptance. Several told me they loved the excitement of never knowing for sure what tomorrow might bring, trusting that it would be something good.

Transfers from one chapter to another were often sudden and unexpected. Cher had an intense romantic crush on Father Orpheus when he was stationed in Boston. She was shocked one evening to discover that he was to be transferred to New York the next day. "I was just numb because it happened so fast! I didn't really have any time to think about it, which I suppose was best. I suppose he had a function in New York." Her voice took on a wistful tone. "I don't know. They had the new chapter there and people were just being transferred out. He didn't have a choice. He just was sent. Staying within The Power, he had no choice whatsoever."

Brother Dagon was transferred like lightning to Toronto in early 1971. "In fact, when I went up there it was the first announcement to anyone that there was such a place!" The Boston Chapter had no idea a branch was being set up in Canada. "It was a complete surprise. I remember I walked in the office, and I found out I was going, and that was the first mention I'd ever heard of a Toronto Chapter. And that night I told everybody I was getting transferred up there, and everybody was quite surprised." Power society thrived on secrets and rumors. Having secrets, keeping secrets, revealing secrets, and discovering secrets were important factors in arousing excitement and maintaining status in the group.

In October 1971, Brother Mark, then a Prophet, gave a formal statement about his life in the church, explaining to an interested outsider what it was like to be without opportunities for individual decisions. "We take vows of obedience. We follow our instructions." Obedience to whom? Instructions from whom? In Power theory, the separate Gods rule through their people. The idea of a centralized church authority is in total contradiction with the theology. Yet the cult's leaders discovered that power could be made to serve their interests. The ideology yielded. In order to exploit the Messengers and Prophets, the leaders adopted several rhetorical devices from conventional religion. The divine purpose to which the cult founders were dedicated was their own transcendence of conventional life. Through sophistry they obscured this truth, hoping to rise on the shoulders of the Messengers, aware they could not make the real situation very clear if they were to succeed. Mark said, "We live communally. We hold no personal possessions, and we have no outside jobs. We hold everything in common." However, cult leaders could dispose of church wealth as if it were their own property. The Omega lived in luxury. The Power was like a feudal kingdom resting on a communist base.

Mark explained, "We work hierarchically, a hierarchy based on function rather than on quality. It's not that the people on top are *better*; it's just that they have a particular function." Nice rhetoric. "I don't decide what I'm going to do, what I'm going to eat, what I'm going to wear. That's not my level of choice. That's decided for me. And it's a relief. My mind isn't taken up with: 'Well, what am I going to do today? What am I going to wear today? Who am I going to talk to? Where am I going to go? What am

I going to eat?' Which is really a lot of wasted time. That level of operation is settled. We agree on it, and it's done, once and for all. And then we operate on another level which is a bit more significant and more basic to everybody. And that's what it amounts to. You know, as you commit yourself more and more to a way of Love, to God, you stop making choices for yourself, because you've already made your choice." The last choice was to submit to The Power. In so doing, "You free yourself from choice, and from conflict at the same time. You don't have to decide, 'Do I want to do this, or do I want to do that?' You've done it already. It's set."

Messengers lived under strict rules against drugs, alcohol, and sex. They were not supposed to indulge their sexual desires, despite the many attractive partners in the cult and despite the free love values of the Gods Lucifer and Satan. Edward once told me the cult had suffered from problems concerning sexuality as early as Xtul, where there were twice as many males as females. Rivalry was disruptive, and if two people were very deeply involved with each other, they were likely to be all the less involved with the group. So after Xtul, the cult experimented with celibacy, then tried out other approaches to the regulation of sex. The leaders did not want to deny themselves erotic enjoyment, but they were quite ready to deny it to the followers. The rule that OP Messengers abstain from sex (unless a relationship were initiated with one of them from someone higher in the system of ranks) cost the leadership nothing, but gave a two-sided benefit. The celibacy rule both trained Messengers in obedience and tested their compliance.

The Messengers responded variously to the regulations. For example, Sister Godiva said sex was her "greatest weakness." She couldn't keep her mind off it. Godiva admitted quite freely that she was gripped by an intense sexual hunger. She did not remain a Messenger long. After a new affair and after being demoted to Initiate rank, she seemed rather depressed but could at least enjoy her sexuality freely. Other Messengers found the celibacy rule to be an advantage. For example, Brother Eros was an extremely handsome young man who had no difficulty in finding willing female partners. He told me that before joining The Power he used to seduce girls, to enjoy them for a while, then lose interest and drop them. He was caught in an unsatisfying vicious circle of seduction and abandonment. Now that he was in The Power, he could turn his natural inclinations into an asset for the church. He still seduced girls, but not for himself. He seduced them for Christ. Rather than having sex with them, he flirted with them to recruit them to the cult. He once said the greatest thing he had gained from the church was "more confidence in a sexual way. And the sexual feeling is always there because sex is around everything. It is a driving force. I've seen through a lot of the degrading negative sides of sex, and the other side is quite incredible, quite a healing thing." He loved "giving people security to open themselves up, giving them some warmth and security to come out and trust and feel that somebody might care for them. And that's what I give to a lot of people, showing them that I care for them. And they respond to it, you know." This, of course, is the basic recruitment process, expressed in baldly sexual terms.

Brother Ariel, always an excellent informant, told me his analysis of the ascetic regulations. "We didn't smoke dope, not so much because it was *bad* but because it was against the law. If we drank alcohol at official parties—Founders Day, Christmas—we got plastered! Mixing our drinks like mad people and suffering accordingly." Alcohol and sex were dispensed by the leadership under strict control. But of course there was an abstract theory behind everything. "The sexual requirements were there to teach us something about our energies; at least that's how we saw it." Sexual abstinence taught them "how we could channel sexuality and use it twenty-four hours a day. And use it constructively, i.e.: make money or heal people."

Why did people follow the rules? Surely the theory alone could not control the Messengers. One strength the leadership had was the ability to *provide* sensuousness, for example in rituals or the therapy sessions, gratifications so appealing and so promising that Messengers would become addicted or overwhelmed by them. A kind of incest taboo developed between Messengers. They were Brothers and Sisters, after all. Many of their romantic crushes were directed at IPs, and since their status of OP Messenger was to last only one year, many of them could defer gratification until they became an IP or were seduced by an IP. I asked Ariel if sexual behavior were closely monitored at Inman Street. "Oh, it was complete monitoring, but in such a way that nobody was conscious. Everybody was on their honor to such an extent that everybody was being watched." Messengers not only watched each other in an informal competition to be good Messengers, but they also watched themselves. When a Messenger broke the rules, he would have something to hide from the others. Having such a secret, he could no longer share himself completely with the others in the psychological intimacy characteristic of The Power. Thus, people who broke the rules "immediately became outsiders, both from their point of view and from the structure's point of view."

The immediate result was guilt and estrangement. In many cases, the infraction was merely moderate sexual foreplay, so the Messengers involved could restore the subjective feeling of good membership standing simply by cooling off the relationship between them. But a complete sexual relationship was a great threat to the Messengers' equilibrium. "And quite often

the consequence was you had to leave. Because the thing you have to remember is how seriously we took it. We might be there for the most ridiculous reasons. People were there because they liked the uniforms, or because
they wanted to be religious, or they wanted a new name, or because they
liked the girls, or they liked the boys, or whatever. But no matter how
ridiculous the reason, they were serious enough to do it." Being a Messenger was a matter of "total devotion."

"And because things mattered, things had meaning. *Everything had a
meaning.* And it was a fabulous feeling." The street work, for example, acquired sexual significance. "The celibacy rule, I felt, was there so that your
sexual hangups could be exposed to the utmost and always built up. You
had this sexual power that you were constantly trying to get rid of, and
yet you had nothing to do with it. So on one hand, it enables you to really
supersell your magazines. When they talk about the *Sex* magazine, they
weren't kidding around! 'Cause that's what it was—purely sexual sell for
the most part." Messengers used their attractiveness and their own sexual
arousal to sell to people on the streets. Beautiful little Sister Eve used
to have great success with businessmen, for example. Ariel comments,
"You're gonna talk to the most attractive person on the street any time,
because even if they say no, you can have for at least ten seconds that *flash*—
as close as you're going to get to sexual fulfillment." He feels the rules
strengthened relationships within the cult, because each Messenger had "a
family as well as lover bond with almost everybody," since he was denied
real sex with anybody.

Ariel admits that the celibacy rule was sometimes broken, occasionally
without dire consequences. "I remember when I was on Messenger line,
there was an incident. Faust, Kafka, Isolde, and I sort-of deviated from
the sexual rules of the time. It involved very extensive body rubs that led to
taking a shower together. I remember feeling very fine about that, thinking, 'Well, I didn't do anything that broke *my* regulations.'" Brother
Osiris told me he discovered it was possible to break any of the rules, so
long as he and the other persons involved could handle "the effects." Ariel
said that it was difficult for Messengers to do this. "Somebody's going to
manifest the guilt. And the minute somebody manifests, then you're all in
trouble. There're so many examples of people not getting caught, but they
gave themselves up, almost. Brother Patrick and Sister Beryl both had
sexual relationships within The Power. They both left. The minute they
started having sexual relationships, their other relationships started crum-
bling, or their Power ties." Only a few were able to beg on the streets successfully after starting a love affair. "Zane and Jezebel had sexual relations,

and they would make mints together. They would use each other to make money."

"When you were having a love affair within The Power," Ariel said, "it was a very special sort of thing. Because The Power was the most important thing in your life. And suddenly, there was something within this most important thing that was even more important. But you really had to walk on eggs around it, because if it got out, you were courting total disaster. If you got caught breaking sexual rules, you'd really blow your image." Ariel and Titania had a relationship for a while, and struggled to keep up their street work. He said, "I felt torn apart by the whole thing, because I had to pretend that it didn't exist, but it did exist." Here the hostility that ultimately drove him to quit the cult first emerged. "It was like: 'I hate The Power, and just to spite them I'll make money.'" It also bothered Ariel and other single Messengers that the occasional married couple that joined the cult was not expected to follow the celibacy rule. One of the nicer rooms at Inman Street was occupied by married couples, such as Lancelot and Flora, Virgil and Leonora. "That was the sort of thing that especially underlined the absurdity of The Power's rules on sexuality for a lot of us. I could understand if a rule around celibacy was in effect to teach us something, but then why weren't married couples included?"

Leadership control over followers' sexual behavior, therefore, was uneven. But the intention was that it be absolute. More than one informant claimed to know that Kitty took personal charge of all relationships of members above Prophet rank, separating any pair that seemed too intensely involved. I do not have good independent evidence on this point. It is true that many couples were separated, assigned to different chapters, while other couples were kept together.

One example of the leaders' involvement in a Messenger's personal life is the experience of Sister Norma. When she was only an Initiate, she and Brother Patrick developed a romantic relationship that was just about to become physical. Mother Amaranth discovered what was going on, called Norma into her office, and, Norma says, "really laid me out in lavender." After this lecture, Norma and Patrick cooled off their courtship. Months later, when Norma was a proven Messenger, Father Adam called her into his office. He said it was time she got betrothed to marry. "Of all the men in the chapter, which one would you like to have?" he inquired. She said Brother Patrick was her first choice, and Brother Eros was her second choice. Adam promised to give Patrick various hints that Norma was the woman for him. Patrick did not respond. Then Adam and Norma discussed Eros. "He told me to ask Eros, which I did." When Norma asked Eros to marry her, he replied, "Oh, I'm very flattered, but no thank you." Norma says she was devastated by embarrassment. "And then I found out later that he and Amaranth had a thing going."

The sexual rules of The Power appear not really to have had anything to do with spiritual development, but were one aspect of life among many that the leaders wanted to control to their own advantage. Ariel remembers one time Mother Juliet "made advances" to Brother Basil, "who was an OP Messenger and she was a Master of a chapter." If a high-status member of the cult started an affair with a Messenger, it was okay. But if two Messengers got involved with each other, they stood the risk of demotion to Initiate rank. One incident that was so blatant that it actually changed the rules was the affair between Brother Mark, a Prophet, and Sister Leah. When Leah got pregnant, the pair could no longer hide their affair. They were demoted. In the past it would have taken months for them to work their way up again. But Mark was one of the brightest American IPs. The church married the couple and reinstated them in their ranks within a week. After this, the penalty for breaking the celibacy rule was not severe. Messengers begging on the streets would be given occasional breaks in which they might enjoy candy or ice cream. Ariel says, "I remember when Patrick and Arcadia had to donate without taking treat breaks, when they'd broken the celibacy rules." Despite the formal regulations, Ariel says, "We were certainly not a celibate group. Our whole orientation was sexual. One of the basic premises of The Power is that sex is the greatest healing force there is. Use it."

PROMOTION AND DESERTION

An OP Messenger would automatically be promoted to IP Messenger status if he followed the rules, participated in two courses of Messenger Training, and displayed no alarming flaws. Not great talent, but a clean record was all that was required. Each level of the hierarchy kept secrets from the levels below. Roxana, an OP Messenger, once asked Eros, an IP, "What's most important to you about being an IP Messenger?" He replied, "That is classified information, sweetie." Actually, the differences between the two levels were slight. The IP Messenger participated in a few more advanced training and therapy exercises, and was given a Magickal Name to add to his Sacred Name, using it only in private IP meetings. Most of the Magickal names seem to have been taken from classical mythology, the names of deities and demigods.

A Powerite might hold the status of IP Messenger for the rest of his life. But if he showed some leadership ability, completed all Messenger training, carried out difficult assignments successfully, and waited a long and indefinite period, he might be elevated to Prophet rank. In a private ceremony he would receive a silver Prophet's ring bearing the Power Sign to wear on the first finger of his left hand. There were two levels of Prophet training. Junior Prophets' Training consisted of fifty-two sessions, covering a whole year, educating the student in the more complex aspects of the doctrine. Senior Prophets' Training, only eighteen weeks long, was concerned with administrative problems. It covered about seventy-five regulation documents and gave experience in communication. Here the Prophet was given instruction in "contact situations," "telepath training," and public speaking so he could take the role of Evangelist in the Sabbath Assemblies and give good Revelation sermons.

There was a formal examination, strict and intensive, before a Prophet could be promoted to Superior (Priest) rank. It was conducted orally by two Masters and had several sections. I will describe two. The first part confronted the Prophet with five difficult social situations he had to handle satisfactorily. One of the Masters would play the part of a disruptive person, and the Prophet was supposed to use all his training in dealing with the person. The examination outline says, "What is basically required of the candidate is good contact and control. He is not expected necessarily to fully satisfy the subject in terms of resolving his problem." The first of the five troublesome characters would complain and insult, the second would present a personal problem, while the third would express pain or tension. The fourth and fifth would act like aggressive outsiders trying to get damaging information about the cult through aggressive questioning.

The last part of the examination was "An unprepared inspired Revelation lasting between five and ten minutes, channeled by the candidate, as though to an Assembly, on a subject chosen by the testers." The candidate could rely on both the doctrinal training he had received and the experience he had gained in public speaking. Father Adam once gave me an impressive demonstration of the seemingly inspired but actually quite calculated performance that made a good Sabbath Assembly Revelation. I wanted to photograph a Sacrifist and an Evangelist in full color, so Adam and Paul dressed up in the proper costumes. The three of us went into the Alpha ritual room. My color lights were hung from the beams in the center of the room, and my Nikon camera was full of film. Adam stood in front of the black curtain with its red goat's-head symbol, his long blond hair flowing down over his scarlet Evangelist's tabard. He went into his act. Adam shouted, cajoled with a whisper, spoke logically in a metallic voice, pleaded emotionally, laughed in joy and triumph! His body moved to accent the speech. He spoke in a negative tone and waved his fingers dismissingly before his face.

He clenched his fist in anger and growled. He pointed to one side, then forward and above. A great performance! But what was he actually saying? In fact, he was merely reciting the letters of the alphabet.

If the Prophet had met all other requirements for promotion and passed his exam, the High Master of the chapter could send a recommendation to The Omega urging that the candidate be "ordained" a Superior. With this rank, the person would receive a second silver ring, this one bearing the Sign of Union, to be worn on the first finger of the right hand. No longer a Brother or Sister, the Superior would be a Father or Mother of the church.

I knew of no cases in which a person who joined The Power after Xtul was elevated to Master rank. All the Superiors I knew had joined no later than 1968, and had participated in the Matthew 10 wanderings. Promotion to the highest ranks meant admission to the inner core of cult society, rather than a mere bureaucratic advance. The Council of Masters, the dozen or so ruling Powerites under The Omega, is identical with the original heart of Power society created in the social implosion of 1965 and 1966. As much an elite caste as an upper class, this group lives off the labors of the lower-status members.

The cult did not make it particularly easy for Messengers and IPs to drop out, but many did over the years. A defecting insider had no right to take any money away with him when he left. Sister Norma was in New York when she decided to quit, but her family lived in Boston. She had to conceal her intentions and beg to be sent home on holiday. There was no other way she could get traveling money. Sociologist Rosabeth Kanter believes this practice of refusing to refund any of a member's contributions when he defects from a cult adds strength to the movement.[3] If a member knows he cannot get anything back on his investment unless he stays with the cult, he is more likely to stay. Furthermore, it may be practically very difficult for a person to leave a cult if he has no money. But Brother Ariel feels that members were not trapped in the cult by this practical problem, because a little patience usually would turn up an alternative. Unlike many communes, the Power's chapters were set up in major cities, and members could make friends on the streets with people who might help them if they decided to leave. Ariel left with only one dollar in his pocket. "The thing that kept me from leaving earlier was I had no place to make any money. The minute I found some money coming in, I left." He quit in Toronto, but says the New Orleans chapter was a cauldron of desertion, both because the chapter itself was relatively unpleasant, and because of the ready opportunities for a Messenger to arrange a job before quitting. "The classic means of making

[3] Rosabeth Moss Kanter, *Commitment and Community* (Cambridge: Harvard University Press, 1972), pp. 80–82.

money was to work at the various strip places around Bourbon Street, because that was what they could easily do. Get a lot of money together and then leave." The jobs included "dancing . . . selling drinks, serving drinks, whatever." Some women were able to move in with boyfriends when they quit the Messenger Flat. The coffee house crowd of Disciples and Initiates also provided a bridge to the outside. Those that had apartments often permitted friends and even strangers to live with them for brief periods.

The rules of the cult on "desertion" had some elasticity, encouraging the deserter to reconsider. He would be demoted progressively down the steps of membership as the days passed after his departure. A deserter who was gone long enough to fall to Disciple rank had to work his way up again with the same painful slowness as before. Edward comments, "He will have a harder time, because having put his hand to the plough and then turned back, it will not be easy to reestablish the confidence in him which has been lost." Conversely, the individual rising for a second time through the ranks already knows the mysteries that are withheld from other low-status members. Although he has insider knowledge and proven capabilities, yet he is not an insider. Edward says, "By his own decision, he has become an outsider and must be treated as such."

IP SEX AND CHILDREN

My information on the sexual practices of IPs is mostly secondhand. I will report what I have been told, with the understanding that I was seldom able to verify informants' statements. Brother Faust says that many rumors spread among Messengers about the sexual practices of Superiors and Masters. "Logic dictated that they should be allowed to do what they wanted." According to the group's theory, "sex was a powerful force used positively or negatively. We were being celibate not because sex was evil, but because we were learning how to deal with it." As Powerites progressed, they should gain control over these forces, so "it would seem logical that Superiors could do what they wanted." Edward told me that one outcome of the cult's experimentation with sex after Xtul was the invention of Power *Unions*. These relationships were presented to the world as marriages but clearly did not have as much force as conventional, exclusive marriages.

Father Paul told me about his Union with Sister Eve. "I met Eve in Boston, and I guess somewhere I'd been trained to look out for the right one, as we all are, and I've always been very romantic and imagined that there would be a right one for me. And I was very thrilled to meet Eve! We had a very conventional and romantic courting, very proper, and we got married in Boston." I attended their Union Ceremony and the very conventional dinner party held afterwards at a nearby hotel, and took photographs. Paul and Eve spent the night in a suite at the hotel, just as any ordinary couple might. Several Powerites wear wedding rings.

Paul explains, "It's very different from the nuclear type marriage, because our primary marriage is to the church. And what this means is if the church requires us to do particular things which might separate us, we're both very well adjusted to that. We have gone through a number of separations in terms of location, and have always found that it has strengthened our bond rather than weakened it." Unlike conventional couples, Paul and Eve do not make decisions based on what they want for themselves or their two children, but on what the group as a whole needs. "I think the marriage relationship I have with Eve is a very special relationship, but it's one of a number of very special relationships I have. I'd say I have a very special relationship with Mother Isis, since we've spent a lot of time together throughout the world, and I would go to her for advice on a number of things where I would never go to Eve, because Mother Isis could counsel me." His relationship with Father Elijah is also close, but in a different way, because they work together.

High-ranked Powerites have experimented with different sexual structures and degrees of freedom at different periods in the development of the cult. I have never heard of a formal divorce in The Power, but do know of two couples that have been separated for years. Certainly there have been affairs of all kinds among the top members, as there would be in any contemporary, intensely interacting group of ideologically liberal people.

Brother Osiris told me that the cult had a practice, called *spiritual relationships*, that bordered on organized group marriage. I will explain it through an example for which I have independent testimony. Sister Amaranth, recruited to The Power by Father Cain, saw him as a father-figure. After she discussed her feelings with other senior people, she announced that a *spiritual relationship* existed between them. He was her spiritual father. This tie was expressed through sexual relations. Now it happened that neither was married, so they were given a Union Ceremony. Then along came Brother Eros. He came to feel that Amaranth was his spiritual mother. He, the junior partner in their developing relationship, discussed it with other superior people and then announced there existed a spiritual relationship between them. It did not interfere with the other relationship between Amaranth and Cain. Both Eros and Cain produced children with Amaranth. According to Brother Osiris, a spiritual relationship always links individuals of different sexes, one a child the other a parent, and is announced by the junior member after consultation with superiors. A Powerite may have one parent and as many as four children. Thus, a network of nonexclusive relationships could develop, perhaps strengthening the cult's cohesiveness rather than disrupting it. I have been told that Mother Isis produced children by three Powerites: Father Adam, Father Baal, and Charlie Green. Adam has also fathered a child with his formal wife, Ishtar.

I told Edward de Forest what Brother Osiris had said to me about spiritual relationships. All he would say was that cult sexual relationships were even more complicated than that. A church document issued to insiders on November 13, 1970, says, "Information about personal spiritual relationships between Powerites is NOT for divulgence to Outside Powerites or members of the general public." Why? "If such information 'leaks out' it is almost certain to be distorted and incomplete, in spirit if not in fact."

However they arrange it, senior Powerites do produce children. Troy, the son of Isis, was born in Mexico in 1967. After 1970, Power children began appearing in some numbers. At the end of my study there were fifteen or twenty children. The word for children in this cult is *The Littles*. In many respects, the lives of the Littles were quite normal. The babies had the usual juvenile equipment: toys, playpens, walker chairs, even kiddie animal pictures on the wall. They wore bibs and diaper-service diapers. They had fuzzy bunting and infant pacifiers. They sucked formula from nipple bottles and took pablum from little spoons. Baby tonic and pediatricians protected their health.

They were supervised not by their mothers, but by *Nannies*, low-status members of both sexes given the job of child care. Often a Little's parents would be stationed at a distant chapter. Mother Isis, traveling a good deal at the time, came to the Boston Chapter to give birth to her third child. She stayed for a while with the new infant, then continued her travels, taking over the Miami Chapter. When a number of Littles had collected in Boston, the chapter rented an extra apartment in the building next-door to the Chapter House, just for the children. The Littles and the Nannies could carry on the business of growing up without disturbing cult activities. A bit later, when there were many children, different chapters specialized in different age groups. The oldest Littles were concentrated in New York, while the toddlers were in Chicago. This way the Littles could grow up in readily manageable cohorts. They did have special relationships with their biological mothers and fathers but treated all the adults of the chapter as parents.

Elaborate administrative rules were written concerning the Littles' Power training and hierarchical status. Edward condensed the adults' Evening Assembly to produce a short version suitable for children. Officially, the Littles were Little Messengers, possessing even Sacred and Magickal

Names. "On his seventh birthday," document S-57 says, "an IP child automatically reverts to the rank of Initiate. . . . If he so desires, he then immediately begins to work his way towards being Baptized again, this time
as a Young Messenger. . . . On his fourteenth birthday, an IP child once
more reverts to the rank of Initiate." Now he can go through procedures to
become a regular adult member. These complex regulations do not deserve
close analysis, because the Littles were still very small at the end of my
study, had not gone through these stages, and certainly had not yet presented the cult with the problem of an adult second generation, radically
different from the first.

ECONOMICS

The largest source of church income was the money collected on the streets
by middle-status members engaged in *donating*. As explained earlier, this
practice was developed in New Orleans in 1967 or 1968 as a substitute for
the original sources of income, fees for therapy sessions and the members'
savings and inheritances. Although Disciples were sometimes included in
donating activities, only Messengers and Prophets regularly worked the
streets. They would go out in groups, usually in the morning, led by an IP,
and keep at it until suppertime. The groups always wore their uniforms,
presented themselves as ministers or members of a church, and in later years
were provided with photo identity cards to show to police or other officials
in the event they were questioned. About every hour, the donators would
take a five- or ten-minute rest break, perhaps smoke cigarettes, and total up
their income for the past hour. They carried black purses, shoulder bags,
really, the men as well as the women. In them they kept personal effects, the
money they collected, and a little notebook in which they tallied magazines
sold and money received. Each donator started out the day with a stack of
magazines about six inches thick, usually protected from rain by a plastic
bag.

Power magazines often contained photographs of happy donators, and
the cult's propaganda about the street work made it sound rewarding and
colorful. On one of his radio shows, Father Paul said, "We do meet all sorts
of people on the street. It's a very good training ground. And in New Orleans once, one of our ministers, Constantine, saw Paul and Linda McCartney coming along the street on their bicycles. So he invited them into our
coffee house. . . . And Paul's reaction was: 'Well, a bleedin' Britisher!'
That was the last thing he expected to find in the French Quarter of New
Orleans." Paul McCartney, of course, was a member of the famous Beatles musical group. An article in the March 1973 issue of *The Powerites*

claimed that street donators had spoken with 75,000,000 people during the previous year. That is a huge estimate, something like 3,000 per donator per day, perhaps one every ten seconds. "Hello, can you help us? Hello, can you help us?" a donator would say to the passing throng, investing less than ten seconds in most unsuccessful attempts to get attention. Many people would be asked more than once, but the total number seen by Powerites was undoubtedly very large. So it is not surprising that donators met many famous or interesting people, even though most of their work was completely routine. The magazine article also claims, "In the course of one day recently, Powerite ministers in New York spoke with The Red Chinese Ambassador, Senator Jacob Javits, Senator Eugene McCarthy, Jackie Onassis, Joan Kennedy and Rose Kennedy, Rod McKuen, Bob Dylan, Neil Diamond, Minnesota Fats, Joe Frazier, and Muhammad Ali. And Marjoe!" All celebrities.

Most of the time, donating was agonizing drudgery. In the winter, the donators wore long cloaks over their uniforms and long-john underwear beneath. But the cold still penetrated. The hourly progress checks were not supposed to be competitive. But a rate was calculated for each donator, each group, and each chapter, called the DJ. These initials stood for Dow Jones, the well-known Wall Street financial index. It was the number of dollars per donator per hour. In theory, each donator was competing only against his personal DJ, but in practice the competition was general and harsh. As we mentioned, in 1973 this system evolved into an obsessive scheme that set income quotas that donators had to meet before they could come home for supper or sleep.

Brother Faust complained to me that the Masters did not seem to realize that donators were exhausted by their work and needed normal amounts of sleep. "People at the top stay up much of the night and get little sleep." He said that the New York Chapter in 1973 had dinner at 11:30 at night, followed by an evening meeting that might last more than an hour, followed by individual chores. Much of the "work" of the cult leaders consisted of physically inactive discussion sessions, so they had little understanding of the strains of street work. As I have mentioned, the "work" of The Omega and other top leaders was a kind of 24-hour-a-day encounter-group stew, supposedly braving and discovering new religious and psychological territory for the sake of other Powerites. To support this intense sociation (defined as labor), the leadership exploited the Messengers and Prophets.

A 1971 administrative directive from Father Pius, the High Pontiff, suggested, "A money thermometer and/or graphs in the private part of the Chapter, with previous ones for comparison, adds to the excitement and validation of the total." The chapters followed the directive and posted DJ figures on a weekly basis. When I observed donators in 1971, each individual was collecting between $40 and $50 per donating day, but the work time was fairly short, around five hours. In peak periods, in 10-hour donating days in 1973 at the New York Chapter, for instance, the total would surpass $100 per day. A superdonator on a great day might make up to $300.

There were some other sources of income. A little money came from admission fees to chapter activities. The Telepathy Developing Circle cost $1.50, or whatever a person could afford. If twenty paying customers attended, it was a hot night. Admission for the Midnight Meditation was seventy-five cents. If a chapter made fifty dollars a week from these activities it was lucky. Initiates were asked to contribute something for their cheap chrome-plated crosses; a dollar or two was typical. There were occasional special events, such as auctions of leftover junk. At one of these I paid thirteen dollars for two pieces of discarded ritual equipment.

Disciples were expected to tithe from their outside incomes. A few held decent jobs, but others were unemployed. More than one attempted to tithe out of a welfare check. Few Disciples tithed dutifully, and there was never a well-developed system for extracting money from them. The income from Disciples was probably not significant in comparison to the money brought in by donators.

Inside Powerites were expected to turn all their worldly possessions over to the church. In several cases, as administrative documents note, IPs were "the beneficiaries of trusts or other sources of private income." I understand that Siegfried, Moses, Opal, and several others had contributed family wealth, and even some who joined as late as the 1970s came from rich families, Brother Faust for example. The HQ Treasurer was supposed to take charge of these investments and whenever possible arrange for the income to be "covenanted or made payable direct to The Power by some other recognized legal procedure." One advantage was the circumvention of individual tax liability in a way that the Internal Revenue Service could not challenge. Income from these trusts was paid directly to the central church organization, rather than to the chapters. In some cases it was necessary to keep investments in the names of individual members, and under such circumstances it was thought advisable "for the Powerite concerned to sign a statement to the effect that he is holding the asset on behalf of the Church, and as its trustee." Because OP Messengers were only trial members of the community and had not yet been admitted into the core of cult society, they were not asked to give over all their property. Financial guideline PS-50-VIII-A-2 states: "OP Messengers are not obliged in any way to hand over any personal money (gifts, income from trusts, etc.), and Inside Powerites should not suggest to an Outside Powerite that he should do this. If an Outside Powerite wishes to donate personal money or assets to The Power, and is certain in his own mind that this is what he wishes to do, it is treated as are all donations to the Church."

One source of income that was never figured into the financial accounts was *retrieving*: scavenging or begging for goods rather than money. Powerites were not only able to collect money through begging, but also had considerable success in convincing people to donate things, even food, directly. One day in 1971, for example, a street donator stopped a man in Boston, asked "Can you help us?" and was immediately offered a piano. I tuned the instrument in the Alpha ritual room a couple of weeks later and found it to be a perfectly fine, almost new spinet, probably worth about $300. One of the cult's administrative guidelines discussed automobile purchases, commenting "Remember that RETRIEVING IS PREFERABLE TO BUYING." There was one period at the Boston Chapter when several dying wrecks of automobiles were parked by their owners on the lawn of the Chapter House as donations. One of them was sold as a mystery prize at a coffee house auction, and to everyone's embarrassment sold for about fifty cents. Another cult memo urges Chapter Treasurers to seek every possible means to keep the chapters solvent, ordering them to look for ways that "retrieving could contribute to the HQ's solvency. How it could be expanded." The term *retrieving* was commonly in use in the counterculture at the time. In most cases for The Power it meant begging for goods, rather than scavenging from junk piles as it did for other groups. Often, the retrieving target was a commercial business. For example, visits were made to butcher shops to ask for free bones for the dogs.

The group's leaders developed a complex system of financial procedures, explained at great length and excruciating detail in a collection of administrative documents dated October 1973. The cult had at least two former accountants, Cain and Hannah, and one management consultant, Abraham. The approach was conventional, although occasionally the language was novel. Receipts filled out by church leaders were called P-Vouchers, for example. British translations of American business terms were inserted at several points in the documents, so that all members could understand.

Each chapter kept income records, day by day, and summarized the information each week. It was supposed to send a thorough financial report to the church headquarters each month. An annual report was prepared with the help of professional auditors. There was an elaborate system for allocating income to different "funds." It clearly specified the amounts to be contributed to central church projects. As one of the documents stated, "A basic principle of Power finances is that contributing 'up the line' in hier-

Table 3: **Income Allocation Structure, 1973**

Percent of income	Name of fund
20%	Central Fund
16%	Publishing Fund
15%	Chapter Expenses Fund
15%	Matriarchs and Patriarchs Fund
9%	P-Gear Fund
8%	Masters' HQ Fund
5%	Transport Fund
4%	Omega Chapter Fund
3%	PR Fund
2%	DR Fund
1%	New Chapter Fund
1%	Building Fund
1%	Music Fund
100%	Total

archy terms is of prime importance. Payments 'up the line' are made in the form of percentage allocations and are deducted from all 'real' income before any other payments or allocations are made." If these procedures were strictly followed, the central organization would be assured of economic support by the rank-and-file members.

Table 3 shows the official system for allocating cult income. The names of several of these "funds" describe them adequately. The PR fund went to "public relations" or advertising, while the DR Fund seems to have gone to lawyers and accountants. The Omega Chapter Fund was sent directly to Edward and Kitty, as their income from their cult. Edward told me the gross monthly income of The Power in this period was between $80,000 and $100,000. Four percent of that, or between $3,200 and $4,000 went to Kitty and Edward.

A Marxist would have no trouble analyzing the economic system of The Power. The Omega would be described as the leisured upper class living off the labor of the working-class Messengers and middle-class Superiors and Prophets. The emphasis of a Marxist analysis would be on the blatant oppression and exploitation of the Messengers, who derived precious little benefit from the thousands of uncomfortable hours they spent begging on the streets. The elite founding members of the cult claimed they contributed greatly to the well-being of their lower-ranked followers because of the doctrinal "information" and spirituality they "channeled" downward. The Marxist would say Messengers' belief in this was false consciousness, that the Power's upper class was of no social value and ruled through the illusion that their self-indulgent games were somehow essential for the well-being of the poor folk they exploited.

Classical economics would look at the participation of the cult in a larger market and ask what the cult sold and at what price. If The Power grossed $100,000 a month and included one hundred full-time members at its height, then the per capita annual gross income would come out to only $12,000. Many Powerites could easily have earned more than this on the outside, and those who could not were young members prevented by their cult involvement from gaining valuable skills at college or in occupational settings. In return for these unexceptional incomes, the group had to give a service. They initially collected donations without returning any definite service, except perhaps putting on an interesting show. Their claim that outsiders should support them because the cult mediated usefully with Lucifer, Jehovah, Christ, and Satan was not believed by the general public. In the early 1970s, The Power took on social service work of various kinds and advertised this contribution to society in its literature. The failure of the cult to grow after 1972 suggests that the market found the Power's product overpriced and that the low hourly wages paid cult workers (Messengers) were not sufficient to attract a large, high-quality work force.

Both the Marxist and Classical perspectives would agree in their general view of the Powerite system of ranks and regulations. The social system described in this chapter was the means by which The Omega and other top leaders of The Power exploited their economic environment in service of their collective desires and ambitions. Messengers and other middle-ranked members did not invent their own social customs, experimenting with alternate schemes in search of the highest personal gratification. Only the leaders of the cult were permitted such freedom. Messengers were given a rigid system of life composed of some gratifications and many demands. Fantasy and festivity gave relief from the drudgery of daily work and gave promise of better times to come. But only through defection or very slow promotion could a low-ranked Powerite escape his exploited status. The cult existed for the sake of its founders, and therefore the social system functioned to channel wealth, power, and pleasure in their direction.

SEVEN

The Gods and Their Symbols

> JEHOVAH is Strength.
> LUCIFER is Light.
> SATAN is Separation.
> CHRIST is Unification.
> They are the Great Powers of the Universe,
> and all mankind is subject to Their Will.
> —Power Sabbath Assembly, 1973

The Power had four Gods, several emblems, and innumerable rituals. These were not a collection of discordant images, but a coherent, unified world-system expressed not only in carefully chosen symbols, but most importantly in the structure of relationships between them. The Great Gods of the Universe were as much a psychological system as a theological one. Each defined a personality type, and together they expressed a sociology. The rituals, emblems, and God-pattern scriptures were intended not only to bring members closer together in expressive communion, and not only to impress and instruct newcomers, but also to create a new reality through the magical effects imputed to the system. In describing a spiritual world, it sought to create one.

THE MIND OF EDWARD DE FOREST

Power theology was not the product of a committee. The Great Gods of the Universe were invented by Edward de Forest. Anthropologist Franz Boas has written:

The esoteric doctrine must, to a great extent, be considered as the product of individual thought. It expresses the reaction of the best minds in the community to the general cultural environment. It is their attempt to systematize the knowledge that underlies the culture of the community. . . . [I]t is the expression of thought of the exceptional mind. It is not the expression of thought of the masses.[1]

Although Edward drew upon the experiences of the entire cult and adapted many notions prevalent in the outside culture for his own use, he

[1] Franz Boas, "The Ethnological Significance of Esoteric Doctrines," in *Race, Language, and Culture* (New York: Free Press, 1966), pp. 313–314.

was not merely the passive compiler of group culture. His intellectual assumptions transformed the cultural elements he took from disparate sources, welding them into a unified whole. Power theology was a coherent *structure* of related concepts. Its basic pattern was the *transcendent duality*—the union of pairs of opposites defining the extremes of reality and brought together in theoretical reconciliation. For example, the cult existed beyond Good and Evil. Good is the opposite of Evil, yet neither can exist without the other. Thus they define an essential duality. In cult theory, Good and Evil are similar in their equidistance from *blandness* (insignificance, meaninglessness). Good and Evil are united in their mutual opposition. The Power embraced both of them as living alternatives to the deadening average. One Power Precept states, "There is no alternative to opposition in this inevitably two-pole universe. The choice is between harmony and conflict." Edward believed opposites could be brought together in harmony. Another Precept states, "The awareness of a fundamental unity preserves harmony in a duality." In Hegelian terms, Good is the thesis, Evil the antithesis, and The Power is the transcendent synthesis beyond Good and Evil. Perhaps this idea is impossible. But Edward believed it and made this principle the basis of his entire intellectual system. He saw himself as the great reconciler of opposites, the transcender of conflict, the Unifier.

Edward's *structural* orientation is very similar to the *Structuralist* approach to anthropology of the French theorist Claude Lévi-Strauss. This analytic technique assumes that beneath the particulars of any cultural system lies a basic message concerning essential categories of thought usually arranged in pairs of dichotomous concepts. Lévi-Strauss claims to find dualities in mythologies, kinship structures, and practically everything else. French Structuralism is an extremely controversial school of thought, attacked as pure mysticism by some anthropologists, ignored by most American sociologists. It is possible that Lévi-Strauss is completely mistaken in his analysis of Amazonian Indian myth, yet his system does seem to be the best for understanding the Power's theology. Therefore, I suspect that Structuralism does properly apply to some cultural systems, perhaps those like The Power, created by minds similar to that of Lévi-Strauss. In his book *The Raw and the Cooked*, he responds to his critics:

If the final aim of anthropology is to contribute to a better knowledge of objectified thought and its mechanisms, it is in the last resort immaterial whether in this book the thought processes of the South American Indians take place through the medium of my thought, or whether mine takes place through the medium of theirs. What matters is that the human mind, regardless of the identity of those who happen to be giving it expression, should display an increasingly intelligible structure as a result of the doubly reflexive forward movement of two thought processes acting one upon the other, either of which can in turn provide the spark or tinder whose conjunction will shed light on both.[2]

This radical statement expresses three assumptions common to the thought of Lévi-Strauss and Edward de Forest: (1) each believes he is capable of discovering the universal nature of the human mind; (2) the structure of the mind is a system of dualities; (3) the basic duality from which all wisdom flows is that between the theorist himself and other persons. For Lévi-Strauss the basic key to knowledge is the relationship *Lévi-Strauss:native*, while for Edward it is the relationship *Edward:Powerite*.

Before we look at Edward's analysis of the relationships between the Gods, let us look at his conception of relations between people. Because the Gods are a projection of Edward's intimate personal relations, we should start with his analysis of the most important relationship in his life, his romantic bond to Kitty. He has written that they were "extremists, the pair of us, and at opposite ends of every conceivable spectrum." In their early relationship, he continually sought to keep close to her, while she periodically tried to break off with him. "Life was always a contest for Kitty. There was always an opposition, an enemy—or a potential enemy—and if none showed itself, she created one." Thus, Edward's principle was *unification*, while in this respect hers was *separation*. This difference is not only in itself a dichotomy, but also a disagreement concerning dichotomies. He wanted to unify opposites, she to separate them.

In an unpublished autobiographical sketch, Edward mentions a second important dual relationship. He says two of his closest male friends became the first permanent converts to Compulsions Analysis. I believe he is talking about Father Pius and Father Elijah. While Edward and his friends shared the same class and cultural background, as Edward and Kitty did not, he says "three more utterly different characters it would be hard to find. They were at opposite ends of the universe from one another, and I was at the opposite end from both of them." The following adjectives describe Pius: quiet, conscientious, reliable, unadventurous, meticulous, predictable. The opposite adjectives describe Elijah.

"They were a strange pair," Edward says, "constantly at odds and yet drawn together by their very oppositeness—just as Kitty and I were." Edward believed Pius and Elijah were not natural friends, however, and it was their common bond with him that really kept them together. "Neither

---

[2] Claude Lévi-Strauss, *The Raw and the Cooked* (New York: Harper and Row, 1969), p. 13.

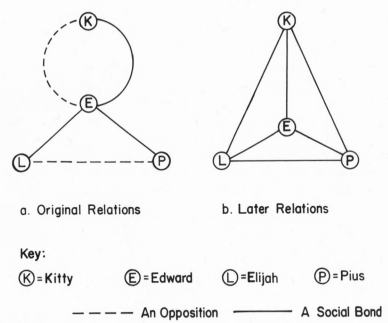

a. Original Relations   b. Later Relations

Key:

(K) = Kitty   (E) = Edward   (L) = Elijah   (P) = Pius

— — — — An Opposition   ——————— A Social Bond

Figure 5. The Structure of Relationships among Edward and His Three Associates

of them thought much of Kitty," and she "was a threat to their masculinity." Figure 5a diagrams their relationships as two dualities, connected by Edward.

Edward acted as the unifier in both dualities. In the duality *Edward: Kitty*, he was a partner to the opposition while working to unify it. In the duality *Elijah:Pius*, he stood outside the opposition while working to unify it. These are the two possible positions of the unifier to an opposition; we can call them the *internal* position and the *external* position. Once all four were deeply involved in Compulsions Analysis, the "therapy" acted to produce strong positive bonds connecting all of them. The social structure then became that diagrammed in Figure 5b. It can be viewed as a three-dimensional tetrahedron in which four people are connected by six equal bonds.

In developing the cult's theological system, Edward used the same style of thinking outlined above. If we replace Pius by Jehovah, Elijah by Lucifer, Kitty by Satan, and Edward by Christ, we get the basic system of Gods, which by 1974 was a single, unified structure. In the beginning there were two separate systems. The one I will call *System A* is composed of two dual relationships: *God versus Humanity* and *Christ versus Satan*. *System B* is composed of Jehovah, Lucifer, and Satan, arranged in two dualities.

SYSTEM A

God is the supreme being, incorporating all other beings and forms of being into a single entity, without limit and therefore beyond description or measurement. In its early years, The Power detached from and came into opposition with "the world," which Powerites called "Humanity." In *The Tide of the End*, Edward attacked Humanity and accused it of being opposed to God. Humanity is a snare of confining inhibitions, while God is limitless. Since God is perfect, He cannot exist in the imperfect world of Humanity, but stands outside time, a memory from the past and a hope for the future. Edward's scripture teaches that God transcends all dimensions. BI-19 states, "This fundamental life force, which is GOD, is infinitely small and has infinite scope. This is the basic nature of the two-pole universe; zero and infinity; nothing and everything. GOD is a non-existence with awareness of all existence."

Humanity exists in the here-and-now, but will soon cease to exist, Edward says. One section of *The Tide of the End* explains, "The tide is now destruction, by God's will; to go against it is to go against God." The duality between God and Humanity is the basic alternative. "And our choice is to include GOD or to exclude GOD. To acknowledge GOD or to reject GOD. To see GOD or to be blind to GOD. To know GOD or to be ignorant of GOD. To worship GOD or to defy GOD." In early cult writings, Humanity is also called the unGod, and is represented by the symbolic figure John Grey. He is the stereotypical, bland, spiritless, modern man. Among several Power "Chants of the unGod" is one which is simply the phrase "living death" repeated over and over. Another chant proclaims, "John Grey's code is hypocrisy, mediocrity, blasphemy." Another asks a profound question, then gives its own answer: "Where are you going? What are you knowing? Can you feel your death? . . . Devoted to the unGod, facing the End. He is chained to Death."

In Edward's book *Humanity Is the Devil*, God spoke to man, saying: "Follow in your heart the concept of evil, and you will go further and further from Me. For though I have created evil for your choice, evil is not of Me; it is of Satan, who is the Devil, and must for you be the Enemy so that you do not follow Him. For the path of evil will lead you to the Devil and you will find yourself in Hell." This is a traditional kind of statement. Satan is the enemy of God although He was created by God. But, according to The Power, because we are entering the Latter Days, nearing the End, there has been a radical change. "Satan is free, for His work is done. Satan is no longer the Devil, for He has passed the poison on to that which chose to take it and become it. Now there is nothing more evil in the Universe than man. His

World is Hell, and he himself the Devil." The "burden of negativity," which it had been Satan's task to bear, has now been bequeathed to Humanity.

Similarly, God has bequeathed his own task to Christ. The Power believed that "God is love" and that God so loved man that He sent His only begotten Son, Christ, into the world. Christ, whether identified with Jesus or de Forest, was a gift of love given from love. So the "blessing of positivity" that had been God's property is now carried by Christ. The relationships between God, Humanity, Christ, and Satan are diagramed in Figure 6a.

In his book *The Two Pole Universe*, Edward stated the social-psychological basis of his theory that all reality can be interpreted as the intersection of pairs of polar opposites. Christ is Unification, Satan is Separation, and the sources of these opposing principles can be found in the emotions Love and Fear. "So there is Love and there is Fear. And Love and Fear are opposites— and more than opposites, for Love and Fear are the two poles of the mind. They are the root of the conflict that divided the mind. They are the fundamental dichotomy, the very core of the struggle that rages within every human being. The battle between these two is the source of all human anguish, all pain, all suffering. All disaster stems from the conflict between Love and Fear." Although opposed to each other, in this world Love and Fear cannot exist apart from each other. If we love someone, then we must fear to lose them. We cannot fear unless there exists something we love and are afraid of losing. Love and Fear, like Christ and Satan, and like God and Humanity, "are two sides of one coin."

The two dualities of *System A* can be expressed as the intersection of two dichotomous variables: Love and Fear, Being and Non-Being. Christ and Satan are modes of being, styles of social relation. Christ is coexistence with another individual in a state of unification; Satan is solitary existence in a state of separation. God and Humanity are states of non-being, states in which a person has lost all individual strength, consciousness, and identity. The Power fled Humanity but has not yet achieved God. Incorporation into a fully realized God is a mode of positive non-being—pleasurable, womblike, loving. Humanity is a mode of negative non-being—painful, dispersive, meaningless. In the short piece *What is God?*, Edward explains that "God and Anti-God are embodied in Christ and Satan." The pair of contending spirits, Christ and Satan, act directly in the world. They are embodied, immanent. Figure 6b diagrams this intellectual structure.

The relationships between these terms can be compared to Edward's personal social relationships and expressed as formal analogies of the type: $a:b::y:z$ (a is to b as y is to z). On the concrete level, the social origins of the

```
GOD bequeaths to CHRIST                    LOVE versus FEAR
                                          ┌─────────────────────────
 *                    *          NON-BEING │ God        Humanity
 v                    v
 e                    e          versus
 r                    r
 s                    s          BEING      │ Christ     Satan
 u                    u
 s                    s
 *                    *

HUMANITY heir to SATAN
```

a. First Analysis   b. Second Analysis

Figure 6. Structure of System A

four entities are as follows. *God:Humanity::Powerites:Outsiders. Christ:Satan:: Edward:Kitty.* We can state the same conceptualization on a more abstract level. *God:Humanity::we:they. Christ:Satan::I:Thou.* In the Power's system of thinking, the relationship *a:b* is one of *both* separation and unity. In October 1975, Edward wrote, "One of the basic tenets of The Power has always been the reconciliation of opposites. Emotionally and psychologically, this means the resolution of mental conflict. Spiritually, it means the harmonizing of opposing cosmic forces."

SYSTEM B

In December 1967, Edward introduced the Three Great Gods of the Universe—Jehovah, Lucifer, and Satan—in a brief essay, *The Hierarchy.* The Gods "represent three basic human patterns of reality," and "each one represents a fundamental problem." Conversely, each "God" can be seen as a basic perspective on the best way to live, or, in the terms of Lofland and Stark, a "problem-solving perspective." Collectively, the three Gods constitute a psychological theory of personality. Each God is a type of person, an attitude toward relations with others, and a cosmic principle.

JEHOVAH, the wrathful God of vengeance and retribution, demands discipline, courage and ruthlessness, and a single-minded dedication to duty, purity, and self-denial. All of us feel those demands to a degree; some more strongly than others.

LUCIFER, the Light Bearer, urges us to enjoy life to the full, to value success in human terms, to be gentle and kind and loving, and to live in peace and harmony with one another. Man's apparent inability to value success without descending into greed, jealousy, and an exaggerated sense of his own importance has brought the God LUCIFER into disrepute. He has become mistakenly identified with SATAN.

SATAN, the receiver of transcendent souls and corrupted bodies, instills in us two directly opposite qualities: at one end, an urge to rise above all human and physical needs and appetites, to become all soul and no body, all spirit and no mind; and at the other end, a desire to sink BENEATH all human codes of behavior and to wallow in a morass of violence, lunacy, and excessive physical indulgence. But it is the lower end of SATAN's nature that men fear, which is why SATAN, by whatever name, is seen as the Adversary.

The origin of *System B* can be traced from the basic separation *God:Anti-God::Powerites:Outsiders* produced in the social implosion of 1965–1966. *System B* evolved as an attempt by Edward to understand his own social relations within the group, so all the elements are good, pro-cult Gods. In a way, the Great Gods are the endpoints of the Adlerian analysis, compulsive archetypes and ultimate goals.

When the God of Nature appeared at Xtul, Kitty called Him Jehovah. He was Kitty's God. It was she who demanded firm dedication to duty. She had long admired Jehovah, was a vocal fan of Israel, and had gone so far in her Jehovian devotion to have twin wedding rings made for Edward and herself that bore the Star of David, Jehovah's symbol. Edward remarked to me that the points of the star dug into the flesh of his finger. Edward did not like Jehovah, but for a while Jehovah was identified as God.

Many of Edward's values were opposed to Jehovah's commandments. He wanted sensuous liberation, experimentation. Jehovah's law, represented by Kitty and by the Old Testament of the Bible, said these urges of Edward's were un-Godly. As an intellectual strategy to strengthen his own position, Edward postulated the existence of another God beside Jehovah. He chose the name Lucifer. He had run across biblical commentaries which noted that Lucifer and Satan were not the same, wrongly confounded by such theologians as St. Jerome. Jehovah, as is well known, is a jealous God. In order to be accepted as the one true God, Jehovah had to discredit His chief rival, Lucifer, so He spread false propaganda that Lucifer and Satan were the same.

At this point in its development, *System B* is of three elements: God in two equal but opposite parts (Jehovah and Lucifer) and a residue that is not included in either and remains Anti-God. But Edward observed that two parts of this residue were antagonistic to Humanity, a mystical part and a ferocious part. Separated from Humanity, they also must be parts of God. In *System A*, Satan was identified with separation, so it was a simple step to name these two other elements of God after Satan.

If God exists in three parts, why did He so divide Himself? Why do all the interlinked dualities of polar opposites exist? In BI-13, Edward wrote, "The answer is: 'the game.' . . . The game is conflict; creating and destroying, building and demolishing, separating and coming together, rising and falling, disintegrating and reuniting, failing and succeeding, living and dying, winning and losing, loving and hating. That is the game, and the game is the essence of existence." Without The Game, without separation, there would exist no universe.

Satan, separation, is therefore the most creative and active part of God, even though Satan is also destructive. Satan, like all beings, is subject to The Universal Law, most basic of Power causal principles, which states, "As you give, so shall you receive." This sounds like a restatement of the Golden Rule, but it is not really a moral commandment. It is a magical, Newtonian principle, as Edward states in BI-31. "The Universal Law works on the basis of reflection. Every action brings about an equal and opposite reaction. Whether there is conflict or harmony, there is always opposition." Thus The Universal Law is a dynamic extension of Edward's key concept of duality. It stresses the absolute importance for him of personal relations, claiming that nothing can be lost in the process of social interaction, postulating a perfectly moral universe. In BI-7, he writes, "The principle of self-judgement is this: a person may accurately judge what he gives, by what he receives." In two manuscripts, Edward explains how this applies to Satan. "Satanists separate. Therefore, by the Universal Law, they are separated." "Due to its propensity for division, separation, and differentiation—apparent on all levels both positive and negative—the Satanic line is characteristically divided! The Universal Law: divide and you are divided." This explains why Satan continually plays a double role; He takes part in *System A* and *System B*. In *System B* He is divided into two aspects. As separation, Satan draws His opposite, Christ (the spirit of unification), into the system of the three Gods. A Power Precept states, "Whatever you demand, expect the opposite." Since nothing can exist without its polar opposite to define it, Edward's theory introduces Christ into *System B* to balance Satan.

Before about 1970, Christ was not described as one of the Gods, but as a being of another kind. "Christ is the Unifier. He brings together all the patterns of the Gods, and resolves them into One. He is the Emissary of the Gods upon earth; Their link with men, by which men have the opportunity to know and understand Them." In Figure 7a, I show one way Powerites often diagramed Christ and the Gods. Lucifer is the polar opposite of Jehovah. Satan contains in His separation two opposite aspects. These dualities are graphed at right angles to each other, forming a cross. Christ is nailed to the cross, at the center, stapling the extremes together.

We can analyze the relationships of Christ and Edward to the theological and social structures, demonstrating that they are parallel. Recall my distinction between two positions an actor may hold with respect to a dispute:

Relationship
of Mediator

	INTERNAL	EXTERNAL
	Christ versus Satan	Jehovah versus Lucifer
	Edward versus Kitty	Pius versus Elijah

```
SATAN
   *
   C                        C
   H                        H
LUCIFER*R*JEHOVAH     M     R
   I                 e     I
   S                 d     S
   T                 i     T
   *                 a
 SATAN               t     E
                     o     D
                     r     W
                           A
                           R
                           D
```

a. The Cross of the Gods   b. Mediators to the Disputes

Figure 7. Structure of System B

Table 4: **Words Describing the Three Gods and Their People**

Satan (Lower Aspect)	Lucifer	Jehovah	Satan (Higher Aspect)
Lust	Enjoyment	Duty	Detachment
Abandon	Permissiveness	Discipline	Mysticism
Violence	Harmony	Struggle	Otherworldliness
Excess	Success	Sacrifice	Magic
Indulgence	Satisfaction	Self-denial	Asceticism

internal (a party to it) and *external* (outside but connected to it). Figure 7b compares Christ's relations to the three Gods with Edward's relations to his three intimate associates. Each is external to one dispute and internal to the other. Each tries to mediate both. Not merely the forms, but also the contents of the two structures are identical. Elijah was Lucifer. Pius was Jehovah. Kitty was Satan. Elijah and Pius represented two opposite styles of dwelling within respectable society. Lucifer and Jehovah were two basic Human alternatives. Kitty, in her intense fickleness, scintillated outside the bounds of conventional society. At times Edward felt she was spiritually superior to average people; at other times he felt she was carnally inferior. Satan, also, has two aspects, one super-Human, the other sub-Human. Table 4 lists some of the qualities associated with the Gods and therefore also descriptive of the people who followed each of the cosmic principles.

EDWARD'S CULTURE ENGINE

As the years passed, Edward's system of dualities expanded into an immense intellectual structure explained in a thousand pages of scripture, providing a complex interpretive scheme. Supported by emblems, symbolic rituals, therapy exercises, and day-to-day customs, it evolved into a rich and ornate culture. There was no clearly marked stopping point at which Edward might decide he had invented enough. The assumptions and social reality that lay at the base of his creativity demanded the unceasing production of new ideas. The creative configuration that Edward worked within was what I call a *culture engine*.

Any social-psychological situation that automatically and perpetually generates new elements of culture is a culture engine. There may be many kinds, but I have seen innumerable examples of one specific variety in my studies of magical and psychotherapeutic cults: the *compulsive striving* engine. Edward's unremitting struggle to resolve human conflicts through an analytic system based on polar opposites is one example. Gordon Rogers' attempt to transform ordinary humans into ideal-human *supers* is another. In the compulsive striving culture engine, an individual or group commits itself irrevocably to the accomplishment of impossible goals with insufficient means. Rather than abandon either goals or means, a person gripped by such compulsive striving continually seeks to improve the means. Rogers kept inventing new psychotherapy techniques. Edward kept inventing new dichotomies. Both Rogers and de Forest held status in their cults because of the culture they had already produced, so they could not risk abandoning old ideas and assumptions while they added new ones. Consequently, both of their systems grew steadily. A necessary step in the culture-manufacturing process is the testing of the old ideas against reality and the discovery that they are not yet perfect. If Rogers and de Forest had been entirely cut off from reality-testing, they would not have continued working. Each cult's theoretical system grew because it was continually being applied and found to be deficient.

The theory of the Gods was intended as a cosmic theory of personality. Each human being was supposed to be closer to one of the Gods than the others, to manifest one of the patterns as an extension of its God. In the *Fear* and *Death* issues of the magazine, individual cult members wrote as advocates for one or another God. David and Adam were advocates for Jehovah; Palestine and Pan represented Lucifer; Amaranth and Abraham spoke for Satan. Edward himself expressed the Christ spirit, in his Christ-like appearance as well as his words. Every older Powerite recognized a special tie to one of the Gods, and members often discussed each other's *God patterns*, considering them useful analyses of personality style.

Brother Lot was a Satanic Powerite. He once explained to me that Satan had given him the power to find lost objects psychically. That day he had found a tarnished silver object; another time he had located a lost hammer. He was particularly successful in finding missing Mendes Goat badges. How does he do it? First he calls upon Satan to help him. The other Gods are of no use. Then he gets a picture of the lost object in his mind and tries to feel where it is. Satan comes and leads Lot to the missing article. Lot held his hands up on either side of his head while explaining this procedure, extending his fingers to simulate Satanic horns. Satan uses his horns like antennas to radar-out the lost object.

Brother Thomas was a Luciferian. In March 1971, he read a short poem about Lucifer in a Powerplay dramatic show: "Bringer of purpose to ease the despair, bringer of joy to ease the pain, bringer of Light to ease the Darkness, come, Lord Lucifer, come." Sister Roxana was also a Luciferian. "I know that he doesn't exist as an anthropomorphic entity or as a person. To me, Lucifer is a name for a whole presence, a whole force, everything that Beauty is, everything that Poetry is."

These examples are very poetic themselves, artistic and occult rather than practical. Of course, the number and intensity of human conflicts within the cult did not decrease merely because of the introduction of the theory of Gods. It permitted many kinds of aesthetic expression but was not effective in controlling or transforming social life. Edward's compulsive, intellectual response was to invent more dualities.

About 1971, Christ was promoted from the emissary of the Gods to the status of a fourth God, representing a fourth basic personality pattern. In promoting Christ, Edward sought to promote himself. As we already mentioned, in 1970 Edward attempted to give Lucifer dominance over the previously dominant Jehovah in determining the style of the cult. Both Christ and Lucifer were Edward's deities, while Jehovah and Satan belonged to Kitty. In BI-34 and a pair of unpublished manuscripts written in 1971, Edward explored the dual relationships between these four entities. The duality *Jehovah:Lucifer* described two alternate social approaches to human life, rather similar to the *Apollonian:Dionysian* dichotomy of Nietzsche, or the familiar *cold:hot, rigid:flexible, conservative:liberal* dichotomies of common language. The struggle between the two was called "The Conflict of the Mind," and their duality was of the mind. The spiritual conflict between Christ and Satan categorized theirs as the "ex-mind" duality. Having noted that no one fitted a single God pattern perfectly, and having seen that the original system of patterns did not solve all problems, Edward decided that each person possessed a *combination pattern*. Each person was close to one polar opposite in each pair: Jehovah or Lucifer and Christ or Satan. His own combination pattern was Luciferian-Christian, while Kitty's was Jehovian-Satanic.

Powerites did in fact adopt the new combination patterns as their universal personality theory, although it was not more successful in influencing social reality than the old theory. The four types were usually named by their initials: Jehovian-Satanic (JS), Jehovian-Christian (JC), Luciferian-Satanic (LS), and Luciferian-Christian (LC). As part of my field research on the 1975 Waltham, Massachusetts, Chapter of the cult, I asked members of the chapter commune to list each person's pattern. Table 5 shows the distribution and demonstrates that Powerites were able to apply the categories to all kinds of people and even animals.

In its magazine the cult published three different questionnaires designed to uncover the reader's God pattern. To test their utility, I asked students in my social-psychology class at Wellesley College to administer the longest cult questionnaire to members of the college community. Each of its nineteen questions had four possible answers, one for each of the God patterns. For example, the first was: "Whom do you identify with? a) Adam (Jehovian); b) Eve (Luciferian); c) The Serpent (Satanic); d) A fourth party eager to patch things up and please everyone (Christian)." Another question was: "Where do you most like to make love? a) Under the bedclothes and in the dark (Jehovian); b) At a Bacchanalian blast-off (Satanic); c) In a gentle summer blowing meadow (Luciferian); d) Wherever your partner prefers (Christian)." The forty-four questionnaires were coded in terms of which God had the most responses on each and which God had the second greatest number. Mother Lilith predicted that the Wellesley respondents would tend to be Luciferian-Christian, intelligent and dutiful young college women that they were. If we assume that individuals' combination pat-

Table 5: **Combination Patterns in the Waltham Chapter**

Type	Men	Women	Children	Animals	Total
JS	6	3	0	5	14
JC	4	1	0	0	5
LS	3	2	0	1	6
LC	2	2	1	1	6
Total	15	8	1	7	31

Table 6: **Combination Patterns from the Wellesley Questionnaire**

Type	Number	Percent
LC	21	48%
SC[a]	7	16%
JC	6	14%
x[b]	4	9%
LS	3	7%
JL[a]	2	5%
JS	1	2%
Total	44	101%[c]

[a] Theoretically prohibited
[b] Impossible to code because of ties in ranking of "Gods"
[c] Rounding error

terns would emerge as the Gods that scored first and second on each questionnaire, then we can test Lilith's hypothesis, and also Edward's hypothesis that two patterns, the Jehovian-Luciferian (JL) and Satanic-Christian (SC) do not exist. The results, shown in Table 6, support Lilith but do not support Edward, since the LC pattern is most common, but the SC and JL patterns also appear.

The Power did not use its questionnaires to discover members' patterns, but merely as diversions for the magazine readers. Members would discuss their personalities with each other and with their superiors in the cult, would interact and observe themselves, and gradually decide what pattern they were. Sometimes there was disagreement. I myself decided my pattern was Luciferian-Satanic, and several of my cultic friends agreed. However, Mother Ruth, Mother Lilith, and Edward de Forest were all convinced my true pattern was Luciferian-Christian. Sister Norma explained to me that "the LS pattern is just about the hardest to pick out anyway, because LSs are so good at disguising themselves." Norma is an LS and felt sure I was not one but an LC. However, she agreed it was hard to tell. "For the longest time everybody thought I was an LC because I acted like such a victim before I became a Messenger. They realized in New York, finally, that I wasn't an LC, and I looked at them all and I said, 'What? I'm not an LC? All this time everybody was telling me I was crucifying myself! I'm not an LC?' And they said, 'Mm-mm. Awfully good image, kid, but you can't fool us.' I guess it takes an LS to see an LS. It was Amaranth that told me I was an LS, and Ruth agreed with her. In Boston, at first they were convinced I was a JC, and then I turned out to be an LC." If we can believe the experts, Amaranth and Norma are LSs, while Ruth and I are LCs.

The dualities proliferated and became ever more interconnected. Perhaps because Kitty's pattern was JS while Edward's was LC, Jehovah and Satan came to be described as Female deities while Lucifer and Christ were male. The basic dichotomy refused to be transcended. Building on some ideas dating from 1968, Edward decided that every pattern had a top end and a bottom end, not just the Satanic. "On the bottom levels, all the patterns are destructive and negative and oriented towards death. And on the top levels, we are positive and life-oriented. At the top, our effects on others are positive; and on the bottom, our effects on others are negative." According to a training document, one can identify lower-end patterns of the four basic types by a few descriptive words, as shown in Table 7.

When the God pattern doctrine had evolved to the point at which all four patterns had upper and lower aspects, then the structure of the Gods was no longer a configuration of canted triangles, perhaps a tetrahedron as in Figure 5b, but a cube formed by the intersection of three dualities: *Jehovah:Lucifer*, *Christ:Satan*, *Higher:Lower*. Human personalities could be graphed as the four side faces of the cube; for example, the LS personality shared by such people as Amaranth, Norma, and Ariel would be represented by the right-hand face of the cube shown in Figure 8.

The new theological system was expected to work better in daily applications. It explained changes in a person's mood as temporary movements across the face of the cube that graphed his pattern. But it was no more successful in actually solving human problems, and had the disadvantage of intellectual complexity. Edward's response, incomplete because he was expelled from his own cult in 1974, was to invent subtypes within each of

Table 7: **Words Describing the Lower-End Patterns**

Jehovian	Luciferian	Christian	Satanic
Cruel	Sentimentality	Compulsive-Responsibility	Lust
Arrogant	Self-Pity	Masochism	Abandon
Self-righteous	Sloth	Feeling weak	Violence
Blameful	Justification	Ineffectiveness	Excess
Bullying			Indulgence

Key:

J = Jehovah	S = Satan
L = Lucifer	H = Higher Aspect
C = Christ	L = Lower Aspect

Figure 8. Cubic Structure of the Combination Patterns

these. As usual, the first type to split was the Satanic. In slang developed by Edward and Kitty, Lower-End Satanists came to be called Goats, and Upper-End Satanists were Snerps (serpents). Then dichotomies were discovered within Snerps and Goats.

The system also ramified into a collection of four-element symbolic structures, some formally adopted by The Power, others merely toyed with by various members. Table 8 shows some of these symbolic tetrads. Color symbolism varied over the years, and the four handicaps were never more than a speculation that interested The Omega. Edward has described his method of structural analysis and its struggle to arrange the chaos of human experience in simple categories. "It's rather like unraveling a ball of wool after a playful kitten has been at it. Or perhaps a better analogy is sorting a shuffled pack of playing cards into different suits."

The structural evolution of Edward's system followed exactly a general principle stated by Lévi-Strauss: "A four-section system can be explained only as the sociological process of integration of a double dualism (without the one being necessarily historically anterior to the other), and the eight-section system as a reduplication of the same process."[3]

POWER SYMBOLS 1965–1973

The Power used several different emblems or symbols over the years, all having a dual nature. The last two symbols are discussed in Chapter Ten; here we will discuss six earlier emblems. The first Power Sign, invented by

[3] Claude Lévi-Strauss, *Totemism* (Boston: Beacon Press, 1963), p. 51.

Table 8: **The Gods and Their Symbols**

God	Element	Color I	Color II
Jehovah	Earth	Black	Gold
Lucifer	Air	Blue	Sky Blue
Satan	Fire	Red	Bright Scarlet
Christ	Water	White	Silver Grey

Mother Sibyl in London, is shown in Figure 9a. It represents the letter "P" for *Power*, seen from the four cardinal directions, and expresses the idea that The Power brings together people of very different perspectives for a common purpose. Some time after its invention, Edward redesigned the Power Sign, giving it flair and elegance. The improved version, shown in Figure 9b, possesses, Edward says, "an ecclesiastical and mathematical flavor." The first version looks rather like a Nazi swastika, while the second is reminiscent of the Iron Cross also associated with the German war machine and worn proudly by American motorcycle gangs. One newcomer in 1971 saw Edward's version as the trumpets of the four Gods. These interpretations were not entirely frivolous. I am sure part of the appeal, intended and unintended, of the Power Sign was its power to suggest meanings.

When Powerites first began presenting themselves as a "church," in New Orleans around 1967, they wore Christian crosses, and as the concept of Satan emerged the following year, they decided to add a symbol for Satan. The best-known image of Satan is the famous illustration by Eliphas Levi of "The Sabbatic Goat" in his nineteenth-century occult book *Transcendental Magic*.[4] This picture has been frequently reproduced, and my collection of Power artifacts includes two paintings of Satan based on it. The Badge of Mendes worn by Powerites consisted of a black triangle, point downward, bearing the head of Levi's goat in red. The face is half-man, half-goat. Between the two spreading horns is a crown, while the forehead is imprinted with a magical pentagram. The Cross and the Goat, shown in Figures 9c and 9d, always went together but were always kept physically separate—for example, at opposite ends of the Alpha ritual room or at separate points on the Powerites' uniforms.

Edward invented another symbol, the Sign of Union, shortly after redesigning the Power Sign. Shown in Figure 9e, it is a combination of the Alpha and the Omega, first and last letters of the Greek alphabet. Three

[4] Eliphas Levi, *Transcendental Magic* (New York: Weiser, 1974), p. 186.

Handicap	Season	Direction
Blind	Winter	North
Deaf	Summer	South
Dumb	Fall	West
Lame	Spring	East

times in the Book of Revelation (1:8, 21:6, and 22:13), God speaks and uses these letters to describe himself: "I am Alpha and Omega, the beginning and the ending, saith the Lord, which is, and which was, and which is to come, the Almighty." The ritual room of any Power chapter was called the Alpha, while the supreme leadership was called the Omega; as steps in a hierarchy, they were the beginning and the ending. The Sign of Union is also a sexual symbol. In the Sabbath Assembly, the Sacrifist, who wears the Sign of Union on his chest, asks, "What is the Sign of the End and the New Beginning?" A member of the congregation is supposed to reply, "The Sign of Union." "Whose is the Union?" the Sacrifist asks. The reply is: "The Union of the Lord Jehovah and the Lord Lucifer." The Sign represents the *marriage* of Jehovah (female) and Lucifer (male), extensions of Kitty and Edward. The Power's marriage ritual is called The Union Ceremony. Married couples are "joined in union." The cover of a cult booklet about marriage carries the Sign of Union. The round outer part of the emblem is an Omega representing the womb of Jehovah. The elongated, inner part of the emblem is an Alpha representing the phallus of Lucifer. The Sign of Union depicts the copulation of these two Gods, their coming together as erotic opposites that can only be fulfilled together. Rank-and-file members of the cult were completely unaware of this meaning. High-status members confirmed my conjecture that this was the proper interpretation of the Sign of Union.

The last symbol introduced in the classical years of The Power was the Unity Cross, shown in Figure 9f. It is a simple, large Christian cross, silver in color, bearing a red serpent, a new symbol of Satan. In 1972, it replaced two separate symbols, the Cross and the Goat, marking a major theological step in the progressive unity of Christ and Satan. As we mentioned a few pages earlier, Edward had just conceived of two types of Satanists, the violent Goats and the mystical Snerps (serpents). The use of a serpent on the Unity Cross signified a transformation of Satan, or at least a change in emphasis, with Satan's more mystical side dominating in His unity with

Figure 9a. Sibyl's Power Sign

Figure 9b. Edward's Power Sign

Figure 9c. The Christian Cross

Figure 9. Six Symbols of the Classical Power

Figure 9d. The Satanic Goat

Figure 9e. The Sign of Union

Figure 9f. The Unity Cross

Christ. Members of Disciple, Messenger, and IP rank were given little Unity Crosses to wear around their necks, made of chrome-plated steel bearing a red serpent decal. Masters of the church wore Unity Crosses on which the serpent was yellow rather than red in color. Not only does the Unity Cross represent a duality, *Christ:Satan*, but it attempts to symbolize the coming ever closer together of the two halves of the duality.

SABBATH ASSEMBLY SYMBOLISM

Power symbolism received clearest physical expression in the Sabbath Assembly. This ceremony, dramatizing the cult's dualisms, changed during the period when the cult struggled to accommodate itself to the world. The weekly Sabbath Assembly, usually held early Saturday evening, was the chief ritual gathering of all members of the cult. It was this ritual, before all others, that expressed the basic premises of the cult to its members and registered alterations in these fundamental assumptions.

Two priests presided over the Sabbath, a Sacrifist and an Evangelist. After the congregation was seated, they would march into the Alpha, accompanied by two other Powerites carrying the fire and water bowls, in a grand procession. The ritual would last between an hour and an hour and a half; then the priests would march out. It was as if the priests brought sacredness into the social gathering, expressed it, then carried it out with them again. Figure 10 shows the layout of the Sabbath Assembly as it was performed in the spring of 1971. Except for newcomers and Initiates, all participants wore black clothing. The only light came from flickering candles and the flame rising from the bowl of fire. The air was hot, filled with incense, an atmosphere either stifling or psychedelic, depending on the degree of one's involvement in the cult.

The congregation sat on cushions placed in a large oval pattern on the floor. Everyone faced inward, toward the circular altar at the center. Their backs were to the outside. The windows were covered. All attention was focused inward, and the outside world was ignored. The Sacrifist and Evangelist sat facing each other from opposite ends of the congregation. They were raised up from the group, seated on crude chairs made from tongue-and-groove floor planking, yet sat within the group. They belonged to the group, expressing qualities of the group, rather than being religious professionals who acted upon the group from outside.

Over their black robes, the two priests wore *tabards*, cloth vestments that hung down over their chests and backs. The Sacrifist's tabard was purple and carried a circular emblem over the chest: the Sign of Union in gold on a

Red Satanic Goat's Head

White Christian Cross

KEY:

E = Evangelist   S = Sacrifist   1 & 2 = Responders

W = Water Bearer   F = Fire Bearer   R = Reader of Scripture

A = Acolyte to be initiated

Black Curtain :   Purple Curtain :

☐ chair, with triangle   ◯ cushion on floor for
   showing direction   member of congregation
   person faces

Figure 10. Layout of the Sabbath Assembly, Spring 1971

black background. The Evangelist's tabard was scarlet and bore a different emblem: the Power Sign in silver on a black background. Behind the Sacrifist, a dark purple curtain hung on the wall. On it was placed a white Christian cross, about a yard high, made from stiff cardboard and painted in an ornate design. Behind the Evangelist hung a black curtain, carrying a red Mendes Goat head.

Most of the service was conducted by the Sacrifist. It was he who engaged the congregation in recitation, he who twice blessed the group, and he who performed initiations. The mood of the Sacrifist was restrained, controlling. The main duty of the Evangelist was the emotional sermon, the Revelation that came near the end of the service. It was free-flowing, in contrast to the studied composition of the rest of the Sabbath, and roused the feelings of newcomers to come forward and join the cult. Both priests carried blackbound Missals bearing the Power Sign in red on their covers. These books contained all the cult's teachings, as well as the formats of the rituals. The Sacrifist read frequently from his Missal. The only use the Evangelist made of his book was when, at two points in the service, both priests recited The Declaration, alternating phrases. We quoted this important doctrinal statement in Chapter One. It announces the coming Unity of Christ and Satan, "The Lamb and the Goat. Pure Love descended from the pinnacle of Heaven, united with pure Hatred raised from the depths of Hell."

The symbolism of the Sabbath is all concerned with *The Power*, in the theological as well as the social sense of the name. It represents the dual relationships between the Gods, particularly the Unity of Christ and Satan, and the process by which they are coming together for "An End and a New Beginning." The Sacrifist represents Christ; the Evangelist represents Satan. They come from opposite ends of the universe, sit at opposite ends of the congregation, but work together for the common purpose. They divide the labor between them, according to their personalities.

The altar at the center was black and red, the original colors of the cult. Circular, with a glass top, it carried the Power Sign at the center. Candles were placed at the four corners of the sign. It was the focus of the circle and of all interactions between the Sacrifist and Evangelist, representing the purpose and social focus of the cult, the joining together of all beings, all principles, for the transcending of all differences and the realization of God.

It is interesting to note the spatial location of the Gods in the ritual. There were no prayers to a distant deity. At no point did a priest speak to any lord located outside the circle. There is a moment in the Evening

Assembly, held for Messengers and IPs only, which states precisely the location of the Gods: ". . . to the Gods who are within us. . . ." The layout of the Assemblies clearly assumed that the Gods were indeed *within* the congregation. At one point in the ritual, the Sacrifist interacts with two Responders who state the natures of Jehovah, Lucifer, Satan, and Christ. At another point, a Member of the Brethren reads a passage from cult scripture. They speak in essence about themselves, reciting interpretations of their social reality while remaining seated within the congregation. Acolytes to be initiated sit in the circle, like all other Brethren, except for the moment of initiation when they briefly kneel before the Sacrifist.

Although the main axis of the Sabbath is the line from the Sacrifist through the altar to the Evangelist, there is a secondary axis at right angles to it. The altar was flanked by two identical stands, each a little over three feet high. During rituals they supported the ritual bowls, one filled with water to symbolize Christ, the other producing fire to symbolize Satan. The original idea for these stands undoubtedly comes from the Biblical description of the two brass columns made by Solomon for his great temple.[5] One was called *Jachin* ("He shall establish") and the other, *Boaz* ("In it is strength"), according to the Bible. Lewis Spence writes that in Kabalistic tradition, the two are supposed "to explain all mysteries." The two columns symbolize the concept of duality. "The one was black and the other white, and they represented the powers of good and evil. It is said that they symbolize the need of 'two' in the world: Human equilibrium requires two feet; the worlds gravitate by means of two forces; generation needs two sexes."[6] This is, of course, the basic concept of Edward's intellectual system. Pictures of the two columns are very common in occult literature. Francis King has reprinted an eighteenth-century engraving which portrays the pair flanking a circular altar reminiscent of that used by The Power.[7] Often, Jachin is shown belching fire, and Boaz gushing water.[8]

Over the years, as the cult attempted to improve its public image and simultaneously to achieve decisive evolution toward the Millennium, the arrangement and symbolism of the Sabbath Assembly changed in parallel fashion. The adoption of grey uniforms in 1971 lightened up the Alpha.

[5] I. Kings 7:15, 21–22; II. Chronicles 3:15–17; II. Kings 25:17; I. Chronicles 4:12; Jeremiah 52:21–23.

[6] Lewis Spence, *An Encyclopaedia of Occultism* (New Hyde Park, New York: University Books, 1960), p. 234.

[7] Francis King, *Magic—The Western Tradition* (New York: Avon, 1975), plate 44.

[8] Manly Palmer Hall, *An Encyclopedic Outline of Masonic, Hermetic, Qabbalistic and Rosicrucian Symbolic Philosophy* (Los Angeles: Philosophical Research Society, 1945), illustration facing page CXIII.

When blue uniforms were introduced in 1972, the walls of the ritual room were painted light blue. Electric lights were hung on the side walls. The two dark curtains were replaced by light blue ones. The altar was no longer a red symbol on black cloth, but became a silver Power Sign on light blue cloth. Finally, the white Christian cross and red Satanic goat's head were retired, and two identical huge Unity Crosses, red and silver, were hung at opposite ends of the room. Presumably this symbolized not only the Luciferian Era, but also the progressive coming together of Christ and Satan. After these changes, I predicted a rearrangement of the positions of Sacrifist and Evangelist. If their Gods were coming together, they also should come closer.

On April 21, 1973, the predicted change took place, as shown in Figure 11. The symbol at the north end has been removed, leaving a single Unity Cross. Both priests now stand together on a low stage, facing the congregation from outside it. The congregation now faces forward toward the priests, rather than inward toward themselves. The altar sits awkwardly between the stage and the congregation. It has lost its role as the focus of the ritual, taken now by the lectern at the center of the stage. The altar had become vestigial, and I predicted it would have to be removed or greatly changed to achieve ritual coherence. Chapter Nine explains how it was changed.

The role of the priests and the location of the Gods had changed. The priests were now separate from the congregation, presiding *over* it and mediating *between* the Gods and their people. The symbols of the Gods were no longer in and around the congregation, but in front of it. If we conceive of the Gods as dwelling in the symbols, they were now located in a territory outside the congregation and dominated by the priests. The Power had become a formal church, rather than a community. It was an institution separate from the social group of all the members, a bureaucracy that had come to treat most members as clients and servants, rather than as participants in an intimate social reality.

The dualities were transformed, both in the ever more rigid hierarchical structure of the group, and in the ritual symbolism. Edward's attempt to reconcile the dualities was not, however, successful. Under the control of its Masters, The Power was getting ready to abolish the concept of duality, rather than fulfill it.

Silver Unity Cross

KEY:

E = Evangelist   S = Sacrifist   1 & 2 = Responders

W = Water Bearer   F = Fire Bearer

A = Acolyte to be initiated

〰〰〰〰〰 light blue curtain

◁ chair, with triangle showing direction person faces

○ cushion on floor for member of congregation

Figure 11. Layout of the Sabbath Assembly, April 21, 1973

EIGHT

A New Cure of Souls

The Wrath of the Lamb has come,
The great Spirit of the Son,
To heal the wounds
That the conflict of the mind
And the pow'r of death
Brought to the sacred land of the Gods.
— Power Chant Number One

Psychotherapy is a kind of magic. It seeks to accomplish changes in the real world by the mere manipulation of symbols. The more academically or medically oriented brands of therapy do not seem magical, because their ideologies do not violate the assumptions of the physical sciences. But all current psychotherapies, no matter what the rhetoric of their practitioners, operate quite independently of the findings of social sciences, often in open violation of scientific findings.[1] The effectiveness of all brands of psychotherapy is in doubt. There is every reason to believe that the most sophisticated approaches are not the least bit superior to the most primitive. The evidence suggests (without being conclusive) that every brand of therapy, conventional or deviant, is of moderate value. The therapies preferred by doctors or by the educated upper classes are not any better than the most rustic faith healing or shamanism.[2] A number of studies demonstrate that

[1] The literature on this point is voluminous and disputatious. The behaviorists attack the psychoanalytically-oriented approach; see Hans. J. Eysenck, "The Effects of Psychotherapy," *International Journal of Psychiatry* 1 (1965): 99–144; Richard B. Stuart, *Trick or Treatment* (Champaign, Illinois: Research Press, 1970); Stanley Rachman, *The Effects of Psychotherapy* (Oxford: Pergamon, 1971); Joseph Wolpe and Stanley Rachman, "Psychoanalytic 'Evidence': A Critique Based on Freud's Case of Little Hans," *Journal of Nervous and Mental Disease* 130 (1960): 135–148; and Albert Bandura, *Principles of Behavior Modification* (New York: Holt, Rinehart and Winston, 1969), pp. 52–61. But the behaviorist approach itself is limited in applicability, and its apparent successes may have nothing to do with its alleged basis in experimental psychology; see Nathaniel McConaghy, "Aversive Therapy of Homosexuality: Measures of Efficacy," *American Journal of Psychiatry*, 127:9 (March 1971): 1221–1224. See also: Andrew Salter, *The Case Against Psychoanalysis* (New York: Harper and Row, 1972).

[2] Jerome D. Frank, *Persuasion and Healing* (New York: Schocken, 1961). Wolfgang Lederer, "Primitive Psychotherapy," *Psychiatry* 22 (August 1959): 255–265.

the popularity of any therapeutic approach is determined by social factors quite unrelated to its objective effectiveness.[3] Consequently, in a study such as mine, the question of the therapeutic effectiveness of Power techniques is not of primary interest. It is extremely difficult to gauge the value of a cure even in controlled clinical settings. In the field it is next to impossible. We can conjecture about the value of the cult's techniques. Perhaps it is useful to do so. But three other important questions can be engaged more easily: (1) What are the Power's techniques? (2) How do they relate to Power doctrine? (3) What are the likely social consequences of the techniques, quite apart from the question of cure? With these questions guiding our analysis, we will discuss several Power therapy exercises, in roughly the order a newcomer would have encountered them around 1971.

THE TELEPATHY DEVELOPING CIRCLE

This group encounter, familiarly called the TDC, was the most basic therapy process, participated in by any visitor to the cult interested enough to pay the $1.50 admission. It was held in the Alpha ritual room and lasted an hour. I observed many TDCs as a participant, tape-recorded one, photographed another, and even led a few Circles, so my documentation is quite complete. Here I will describe it combining my observations from four Circles run by Sister Amaranth at the Boston Chapter, March 5, 19, and 26, and April 2, 1971.

The cushions were spread out in a single large oval pattern on the floor. The room was dark. Incense spewing from a chalice gave the air a translucent quality, like a warm liquid. Physical objects seemed unreal. The amber glow of the candles was lost in the dark walls and clothing, but it illuminated faces with a magical radiance. Two or three dozen people sat in the Circle, touching each other, pressed closely side by side. We fell silent.

[3] Ari Kiev, *Transcultural Psychiatry* (New York: Free Press, 1972). David J. Rothman, *The Discovery of the Asylum* (Boston: Little, Brown, 1971). Anselm Strauss, et al., *Psychiatric Ideologies and Institutions* (New York: Free Press, 1964). Robert B. Edgerton, "Conceptions of Psychosis in Four East African Societies," *American Anthropologist* 68 (1966): 408–425. Jozef Ph. Hes, "From Native Healer to Modern Psychiatrist—Afro-Asian Immigrants to Israel and Their Attitudes towards Psychiatric Facilities," *International Journal of Social Psychiatry* 13:1 (Winter 1966–67): 21–27. Masaaki Kato, "Report on Psychotherapy in Japan," *International Journal of Social Psychiatry* 5:1 (Summer 1959):56–60. Richard F. Larson, "The Clergyman's Role in the Therapeutic Process: Disagreement between Clergymen and Psychiatrists," *Psychiatry* 31 (1968):250–263. Lawrence S. Linn, "Social Identification and the Seeking of Psychiatric Care," *American Journal of Orthopsychiatry* 38:1 (1968):83–88. Shashi K. Pande, "The Mystique of 'Western' Psychotherapy: An Eastern Interpretation," *Journal of Nervous and Mental Disease* 146:6 (June 1968):425–432.

Then Amaranth entered, dramatic, reserved, and haughty, and took her place on a purple cushion directly under the cross at Christ's end of the room.

After a brief introduction, Amaranth divided us into groups of six and had us sit in little circles. We meditated on our "aims for the evening." What did each of us want to contribute? What did each of us want to receive? "Relax," she said. "Close your eyes. Make no effort. Let it come. Now begin the meditation." After a minute of silence, she said, "Come in now." We opened our eyes and then told what aims had emerged in our meditations.

Some of the aims expressed in the April 2 TDC were the following. Brother Gregory wanted "to give understanding and to receive something that I really ought to know." Shorty wanted "to give strength and receive strength." Betty parroted Shorty, "I'd like to give strength and receive it, too." Arnold said, "I'd like to give thinking and reason, and receive purpose." My own aims were "to give intensity and receive acceptance." Brother Simon finished "the round on aims" by saying, "I'd like to give and receive communication."

The next activity was also conducted in the small groups. Amaranth announced, "We'll have rounds in each of the circles now on how your awareness and sensitivity have been since your last Circle. How it's been developing, what kind of things have been happening." Supposedly, our work in the TDCs would improve our sensitivity and awareness, from week to week. Our contact and communication with other people would constantly improve. But the level on which this progress would take place was seen as occult, psychic, or at least subconscious. The Circles were supposed to develop our powers of *Telepathy*. On a radio show in 1972, Amaranth explained what The Power meant by this word.

"When we say *telepathy*, we don't mean mind reading, sort-of picking words out of somebody's brain. We don't do that. But what it is is becoming more aware, increasing sensitivity around other people, around objects, around environments. Being able to understand what a person's feeling, going through, without talking to him about it. Just by being near him, picking up his moods and emotions." Amaranth's definition is on the borderline between the psychic and the psychological. Cult theory did not recognize any clear line between these two different traditions for interpreting human experience.

In one TDC, Brother Simon said, "My sensitivity around people seems to be very good, especially donating, and really knowing if they're going to say yes or no, and knowing what people to ask. Picking up how people are feeling, spirits, vibrations." Sometimes, Messengers donating on the streets would try to guess the home towns of people they met, or their ages. No clear distinction was made between subliminal awareness of another person's emotions, and extrasensory perception of his thoughts or hidden information about him. Brother Grieg reports he was in Harvard Square hawking literature when a young couple stopped to speak with him. He claimed he immediately knew all about them, even though he had never seen them before. Grieg told them they were from Michigan, that the guy was 22, and the girl 17. "Yes!" they exclaimed. He was right. Grieg said the incident frightened him. He didn't know what to do with such power and wasn't sure he'd be happy if it came to him again. Sister Marie mentioned a similar incident in which she had performed the same trick while donating. The person was amazed and asked if Powerites were telepathic. "That's not really in our line," she said.

The TDC rounds on sensitivity and awareness were always followed by a Meditation. As we said in Chapter Three, in this cult *meditation* means *directed fantasy*. It is often performed and discussed in group settings. Powerites are given a topic to meditate on—that is, to free associate about; then the participants discuss the images they received. Some of the TDC meditation topics Amaranth gave us were: "the future of Humanity and your part in it," "mass destruction," "the end of the world," and simply "self."

Many people reported extremely vivid images of terrestrial annihilation, often science fiction and surrealist pictures. One fellow saw spaceships shooting death rays at Humanity. Another saw King Kong smashing city buildings. Somebody else saw a setting sun with the words THE END written on it. Another said he had also seen a setting sun, but his had a face on it. When the solar face set, it stuck its tongue out. One young man had a vision of the world disintegrating into anarchy, with only the holy cities Rome and Jerusalem remaining to preserve order in the chaos. A young woman described earthquakes, floods, and blizzards. Sister Roxana saw everyone strung together like a chain with bands of light. Brother Origen saw the earth topple, flip over slowly end for end, while the people shrieked. He heard himself addressing terrified multitudes, telling them there was nothing they could do to save themselves. This was the end! In the vision, he waved his arm, and a vast image of Satan appeared in the sky.

After the groups had briefly discussed the participants' meditations, Amaranth asked their leaders to report some of the images that had come through. She then summed them up into a coherent picture. The Power assumes each participant is in touch with part of a reality, and that the entire truth can be discovered by adding together the pieces received by different participants. The same approach had led the cult to Xtul when fragmentary meditation images had proved to be parts of a single, collective vision. On the social level, this practice followed from the desire to make the personalities of the members fit together, to create a psychic unity so the group would be strong and cohesive.

The chief activity of the TDC, *Psychometry*, followed the Meditation. It is a traditional occult practice, adopted without modifications by The Power.[4] We divided into pairs. One time I photographed Ron Forbes and Larry Spiegel, two Initiates, performing Psychometry. Ron did the first reading. Larry gave Ron his Initiate's cross. Ron held it to his forehead and closed his eyes. Supposedly, the cross would have absorbed psychic vibrations from Larry, the only person who has ever worn it. Ron opened his mind to images, letting the "aura" of the cross penetrate his mind and produce pictures. He might see Larry's past, his future, or an allegory concerning some aspect of Larry's nature. These images came from the cross, it was said, not from Ron's imagination. For more than five minutes, Ron described what he saw. Larry commented and asked questions. After a while, they would switch roles and Larry would do Psychometry on an object belonging to Ron.

Amaranth would instruct newcomers, but only in the most superficial and general way. She might, for example, tell a couple that they could read each others' hands if they did not have any suitable objects. She could not tell participants how to come up with visions, but would usually say something like the following, supporting an occult interpretation of Psychometry: "When you're doing the reading, don't worry about whether you're picking up something about the person you're reading. Because you *will* be picking up something about the person you're reading. The main thing is to relax. Don't place any demands on yourself. Just relax and let the things flow in. They'll come. If you come up against a block, the block is probably in the person that you're reading. So describe the feelings around the block. If you draw a complete blank, describe what you yourself are feeling, because you'll probably be picking it up from the person you're doing the reading on."

This Psychometry is clearly another technique for producing directed fantasy. In this case the topic is the person being read and the reader's feelings about him. The reader is encouraged to explore and express his feelings by the occult definition of the situation, which denies they are his feelings. According to Psychometry theory, the images come not from the mind of the reader, but from the object pressed to his head. He is not to blame. This psychic exercise may in fact have the effect of liberating the reader from excessive inhibitions and encouraging him to express himself.

[4] Lewis Spence, *An Encyclopaedia of Occultism* (New Hyde Park, New York: University Books, 1960), p. 333.

The cost is the requirement that he accept a psychic explanation for the things that happen.

The occult interpretation of Psychometry used by The Power may be called a *facilitating definition*. If we take a narrowly pragmatic definition of *truth*, then there can be many competing truths about any complex phenomenon, each serving a different purpose. Pragmatically, truth is whatever works. Regardless of its scientific value, one definition of the situation may *work* better than the others, may accomplish some specific task better than the other. If our purpose is to reconcile Psychometry with the findings of academic psychology, then we must reject the occult interpretation and describe Psychometry as an exercise in directed fantasy. But the Powerites have no such purpose. They want to develop and experience exciting human relationships and personal emotions. The occult definition of the situation works better for them, considering their goals; therefore it is pragmatically true. Occult statements about the procedure are true in the sense that they are loyal (true) to the purposes of The Power. *A facilitating definition is any interpretation of the situation, regardless of its objective truth, which contributes to successful social interaction in pursuit of certain goals.* The occult orientation may be the facilitating definition in many situations, because it validates expression of questionable feelings and ideas, and reduces the sense of risk and blame.

The quality of Psychometry readings varied. The first Powerite who did a reading on me was Brother Lot. He took my wristwatch, held it to his head, and described the visions that came. A paper punch. Drafting tables with papers, drawings, drawing tools. The sun shining in windows on a nice day. A scene in the country. Trees. He saw me walking down a road with a stick or fishing pole over my shoulder. A woman. Distant. In the past or the future. Lot guesses I am not married. The river in Boston. The Charles River. At the university, where he and I have met a couple of times. Lot says I want freedom. Freedom is very important to me. He sees me burst out of a university building and pull off my tie. I want to leap into the cool water. A piece of paper. Maybe a school degree. I was working for it, he said, but was really using it as an excuse to postpone living. I was working for a degree, believing my life would really begin as soon as I had it. But, Lot said, the beginning of life should come now. He is conscious of my wristwatch. He senses it is time for the Psychometry to end.

Lot's was a typical reading. Many physical images, usually connected to the person being read. Sometimes conjectures about his feelings. Sometimes an analysis of his life. Sometimes advice. I frequently observed couples engage in courtship during their Psychometry. They may report sharing visions of a highly intimate nature. Often the result was uninspiring. Often participants expressed dissatisfaction at the quality of a reading, but never in my experience questioned the validity of the exercise.

After each Psychometry, Amaranth would "do a round of the room," asking each person by name how the reading had gone. A few actual comments follow. "It was like reading a book." "Yes, it's like he's known me for years." "It made a lot of sense to me." "I almost felt like I was preaching a sermon at him, but somehow it felt right." "It was really good. I really feel a lot better." "It was much more flowing than in the past. It seemed real." "Yeah, it had quite a bit of meaning." "I'm getting more confidence, now." "Shocking." "Very emotional." "It was very intense." "Ummm. I was really getting into it." "It was very intense, so intense that I didn't realize I was here while I was doing it." "It was terrible. It was very superficial." "Everything I have always wanted to know about him but was afraid to ask. It was super."

Next, the group would move back into the large circle. We held hands all around, closed our eyes, and meditated on what we had achieved that evening and on the mood in the room. After a minute, Amaranth said, "All right. Come in now." She did a round on what we had seen. At one TDC, Brother Thomas said, "I got an image, like a white stallion just bursting forth and galloping off." Larry saw "a roomful of mirrors that all-of-a-sudden smashed and then went back together again." Grieg "got the feeling that there was a great deal of retreat from a great deal of intense emotion." Others picked up "subdued sadness," "a sense of God," "More unity," and the obscure sound of "muffled chimes." I said I felt "that we're all part of a single, living being, here in this room." Amaranth completed the round by saying her image was "like Bill's," a feeling of unity among the participants. Certainly, this was what was supposed to emerge. The Telepathy Developing Circle encouraged a controlled intimacy among participants, the development of social bonds, and the emergence of a mystically understood group consensus.

MIDNIGHT MEDITATION

Every Friday and Saturday at Midnight, a Meditation ritual was held in the Alpha, lasting half an hour. The circular altar was placed a few feet in front of the Sacrifist's chair, becoming the focus of a circle of participants seated as usual on the floor cushions. A single priest, the Sacrifist, conducted the ceremony. His format instructions said, "The Sacrifist creates and maintains an atmosphere which is relaxed, quiet, contemplative, and dignified." The Meditation is intended "to relax tensions, worries, problems, conflicts, depressions" and "to engender a feeling of peace, confidence, security, contact, and healing."

The main business was a pair of meditations, relaxed focused fantasies on given topics, separated by Power chants. The subject of the first meditation was a negative concept, the second was the positive opposite of the first. In one Meditation I attended, for example, the first meditation was on *confusion*, the second on *clarity*. The pairs were probably taken from a list of burdens and blessings made up by Edward. Burdens are negative qualities that a person may have, often without being aware of them. He writes, "A burden cannot be eliminated until it's been seen and acknowledged. . . . When a burden is recognized, it loses most of its hold on us (which depended largely on our own unawareness of it as a burden), and therefore, if its opposite blessing suddenly emerges, the burden is eliminated with ease, *without* losing the presence of the blessing." The Meditation sequence sought first to expose participants to a burden that might be causing them significant personal problems, giving them a chance to become aware of it, then exposed them to the corresponding blessing. In theory, this procedure would be psychotherapeutic, lessening the power of the negative burden and increasing the strength of the blessing. A series of Meditations, covering all pairs, would improve participants in many areas. Perhaps the Meditations merely functioned to give Powerites one more enjoyable group experience, but the theory extended Edward's idea that the resolution of conflict between polar opposites would be possible. Burdens were like the compulsions that Edward's therapy business was originally founded to cure. In meditation a person might discover that he need not forever enact a particular burden, but might better achieve his life's goals if he substituted the corresponding blessing. Table 9 gives a list of twenty-five pairs of burdens and blessings, twenty-five minor dualities of the human psyche that deserved therapeutic attention.

PROGRESSES

The main group educational and therapeutic meetings for Initiates, Disciples, and OP Messengers were called *Progresses*. They were the outgrowth of the original Compulsions Analysis *Communications Course*, based in turn on the Technianity *Communications Course* Edward and Kitty took in London years before. By the early 1970s, there were several formats for these meetings. Usually held Monday and Wednesday evenings, they lasted three hours, with a 20-minute break in the middle. The first half would be devoted to activities, the second half to the study of Power teachings. At one

Table 9: **Twenty-Five Pairs of Burdens and Blessings**

Burden	Blessing	Burden	Blessing
Unawareness	Awareness	Misery	Happiness
Blame	Acceptance	Confusion	Clarity
Hatred	Love	Cowardice	Courage
Doubt	Certainty	Arrogance	Humility
Vulnerability	Invulnerability	Tension	Relaxation
Futility	Purpose	Insecurity	Security
Ignorance	Knowledge	Stupidity	Intelligence
Anxiety	Serenity	Hypocrisy	Honesty
Inhibition	Freedom	Greed	Generosity
Frustration	Satisfaction	Pessimism	Optimism
Weakness	Strength	Cruelty	Kindness
Apathy	Enthusiasm	Insensitivity	Sensitivity
Exhaustion	Energy		

time, Mondays were devoted to the development of communication skills, while psychological problems were dealt with on Wednesdays. My information about Progresses comes from three sources (1) my own participation in several in 1971; (2) interviews with Sister Norma and Brother Gregory conducted by my assistant, Carol Fisler; and (3) my own participation in the Technianity Communications Course in 1970.

Each half of a Progress would be run by a Controller, a senior Powerite, aided in the first half by two or three others who helped supervise the exercises. The Controller would begin each session by reciting a Power Precept, which the congregation would repeat in unison. Some Precepts encapsulated various aspects of Edward's therapeutic theory. "Our dissatisfactions are born of ignorance. Our problems stem from blindness." "Humanity is a trap, and human beings are caught in the trap." "The basis of all healing is the lifting of guilt." "We cannot change ourselves. Others can change us." "The first step is to know that we are greater than the pain we feel." "Where love is real, the gift of love is the healer of all ills." "We must go through weakness to reach strength." "We must have known despair before we can find fulfillment." After the Precept, the participants would be guided through three or four exercises taken from a large collection.

Several activities were clearly derived from Technianity, although the meaning given to them and the exact procedures were changed radically.

Examples include: *Acceptance*, *Reflexes*, *Articulation*, and *Acknowledgement*. The first was derived from the very basic Technianity exercise TR–0 (Training Routine Zero), in which one is instructed to sit for up to two hours, motionless, unresponsive, eyes glued on the eyes of another student who is sitting three feet away, following the same instructions, gazing back. TR–0 trains a student to "be there." In 1961, Gordon Rogers wrote, "Anything added to BEING THERE is sharply flunked by the coach. Twitches, blinks, sighs, fidgets, anything except just BEING THERE is promptly flunked, with the reason why. Patter: Student coughs. Coach: 'Flunk! You coughed. Start.' " The Training Routines involved very strict discipline. A second part of TR–0 was called "bull baiting." The student sits in the catatonic immobility of TR–0, and the coach tries to make him react against his will. Rogers says, "This TR should be taught rough-rough-rough and not left until the student can do it. Training is considered satisfactory at this level only if the student can BE three feet in front of a person without flinching, concentrating or confronting with, regardless of what the confronted person does." In theory, the student is said to be vulnerable at certain points, to have "buttons" which if pressed will make him react. Sensitivity about being overweight, for example, may cause the person to blush when his fat is poked. These psychological buttons are to be found and "flattened." Sometimes, it seemed to me, the student himself was flattened by bull baiting. At the very least, this and the other TRs are successful in flattening the affect of the student, reducing his emotional responsiveness and his emotional resistance to control by Technianity.

TR–0 also could produce an altered state of consciousness. One time I did it with a young man from Kentucky, an English teacher I happened to like. We sat staring at each other for two hours, which is 120 minutes, which is 7,200 seconds. A long time to stare into someone's face, allowed to breathe and blink occasionally, but never look away, never smile or fidget. Afterward my partner exclaimed excitedly that he had seen me change before his very eyes! I had become different persons—a savage with a bone through my nose, then a decayed corpse covered with filth and cobwebs. He was sure these were glimpses of my previous incarnations. Everyone in the Technianity center was pleased and complimented him on his perceptions. His interpretations fitted the cult's ideology exactly.

I did not tell them what I had seen. He, too, had changed. A halo of light had grown around his face. He had become pale and two-dimensional, shimmering, covered with dark spots. Of course, I interpreted what I saw as simple eye fatigue. He and I had experienced the same stimuli but understood them differently. Unusual experiences like his, perceived within the definitions provided by the cult, are powerful conversion mechanisms. Technianity converts people slowly to its perspective, following a *reality gradient*. This is Rogers' own terminology, but ideal for social scientific use as well. A reality gradient is a gradual introduction into a new ideology, step by step through a series of ever more alien experiences and a progression of ever more deviant ideas. The therapy processes of Technianity gradually committed my friend to ever more deviant levels of cult belief, drawing him into its reality and away from that shared by conventional outsiders.

I remember the exam I passed in Technianity to prove I had mastered TR−0. The secretary of the center, a pleasant young woman who happened to be the daughter of a dean at the university I was attending, gave me a "check-out" on TR−0. We sat in straight chairs, facing each other, our knees almost touching. "All right," she said, "start." I sat upright, my hands on my knees, gazed into her eyes, and went into TR−0. "Hi, Bill! How ya doin'?" She bounced up and down in the chair and waved. She pretended to be insulted and hurt that I wouldn't react to her. She acted mad. She pouted, then cracked a few stale jokes. Smiling, she brought her face close to mine and rocked from side to side.

She took my hands in hers and waved them through great circles in the air. She let my arms drop, and they fell at my sides. She said she was going to poke out my eyes and described how she was going to do it. She remarked she hadn't had the fun of poking out an eye since last week. She said the poor fellow she had blinded then was still in the hospital. She pretended to gouge out my eye with her thumb. She held my fist, pretending it was an electric shaver. "Bzzzzzz." She shaved my face. She placed my hands on my knees, then played with my sideburns. She fluffed them up and said I was a bear. She took my hand, noted it was sweaty, and said, "Ah—a wet palm! Do you come from Wet Palm Beach, Florida?" Through all of this, I gazed straight ahead and reacted not at all to anything she said or did. "Okay. It's a pass. That's it."

Some participants say they "exteriorize" while in TR−0. When a person exteriorizes, his spirit leaves his body temporarily, perhaps hovering a short distance from his head. The concept is akin to "astral projection." Rogers suggests that the ideal relationship between the spirit and its body is one of moderate exteriorization. The spirit should be outside the body, but near it, operating the body at arm's length, so to speak. In psychiatric terms, this seems to be a state of general dissociation. When deep in TR−0, I noticed that my physical sensations were greatly attenuated. A feather lightly brushing across my face did not tickle. An itch did not matter. I was only dimly aware of the existence of my legs. It seemed as if my personal boundary had contracted. When my hand was touched to my face, I sensed the contact in my cheek, but not in my fingers!

The Power exercise, *Acceptance*, was a significantly modified version of TR–0. Powerites would sit on cushions on the floor in pairs, facing each other. Each would sit comfortably, gazing into the eyes of the other for one minute, trying to accept that person and really permit him to be present. Here TR–0 is radically transformed. *Acceptance* is mercifully brief. The concept is different. Each person is not supposed to block off perceptions of the other, as in Technianity, but to extend quiet warmth to him. There is not a strict rule against the slightest movement. Brother Gregory Watson, a Disciple who attended many Progresses, recalls Acceptance well. The task was to "look into each other's eyes for a full minute without laughing, looking away, saying anything. This is to learn to feel free about looking at someone without embarrassment, to get over inhibitions about this sort of contact. Learn to accept the other and to feel accepted by removing these inhibitions."

The next step was *Reflexes*, the Power equivalent of Technianity's bull baiting. One member of the pair would take the role of *controller*, the same as the Technianity coach role. Watson explains that "reflexes are gestures, words, attitudes, expressions that cause a nervous reaction—hate, fear, giggles, etc. The controller hits the subject with things he feels the subject is sensitive to so that the subject can learn to accept this, to control his reflexive reactions." Watson himself was particularly sensitive about being overweight, so the controllers would often focus on his reflexes about being fat. But, in contrast to the harsh treatment in Technianity, the Power therapies were predicated on love and acceptance.

Power exercises *Articulation* and *Acknowledgements* were derived from the Technianity procedures TR–1 and TR–2. This pair was also called *Alice Games* by Gordon Rogers, because they drew upon *Alice in Wonderland* for material. In TR–1, the student is supposed to read a quotation from *Alice*, memorize it, and, while "holding his TRs," speak the sentence to the coach as though it were his own contribution to some hypothetical conversation they were having. Sometimes we used actual copies of *Alice*, back in 1970, and at other times we read from sheets of excerpts. How many dozens of times did I say these crazy sentences? I will never forget them!

> *I'll give them a new pair of boots every Christmas.*
> *Four times five is twelve, and four times six is thirteen.*
> *The question is, what did the archbishop find?*
> *You insult me by talking such nonsense.*
> *You're enough to try the patience of an oyster!*

What a number of cucumber-frames there must be.
The master says you've got to go down the chimney.
I didn't know that Cheshire cats always grinned.
She doesn't believe there's an atom of meaning in it.
However, I know my name now, that's some comfort.

I found it singularly appropriate to quote the Cheshire cat at my Technianity coach: "We're all mad here. I'm mad. You're mad." Alice asked, "How do you know I'm mad?" The cat replied, "You must be, or you wouldn't have come here." There is a subtle brainwashing and propaganda effect here. The student becomes inured to crazy ideas. He treats them as detached words, bleached of their meaning, absurd, unconnected to his surroundings. He is confronted by madness and sees it as a beneficial game. He plays the game. After he has accepted the words of Wonderland, he has no difficulty accepting the words of the cult. The student submits to the discipline of the cult, merely by going through the exercise. If he performs poorly, the coach shouts "Flunk!"

TR–2 is a reversal of TR–1. This time the coach recites a quotation from *Alice*, and the student tries to acknowledge it in such a way as to bring the dialogue to a full stop without encouraging the coach to continue. Acknowledgement is a means of control. The student was permitted to use one of the following five acknowledgements: alright, okay, thank you, good, fine. Rogers says that a properly delivered acknowledgement is so powerful it "can take a client's head off." "An acknowledgement is a very, very powerful sixteen-inch gun, . . ." and "it actually staggers people to have an acknowledgement come to them." But, Rogers warns, "We're not trying to reach the ultimate in an acknowledgement, because that would be the end of the universe. If someone could say, 'Yes'—'Good'—'Okay' with enough intention behind it, all communications of this universe from the moment of its beginning would then be acknowledged, totally." Technianity seems obsessed with the idea of *power*.

The Power version of TR–1, *Articulation*, had a very different purpose. Sister Norma says it was "an elocution lesson" in which Powerites were "taught to speak clearly and concisely." In each pair, the controller would give the student a simple sentence to say. The student was supposed to repeat it in a direct manner, without using extreme gestures or other "distractors." If the student made a mistake, the controller would say "Stop," explain what the error was, and tell the student to try it again. In the Technianity TRs, the command was "Flunk!" not "Stop." In every detail, the Power version of the exercises was less harsh than the original Technianity version. Disciple Gregory Watson says the purpose of Articulation was "to ease situations where you have to speak to people, show more confidence, come across more professionally, present a better picture of what you're talking about."

The student's statements were *acknowledged* by the coach, and in *Articulation—Stage B* students learned to use four acknowledgements: right, okay, thank you, fine. One of Technianity's was dropped from the list, *good*, because it was felt to be too judgemental. I remember practicing these exercises in a Monday Progress. Sister Leah was the controller for our little group. We sat in a circle, facing each other. Each of us in turn would say a simple declarative sentence to Leah. We tried to speak clearly and not let the words "disperse." If Leah felt we spoke well, she would acknowledge our sentence. Otherwise, she would ask us to try it again. When Leah had done this with each of us, she passed the role of controller on to the next person in the circle, and we did another similar round. When each of us had been controller once, the exercise was over. We were not supposed to "invalidate" our partners, not criticize the content of their sentences. Rather than firing our acknowledgements like sixteen-inch guns, we were supposed to communicate acceptance of the other person.

Powerites did not play *Alice Games*, training them to tolerate mad sentences. People were urged to express themselves, rather than subjugate themselves to another person's madness. Acknowledgements were used as responses to the answers students gave when asked questions like: "What person or thing in the world makes you get bored the most? What is your greatest wish for the future?" The Power wanted to communicate, not to stop communication.

Two of the Progress exercises called for participants to touch each other: *Physical Contact* and *Physical Therapy*. It is possible that these procedures, particularly the latter, were derived not from Technianity but from another cult, The Alexander Technique. Father Siegfried and Father Adam were the sons of a practitioner of this deviant therapy. Invented early in this century by F. Matthias Alexander, it involves a series of procedures designed to give the client a greater awareness and control of his physical body. When I asked Edward de Forest where *Physical Contact* and *Physical Therapy* had come from, he could not say. He doubted they were derived from the Alexander Technique.

My first experience of these two Progress exercises was on different evenings when I was paired with Sister Roxana, who was then still a mere Initiate. Through this contact we began a rather warm friendship that continued for a long time. One Monday, Roxana and I were paired off by Mother Bathsheba for Physical Contact. In the first round, I was to be the active partner, following Bathsheba's instructions, while Roxana was to be passive and accepting. "Put your hands on the other's shoulders," Bathsheba commanded. I placed my hands softly on Roxana's shoulders. "Okay," Bathsheba said, "put your hands on the other's head." I did so. Bathsheba continued, ". . . forearms . . . knees . . . waist. . . ." Sister Norma has described this exercise as "fun, strange." The idea was to "touch in a manner that gives security." Roxana accepted my touches calmly. Then we switched roles. Bathsheba gave the same set of touching commands. This time Roxana touched me, and I accepted. Around the room there were a dozen pairs of Powerites touching and accepting.

Then we did another sequence in which Bathsheba no longer gave the commands. The person being touched told the toucher what to do. I told Roxana where to touch me, step by step. As Sister Norma has remarked, participants in the Progresses "never touched in the good places." We stayed away from the erogenous zones. Nonetheless, a very special feeling was generated by the alternate touchings, erotic without doubt, but also calm and exploratory. The final section of Physical Contact was another role reversal. Roxana gave me instructions, and I touched her.

Three weeks later, when Father Adam was controller of the Progress, Roxana and I were paired off for *Physical Therapy*. The basic idea was for one person to lie relaxed on the floor. The other would kneel, lift an arm of his supine partner, supporting it carefully at the shoulder and wrist, and move the arm in slow, slow circles in the air. Everything would be extremely quiet and calm. Sensual and spiritual. After a minute, the active partner would move on to the other arm, then each of the legs, and the head.

But the first time we did it, the Boston Alpha was so full of people that there was not room to lie down. Father Adam improvised. He had half of us sit on cushions, relax, and receive back rubs from the other. First, Roxana massaged my back, arms, shoulders, and head for about fifteen minutes. It was a very happy time for me, but hard work for her. Then we switched roles, and I massaged her.

Possible therapeutic effects aside, the chief consequence of all these Progress activities was the development of social relationships between participants. Over the weeks, strangers made friends within the group of habitual participants. Because these relationships developed within the cult, they tended to stay within the cult, thereby contributing to its strength. A reporter who visited the Technianity Communications Course has given a very plausible interpretation of the appeal it had for some people:

For many an alienated person hungry for companionship and structure, this course may be worth the money if only because it puts him for hours opposite to another person who has agreed to look at him straight in the eye and to give or take commands rapturously. Some neurotic inhabitants of big cities have never had even this much interchange with other human beings (even in sexual intercourse you can keep your eyes closed).

P-SCOPE SESSIONS

In Chapter Two we briefly described the use of a Technianity E-Meter in pseudo-psychoanalytic sessions, and the application of the same device, later called the P-Scope, in Compulsions Analysis. Here we will describe the actual procedure in the sessions. There were many different formats, but basically all involved sequences of questions and answers. One of Gordon Rogers' 1951 procedures contained the following questions among many: "What is your most common emotion?" "How do you feel about survival?" "How right are you about what you do?" "What responsibilities are you willing to shoulder?" If the procedure was to be taken seriously, it was important for the subject to give correct answers. But the theory of the subconscious mind held that people could be mistaken about their real feelings. On the subconscious level, they knew and recognized the truth. On the conscious level, they were enmeshed in a web of self-deception. The E-Meter, functioning as a crude lie detector, seemed an effective tool for testing the client's answers, to see whether they were correct or not.

Compulsions Analysis and the later Power sought to uncover subconscious *goals*, using the P-Scope to verify which ones really mattered. The Power technique may be derived from the main procedure that (at least at one time) seems to have been the step before achieving *super* in Technianity. I have not experienced it myself and rely on a somewhat garbled account by a journalist. It seems that Technianity's *Grade VI Release* process, which follows a series of procedures called "The Power Processes" and "The Power Plus Processes," may be the one adapted for its own purposes by Compulsions Analysis. Intended to achieve "return of powers to act on own determinism," this *solo audit* "developed from Rogers' theories about the existence of past goals, how they are implanted, and how we can free ourselves from their negative influences." *Solo audit* means that the client would do the process on himself. He asks himself various questions and uses the E-Meter to validate his own responses. In order to have a hand free to write them down, he holds both "cans" (electrodes) of the meter in one hand, separated by an inch or so. On a sheet of paper he draws a "Line Plot," a list of personal goals and the "oppositions" that block the fulfillment of those goals. Figure 12 is an example listing the client's goals under GOAL TERMINAL and the things that prevent the realization of the goals under OPPOSITION TERMINAL.

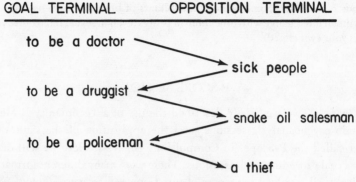

Figure 12. A Technianity Line Plot

All three occupations listed under GOAL TERMINAL are goals adopted by the person being analyzed. He wants to be a doctor but is blocked from fulfilling this goal. Therefore he adopts the nearest possible thing to being a doctor, which is being a druggist. When he cannot do this, he turns to a third substitute goal, being a policeman. So the Line Plot lists a hierarchy of goals and the things that prevent their fulfillment. The Opposition items can be forces external to the person, or internal. For example, a druggist may be forced out of business by an actual snake oil salesman, but the doctor may be forced out of business by the mere fear of sick people.

In The Power, this procedure was called the Goal Line, or line of goals. It was run, using a P-Scope, in regular therapy sessions in which the therapist asked the questions and the client responded. The session would begin when the therapist asks, "What is your chronic goal?" If this question does not mean much to the client, he might phrase it differently. "What are you trying to achieve? What are you after?" Figure 13 shows the actual responses given by Mother Lethe in a session when Edward de Forest was her therapist. She gives several answers to the question: "To die . . . to be bored . . . to feel unaware. . . ." Edward writes these down. When she has run out of responses, they go back to the top of the list and go through the answers again. The P-Scope needle moves when Lethe is on some items and not on others. If there is a response on the P-Scope, Edward makes a little mark in front of the item. Eight of the eleven produced a response. Then they go through the list again. This time, only one item gets a P-Scope response, "To die." If more than one had drawn a response, they would have continued going through the list until they got only a single movement of the needle. Then, the therapist announces the result to the client. Edward would say, "Lethe, your chronic goal is to die."

The next sequence would take the goal, to die, and incorporate it in a question. "What would happen if you failed to die?" Or, "What would you do if you failed to die." She gave (as it happened) eleven responses to this new question. Only four got a strong P-Scope response on the second run-through. The third time through, only one got a strong reading: "to destroy people." Lethe's chronic goal is "to die," but because she cannot achieve this, she has adopted the secondary goal "to destroy people."

The third step was to find the reason she could not die. "What would prevent you from dying?" She replied "People in need . . . crippled people . . . the Pope . . . my mother. . . ." But none of these gave a strong response. So Edward turned to an alternate question, probably one like: "What would destroying people accomplish?" She gave fourteen answers; four got a P-Scope response, and the one that finally emerged was "to make me bigger than everything else." Throughout the therapy session, Lethe continually failed to find oppositions outside herself but found oppositions always inside. Perhaps they can be described as conflicting goals. The line of goals continues, sequence after sequence: "To isolate people . . . to dominate the situation . . . to change the situation."

Brother Osiris, who had been given extensive therapy by Edward de Forest and trained in the techniques by him, was kind enough to instruct me. I received a similar therapy process, Maximum Compulsion, from him,

CHRONIC GOAL:

//   To die.

/   To be bored.

/   To feel unaware.

     To not feel I'm fulfilling my potential.

/   To ruin my chances for an interesting future.

/   To change the situation.

/   To hide myself.

     To undermine my confidence.

/   To cut back my power.

/   To be out of control.

     To be aggravated.

Figure 13. First Stage in Lethe's Goal Line Analysis

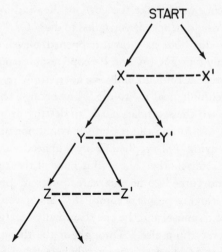

Figure 14. Diagram of Goal Line Analysis According to Osiris

so I could understand what the sessions were really like. Despite the fact that I had experimented with my E-Meter/P-Scope many times before, I was surprised at how effective the device was in forcing me to admit things I preferred to conceal. I cannot say how factually accurate the analysis was, but it did powerfully engage my emotions. The analyses of both Lethe and Osiris strike me as correct descriptions of these two people whom I came to know well. Several Powerites commented to me that Lethe was self-destructive and perhaps harmful to the people closest to her. This observation agrees with her first two goals, "to die" and "to destroy people." Osiris is a very mysterious, frightening person who is nonetheless quite loveable. He explained the results of his own therapy, using a diagram like that in Figure 14.

The letters X, Y, and Z indicate goals, arranged in a hierarchy. X', Y', and Z' are circumstances or things that block the achievement of those goals and force the person to adopt a less desirable substitute goal. Osiris explains: "There are triangles of what you want (now all those are unconscious), and what stops you from getting what you want, and what you do when you get stopped from doing what you want. And it goes on and on and on. Let's say . . . I'll give you some of mine:

"I want *to hide*.

"And what stops me from *hiding* is *people trusting me*, since this opposes my wish *to hide*.

"And what do I do to solve this dilemma? To stop you from stopping me from hiding if you trust me? I *frighten* you. Now *frightening* you becomes my second goal, because I can't get the *hiding*, so I'll get to *frighten*. Maybe that will work.

"And then you can stop me by something. Say, by *loving* me. So I can't *frighten* you anymore. So I go to maybe *killing* you.

"Then you can stop that by something."

In the diagram of triangles, X represents the goal of *hiding*. X' represents *trusting*, which prevents X and produces the alternate goal Y, which is *frightening*. Y' represents *loving*, which prevents Y and produces the alternate goal Z, which is *killing*. The sequence goes on and on. "Then it breaks. You see, I reached the bottom. I tried hiding—I couldn't. I tried frightening you—I couldn't. I tried killing you—I couldn't. Then I jump to a higher goal than the one I started with. Which would be *feeling free*, for example. And that's typical of a cycle. You start at the point which is a basic drive, and you work down. The more you are frustrated with one goal, you go to a lower goal, till you reach bottom and the cycle breaks. And you feel free. You feel good. You go to a positive part of the cycle."

All the time, the predetermined format of the questions and the P-Scope readings guided the process. When the P-Scope "registers a charge," it indicates the item that stimulated the response is "real to you." The entire process may take several sessions. "Eventually you go down to your lowest possible solution which doesn't work, and suddenly you switch to a positive." The purpose is "to find your unconscious goals. To find the pattern you follow. Because if you have in your head an idea what basically you want and how you behave about it and what stops you, it doesn't have as much power on you as it would otherwise. At least you're aware of your pattern." You have "more and more control. So when you're trying *to hide*, you wouldn't be blaming other people for being stupid or aggressive. It's just the fact that you want *to hide*. It loses much of its force upon you."

There are many other therapy processes similar to the Goal Line but designed to uncover hypothetical resistances, inhibitions, problems, or positive areas of compulsion. "Most people get into religious topics, eventually, whether it's in the most positive area or in their line of goals. It might be ultimately they want to be one with God, or they want to destroy the world, or they want to be crucified." In Chapter Three we explained that this discovery of magical goals in Compulsions Analysis was one of the chief factors transforming the therapy into a religious cult. Even as it was practiced ten years later, the Goal Line therapy leads to what participants perceive as religious desires and experiences.

P-Scope sessions were sometimes held in group, mass-production meetings where one *Therapist* would handle as many as four *Questors*, or patients. A half hour would be devoted to each Questor, so a session with four of them would last over two hours. The Therapist would sit at one side of a table, and the Questors would sit on the other side facing him. The Questors are hooked up to the P-Scope, one at a time. The Questors also take turns serving as Scribe, writing down the questions and answers. The participants render themselves psychologically naked not only before a high-status Therapist, but also before two or three peers.

The therapist would ask, "What's going on with you?" Where is your attention?" If the P-Scope indicated any charge on any question, the therapist would follow up on it, getting the Questor to talk through his feelings. A number of formal processes would also be used in these sessions. It should be obvious that these meetings not only served to solidify bonds between participants, but also functioned directly as a mechanism of social control. A participant having deviant thoughts and feelings would have a very hard time concealing them. Presumably, these sessions also functioned to inform participants (particularly the leaders) of the general situation in the chapter and any group problems that may have begun.

PSYCHIC SESSIONS FOR IPS

Several kinds of therapy and self-discovery sessions were held for inner members of the cult, including a number based on parapsychological assumptions. Here we will discuss Telepath Sessions at length, then briefly describe Forum Sessions and Mediumistics.

Like the P-Scope Sessions, Telepath Sessions were designed to uncover the compulsions, fears, and unconscious *agreements* (assumptions) that motivated participants. The controller of the session, the one who does all the psychic work, is called the Telepath, while the others are Questors. The method by which the Telepath uncovers the hidden contents of the Questors' minds is called Subliminal Contact. Power executive document S-44 warns, "Subliminal Contact is not to be discussed, practiced, or taught in the presences of any member of the general public, Disciples, or Powerites below the rank of Messenger." This prohibition acted not only to preserve the secret therapeutic treasure of The Power, but also to protect the cult from ridicule. The Telepath Sessions were among the most thoroughly occult practices of the group. Upon entering the status of Messenger, a Powerite would be given an introductory talk about sessions, in which the basic idea would be explained.

"Everything that we do, think, or feel, or that happens to us, is motivated by an agreement or compulsion in our psyche.

"Our problems stem from conflicting agreements in the psyche.

"Each of the processes that are run in Sessions is designed to bring to the surface a particular set of conflicting agreements."

So far, this sounds like conventional psychotherapeutic thinking, except for the solipsistic claim that all things that happen to a person are motivated by something within him. In one of his earliest writings, *Logic 1*, Edward wrote, "So let us be quite clear that EVERYTHING that happens to us is, on some level or other, our choice, our decision, and therefore our responsibility. . . . If someone throws a stone at you, that is his choice. But if you are hit by a stone, that is your choice." Except for this point, the theory sounds like that of Freud. The Messenger is told that these *agreements* will lose their power once they have been brought to the surface and made conscious. But the therapy reveals itself as occult through the method it uses:

Subliminal contact is the method by which the Telepath uncovers the agreements. He makes telepathic contact with the psyche of the Questor concerned, and asks the particular questions relevant to the process which he is running.

The answers to these subliminal questions come direct from the Questor's psyche, and the Telepath tells the Questor the answers so that he can write them down, explain what they mean to him, and say anything he wants to about them.

A typical Group Session might involve one Telepath and four Questors. The Telepath would be of Master or Superior rank, while the Questors might be Messengers or Prophets. They would take their places in the Sessions Room. The Telepath sits on a chair behind a desk or table, and the Questors sit in a semicircle facing him. The Questors sit some distance apart, as the instructions specify, "to allow the aura of each Questor to expand freely without touching, clashing with, or intruding upon the surrounding auras," and "to cut out any possible confusion on the part of the Group Telepath about whose projections he is receiving at any given moment, which may happen when auras are touching or overlapping one another."

Each of the Questors has a Session Book in which he writes the results of the Subliminal Contact and any comments he wishes to make about the material uncovered. In a series of such sessions, a sequence of nine different processes would be run, each using a different set of questions to uncover different agreements and compulsions. The names of these processes hint at their content: Achievement Problem Cycle, Problem Source Cycle, Intention Cycle, Resistance Process, Consequence Cycle, Line of Decisions, Line of Sources, Line of Monopolisers, and Fear Process. The last of these, for example, contains three cycles: Reality, Fear, and Love. This triad could be repeated several times in the therapy of a Questor. The shortest of these, the Reality Cycle, contains only seven questions:

1. What is Reality?   5. What is unreal to you?
2. When is Reality?   6. What could be real to you?
3. Where is Reality?   7. What is important to you?
4. What is real to you?

In P-Scope sessions, the therapist would ask these questions aloud. In Telepath Sessions, the telepath asks them telepathically. For example, in the Line of Sources process, the telepath would tell the Questor, "Now we're going to find out your most intense emotional state." Thus he informs the Questor of what the question will be. The telepath now asks the question *silently* in his own mind: "What is your most intense emotional state?" The Questor is not supposed to do anything on the conscious level. He just sits there as the telepath makes contact with his aura. The situation is similar to the Psychometry practiced in the Telepathy Developing Circle, except that the expert telepath needs no physical object and is supposedly able to focus on specific topics. After a few seconds, the telepath announces the answer he got to the subliminal question: "Paranoia."

The telepath is a senior member of the cult who presumably knows each of the Questors quite well. Paranoia may indeed be the most intense emotional state of this particular Questor, and the telepath may have observed much evidence of it over preceding weeks. After the telepath has given the answer, the Questor writes it down in his Sessions Book and may comment on it. What happens if the Questor denies that he really suffers from paranoia? One of the multitudes of therapy guidelines written by Edward says what telepaths should do if the Questor "denies the reality of the agreement":

Ask him about it; how it could be real, whether he is retreating from it or suppressing it. Also ask him subliminally for more information which will help him to see the reality. Make suggestions if necessary in question form. Use the other Questors if it feels appropriate. If it is still unreal to him, then say that you will come back to it during the discussion following the Session.

Another set of instructions told the telepath, "Always project certainty and confidence, particularly when a Questor is feeling uncertain or insecure." It is quite common for conventional psychotherapies to handle patients' doubts as symptoms rather than questions. The therapeutic system must not come into question. It is the patient who is on trial, not the therapist. However illogical and unfair, this tactic does strengthen the therapeutic system. Either the client rejects the therapy altogether or he submits to the will of the system. The Power refused to be questioned.

To show how a single cycle might work out, I will quote from one of the many secret bulletins Edward wrote for his therapists. This one deals with

the Line of Sources, a sequence of assumptions the person holds that together support a current emotional state. The bulletin was originally written in November 1965 and revised in October 1968. The set of questions
might be used in either P-Scope or Telepath sessions. For the sake of example, Edward has supplied a likely sequence of answers a Questor might give:

"What is your most intense emotional state?"
"Paranoia."
"Why is paranoia your most intense emotional state?"
"I am being watched."
"What does your paranoia stem from?"
"A need to isolate myself."
"Why does your paranoia stem from a need to isolate?"
"It keeps my attention on myself."
"What does your need to isolate stem from?"
"My knowledge of the future."
"Why does your need to isolate stem from your knowledge of the future?"
"I see things differently from other people."
"What does your knowledge of the future stem from?"
"The world is ending."
"Why does your knowledge of the future stem from the fact that the world is
ending?"
"It has been revealed to me."
"What does the fact that the world is ending stem from?"
"Nothing. It is ending."
"Why does the fact that the world is ending stem from nothing—it is ending?"
"That's the way it is."

The sequence of questions incorporates the answers as the Telepath or
Therapist receives them to produce a step-by-step process. Any kind of
answer can be incorporated. The Telepath is not looking for elaborate explanations. Note that he does not follow up on the claim that "I am being
watched." He does not ask by whom or how the person knows. He tries to
carry through to the basic assumption believed to underlie the entire psychological structure. In this case, the assumption that the world is ending.
Beyond this, the Telepath gets nothing. The impending end of the world is
a "Basic Reality" for this particular Questor.

In principle, the Questor now no longer needs to feel paranoia. His task
is to adjust meaningfully to the conviction that the world is coming to an
end. The obvious course is to accept the coming of the end within the millenarian Power, to join with others in aiding the end, preparing for the New
Age that is to come. The Questor can no longer say, "I see things differently
from other people." Other Powerites see things the same way.

This sequence of questions and answers is a very good example, because it shows the likelihood of a *supernatural outcome* in a therapy process that starts with obsessive assumptions and no anti-supernatural bias. The sequence of questions forces the answerer to search for some ultimate response that can terminate the process. Any answer less than ultimate will call forth another question. Throughout human history, religious concepts have been offered as ultimate answers. We cannot ask the same questions about the *sacred* as we can about the profane. It may be that the chief intellectual function of religious concepts is to block inquiry. The Ultimate enters language only as a semantic trick to stop an unpleasant interaction. But once the Ultimate has been invoked, it takes on the quality of reality. Beginning as a mere "etc." tacked on at the end of a limited description of the world, the supernatural comes to impress us as powerful in its own right. If we encounter the supernatural often enough, we become occultists. Powerites encountered the supernatural daily.

The Telepath Sessions were really individual therapy in a group setting, but Forum Sessions were true occult group therapy. In Forum Sessions the *agreements* held by the group as a whole were telepathically uncovered, not the agreements of individual participants. A Telepath would run the session, and any number of Inside Powerites were free to attend. These Brethren would sit in concentric semicircles in front of the Telepath. They did not have to space themselves out to keep their auras from overlapping, because it was the group aura that the Telepath was to read.

The Forum would last a half hour, followed by an hour's discussion. The main business was the discovery of group agreements. The Telepath would meditate, then speak. He might say, "There is an agreement that we must resist acknowledging fear." Then he would silently ask a subliminal question, "Why? Why is there an agreement that we must resist acknowledging fear?" The Brethren all write the agreement in their session books, and, if they wish, they also write down their "reality on the agreement." That is, each one would note his first thought on what the agreement means to him. The Telepath might announce the answer to his question, supposedly received telepathically from the aura of the group. He might name other group agreements. After the Forum proper, the Brethren would discuss the agreements in turn, their reactions to them, and their feeling about the session as a whole. We might discount the possibility that telepathy exists. But, here as in Psychometry, the belief in telepathy may provide a facilitating definition of the situation. The Telepath may feel free to bring up sensitive issues, shielded from criticism by the claim that he merely discovers an agreement already held by the group. No single individual is responsible for the content or course of the Forum Session.

The practice of Mediumistics, another occult-psychological therapy, was predicated on the existence in each person of four levels of consciousness. Messengers were first introduced to Mediumistics by a Training Officer in an advanced psychic workshop. This could be done in group sessions, but we will describe it in terms of a single Messenger guided by a single Officer. First, the Messenger would lie down and close his eyes. The Officer then spoke, with the same patter as a hypnotist, telling the Messenger: "You are relaxing. Getting more and more relaxed. You are relaxing your body and your mind. You are feeling very peaceful and very relaxed. You are relaxing your consciousness. You are becoming completely relaxed." He tells the Messenger that his next level of consciousness "is coming in." This is a part of the Messenger that he normally suppresses or hides. It is an alternate personality, not a mere fragment. The Messenger answers questions about how he feels, what his "emotions and realities" are. These are the characteristics of the second level. The Officer asks the Messenger what his name is. He will reply with a completely new name, "a word which describes the concepts embraced by the level," such as Nature, Peace, The Wanderer, or The Silent One. The Messenger becomes more acquainted with his second level, even carrying on a conversation between his first and second levels, as if they were independent persons.

In subsequent sessions of Mediumistics, the Powerite will uncover two more alternate personalities, the third and fourth levels. The first is the ordinary consciousness of the person, the second and third are said to be the psychic consciousness, while the fourth is the spiritual consciousness. After Mediumistics, a person would own six names: his Grey Name (civilian name), his Sacred Name received upon becoming a Messenger, his Magickal Name received upon becoming an Inside Powerite, and the Mediumistic names of levels two through four. Some high-status members had other identities as well. Apparently the cult adopted some of Technianity's processes for exploring previous incarnations. The E-Meter (P-Scope) is used to help the individual recall long-buried memories of past lives. Cain had been John the Baptist, while Juliet was Salome, in previous lives. Juliet had also been Queen Elizabeth the First. Cain had been other Biblical personages as well. Orpheus had been William Blake, and Abraham was at one time the Lord Krishna. Father Adam had previously lived as Adolf Hitler, and before that, as Napoleon. It would be wrong to diagnose these alternate personalities as a form of multiple-personality neurosis, an individual hysterical pathology. Rather, and more simply, we can view these personalities as play-acting. They are the projections of wishes and dreams, encouraged to utterance by the occult processes of the cult. I suggest they had nothing to do with mental illness, and I suspect the many therapy processes had very little to do with cure.

CONCLUSION

We can distinguish six closely related functions served by The Power's psychic-psychological pseudo-therapy exercises. The therapy strengthened the cult through *testing compliance*, *training obedience*, *exercising control*, *confirming the ideology*, *providing rewards*, and *increasing social cohesion*.

Although the therapy claimed to be a means that could change anyone in a positive direction, in fact many people did not have great success with it. Some could not subjugate themselves to its demands. If a newcomer was prepared to accept the requirements of the cult, he would prove this by submitting to the regulations of the therapy exercises. If he was unwilling to submit, he would fail in the sessions and be driven away. Thus the therapy functioned as an examination of the candidate for membership, testing his compliance.

Simultaneously, the therapy trained obedience. If the newcomer was compliant enough to submit to the initial sessions, he would gradually be trained to accept ever more rigorous control over his thoughts and behavior, in the end even submitting his entire self-concept and world-view for manipulation by the cult.

Not only did the therapy support the imposition of social control over the client, but in many ways it directly exercised control. Several of the therapy exercises forced the participant to express all his feelings and admit all his actions. Individual therapists, or groups of fellow Powerites, would then bend the person in the desired direction, controlling him in a subtle but absolute manner.

The therapy exercises did not seem like unjust oppression to those who participated, partly because they produced experiences that confirmed the ideology upon which they rested. After a Powerite had experienced telepathy, alternate levels of consciousness, and other psychic phenomena, he was incapable of doubting the reality of psychic concepts and unlikely to reject interpretations of the world provided by the cult. Of course, to the outsider trained in the social sciences, other, nonpsychic explanations of the experiences may seem better. But to the person who actually experienced the phenomena, and did so in a cognitive setting which presented no alternate scientific explanations, the Power ideology was proven beyond doubt.

The therapy aroused the commitment of many participants because of the intense personal gratifications it provided. The range of rewards is great: backrubs, intimate discussions, flamboyant displays, solicitous attention, a sense of glorious insights, magical status, the chance to express forbidden feelings, and the delicious smugness of participating in a world of precious secrets.

Finally, the therapy exercises were the prime strength of the cult, because they produce powerful social bonds. Earlier in this book I said that Powerites developed intense personal ties through the therapy sessions. Here we have seen how it was done. Through revealing themselves to each other, through exchanging gratifications, and through common submission to a powerful and intrusive group consciousness, Powerites were bound tightly together in their magical cult.

NINE

The Separation

Where now is the Light of the
    Lord Lucifer?
Shrouded in the Darkness of Death,
    which hangs over the earth.
Whose Death?
The Death of the Lord Christ, which
    has come full cycle, and returns
    for the Time of Reckoning, that
    the debt of pain and suffering
    might be repaid in kind.
      —Power Sabbath Assembly

I had not visited The Power for several months. My field research was in suspension. A psychiatrist with whom I taught at Harvard mentioned a letter he received from Father Abraham and Sister Ruth saying that the Boston Chapter was closed but that Massachusetts would still be served from New York. I lived not far from the old Chapter House at 46 Concord Avenue, so I adopted the habit of walking past at least once a week, just to see what was happening.

In late June, 1974, there was no sign of activity at the house. Several windows had been broken. Garbage was strewn around the lawn in back. I could see that all furniture and decorations had been stripped from the front rooms. Signs posted by a real estate company said, "No Trespassing."

A few days later, wrecking machines like mechanical tyrannosaurs began chewing away at the large building nextdoor in which The Power had rented an apartment for the children. Dark, shattered, deserted, this huge wooden structure collapsed into splinters.

The angels had been crucified. The wrecking crew found the old paintings of faceless angels. They had first hung in the original Cavern at Inman Street and spent the last three years in storage behind the Alpha bleachers. The workmen nailed them over the openings in the house to keep kids out. One angel was pinned at the very peak of the roof, covering the fire escape exit, spikes through his shoulders.

In July, an enormous steam shovel clawed at the Alpha. It had eaten the roof and was biting into the back wall, Satan's wall where the red goat's head had hung years before.

By August the site had been stripped bare to a level below the old foundations. Over the following winter, a modern brick-and-concrete apartment building rose over the grave of the cult. Leftover Powerites around Boston passed the rumor that the place was cursed and all attempts to lay the foundation of the new building had failed. The ground churned in agony and cracked the cement. But by the spring of 1975, apartments in the new building were ready for rent. By the Universal Law, the prophecy of doom spoken by the cult had returned to devastate it.

THE EXPULSION OF EDWARD DE FOREST

There are several ways to tell the story of The Great Separation. On the personal level, the schism is explained by the domestic fact that the marriage between Kitty and Edward failed, and he "ran off" with another woman, Lilith. A number of former Powerites blame Lilith, incorrectly, for the explosion that devastated their cult, and they believe falsely that her relationship with Edward is entirely destructive in nature.

Lilith says, "My whole history with The Power was very unique." She often lived with The Omega, and except for the brief time that she was head of the Rome Chapter, she was never a part of normal chapter life. She comments, "I have never been a regular Powerite." A native of New Orleans, she joined the church there in 1967. She rose rapidly to the rank of Priest, taking charge of one of the groups wandering Germany. Then she was put in charge of the Rome Chapter. Later she participated in the secret life of The Omega. She says her rise to prominence was unequalled in speed and vigor. I asked her why. "I have been told I have what's called a will to power." After helping to lead the drive to plant new American chapters in 1970, she dropped out of the cult. But in September 1971, she joined Edward and Kitty again in Toronto, only to drop out again a few months later. When The Omega moved into Mount Chi in New York, Lilith joined them once again.

A relationship developed between Edward and Lilith that rivalled his relationship with Kitty. In his terms, they were both Jehovian-Satanic, exciting, aggressive, strong-willed women. He wanted love from both of them, but they competed for exclusive possession of him. Free love became one of the key issues disturbing the upper reaches of Power society. In 1973, Edward again stressed the idea of The New Game, a concept suggested three years earlier by Lilith and connected to Edward's own desire for sexual lib-

eration. With Lucifer's hedonistic morality as his justification, he attempted to liberalize the sexual life of Inside Powerites.

It was an emotionally difficult time for Edward, and he was not able to
carry out a consistent policy. He suffered intense depression and self-doubt
from November 1973 through March 1974. Kitty and the Masters of the
cult found his behavior to be erratic and bizarre. Tension grew. One
Powerite told a newspaper reporter that The New Game was the cause of
the trouble, saying, "I guess you could say it was a sort of community sex
thing with members of the cult. It was really becoming a weird scene.
The sex thing was causing a lot of dissension and jealousy among our
members." Some Masters actually accused Edward and Lilith of having
sex relations with their dogs.

In previous chapters we said that a major crisis had developed for the cult.
The source of this threat to its existence was no single narrow subject like
sex, but the more general issues of which sex was but one aspect—cultural
contradictions which had been with The Power since the beginning. The
cult had sought escape from the world; it had sought glory within the
world. Both quests had failed, but the economic livelihood of the group was
now tied to accommodation with society. Edward represented the imprac-
tical but unrepentant cult desire to transcend the limitations of reality.
He urged liberation, while the Masters had come to demand control. The
cult expected him to help resolve its problems, but instead he disrupted the
social order in obsession with his own troubles.

In March 1974, the leaders of the cult decided that a special attempt
must be made to straighten out the relationships between the members of
The Omega. The church rented an apartment in New York City for Edward and Lilith, where they could work through their affair and decide what
they wanted to do. One informant tells me this was Kitty's idea. Although
the apartment was paid up for a month, the couple stayed only a few days.
Lilith became almost paranoid, afraid that Kitty might resort to violence,
perhaps kidnapping her and her dog Satan.

On March 23, a meeting of The Council of Masters removed Edward
from the office of Teacher of The Power. On the twenty-sixth, Father Moses
and Father Pius tried to get Edward to sign a document giving up his
authority over various assets. On the following day, Edward withdrew
$1,000 from a church bank account to which he had access, and flew to
Mexico with Lilith. They wanted to get away from the complex situation in
New York and think things over. Edward was not inclined to fight the
Masters for control of The Power. Always passive, always introspective, he
needed peace and quiet in which to sift through his emotions. Edward and
Lilith were drawn to Xtul.

Edward of course had been at Xtul with the original group in 1966, but for Lilith the place was only a legend. The first sight of Xtul made a great impression on her. "It was incredible! It really was. It's right outside this tiny Mayan village. You're kind-of walking along this road through the jungle, and all-of-a-sudden you come to this great big stand of palm trees. And palm trees are not native down there. It's this sudden grove of palm trees. And buildings—these deserted ruins that are there—right on the beach, which is incredibly beautiful. Just the most extraordinary place. Very physically beautiful. Very magical. Very calm feeling there. It was a time for us—in fact, the Separation had just taken place when Edward and I went to Xtul—it was like being in the eye of a hurricane. There were all these things happening, and Xtul just seemed to lay a blanket of serenity."

On April 17, Edward and Lilith arrived in New Orleans. They stayed with her family and tried to communicate with members of the local Power chapter. Edward went to the chapter house and spoke briefly with Father Esau and Mother Cybele but was soon asked to leave. Edward attempted to make a statement at a Sabbath Assembly meeting but was barred from the ritual. He phoned Father Cain long-distance and asked for a Masters' Meeting to discuss the situation, but Cain rejected the idea. He phoned the other chapters, but most refused even to accept his call.

At this time, power in the cult was formally held by Cain, Pius, Siegfried, and Moses, because their names were on the church incorporation documents. They called themselves The Four. Edward believed, I think falsely, that the real power was in Kitty's hands. In any case, The Four held the bureaucratic instruments of power. So long as Edward failed to exercise his charismatic power, he was powerless. He hesitated. With every day that passed, the new leadership grew stronger and the possibility that Edward might regain his status with The Power diminished.

Edward and Lilith settled for a time into ordinary civilian life in New Orleans. She took a job in a hospital, but almost immediately fell seriously ill with hepatitis. Edward took whatever job he could, unashamed to become a common laborer for a while, if that was what "the signs" indicated. He helped deliver and install floor carpeting. Then he got a job with an architectural firm. Edward and Lilith stayed in the city through the summer, struggling along without a clear plan for the future.

THE ESTABLISHMENT

In every way, it was a bad time for the cult. Income, spirits, and membership declined. By the end of 1973, Messengers were dropping out in dangerous numbers. The January Blue Sale had failed to replenish the supply of workers. Edward's expulsion magnified the disillusionment and confusion that Powerites already felt, and it nearly caused a final collapse. The leaders decided to close two of the six chapters, Miami and Boston. The New York Chapter could send donating trips throughout New England, while New Orleans could cover the South. The cult was in a state of confusion for perhaps a year after Edward's expulsion, but the first couple of months were the most traumatic.

Kitty and The Four had to complete The Separation from Edward by expelling his works. To eradicate his influence and to protect themselves if he were to assert a legal claim, they decided to cast out his Teachings. As we will see in a few pages, they also quite reasonably felt that the ideology developed by Edward had proven to be a complete failure. The issue of *The Powerites* dated May 1974, but probably edited in March, was the last to contain Edward's picture or anything written by him. There is no mention of him at all in the final issue of *The Powerites*, dated June 1974.

In May, *The Power—Church of Armageddon* was renamed *The Establishment—Church of the Apocalypse*. Members were no longer called Powerites, but Establishers. The monthly magazine became *The Establishers*. The fancy quarterly color publication, *Power—Visions of the Apocalypse* became *Establishment—Visions of the Apocalypse*. The formats of the magazines were kept exactly the same. Old photographs were carefully used for a few months, until new ones were ready. In a press release, reprinted in the first issue of *The Establishers*, Father Siegfried, on behalf of The Four, announced, "There has been a growing doctrinal and personal conflict between the Church's governing body, the Council of Masters, and Edward de Forest, chief theological writer for The Power Church." Notice that Siegfried describes Edward's functions very narrowly. "The Establishment Church of the Apocalypse is an important break with the old and represents the establishment of a new order, which we hope, with God's guidance, will be part of the foundation upon which He builds His millennium."

A cover letter, sent to newsmen with copies of this press release, explained: "We have broken away from the old Power Church, and the new Establishment Church of the Apocalypse has been established. . . ." The Establishment held all the assets of The Power, occupied the remaining chapter houses, and kept most of the higher-level membership. In December 1974, Father Siegfried explained, "In essence what occurred, in a purely legal sense, last summer, was a change of name situation."

For a short time, the cult tried to replace Edward with a new figurehead. Father Adam was put forward to fill the role vacated by Edward's expulsion. The last issue of *The Powerites* and the third issue of *The Establishers* carry brief emotional essays signed by him, printed under a dramatically lit photograph. He looks somewhat like Edward and is sometimes mistaken for a relative. People think the two men are brothers. When Adam lets his blond hair and beard grow, like Edward he resembles the popular conception of Jesus Christ. On the first day of Adam's brief reign as cult figurehead, he appeared at the New York Chapter flanked by two attendants and dressed in a pure white suit with gold jewelry. His star fell as quickly as it had risen. Adam was well liked but had no legitimate claim to leadership. Members thought his white suit was silly. The cult decided it no longer needed a charismatic leader or figurehead.

Most low-status members found out about the Separation abruptly, without warning. Suddenly one Saturday, several sections were cut out of the Sabbath Assembly. In New York, Father Siegfried was the Evangelist. He gave a stormy sermon condemning Edward and his ways, giving the congregation a simple choice. "You're either for us or against us. All those who are for us, please stay. All those who are against us, please leave." A few left.

All Power literature was withdrawn from circulation. Thousands of copies of various writings and magazines were kept in storage in Toronto for at least two years. At the Chicago Chapter, paint remover was used to take *The Power* off the blue plastic covers of the Assembly hymnals, but within a few weeks the hymnals themselves were withdrawn. Many copies of the inner teachings and administrative documents, The Missal, were burned. Melvin Potts was part of the detail that burned Missals in New York. They were carried in piles to an open space behind the Chapter House and burned in a large metal can. Several Establishment leaders told me that all copies of the Missal had been destroyed, but over the next two years a few intact Missals turned up. There was a touching rumor that Father Remus, the brother of Edward de Forest, had hidden a complete copy in an elevator shaft, but this story was never confirmed. I obtained my copy in Canada.

Brother Faust, who was an IP Messenger in New York until just after the split, has described that period to me. The Teachings were phased out over the first few weeks after Edward's expulsion. "Everyone was waiting for the great revelation— what really went on—a spiritual interpretation of the scandal." Fathers Cain and Moses held four days of meetings, explaining radical doctrinal changes. From two in the afternoon until eleven or twelve at night, a few of the key ideas were thrashed out at length. It was explained that Edward was indeed a manifestation of Christ, but that Christ was in truth a negative being. I am told there was even a solemn exorcism ritual in which both Satan and Christ were cast out of the New York Chapter.

Everyone was urged "to overcome their Christ and Satan parts," which were described as "malevolent spirits." Lucifer, oddly enough, simply faded from the scene. Only Jehovah remained, triumphant over the other Gods, now recognized as the one true God.

THE ESTABLISHMENT VIEW

On my first visit to the New York branch of the Establishment, I naturally asked my former Powerite friends why the Separation had occurred. Sister Tamar told me they had tried the old way of The Power and found it "would not work." What did this mean? First, she said, The Power was not receiving a favorable response from the public. People were repelled by the image and doctrines of the cult. Second, members themselves felt they had lost a sense of purpose. What they were doing had lost its meaning. When I spoke with Brother Eros, he stressed these same two points.

Brother Ariel, who left immediately before Edward's expulsion, has given a slightly different explanation. He says the cult had overfished its spiritual sea. The street work became tougher because "our areas were drying up because of misuse and donating. We had overused them, in a sense. Donating was a hassle because people were nasty to us on the streets because they'd been stopped too many times. There was high demand to make more money than we'd ever made before, when it wasn't even possible to make the same amount." Obsessed with its own problems, the leadership was no longer able to give the Messengers security or direction, only demands. Yonge Street, a main donating area in Toronto, was one example of fished-out territory. For over two years, almost every day, the cult sent donators to beg from shoppers and businessmen in the space of a few city blocks. "Everybody insulted you—'Get the fuck out of here!'—so donating was hard, and they kept expecting us to make ten to fifteen dollars an hour."

Many attempts had been made to find glory. Pseudo-therapeutic self-discovery had been very exciting in 1963, but after ten years it had lost all of its attraction for Powerites. They had tried wild, exciting adventures in Xtul, in Germany, and in many public and private settings. Adventure was only a strain to them now. The most recent attempt to find glory had been a bid for warm acceptance by the general public. Success would not have afforded transcendence from the human condition, but at least it would have been success. The group was not ready to give up on the general public, because it had not become economically dependent upon steady income from outsiders. The IPs had returned to a comfortable middle-class lifestyle, complete with television sets and small children. The cult had gone most of the distance toward becoming a church. Forced by failure to change again, it changed further in the direction of conventional church status.

When I last interviewed them, Establishers had had two years to look back and develop their theory of what went wrong in The Power, both to quell painful memories and to provide a basis for future decisions. They often describe it in theological terms, in terms of falling away from the correct, traditional teachings of God. Siegfried says, "Our problems arose with the doctrine of the Unity." The twin theological innovations of The Unity of Christ and Satan and the Great Gods of the Universe are described as vast mistakes. Power theory attempted to define evil out of existence. As I see it, this meant that social control was precarious, and if exercised, created great internal cultural contradictions. One God can represent the authority of the leaders, but several Gods must represent moral chaos. As I did, the reader may find the celestial committee composed of Lucifer, Jehovah, Christ, and Satan attractive. They symbolize pluralism, liberalism, the modern temperament in medieval guise. To follow them, one must be a relatively free, versatile person. The Masters of the cult wanted a God through which they could control their followers, not a collection of Gods each making costly demands on the Masters.

Power theology was too abstract and intellectualized, Establishers now say. To some extent they blame Edward. As Elijah told me, and as I have observed for myself, Edward's thought processes are extremely "paradigmatic," in the sense that he analyzes everything in terms of ideal types and categorical schemes. As Elijah put it, "He would paradigm anything he could get his hands on. The bucket was never a bucket, it was a *Platonic Bucket*." He still respects Edward, however, and calls him an "extremely good theorist."

Establishers take much of the blame on themselves and say that while the theology was primarily Edward's invention, they all participated in producing it, and all accepted it with enthusiasm at first. Moses calls the idea of The Unity of Christ and Satan "a fascinating, very beautiful philosophy." At first "it seemed very good in almost every way," but later it proved "workable in no way." Abraham says The Power had a tendency to seek purely intellectual and symbolic solutions for what were real, practical problems, "to explain something with another explanation, and then to explain *that* with *another* explanation. And I think our theology began to proliferate in a way that was becoming more and more removed from the original. It wasn't theology that attracted us in the first place. It was the concept of being able to *do* something about our situation. You can sit in your armchair and write catechisms, but it actually doesn't produce any change."

They blamed Jesus Christ as much as Edward de Forest. Siegfried says that The Unity of Christ and Satan "looked like a very logical extension of the whole Love Your Enemies teaching. It seemed like a very viable way of overcoming hatred, of overcoming fear." Cain feels that "What we were doing was seeing whether taking what Christ is historically said to have taught to its logical conclusions" would really work. "And we found that it didn't." When the Establishment exorcised Christ along with Satan, it was expelling a particular conception of Christ. "What we were rejecting was the kind of love which is weak and leads to a lowering of standards."

The Christian message, as interpreted by Edward, had weakened the cult both emotionally and financially. As we saw in earlier chapters, in the 1970s The Power evolved into a social service organization, attempting to feed and rehabilitate miserable, unproductive people with few virtues or attractive qualities. I argued that this followed from the cult's need to present itself as a church, and from the exigencies of the history of The Power, particularly its economic and recruitment traditions. But on the theological level, this was what Christ and Edward seemed to demand. Abraham came to ask, "How effective am I, say, spending my evenings sitting down next to some poor old guy who's an alcoholic and who has nothing else in his head but that?" Were the continual visits to Willowbrook and other homes for the retarded really worthwhile? "I've been to Willowbrook or its equivalent until it's come out my ears!" The Power had burned out.[1]

Father David spoke with great feeling, even agony. "In the last six years, we've plumbed the depths, at times, of our own negativity, collectively and individually. That was one of the realities of The Power that we were setting out to [change when we became The Establishment]." When Edward suggested The Unity of Christ and Satan, "he commanded quite a lot of respect from a lot of people. So it was a case of, 'Okay, let's try it.' " Like Siegfried, Cain, Moses, and Abraham, Father David came to feel "It works in theory; it doesn't work in practice." He exclaims, "We tried to make it work! We believed it! We felt, 'It should work! It really should work, you know!' Helping people and loving your enemies. When we tried to help people, they didn't want to be helped. Because what we were putting out was The Unity of Christ and Satan, we would love the enemy and everybody as it were, the kind of people that we attracted were for the most part [disordered people with nothing to contribute]. These people didn't want our

[1] Herbert J. Freudenberger, "Staff Burn-Out," *Journal of Social Issues* 30:1 (1974): 159–165.

message. They just wanted handouts, clothing." It was a terrible strain to try to help them, even worse because it was useless.

"We were out there earning the money, paying for the coffee houses for these people to come in and tear apart. We lost a lot of energy. We lowered our standards to allow people to join, because we needed people. We lost energy going into giving and giving and giving and giving and giving and giving and giving and giving into a big black hole. We plumbed the depths, and that was the major bottom that we had. We almost folded. Almost didn't make it. Oh, awful! Awful! We really had to do something drastic. So we took it to the man and we said, 'Unity doesn't work, Edward. Afraid. Sorry.' Collective, it was a collective thing. Edward was appointed, as I'm sure you're aware, by a Council of Masters. The Council of Masters took it to Edward, and Edward said, 'Well, I still believe in it.' So they said, 'Well, bye. . . .' "

Edward, of course, had been rather thoroughly insulated from the problems faced by his followers, living apart from any of the chapters at places like Key Largo and Mount Chi. "He hadn't done what we'd done. He'd never done it on the street! He'd never done it in the coffee houses. He couldn't understand that it couldn't work. As far as we were concerned, by our fruits we were seeing that it didn't work. It was hard. It was getting harder. We were being hurt. So we had to make a clean sweep. When we did that, when we formed The Establishment, there was a vision of Jehovah again. It was a vision of what it was like at the start. We saw where we were, and I cried. I cried inside. I cried to people. And also I cried in music. I was so involved trying to earn money to support people who didn't want my help. I'd lost my original vision, love, fire in the belly. And when I saw it again I was like a baby. I broke down! I cried! I cried with release and relief. I was also angry. I was angry at Edward de Forest. There was an awful lot of failure. The numbers of things that we tried to achieve! And they all failed. The Power was a complete failure, as far as we were concerned. There was a period there when we were foundering around. We didn't know where we were going. We just knew that we had to get back to God."

The Establishment really dates the Separation from Christmas 1973, rather than from Edward's expulsion three months later, because the major issue was first raised at the cult's year-end meeting of the Council of Masters. Siegfried says, "That conference was the first time that serious doubts had been expressed in a conference-type situation about this whole theology of The Unity." All the important people were there, and Siegfried agrees with David that many Masters felt that the doctrine was a failure. " 'We don't feel it.' 'It's a lie.' 'We're telling ourselves a lie.' 'We're telling other people a lie.' 'This is not what God's about.' There'd been a number of feelings like that. Through the early part of '74, those feelings grew stronger. It came to a head in the spring of '74, when it became quite clear that the vast majority of us couldn't stomach this any longer. It felt to us to be completely alien to what we'd started out with in the first place, way back in Xtul. But to de Forest it was his life's work. He'd suggested this particular theology, and he felt it was the answer for him, so we said, 'Okay, Edward, you have The Power and its doctrines. We will start again.' "

EMERGENCE OF THE ESTABLISHMENT CULTURE

When one cult seeks to imitate the success of another, or when one splits from another, it must balance the need to copy with the need to differentiate. The Establishment had to reject much of the old Power without giving up the strongest aspects of the original culture. The leaders could not discard everything instantly, and they adopted various tactics for achieving change at the least cost. One approach was to rename things; a related approach was to reinterpret them. The Power had developed a public vocabulary of coined words. The Establishment retained much of the reality, changing only the image. Table 10 gives a comparative glossary of Power and Establishment terms, with their common meanings. Most of the new terminology came in during the first weeks of the "new church" and was a very inexpensive way of producing great superficial change.

All of the Power's emblems were abandoned. The badges, crosses, and special rings were "deconsecrated" and either destroyed or sold as simple jewelry. All of the marked ritual equipment, including priests' tabards, were discarded. Only one emblem was invented to replace the several given up. Father Moses says, "I think we played around with quite a number of things that somehow reflect what we are, or were, or wanted to be." The natural symbol for Jehovah was the six-pointed Star of David. Mother Sibyl, who had invented the original, straight-armed Power Sign, drew a very similar new monogram for The Establishment. The first emblem had been the letter P for *Power*; the new one was based on the letter E for *Establishment*. The final result was a six-pointed star with a capital E in the center. Moses says, "When this one came up, it just kind of rang bells with everybody, and we floated it around quite a lot of people, people with either an artistic or symbol-minded type of concern. And everybody seemed to think: 'This is great. That gets it.' "

Moses says the Establishment culture, like that of The Power, was built up eclectically, taking the best from many sources. It "is compiled out of

Table 10: **Glossary of Word Transformations**

Power Words	Establishment Words	Meanings
Ritual Terms:		
Alpha	Sanctum	the main ritual room
Altar	Shrine	the ritual table
Assembly	Celebration	a group ritual
Sacrifist	Celebrant	presiding priest at a ritual
Evangelist	Herald	priest that gives the sermon
Servers	Bearers	ritual assistants
Membership Ranks:		
Master	Luminary	the top leaders
Provisional Master	Minor Luminary	lieutenant leaders
Superior	Celebrant	junior "Mothers" and "Fathers"
Prophet	Mentor	senior "Brothers" and "Sisters"
IP Messenger	Covenantor	lowest rank of "ministers"
OP Messenger	Witness	student ministers
Disciple	Lay Establisher	lay member who tithes
Initiate	Aspirant	new member
General:		
Power	Establishment	name of the group
Chapters	Establishments	branches of the church
IPs	Elect	core members, "ministers"
Donating	Funding	the street work
Baptize	Consecrate	initiate to a new status
DJ (Dow-Jones)	JF (Jehovah's Finances)	financial indicator
The Cavern	The Garden	the coffee house

thoughts, ideas, suggestions, things that people throw in or offer." One day, someone suggested that there should be flowers in the Sanctum for the various celebrations. "Then somebody came along and gave us a white rose, one week. And I thought: Oh, a white rose. A white rose symbolizes purity. We'll put it on the shrine in the celebration. So every week we have a white rose there." In May 1976, at some church festivity, a middle-aged Jewish man named Jerry was "doing a little number." He brought with him a shofar, the Jewish ram's-horn trumpet. He said, "This is a shofar; we'll give it to the Establishment." Moses comments, "So obviously we had to use it. What is a shofar? It's for calling people to God. The obvious thing to do was to blow it at the start of every Sabbath Celebration."

Some hymns and chants were abandoned immediately, because their words and concepts were completely obsolete. Others were merely changed. For example, the second stanza of Power chant number twelve, "Together we are come," expressed the value of community, the coming together of individuals mirroring the coming together of the parts of God. The Establishment version of the same chant stresses the dominance of Jehovah. It preaches dedication to Him rather than commitment to the community.

Power Version	Establishment Version
Alone we are nothing,	Alone we are nothing,
Together we have strength;	With You we have strength,
Strength in our Unity,	Strength in our purpose,
The Unity of God.	The Glory of God.

For two years the church rituals limped along without printed hymnals. Little one-page "hymnlets" gave the words of the specific hymns selected for a Celebration, and the church printed several versions of hymnlets which were rotated for different weeks. Establishers composed many songs, and finally in 1976 a modest hymnal was printed, incorporating suitable old Power hymns, some modified ones, and several new ones. Not all were composed by inner members. Hymn 25, "The Awaited One," was written by a young guitarist named Greek, who was with The Establishment in New Orleans for a while, and who, as Moses says, "wrote this very beautiful atmospheric piece, and then went off his own way."

> In every land there is a song
> From the far horizons of time
> A legend that's told in every tongue
> The Awaited One shall come.

In doctrine, The Establishment is a bland simulacrum of a millenarian Jewish sect. It announces that the Messiah is coming soon, for the first time. Jesus was not the Messiah. Neither was Edward. Until the Messiah comes, we should live virtuous lives according to the laws of the Old Testament. Establishers use a few Jewish terms, several showing up in hymn texts. The group's password is *Shalom*. Gone are the days of "As it is . . . so be it." Establishers never wear crosses, but only their Stars of David. Several months after The Separation, I overheard one of the Establishment children warn a visitor who wore a cross that the man would go to Hell if he followed Christ. The church celebrates neither Christian nor Jewish holidays, and does not follow Jewish dietary laws.

The clientele of the church has changed radically. In contrast to the old days, many of the people served by the church are unhappy middle-aged people, considerably older than the ministers. In New York particularly, the clientele is primarily Jewish. A number of steady customers speak with Eastern European accents and bring in with them many elements of traditional Jewish culture. It is possible there is a market for a psychic-occult millenarian Jewish sect in America today. If so, The Establishment may eventually achieve success. But it must be emphasized that most Establishers do not come from Jewish families. I was able to determine the religious origins of twenty-five dedicated Establishers, and only five were Jewish. An equal number were Roman Catholic, and there was an Armenian Orthodox, a Unitarian, and one with no religious training at all. The other twelve were all Protestants: five Anglicans, two Presbyterians, and five from other denominations. Perhaps the doctrines of the group are so vague because they represent the lowest common denominator of beliefs held from childhood by members.

Mother Amaranth recited the basic tenets of the group on one of its radio shows in early 1975: "The Establishment Church believes that a Messiah will come, not as some supernatural being, but as a person with the qualities of leadership that will inspire people to a new way of living. Meanwhile, our function is to provide spiritual and moral leadership, to assert and affirm the values and codes in which we believe, to help and support people in need, and to offer a cause and a purpose for those looking for meaning in their lives and searching for truth within themselves."

Under such titles as Psychic Workshop, Focus, and Forum, the church presents some of the most basic psychic activities that used to be performed in the Telepathy Developing Circles and the Progresses. I participated in several of the psychic activities at the New York and Chicago Establishments, and discovered that much of the material was left over from The Power. Although the Missals were discarded, I was interested to discover that the leaders of the meetings most like the old Progresses were still using the same Training Synopses of Edward's writings that they had used years before. Edward's psychology theory, much of it at least, is still in use, although the fact is not made clear to any newcomer. Many Establishers still type each other in terms of God Patterns, although they no longer accept any God but Jehovah.

In the summer of 1976, Cain and Moses produced two doctrinal courses. I secured tapes of Cain's five-meeting course and discovered that it was hardly a course at all, but really brief statements followed by free-floating discussions. Titled *The New Reality*, this course covers five topics: love, the mind, God, morality, and the world. The few ideas in the lectures are a mixture of the most sentimental conventional religiosity and a few leftover Power concepts. Occasionally Cain quotes the Bible. At one point he retells the Garden of Eden story. In the third lecture he discusses the different ideas people have about God—mentioning the Power's Gods obliquely—then argues that the only true God is Jehovah, the God of the Old Testament.

Cain's introductory lecture is about love. We all desire love, he says. Love from family and friends is not great enough and not secure. We long for more, for something greater, something more reliable. It is a mistake to depend entirely on human beings. What we really need is love from God: perfect love, complete love, infinite love. We must keep God's commandments, or we will be cut off from Him, from the source of all love. "The ability to love is totally and solely dependent on being receptive to God." We could say that the original social implosion that produced The Power was driven by the hunger for infinite love. Not finding it in each other, not finding it in Edward de Forest, the old Powerites have now turned to Jehovah, an invisible and therefore indisputable source of such love.

Poor in specific doctrines, The Establishment fills the gap with occult and psychic speculations. The church does not commit itself to belief in Astrology, Telepathy, the human Aura, or whatever, but toys with these concepts as tentative, surrogate, low-level doctrine. It has become a psychic supermarket, purveying whatever occult nonsense it can, indulging in whatever psychic activities seem to appeal to people.

When I visited the Chicago Establishment in September 1975, Father Mark took me along with him to a Psychic Fair being held by a number of occult groups in a magnificent lakeside convention center. The fair organizer, an independent entrepreneur, leased convention hall space, then rented booths to about thirty groups and individuals. There were palm readers, sellers of mystic equipment, representatives of Silva Mind Control, and every manner of occult professional. The Establishment had rented a double-sized booth for $150. They propped their big Star of David symbol up on a chair and offered Psychic Readings (Psychometry) for $5 and $10. I paid Brother Dagon $10 to do a reading, using my hand as the Psychometry object, focusing on the question of whether The Establishment would like my book when it came out. He said yes. I think he was wrong. Mark told me at that time that the church is not and didn't want to be known as "a group of psychics. That's not our shtick." Rather, he said, it is a religious group interested in psychic phenomena.

In its early days, The Power presented its own message and was not hospitable to people who wanted to use the cult as a forum for their own non-Powerite beliefs. Today, however, The Establishment invites many occult lecturers to give presentations. The Establishment refers to itself as a "psychic center," if not exactly a psychic supermarket, and uses the contributions of famous occultists to build its own fame and make a little money. Among the subjects covered in lectures and demonstrations given by outsiders at the New York Establishment in 1976 were: Acupuncture, Alchemy, Astrology, Auras, The Bermuda Triangle, Biofeedback, Dowsing, ESP, Etheric Movement, Eurythmy, Hindu Astrology, Huna, Hypnosis, Iridology, Jungian Psychotherapy, Kirlian Photography, Naturopathy, Numerology, Psychotronics, Pyramid Power, Reflexology, Sufism, The Scudder Method of Healing, Telekinesis, Tibetan Buddhism, UFOs, and Zen Meditation. The Establishment has held its own Psychic Fairs, a Psychic Festival, a Spiritual Technology Conference, Psychic Weekends, and an occult boat cruise around Manhattan.

The church tries to make money at all its activities. It passes collection plates in the Sabbath rituals, something The Power never did. It charges admission for the guest lectures, then splits the take with the lecturers. Admission to the Focus or Forum (Progress) activities is $2. Psychic Readings, such as the one Sister Tamar gave me in New York, generally run $5 for fifteen minutes. Sister Samaria does Psychic Sketches, pastel drawings that go for a few dollars. More money comes in from individual healing sessions, aura readings, and Spiritual Consultations which cost $30. The Establishment holds courses in occult practices. The fee for Sister Roxana's course "An Introduction to Astrology" is $70, while Mother Isis' eight "Spiritual Healing" classes have a $100 fee.

TRANSFORMATIONS OF RITUAL

The Sabbath ritual evolved rapidly after The Separation, but the changes merely continued the trends in the last year of The Power. Figure 15 shows the layout of the New York Sanctum for the Sabbath Celebrations held there after mid-1975. Both the physical layout and dramatic performance made it entirely clear that the priests had become professional mediators between the congregation and God. They were no longer extensions of the

KEY

C = Celebrant (Sacrifist)   S = Lead Singer
W = Water Bearer   cb = Collection Bowl
F = Fire
              chair, with triangle showing
              direction person faces

Figure 15. Layout of the Establishment's Sabbath Celebration

congregation, expressing the Gods that dwelled within, as they had been in the classical Power.

The rituals, strangely, had also lost their mysticism, their sacredness, and their profundity. The Celebrations had become *entertainments*. A year after The Separation, on February 22, 1975, I wrote in my field notes, "The Sabbath Celebration was more like a religious variety show than a group ritual. Father Pan started it off, pacing back and forth in front of the stage during the beginning like a warm-up MC from a TV show. He even began with jokes." At several rituals I attended over the next year and a half, the priests would suddenly drop character and explain to the audience what was going on, particularly when they were introducing a change in the ritual or a new song, but also at other times as well. The Celebrant (Sacrifist) acted like a Master of Ceremonies, introducing the Herald (Evangelist) and musical soloists by name. In the old Power, the Sacrifist and Evangelist almost always kept a haughty detachment, seldom making eye contact with members of the congregation, never smiling except in the Revelation, infusing the ritual with as much drama and mystery as they could muster. The Establishment seemed more amateurish in its theatrics, perhaps because they were now conceived as theatrics rather than something more real.

I observed the ritual room of the New York branch evolve into a small theater from the time the building was first occupied at the beginning of 1975 until September 1976, when I terminated my field research. In early 1975, the ritual took place on a broad, low stage, covered by a carpet. Over the months, the Establishers built four tiers of risers on three sides, transforming the room into a modern small theater with a sunken stage. They set up theatrical lighting controlled from a booth at the back. There was even a sound system. The audience for these presentations seldom surpassed seventy-five, however, including all the Establishers. The smaller Chicago branch, with a miniscule clientele, continued to use a low stage and did not invest in elaborate remodeling of the ritual room.

The Shrine (altar) was a table, of various construction at different times and chapters, supporting small pieces of ritual equipment, including two custom-made seven-candle candelabras. I hesitate to call them menorahs, because I never heard an Establisher use this Jewish term. Hanging behind the Shrine, a few inches in front of the back wall, was a gold Star of David, about a yard across, with a huge, blue capital *E* in the center. Stage lighting was set so that at certain points in the ritual colored shadows of this emblem were cast on the white wall, symbolizing the presence of Jehovah.

Several old symbols were reinterpreted. The best example is the traditional use of fire and water. The New York Establishment took over the old Boston altar stands and the two silver bowls that had been contributed by Ron Forbes. One held water; the other contained a flaming sterno can. Near the entrance of the ritual room, the Establishers placed a second set of fire and water bowls on a little table. In the early days, Edward had introduced the use of fire and water to symbolize Satan and Christ. Every initiation ceremony, at every level, administered fire and water to transform the candidate into his new status. The Establishment retained these evocative symbols but reinterpreted their meaning. As Moses told me in 1976, "They symbolized something different then from what they symbolize now, but they're still as symbolic and as usable. It's such an old, original, basic symbolism of God—the fire and the water, those two basic elements—the one representing the spirit and the other representing the physical." In Power initiation rituals and the Union Ceremony, The Hymn of Consecration would accompany the anointing with fire and water. One phrase was chant-

ed many times: "May the Water give me Life, Purify me with the Fire."
One verse sang of water and Christ, while another chanted to Satan:

> Purify me with the Fire,
> Satan, test me in Your Pit of Fire, desire. . . .
> Purify me with the Fire,
> Tell me how to give my life to You.

After The Separation, The Establishment quickly dropped the Christ
and Satan verses, and The Consecration Chant became the simple repeti-
tion, over and over, of "May the Water give me Life, Purify me with the
Fire." There was no longer any explanation of what the fire and water
represented. In February 1975, a new chant was introduced, with fresh
music that gave new meaning to the symbolic elements:

> By the Fire of Purification
> And by the Water of Life
> May the Great Lord Jehovah
> Be with us now and forever.

One important piece of stage business used by The Power and modified
in several forms by The Establishment was the blessing of the congregation
using the fire and water. Called *The Invitation*, this blessing was spoken in
the Sabbath Assembly by the Sacrifist. He rose to his feet, standing at his
end of the circle of participants, facing the altar with the two bowls on
stands at either side. As he spoke, he raised first one arm, then the other,
pointing with two fingers of one hand straight at the water bowl, then with
two fingers of the other hand at the fire:

> May the life-giving Water of the Lord Christ
> and the purifying Fire of the Lord Satan
> bring the presence of Love and Unity
> into this Assembly

Immediately after The Separation, The Establishment changed this to:

> May the Fire of Purification
> and the Water of Life
> bring the presence of love
> into this Celebration.

Again, Christ and Satan have been removed from the symbolism, but the
theatrically successful blessing with fire and water has been retained. A year
later, the relevance of the symbols to the Lord Jehovah was stressed, and the
complexity of the stage business was greatly increased. Early in the Sabbath
Celebration, the Celebrant (Sacrifist) would stand in front of the Shrine
(altar), facing the congregation. The two Bearers of the bowls would come

forward and stand on either side of him. The fire was not yet lit, and the water bowl was still empty. As he spoke, the Celebrant would take a burning taper from the altar and light the fire, then pour water into the other bowl from a flask that also had been resting on the altar. His words were an explanation to the congregation:

> This is the Fire of Purification through which
> our Lord Jehovah shall purge all sin and
> sickness from the world and from each of us.
> And this is the Water of Life through which He
> will invest in us His Spirit for the Millennium.

Another version of this blessing was used in Midnight Celebration rituals, the successor to The Power's Midnight Meditations. By the end of my observation period, September 1976, the original Invitation had been altered to dramatize explicitly the transformed theological universe of the church. The Powerite Sacrifist pointed his hands toward the center of the encircling congregation as he spoke The Invitation. As we have seen, the focus of attention in the rituals before 1973 was at the center of the congregation. All the cosmic principles were conceived of as dwelling within the social group that comprised the cult. The Establishment worships a distant God, Jehovah who dwells in Heaven. When priests speak to Jehovah in the Establishment rituals, they either gaze upward or face the altar where His symbol hangs. The focus is above and beyond the social group, in some cosmic realm quite outside the congregation. In the Midnight Celebration version of The Invitation, the Bearers come forward with their bowls, the fire already burning brightly and the water sloshing. As in the old Power initiation rituals, the priest passes his fingers through the fire and dips them in the water as he speaks. But instead of pointing into the congregation, he raises his hands, two fingers of each extended as before, and points upward, at Heaven. His words stress the new theology:

> By the Fire of Purification
> And by the Water of Life
> May this Celebration be filled with
> praise and exaltation to
> Our Lord Jehovah
> and to his Messiah.

ESTABLISHMENT SOCIETY

The social organization of The Establishment is based on traditions developed by The Power, but there have been changes. The first eighteen months after The Separation were a time in which Establishers concentrated on re-

newing their internal society and paid relatively little attention to those
who used to be called OPs. The rank of Acolyte was dropped, and the rank
of Initiate, now called Aspirant, was restricted to those few individuals
working to become Witnesses (OP Messengers). The Witnesses lived in
their own apartment, as had OP Messengers before them, but very few new
people were recruited during the months of crisis. The most troublesome
Disciples were driven away, and those few that remained were called Lay
Establishers. Asserting a distinction between clergy and laity, this name
indicated a further step toward conventional church status. Formerly there
had merely been several steps in increasing commitment. Witnesses were
often described as "student ministers," while those above Witness rank, the
Elect, were "ministers." In mid-1976, another status was invented, that of
Friend of the Establishment, similar to Lay Establisher except that Friends
did not have to tithe but merely to make significant, continuing contributions in labor or money. The great mass of the people who attended Establishment psychic activities had no status in the church and tended to be a
fluid population.

One important change was the emergence of the New York branch as a
supreme headquarters. The Westchester County hideaway, formerly called
Mount Chi but now Shiloh, was retained, but instead of being The Omega,
it was merely an adjunct of the New York headquarters chapter. At the
beginning of 1975, The Establishment took over a four-story Manhattan
building and began paying off the $900,000 price the owner demanded.
For about a year, there was tremendous pressure on street donators to bring
in great sums of money, but when a good bit of the price had been paid
off, and some spaces were rented to businessmen, the pressure let up. The
three smaller chapters, in Toronto, New Orleans, and Chicago, were not
centers of great cultural activity nor particularly good recruiting grounds.
I think they mainly served as sources of money, centers for donating over
wide geographical areas, but they also gave Establishers the possibility of a
more varied life through occasional transfer to different cities. In August
and September 1975, I performed censuses of the New York and Chicago
branches; the basic information obtained at that time appears in Table 11.
We can see that the New York chapter was three times the size of the one in
Chicago, and contained far more high-status members. The status differen-
tial of males versus females in New York is explained by the fact that all
the Luminaries and Minor Luminaries had been at Xtul, where there were
twice as many males as females.

Edward believes that The Establishment is completely dominated by
Kitty. But when I asked Father Cain to describe the governmental structure

Table 11: **Census of the New York and Chicago Establishments**

Rank	New York			Chicago		
	Males	Females	Total	Males	Females	Total
Luminary	4	1	5	0	1	1
Minor Luminary	3	0	3	0	0	0
Celebrant	4	4	8	2	0	2
Mentor	2	6	8	2	3	5
Covenantor	1	4	5	2	1	3
Witness	0	3	3	0	0	0
	14	18	32	6	5	11

of The Establishment, he told me what I had heard many times. "We have a board of directors which is composed of the Luminaries, both male and female. We have a kind of executive committee of four, of which I'm one." The other three are Pius, Siegfried, and Moses. Cain says this formal structure does describe the way things work. He denies there is any hidden power structure in any way different from the explicit arrangements. The Four and the council of Luminaries are certainly capable of running the church.

Brother Pan says Kitty is an exceptional person. "She has a vision. It's almost like a voice. One could say that she has an amazing perception of life, amazing perception on the direction" The Establishment should go. He acknowledges that she gives vital guidance. "To describe her, she is like a channel. How do you describe a channel? I think the biggest thing that I feel personally around her is the love of God. The amount of care. And that is probably the biggest thing, that she cares. She cares about us. She cares about the direction that we are heading."

Siegfried knows Kitty well, and says he has a clear perspective on the role she played over the years. "She was, I would say, very much Edward's wife. She never was an out-front figure in any sense. She was enormously helpful in the original setting up in London. But I would say that over the years he was always the out-front one. She was never involved in the organization of The Power. She was always very supportive of him." I asked Siegfried if she received any financial support from The Establishment. Hesitantly, haltingly, he said, "No . . . No . . . No." What is her role today? "She is now a friend of ours, but she lives a very private kind of life. She does a lot of traveling around. She's sometimes in town, but not very often. And she has no official connection with us at all." Elijah agrees. He says Kitty has "always remained a good, true friend. A constant companion and true friend, and I think reasonably stays in the background." Her only participation with the church is "in a very loosely advisory capacity."

I must leave to someone else the task of writing an ethnography of The Establishment Church of the Apocalypse. In the following chapter we will examine the rebirth of The Power after The Separation. For Establishers, The Power failed and was discarded with Edward de Forest. When Edward and Lilith fled the group, they lost the social structure of The Power but took the culture with them. Edward and some of the chief Luminaries of The Establishment say he took *The Power* with him. The history of The Establishment, from 1963 through 1976, is the story of a social group that became a cult that developed into a sect that has nearly completed a transformation to the status of conventional religious denomination.

Although The Establishment is not a product of the contemporary occult revival, it exploits current public interest in psychic experiences. We may well wonder if the group's new adaptation will prove more satisfactory than its earlier attempts. Traditionally, the occult market has been served by individual psychic practitioners, and there is some question whether a "psychic supermarket" or "occult clinic" has any economic advantage. My observations show that The Establishment is not attracting large numbers of interested people to its occult activities, and many of the people who do come are not cultic seekers but merely unhappy, isolated middle-aged folk. For the time being, The Establishment seems to have given up any plans for evangelical expansion. Most people now attracted to it are not eligible for membership in the core community, and a source of a stable lay congregation has not been found. One very important radical change deserves mention. For the first time since the beginning, individual members of the group have begun developing close social ties with persons on the outside. Father Elijah, for example, has a deep friendship with a woman clairvoyant associated with the group but not a member of it. This social change may finally mark the end of the isolation caused by the original social implosion, and therefore the end of the social reality that was The Power.

TEN

A New Beginning

There is nothing left now with the world of men, but to
take from the midst of humanity the few, the very few
who do not belong to humanity, and to allow the Devastation of the Latter Days to take its inevitable course.
—*And Now the Judgement*, Power scripture

In the year after The Separation, small groups of former Powerites gathered
in New Orleans, Chicago, Boston, and Toronto. Inspired by their interest,
Edward de Forest attempted to create his cult anew. Because he felt the
old cult was a complete failure, he refused to use the same methods a second
time. Therefore he did not start with a therapy process or any other mechanism to strengthen social bonds between the people who came to him.
Rather, he encouraged them to begin with the sudden creation of new functioning church chapters. Had they been orderly people enjoying economic
security, they might have been able to form a cohesive group through living, working, and studying together. But, for the most part, they were
unruly and unproductive: disruptive street hippies, depressives, alcoholics.
The many pathological Powerites drained the vitality of the few talented
ones. The Power's Renaissance was really a Dark Age.

REBIRTH OF THE POWER

The Power was dead, but there were many who wanted it brought back to
life. Some had left the cult in the most painful days, dissatisfied but not
yet thoroughly disillusioned. They wanted bigger roles in a better cult. A
larger group consisted of the rejected would-be Powerites, people who had
not been allowed to enter the high-class world of inside members. They
wanted a cut-rate cult that would confer on them the high status jealously
guarded by the people now in The Establishment. And there was Edward
de Forest. He wanted his Power back.

Edward offered a weekly Power seminar to New Orleans peripherals and
contemplated expanding it into a Power College. Author of the Teachings,
he felt they were the heart of the movement. He incorrectly believed that

the mere dissemination of his doctrines could create a new church. Attendance at the seminar was irregular. The people who came had little concept of the theology and were neither intelligent nor intellectual. Edward tried to teach them from his unpublished 1971 book manuscript, *Blame and Demand*.

At one seminar, attended by only four peripheral Powerites, there was a lengthy debate between Edward and a fellow named Rock, who wanted to tour the country with the status of Power minister. But Rock was not sure he should try to sell the whole package. The head of the New Orleans Establishment, Father Siegfried, had lectured his flock on the failings of Edward's teachings. "Now Siegfried had a point when he said that the Unity of Christ and Satan got in the way" of public acceptance. "A number of people that I've talked to were under the impression that Powerites had sexual intercourse with the Devil."

Edward exclaimed, "Does one abandon a set of beliefs and teachings because there are people who have difficulty with them?" Rock, who cared little for the doctrines but much for the status of minister, was unmoved. Edward continued, "But, you know, I've found, and I think many, many Powerites have found, that on personal contact, with a little explanation, there are very few people who don't at least begin to understand that it's not Devil worship, not paganism, not black magic. It's something basically good." Other seminar participants agreed with Rock that the doctrine was hard to sell. Edward argued passionately. "Could you imagine that *Jesus* would have scrapped his teaching because the Pharisees regarded it as the work of the Devil?" But Rock replied that they would have to compromise if they were going to build a successful church organization.

Lilith leapt into the debate. "This is the basis of the split between The Establishment and The Power, because The Establishment, in my terms, became identified totally with the structure, with the organization, and completely negated the teachings. Those became secondary." She and Edward spoke almost in unison: "And therefore, of course, if there was any block to the expansion of the organization in the teachings, you scrap the teachings!" Nobody was convinced. Edward failed to get a dedicated group together in New Orleans. Former Powerites in other cities wrote, called, and even visited him. He decided to explore the situation.

Edward flew to New York City for the weekend of July 27–28 in order to meet with many northeast Powerites, say his piece in the shadow of the Establishment headquarters, and test the possibilities for the future. Disciple Ben Jacobson made arrangements for Edward to speak in a Victorian church in Greenwich Village on Saturday evening. A large audience attended, most of them former Powerites who had never actually seen Edward before. The next day, Edward met with two dozen of these people at Washington Square Park. They sat on newspapers on the ground, sang cult songs, and talked. Finally they held a Meditation, then the nostalgic gathering broke up. There had been no formal discussion of a rebirth of The Power, but enough people had shown an interest in Edward to convince him that the cult could indeed be revived.

Edward flew back to New Orleans and contemplated his prospects. What he really wanted to do was spread his teachings and receive honor and support from readers. He submitted his manuscript *The Matthew Commentaries*, an exegesis of the New Testament, to commercial publishers, but none were interested. The Power College never materialized. A month after the New York trip, he sent an open letter to his fans, saying: "You may form ANY kind of group or corporation or commune that suits you." Hinting that a rebirth of the cult was on the horizon, he said his fans were free to wear uniforms, take ranks and titles, and hold rituals. He promised to provide material for doctrinal seminars.

All the people Edward had met in New York were strangers to him. The most able and mature of them was Osiris, a talented ceramic artist and former architect. Osiris was a Coptic Egyptian who was living near Boston with his American girlfriend Lisa and her little boy. He had joined the cult in Boston, was assigned to the Miami Chapter, then quit after nearly a year of Messenger status. "I discovered it ceased to be what I wanted." Osiris is a really remarkable man. As a boy, he had organized a hashish club dedicated to experiencing everything of which the spirit was capable and gaining complete mastery over every mode of consciousness. He had investigated a number of religious organizations, including Rosicrucianism, not as a religious seeker, but as a spiritual connoisseur and epicure. Osiris joined The Power because it seemed dedicated to "adventure, fun, growth, expansion. The main attraction to me was the feeling of: We're a group of people who are willing to follow our stars—no matter where it leads—up or down or sideways."

In a series of phone calls, Osiris and Edward discussed the future of the cult and ultimately decided to launch it again in Boston. In New Orleans, Chicago, and Toronto, there were small groups of former Disciples who had longed to be Inside Powerites but had never made the grade. But there were also Establishment chapters in all three cities, which would have been uncomfortable competition for a fledgling Power. The Establishment had pulled out of Boston, leaving many OPs high and dry, ready to link up with any version of the cult that might appear.

There seemed to be the beginning of a Boston Chapter already in existence. Disciples Bob Stone and Sam Rhodes, with Bob's wife and several

friends, had been talking about reincorporating the church and had been
holding regular meetings. A second group consisted of ex-Messengers living in what had been the old Disciple commune on Suffolk Street. These
two groups had nothing in common, disliked each other, but seemed to be a
promising beginning. Osiris contacted many of the former cult members in
and around Boston and told them that Edward de Forest was coming to
gather his followers. On October fifth, Edward was "on my way to Boston
to find out what the Game has in store for me there. The strongest Power
contingent is in Boston. And the time has come to discover whether I'm
meant to be directly involved in the recreation of a physical Power structure. The signs, of course, are ambivalent."

Edward moved into Lisa's house with Osiris and held a series of seven
organizational meetings with the Boston cliques. On October eighth, Edward's birthday, Sam Rhodes held a huge party for everybody at his parents'
home. Old friendships were reestablished, and many people met for the first
time. There were many unattached former cult members in the area, but
Edward tried to work primarily through the two main groups.

Bob Stone had been holding meetings and rituals, often at a casual furniture shop, The Bean Bag Store. On the average, eight people attended,
and a total of fourteen different folk came to one or more of his meetings.
None of them had been Messengers for any length of time. Osiris had a
definite opinion of Stone's bean baggers: "They had some connection with
The Power in the past, and they missed that very much, and they wanted
to keep it going as long as possible. Like: Daddy and mommy left home
and haven't come back. It feels lonely without daddy and mommy, so we'll
play-act daddy and mommy and do exactly the same things that were going
on. So we'll have this nice, warm security feeling. And hopefully if we keep
doing that, daddy and mommy will come back." Daddy Edward was home
again.

The Suffolk Street ex-Messengers, Ariel says, were "people who had left
The Power on rather a sour note." It was a colder group than Stone's, reserved even in its skepticism. Sue Knowles, former proprietor of The Power
Thrift Store and now a teacher, was unnerved by Edward's style of communication as she observed it in his Suffolk Street conferences: "He doesn't
listen to what other people are saying. He has his vision, and that's where
he's at. He laid out his latest vision of where he wanted The Power to go.
And I think Brother Patrick said something about: Well, that wasn't exactly what he wanted. He wanted more openness, more freedom, and more
New Game type of playing. And Edward again repeated his vision. No
one said a word. And he said, 'I think everybody agrees with that.' And no
one said a word. He did that about three or four times, the whole silent

Table 12: **Three Categories of Waltham Powerites**

Ex-Messengers	Stone's Group	Others
Ariel	Bob Stone	Ron Forbes
Vita Cordova	Maude Stone	Mark Lembert
Isolde	D. Lord	Al Capone
Woody	Rose	Roger Bergman
	Marsha	Rico Sorbo
	Sam Rhodes	Quincy Adams
	Julio Famagusta	Wendy Adams
		Melvin Potts

consent thing, and just went on that everyone had accepted it. Everybody was just so awestruck with him."

The plan that emerged from all these conferences was that Osiris would find a house the cult could rent, people would all move in together, and a new Boston Chapter would come into being. Osiris located a renovated but scruffy house in Waltham, west of the city, that was divided into four apartments. He and Edward went through the list of those who wanted to move in, and selected only those with jobs or very good employment prospects. Most of the old Messengers withdrew from the project when they saw what the other Powerites looked like and learned what Edward expected of them. The group assembled only enough cash for two of the four apartments, a third was taken by a pair of nonPowerite women, and the fourth was left empty. The chosen people moved in at the beginning of November, but Edward and Osiris continued to live with Lisa.

Two weeks later, a group of rejected, unemployed Powerites, acting without official sanction, scraped up a few dollars and rented the fourth apartment in the house. Ariel says the main group deliberated, and "it was decided that it's silly to have them living in that apartment next-door, and be separate from us. So we absorbed them, but in absorbing them we had to open up the doors to everyone." Although no one knew it at the time, this decision assured failure of the entire project. The three apartments filled up. There were two married couples: Bob and Maude Stone, Quincy and Wendy Adams. Three couples paired off informally: Vita Cordova and Ariel, Isolde and Woody, Rose and D. Lord. One woman, Marsha, lived by herself. The remainder were unruly, unattached males. There were really three divisions: the ex-Messengers, Bob Stone's group, and a fluctuating collection of leftovers, as listed in Table 12. Although the ex-Messengers sometimes used their old sacred names, there was such confusion over the relative statuses of the house members that the group did not adopt the old system of ranks. The imposition of such a system might have introduced a measure of coherence to social relations, but at the cost of acute resentment by those who would wind up at the bottom. The group talked about ranks as a thing of the future, a fantasy that never did emerge.

The ex-Messengers were able people of middle-class background. Except for Bob Stone, none of the other people were regularly employed and did not care to be. When the Power had come into existence back in London, a social implosion stimulated by many powerful therapy sessions brought individuals together into a cohesive group. This time, people with little in common and no history of developing cohesion were thrown together in an ambiguous living situation in the vain hope that something grand would develop. Had Edward immediately begun therapy sessions, had there been some selectivity in admitting candidates for membership, and had there been a more favorable economic base for the Waltham Power, the social cleavages might have been overcome. But Edward was done with formal therapy. He wanted his teachings to be the seed for the new cult. Waltham was like a sackful of wild, hungry cats. In four months it tore itself apart.

THE WALTHAMITES

Quite apart from their unsatisfactory relations with each other, the new Powerites were individually disorganized people. Victims of unfortunate pasts, they created unfortunate futures for themselves. They suffered persistent medical, interpersonal, and psychiatric problems. They were people with "enduring, acutely felt tensions," as Lofland and Stark put it, but they were also people who generated a tremendous amount of tension for those around them by their disruptive behavior. Edward felt that few had character, and said most were "tatbags," "street people," "the dregs of the earth." I will briefly tell the life stories of six of the most stable: Bob Stone, Sam Rhodes, Marsha, and Rose, all full-time Walthamites, and Cher and Spic, the two most active outside participants.

Bob Stone

"I grew up on a farm in Pennsylvania," Bob Stone says, "until I was almost fifteen." He feels it is significant that he was born on the birthday of one of the Beatles, Paul McCartney, and also significant that he left home on the day The Power was founded. "I went to a private school in Hershey, which is also in Pennsylvania. It's an orphanage. I'm a half-orphan, because my father died. The school owns Hershey Chocolate, so it's kind-of rich. It's a strange school. It covers 14,000 acres. It's a vocational school. I was

into school. I loved tests. Everyone hated me at school because I was one
of *those* guys. A lot of people thought I was weird because I enjoyed school.
They had so many great teachers." Bob was really good in math and science,
and was admitted to the Carnegie Institute of Technology in Pittsburgh.
Unfortunately, he "couldn't make the high school to college switch," did
poorly his first year, then dropped out.

Over the next five years, Bob Stone invented his own personal religion.
"At one time I was a Methodist, but I decided Methodism wasn't doing
what it should be doing for me. Because my main thing was around *fear*."
Although Bob is a superficially calm, competent fellow, he says he is terrified most of the time. "Then I became an atheist. I realized, after being an
atheist for a while, that there is religion, somewhere. That it can be found
within a person. I started making my own religion. I figured I'm as good a
source as anybody, because nobody knows my head like I do. I figured my
religion would be a personal religion. It would be one of a kind. Nobody
else would have this kind of religion. And so I started writing it down. I
gave it a name. It was called Durism." Durism would give him the power to
endure his fear. "I even invented a Durist Cross. Do you know what a carpenter's square looks like? An L-shape? Well, it had a white L-shape and a
black L-shape, interlocking to form a square."

In Vietnam, serving as a Marine, Bob read a little about Buddhism and
decided he had really discovered the same thing independently. Durism
was Buddhism. But he did not discuss his religion with any actual Bud-
dhists. "For a long time I couldn't even tell people what I was doing in my
head. And whenever I tried to explain to people that I was working on a
science in my head, it would go away, for months. It wouldn't come back
for a long time. Finally it got to the point where I could tell people about it,
but I couldn't write it down. In 1970, I finally got to the point where I
could write part of it down. It was really crude." He discarded the name
Durism and expanded the system. "I called it a science. To me it's a religion.
It's a religious science. And I call it Bobbycraft. And I believe that Bobbycraft was dumped into my head by some Force. It was put there on purpose." Bobbycraft reduces Bob's fear and gives him a framework for understanding the abnormal experiences that he has quite often. "I have a thing
which I call Superconsciousness, which I can at certain times attain. And
when I am in a state of Superconsciousness, I am in touch with a channel to
what I would call an Angel." This Angel has proven his existence to Bob by
helping him manage his day-to-day life. For example, Bob says he is able to
drive his car very fast in bad weather, at night, or on winding roads, without fear of crashing. The Angel warns him if there is danger ahead.

After Vietnam, Bob took a job installing computers for Univac. "I love

computers. I've got computer karma." Bobbycraft helps him communicate
with the computers, and his science is organized according to computer
logic. Computers have no fear. "The people that I work with on computers,
I've never been able to get in with. I've never been able to tune into those
guys. They're very straight, very conservative. They think I'm a hippie
freak. They don't listen to anything logical unless it follows their particular
pattern of thought."

Univac transferred Bob to Boston, where he met The Power. He decided
that the doctrines of The Power were almost the same as those of Bobbycraft, except that the cult did not understand things as well as he did. "By
the time I'd met The Power, I had written maybe four or five thousand
pages. It's a secret book that I have. Just about everything I've written is
exactly the same, with different words, as what The Power believes." The
Durist Cross was like the original Power Sign. The chief diagram of Bobbycraft was a circle with tangent lines, like the Power Sign, showing how
opposing forces can shoot out in all the directions of the compass. When
Bob speaks about this, he always draws a picture, explaining that these
forces were like the four Gods of the cult. "I believed in a thing which I
called Roto, which went this way, and out of Roto stemmed another force
which I called Toby, and out of Toby stemmed another force. You see I
gave everything names. Before I met The Power I believed that the Beatles
knew my science. The same force that came through them is working
through me. If you take the Beatles' words, and if you substitute a word for
each of their code words, every word except for one works out identical.
There is one word that they use that they have two meanings for, which I
have two separate words for."

But Bob is not ready to publish his great book. "It's all written in para-
bles. It never means what it says. I'm the only person who knows what I
meant when I said: Time is a circle. It's fruitless to try to explain to people.
Now this science has given me the ability to create a new language. It's
based on a new alphabet and everything. All the words are new. Like I have
one word which means the concept of learning new words, and that's Doli.
And each word that I have explains a fairly large concept. Now I can take
this book that I've written and convert it into my language. You would
never be able to convert it into English. If a person took the time to study
the words, he would be able to read my book."

Bob met Sister Claire around The Power coffee house. She was a brand-
new Messenger, a pleasant but unattractive woman who says, "My biggest
fear was that I'd be an old maid." She found she could not make it as a Messenger, dropped back to the status of Disciple, and became just plain
Maude. No longer able to live in the Messenger Flat, Bob says, "She needed

a place to stay, so I let her stay over at my house for *two days*, and she never left. So we got married in the church." When I first met the two of them in 1972, they were about to visit the Toronto Chapter, where the Union Ceremony was carried out. Bob spent half an hour explaining Bobbycraft to me, until Maude made him stop. It was her policy not to let him disturb people with his crazy ideas. What does Maude think about her husband's personal religion? She giggles, "I don't understand a word of it!"

Bob Stone wished he had his own religious cult but was far too withdrawn a fellow to create one. When The Power abandoned Boston, he saw his chance. In organizing meetings of former Powerites under Edward's banner, he was actually attempting to build his own group. He never accepted many of Edward's doctrinal statements, and used the cult merely as a vehicle for his own ambitions. While he was living in the Waltham house, Bob began collecting discarded computer parts from his job. He plans to build a computer that can be plugged into his brain, to complete Bobbycraft and finally end his terrible fears. In the future, he believes, everyone will have a microcomputer implanted inside his skull, and people will be linked by mental radio. "We're moving into an age now where we can get into a mass mind." In a few years, according to Bob, the earth will be expanded into a vast, hollow computer, with each person dwelling physically isolated from others in a little room. The world "will become an animal, and each of us will be the nucleus of a cell."

Sam Rhodes

Sam Rhodes was the son of a university theologian, a pathetic, frail fellow with poor health and low self-esteem. "When I was in school, I didn't really have what you would call close friends. I'd come off like a real punk. After I got out of high school, I went into a real inferiority cycle where I just figured everybody must hate me, everybody must not be able to stand the sight of me. So instead of forcing myself on people, I was being very withdrawn and shy. My teeth were falling out of my mouth. I was really overweight for my size, and really looked icky. I was going from one crummy job to another. I would think: 'I'm nothing! How can I go around being sociable with girls?' Instant rejection." Sam got into drugs, marijuana mostly, and made some tenuous friendships. "Dope fiends like me."

He developed cataclysmic intestinal difficulties, which his family at first interpreted in psychiatric terms. "I was just hanging around, going from one shrink to another 'cause they thought my colitis was related to psychosomatic problems. Mine was organic. Once I got the thing started, psychological stuff could bring it on. Like when I was going through all that messy stuff with feeling really rotten, and then having my motorcycle accident, getting plastered all over South Boston, and then getting busted four days later. That's what brought on my last attack!" The doctors decided to operate. In such cases, particularly when the patient is young, the surgeons act cautiously, snipping out pieces of the person's insides bit by bit in a long series of operations. Each time they hope they have removed enough. Sam was given a second anus, an opening in his side that permitted the waste to flow out into a plastic bag, instead of continuing on through his damaged system. Naturally this did not help his problem of self-esteem.

Then he met The Power. "I walked into the coffee house, and all of a sudden: BOINNNNG! People with open arms said, "Hi! I'm glad you're here. I hope you'll come back all the time.' I was dumbfounded to find people who were like this, because one of the fantasies that I'd always had was some kind of atmosphere, or environment, or world, or community where people could really be open, could really give to each other." He had found glimpses of such worlds in science fiction novels, notably Robert Heinlein's *Stranger in a Strange Land.* Sam said The Power was like Heinlein's fiction come to life. "Although I felt an inch high when I came in, all of a sudden I was thinking: 'These people will accept me.' "

Marsha

Marsha's family lives in one of Boston's western suburbs, her father an underpaid accountant and her mother a department store employee. Her sister is "a Jesus freak" who hates The Power. Her two brothers have attended college. Marsha herself lasted only one semester at Northeastern University, a mammoth working-class school. By nature "a wallflower," she could achieve relationships with men only by being very easy. To have any kind of romance she has to give herself entirely to the other person's whim. She does not receive love and respect in return. Except for rare moments of surprising decisiveness, Marsha is passive, withdrawn, and self-despising. She is large and lethargic. She feels "hopeless, depressed, suspended animation, blasé, blah!" In school, she was the "class yecch." She has worked intermittently at several jobs, including one as a hospital attendant, and sometimes dreams about becoming a registered nurse. Marsha claims to be handicapped by poor vision, although her friends suspect this is an excuse for poor reading ability and general introversion. She constantly broods about her weight.

Early in 1972, she was living on her own in a Boston apartment. She had met Powerites on the streets several times but had never visited the cult. In mid-February, she let Hank Fraser and his wife crash in her place for a few days. Hank was a drug runner and bag man. He became Brother Calvin, Messenger of The Power, a year later. Marsha decided to visit her older brother for the weekend, leaving Hank in charge of her apartment. She left Boston on Friday, assuming it would be quite easy to hitchhike across to Amherst, where her brother was attending college. "Never quite made it!" She got as far as Springfield, frustrated by the difficulty of her manner of travel, ready to take any ride she could get. "I was really tired and upset. I didn't care *where* they were going!" One trucker gave her a lift to Danbury, Connecticut, quite in the wrong direction; then another dragged her to Pennsylvania. "Actually it was a succession of two different rapes by two different truck drivers." These trucker abductions were not only unpleasant but left her in a terrible plight. She had to get back to Boston by Monday if she wanted to keep her job, but she had no money. "Finally this one trucker picked me up . . . and wound up giving me the money to get to Boston by bus." She didn't make it back until Thursday. "I lost my job. I'm good at losing jobs." She discovered that Hank had run off with all the money she had left in her apartment. The rent was due soon, and she was broke.

A few days later, "we had a party to celebrate my twenty-first birthday," many street people whooping it up in the apartment. She left for about an hour, "and a couple of people who were invited wrecked the place. I think it was in a fight. All this damage was done. Broke in the bathroom door. And they attempted to clean it up and threw all the stuff down the toilet, and stopped that up. And I think they punched in a couple of other doors. Needless to say, the next morning the landlord came up with the police. I was chicken and I didn't want to face them, so I just left. So therefore I wound up on the streets. February. Cold." She crashed with strangers for a while. Street people told her about the Power coffee house. It was "a day-time place," a warm, free location they could go, keep from freezing, and have a good time.

Marsha was "ecstatic" at joining the cult. "It was the first time that things went together." The Power became her dating bureau. "For the first time I had friends." In the first few days she met Dwight Lord, who preferred to be called "D. Lord," and became his girl. D. Lord had been trained in commercial art, and he had been a cop, a Vietnam soldier, a merchant seaman, a carpenter, a convict, a biker, and a street person. He was also an alcoholic. He often slept under one of the bridges on the Charles River, sometimes in people's basements, and sometimes under a Cambridge bush. He spent his best nights on the floors of friends' apartments. At the time Marsha went to live with him, he had staked out quarters in an abandoned Boston building.

There was no heat. "Really a mess. All torn down. A whole mess of mattresses." Until recently, another Powerite woman, Vita Cordova, had been living with D. Lord. They had fought. In a rage, Vita ripped out the bathroom sink. Now Vita was living with another Powerite, Abe Rimbaud. D. Lord was "on line" to become a Messenger, so he was trying to keep celibate and abstain from alcohol. For the first two nights, he and Marsha did not have sex. On the third, they did. D. Lord had started drinking again, anyway, so he postponed becoming a Messenger until some later opportunity. He and Marsha were not alone in the wrecked building but shared the space with "a whole bunch of runaways," as many as a dozen of them. D. Lord was their protector. "At that time, there was a great craze for thirteen-year-olds to run away. It was better for them to stay there. There was this nutty guy running around raping all the girls."

Eventually, Marsha and D. Lord broke up. Vita Cordova gave Abe Rimbaud to Marsha. Then there was a long sequence of other men. Marsha became a Power regular, a Disciple. "My dream was to go to Toronto and become a Messenger." She never did. At the beginning of 1973, a man she refuses to name got her pregnant. The daughter was given away. After the cult left Boston, in the spring of 1974, things turned very bad for her again. "I was doing speed [amphetamine drugs]. I was really wiped out on it." The speed was supposed to help her get thin and let her work at a night job while playing all day. She lost her job. Her current boyfriend dropped her. It had become her habit to pick up new boyfriends, men of low quality looking for quick sex, at the Power coffee house. It was gone. "I took a bottle of sleeping pills." Then she decided she didn't want to die after all. "So I checked into Boston State for about ten days. Nice vacation, but it really didn't do me much good." When the cult started up again, she naturally wanted to be a part of it. Not only was D. Lord in the Waltham house, but two of his other girlfriends were there as well. Marsha tried to be friendly with all of them despite the old hostilities and buried longings irritated by every contact. She had no friends outside The Power.

Rose

Rose grew up in a suburb of a middle-sized city in Connecticut. Her parents were poor, but the intercession of other relatives made it possible for her to attend a religious women's college. Her relationships with men were fleeting and precarious. Picking guys up in bars "was the big thrill of the time. I was trying to show off to my girlfriend, my roommate then, and bring her out into the world. It was the college thing to do. Going to a girl's school, the only time you meet guys was to go out, and if they didn't pick you up, you have to pick them up. The girl I was best friends with and I would go out and wait to get picked up, and then get drunk enough so we didn't care either way and go pick up somebody, if we weren't already. And we had our ways of playing little games doing it. We'd go around to guys we liked the looks of and ask them if they'd seen somebody, and give them a description of somebody that didn't exist. It was all superficial. You didn't worry too much about relationships. Because it was just usually one-night stands. You meet the guy that night, and you're with him that night, and that's it. And you never see him again. You don't have to get involved."

These "one-night stands" did not involve sex. Rose would give the guy a false phone number so he couldn't pester her for a second date. The idea was to be entertained by a fellow who was basically only after sex, maybe engage in some petting, but not go further on this first date. The victim would be led to expect sex on the second or third date. Rose usually avoided a second date, so she got food, drink, and entertainment, all paid for by him, without having to give much in return. It was a game played against the boys, a game she usually won. But not every time. One evening she went through this routine with a guy, wound up in his car, and suddenly there was a knife at her throat. He raped her, making her perform various sexual acts which she found agonizingly disgusting. Rose says this night was a traumatic event that soured her on sex forever. But it was the natural outcome of the deceitful mutual exploitation that had marked male-female relations for her since the beginning.

She met a nice fellow at a discotheque and married him. She gave up on college, expecting to have no need of labor skills. Marriage was supposed to solve her financial problems as well as take the place of her one-night stands. Her husband had a good job and supported her decently for a while. But Rose loathed having sex with him. Before the end of its first year, the marriage collapsed over the issue of sexual relations.

The only job she could find for a long time was employment with a professional picket agency. Rose used to march up and down carrying a sign and shouting the day's slogans. She often met Powerites while on the job. The cult sent donators to her city, and they made a great impression on her. She became a Field Disciple and supplemented her self-esteem with the somewhat hollow claim that she was a member of a marvelous religious group.

At the end of June 1974, when vacation time rolled around, she and her girlfriend went to New York City. Rose had told her friend all about The Power, and dragged her to the headquarters to show it off. Surprise! The sign said: "The Establishment Church of the Apocalypse." Rose was very embarrassed. But she attended some Establishment activities and began making friends. Melvin Potts arranged for Rose to stay without cost with his group of street people. She attended a Focus activity run by Father Remus and Mother Beryl on the subject of male-female relations. She was paired off in a discussion exercise with D. Lord, who had followed the cult from Boston to Manhattan. "We ended up comparing our ex-spouses. And we got along pretty good. We just had a good conversation. Had good fun, making jokes of our ex's and: 'I had that problem too.' And: 'I know how you feel.' "

It turned out that D. Lord was one of Melvin's group, crashing collectively in whatever place one of them could arrange. Sometimes they got enough money begging on the streets—"spare-changing" they called it—to rent a room in their "favorite cockroach haven." Otherwise, they would beg floor space from someone or wind up on the streets. They even slept in Central Park! One evening, D. Lord and Melvin Potts had a kissing contest, alternately kissing Rose as passionately as they could. She decided D. Lord was the winner. The first night that she slept with him they didn't touch each other. The second night they made out. He became her protector, not really her lover. They never consummated the relationship sexually, although she lived with him for the next eight months. Her frigidity and his alcoholic ill health combined to exile sex from their bed. Each used the other as a token of social worth rather than as a love object. D. Lord was desperate to be able to say he had an "old lady." Sometimes he became confused and thought Rose was one of his former wives.

Rose decided to join The Establishment. She'd always thought it would be great to be a minister, to have respect and security in a pleasant occupation. But The Establishment had little use for D. Lord. One evening, Brother Eros called him a lousy drunk. Rose and D. Lord saw Edward de Forest when he came to the city, and heard that Bob Stone's group was trying to start The Power going again in Boston. The pair moved to Boston. They stayed where they could, crashing with friends or living on the streets. There was a cluster of bushes in a street divider near Harvard Square that was a good place to sleep in dry weather. When it rained, there was always D. Lord's favorite bridge on the Charles River or a vacant Harvard dormitory. Rose would beg on the streets by day, collecting enough cash to buy drinks for her man in cheap Cambridge bars. The only things D. Lord ever gave her in return were stray dogs. He seemed mindless of the fact that the animals were burdens, not benefits. When the Power commune opened up in Waltham, Rose and D. Lord were happy to move in.

Cher and Spic

Many later Powerites were drawn to the cult because in some series of life experiences they had come to prefer colorful fantasy over drab reality. Many had left the square world in the psychedelic glory of the late 1960s, had lived in OZ or some other Wonderland, and had lost touch with and taste for conventionality. Alienated from the Grey Forces, they were natural cult members. Cher and Spic fit this description exactly.

Cher is a Jewish American from the Boston area who spent her late teens living with her mother in Spain. Cher became deeply involved in the marginal Spanish counterculture in the late 1960s. She began doing drugs when she was fifteen, mostly methedrine and hashish, and rejoiced in a wild succession of passionate sexual adventures. When she was seventeen, she toured the country as a dancer with a rock music band, visiting all the dives and resorts of that corner of Europe. Near the end of her Spanish career, she ran a youth-culture coffee house on the island of Gibraltar. She returned to the states, married, and then divorced after two very sad years. Cher suffered a nervous breakdown at the end of the marriage and was afraid to leave the house for many weeks. She is a very competent worker and never has any difficulty finding some sort of job, even during hard times.

Cher suffers terrible headaches and other miseries. I cannot say to what extend they are psychogenic. Suffering is a prime axis of her life. She daydreams about sexual relationships with romantic, charismatic men, usually men who project the image cultivated by rock music stars. For many years, she and her childhood friend Sister Norma have concocted a running fantasy in which they are jet-set, superspy superheroines, dashing about Europe on secret missions. They act out this fantasy in little skits they produce for their own amusement.

When Cher first met The Power, she was deeply aroused by the attractive men running the Boston Chapter but repelled by the Christian content of the doctrine. Then she saw the rock-opera movie *Jesus Christ Superstar*. It changed her feelings, and she developed passionate ties with several Powerites. She and Norma lusted after Edward de Forest, as well as several of his henchmen. Cher did succeed, in the last days at Waltham, in having a romantic weekend with Osiris. The only decent man who was prepared to be faithful to her was Spic, a useless but calm guy she met in the coffee house. They live together in East Boston. Spic says Cher is his wife, but she denies it. Cher pretends to despise Spic. He is convenient and harmless, usually out of work, usually cheery. Cher supports him. She has not married him because she still hopes to be swept away by a charismatic rock star. She pursues studs constantly, usually failing to catch up with them. So long as Spic fills the void at home, willing to put up with anything Cher does, she can manage in the conventional world without giving up her impossible dreams. One time I heard her express her boredom with him: "Spic, I think I'll put you out with the garbage." He calmly replied, "It's only Saturday and the garbage man doesn't come until Tuesday. You'd better wait."

Spic is a rather short and slim fellow. He has little physical strength but hints at vast magical powers he holds in check with a resolute will. He says his real name is Edgar Allen Poe. He sports a pointed goatee and has a Satanic twinkle in his eyes. On one hand he wears a huge ivory ring carved with the face of Satan. Spic says the ring is magic and changes color when disturbed by the atmosphere around it. One time the ring was lost and picked up by a neighbor. Although the finder knew the ring belonged to Spic, he put it on his own finger. Within a few hours, the color of the ivory had changed markedly, terrifying the man and forcing him to return the ring to Spic.

Spic says he has two fathers. His spiritual father is Satan, "our Father who art in Hell." Spic says his biological father is seven feet two inches tall and lives in Canada near the Arctic Circle. Spic is one of sixty illegitimate children of this formidable Dad. All the mothers were different. Exactly equal numbers of both sexes were produced, so he has thirty half-sisters and twenty-nine half-brothers. His family is Basque and has always kept to the old Satanic religion to which all Basques belong, Spic claims. He talks with a quite ordinary American accent, although he says he grew up in Europe—Basque territory and Palermo. He explains that English is the international language, so his family taught him no other. "I know many of my relatives, my ancestors were put to death because they were of the ancient religion. Just because they would not say, 'I believe in Jesus Christ,' several of them were burned at the stake, several of them had their heads chopped off. We were subjugated to the witch purges of Europe." Spic is quite a hero, one of the leading Basque revolutionaries. "I was in a riot in Madrid. I was one of the organizers for The Basque Liberation Movement, and when we rioted in Madrid the troops came. And they didn't fire over the crowd—they fired at the crowds with their Spanish rifles and machine guns. We were told to disperse first, and then they fired, and four or five hundred people were killed." Of course, this is pure fantasy.

Spic can recall several of his previous incarnations, and in each one he participated in violent military action. He was "with Napoleon and his French regiments," fought in the "Spanish-American War in Cuba," and in "both world wars, and I knew how I died each time. Through explosions, either through cannon, dynamite, or whatever." In this life, Spic has had wonderful adventures. Not only did he organize Basque resistance in Spain, but he was also a blockade runner taking medicine into North Vietnam during its war with the United States. His only child was fathered in Hanoi. Perhaps his greatest brief adventure was the time he fell out of an airplane without a parachute. He fell from a great height. It seemed he fell forever. Then he splashed into a lake that happened to be under him, and emerged from the ordeal unhurt.

He was a violent, crashing street person in New Orleans, met The Power when it offered him a free meal, then wandered up to Boston. He met Cher in the Boston coffee house and eventually moved in with her. The two of them visited the Waltham house often but declined to live there. Cher was disgusted with many of the people in the house. The last meetings of The Power in America were held in Cher and Spic's third-floor apartment. At last report, Cher's mother and little sister had come over from Spain to live with them, and Spic had continued to fail to hold a job.

WALTHAM ASPIRATIONS

The Walthamites had high hopes. For the first and probably last time in their lives, they had a chance to make history. They thought it was just barely possible that they were like Christ's disciples, never-to-be-forgotten founders of a new age. Julio said Waltham was really a "training camp." He said, "This is boot camp for the Army of God." He wanted to be High Pontiff in charge of designing rituals for the new church. Marsha was content to become an IP, while Rose's ambition was to be a "minister." D. Lord desperately longed to be a Messenger. Melvin Potts expressed a philosophical attitude: "If it's meant for me to go into the Hierarchy, I think I'd like it. The entire idea of this house is basically: The majority of those who go through this will be the new Hierarchy when we reopen."

The Waltham house built the semblance of a Power church. A great communal feast was served on Thanksgiving, and everyone gorged on donated turkeys and other goodies. Sam Rhodes entertained with a magic show, and there was singing. Late that evening, the house was formally consecrated by Edward de Forest. The Powerites stood together in black uniforms, holding candles and chanting. They went from room to room, consecrating every nook with fire and water. At every turn, Edward proclaimed, "This House belongs to the Gods!"

At first, the Sabbath Assemblies were rather informal. Then D. Lord invested a week of woodworking to make a complete set of ritual furniture, including a circular altar, two carved priests' chairs, stands for the fire and water bowls, and a gong made from a pot lid. Mark Lembert made a silver and black plywood emblem to hang against a black curtain in the living room of one of the apartments. The room became a holy place, the Waltham Alpha, with the unveiling of the new equipment at the Sabbath, on Saturday, December 14. The Assembly was held in the classical form, with the circular altar at the center and twenty-one Powerites sitting in an oval around it.

December was the time of greatest excitement and hope. Thanksgiving established Waltham as The Boston Chapter. The new ritual equipment and black uniforms elevated the drama of the cult. Edward, Lilith, and Osiris moved into the house around the twentieth. The Christmas Eve party was the high point before everything slid into ruin. There was a wreath on the door, greens on the bookcase, and a nice Christmas tree in a corner of the Alpha. Each resident of the house made a cardboard ornament for the tree. The dinner was wonderful. There was turkey (but no gravy), bread dressing, mashed potatoes, bread and butter, pies, cookies, and fruit punch. After supper, Sam Rhodes put on another magic show, dressed in top hat and tails, using a school desk covered with a black cloth as his work table. His magic equipment emerged from an old suitcase labeled The Great Destroyer. Silk handkerchiefs changed color before our very eyes. Rings linked and unlinked, leaving only the slightest suspicion that one of them might have had a gap in it. Sam poured milk from a gimmicked pitcher into a rolled newspaper, then made it vanish. He drew a coin from Isolde's ear. Too bad his powers were insufficient to restore his own health or that of his cult.

One factor that did not help the chances for the Walthamite church was the poor medical condition of many members. Sam Rhodes was the worst off. His intestinal difficulties threw him into the hospital more than once, and eventually he gave up trying to live a vigorous life and moved out of the Waltham house to live with his parents. The fact that the girls in the house used to kid him about his "shit bag" may also have impelled him to leave. Mel Potts had a problem with his blood sugar and terrible physical awkwardness. He never walked, but rather stumbled around bumping into people and things, and had similar lack of control over his emotional impulses. Isolde complained of several disorders related to her obesity. Maude was operated on for an ovarian cyst, and afterward delighted in displaying her obscenely ugly scar. Her baby son went to the hospital with pneumonia. Blanche, Mark Lembert's girlfriend, went for tests, and a while later suffered a disorder of her "woman's parts." Lisa received a hysterectomy. Marsha said she needed an eye operation. Rose said she needed to visit the hospital, but wouldn't say why. During the hundreds of hours I spent with the Walthamites, never did I hear one person show real concern for another's medical problem. The cult ideology was useful to them in denying any need for sympathy, because it claimed that each person's problem had been chosen by him. When Sam Rhodes' digestive system broke down, they criticized him for "pulling in a limitation" by adopting such an excuse for his laziness.

Several accidents occurred. Vita Cordova splashed duplicator fluid in her eye while working at an outside job. D. Lord stuck his thumb in the power planer that was part of his basement shop. It was a dirty, aged machine with no safeguards. It bit a large chunk out of his thumb. The doctor bandaged it and made him wear a sling and stay away from water. He enjoyed the sling, and it was not his habit to wash, anyway. A few days later, the physician grafted a chunk of flesh from D. Lord's upper arm into the hole in his thumb.

The Waltham house was an unhealthy environment. Many of the rooms were filthy. Cat excrement and garbage filled the cracks and corners. There were not enough towels nor toilet paper in the bathrooms. The diet was very poor. By the middle of January, it was terrible. Julio Famagusta pretended to be the house doctor, but nobody went to him for treatment. I several times saw him caress women's heads, in order, he said, to cure their headaches and colds. His chief methods of treatment were all magical, including rituals and meditation. My able research assistant, George Oberhofer, got the recipe for one of Julio's most potent medications, "red medicine." The ingredients included red wine, kerosene, diced onion, potassium permanganate, and several herbs. It was supposed to be a quick sure cure for the clap.

For a couple of months the Waltham group had a definite plan. Edward wanted them to save up a lot of money and prepare spiritually to leave civilization and set up a Survival Center. Julio says this would be "a place in some very remote part of the country, where we will live and grow. We will also run missions into cities. If we all make it, we'll be the future ministers of the church." Where would they go? Quincy Adams claimed Edward told him all about it. Proudly he refused to divulge the details: "My lips are sealed." Roger Bergman felt the Survival Center would be in New Mexico. Mark Lembert said the Middle West was a possibility. Roger didn't feel he was ready to live off the land. The people in the house were unhealthy, so it was a good thing, he felt, that they had time to build themselves up. Maude didn't like the Survival Center idea. She was squeamish about the snakes, spiders, and scorpions she was convinced infested New Mexico. Sam Rhodes joked that they were probably going to Outer Mongolia: "The idea is something similar to what happened at Xtul eleven years ago. Total isolation and self-supporting, where we can really learn how to go about setting up our Survival Centers." Woody felt it might be a good idea to "get mobile homes, campers" and send musical mobile chapters out from the Center: "Everyone will say, 'Wow! This is a really terrific experience! I've never heard music that really expressed every emotion that I was going through played like that!' Because, hopefully, that's where our music is going to get, where we'll be able to pick up emotions and *play* them."

Edward had come back to his old apocalyptic view that "human structures are collapsing." Of course, his own human structures *had* collapsed. A Biblical analogy helped him explain the purpose of Waltham and allege its divinely ordained importance: "Noah didn't build his ark on water. He was given time—not much but enough—to build it on dry land and solid earth. But he built it to survive when that dry land and solid earth were lost beneath a deluge that he knew was coming. And he didn't stop building until his ark was ready for that deluge." The new Power would be that ark, and in Waltham they needed the security of a solid environment in order to build it. Edward made only the vaguest of plans for the Survival Center, consulting a few governmental pamphlets and checking out The Surplus Property Utilization Program. He admitted that he didn't really know what the group would wind up doing. "Maybe we'll be gypsies."

THE NEW OMEGA

When Lilith joined Edward in Boston, she was presented to the Walthamites as Edward's *Consort*. Many believed that Osiris was the new High Pontiff of the church. The three of them were the new Omega, isolated from the body of the church but supreme over it. Edward never became the leader of the Waltham group but preferred the status of Teacher. He hoped that his Teachings would draw out of the mass of miserable Walthamites a few individuals capable of existing on his plane. Osiris says The Omega did not participate in the life or rituals of the Waltham house, except as observers, because "we were not part of The Boston Chapter." Other chapters might emerge in Chicago and Toronto. All should be treated equally. "The period before we went into living in the Waltham house there was a conscious, deliberate stress on the fact that there is a Power with or without Waltham. This entity was called The Omega." Lisa's little house was a very crowded living quarters for her, her son, The Omega, and Satan the dog. After a couple of months, she became completely fed up, terminated her romantic affair with Osiris, and asked The Omega to move out. Osiris, Lilith, and Edward took up residence in the Waltham house around December 20, taking over the downstairs apartment. Thus the triad moved into Waltham without the intent of asserting true leadership or even becoming involved in chapter activities.

In the last weeks of 1974 Edward and Osiris went to New York City to see Kitty and Edward's brother Remus. This was the only time after The Separation that Kitty and Edward met. For seven hours they exchanged blame and recriminations. The meeting proved there was no hope of reconciliation between Edward and Kitty.

Over the next two months, Edward formally disentangled himself from

The Establishment and from Kitty. He was forced to negotiate with The Establishment to obtain copies of his own writings. In a letter to Cain he also argued that The Establishment owed him a considerable sum of money. "Over eleven years I estimate the income of The Power to be close to $5,000,000, which was made possible in large part by my contribution to its development. In view of this, a settlement on me of $50,000 seems scarcely unreasonable to enable me to continue my work." Cain was not impressed by this argument.

Edward kept these dealings secret from the Walthamites, and they in turn tried to uncover everything he hid. For a long time, several of them were under the mistaken impression that Edward was very rich, the heir to a vast family fortune. He never told them his real situation, one of complete penury. He did not take a job in Boston, although for a brief time Lilith worked as a secretary, and he made absolutely no financial contributions to the house. His rent was paid by the Walthamites, who also provided his food.

Throughout January, there were constant rumors that Edward was planning a mysterious trip, perhaps to Santo Domingo. One time, I observed people listening in on part of a telephone conversation between Edward and a lawyer who mentioned Santo Domingo. Finally, three weeks into the month, Edward vanished. Gradually the people in the house discovered that he had flown away to get a divorce.

Osiris said that Edward had always been distant from his cult. "In a sense, Edward was outside The Power. He was not part of the group. He said many times that many of the Masters didn't have any contact with him." He had never attended a Sabbath Assembly before Waltham. When I showed him my photographs taken four years earlier of the Sacrifist and Evangelist, he was astonished to see the colorful tabards they wore. He didn't have the slightest recollection of such garments. When he did sit in on Waltham Sabbaths, he clutched the Assembly Book, confused as any newcomer. He was unfamiliar with the hymns and the pieces of ritual business. He did not dress like the others. When everyone else, including Osiris and Lilith, began wearing black uniforms, as in the very old days, de Forest adopted a brown uniform for himself. Once in jest he introduced himself as "Mr. Brown." Edward's costume consisted of a brown turtleneck shirt, brown trousers, and brown half-boots. The colors ranged from honey to caramel to chocolate. He wore a large ornate silver cross, and frequently carried a brown shoulder bag filled with personal effects such as his pipe and tobacco.

Osiris explained to me how the three members of The Omega spent their time. "If you could manage to take a peek for a short period of time at what was going on, it wouldn't make sense to you." Mostly they talked, but the content of the discussions was so personal that outsiders would not have understood they were engaged in Power work. What were the norms? "You have to be as open as possible with yourself and with the other two members of the triangle. And that whatever it is, whether it's extremely negative, extremely positive, you have to express it, and you have to force yourself not to avoid it. Which led to activities like exhausting any feelings one might have about something—to its limit. Pushing it, and pulling it, and explaining it, and talking about it until you are completely out in the open, instead of trying to look good or trying to get your point across or trying to influence somebody else."

The work of The Omega was identical to that of an encounter group, except that the benefit was supposed to be for all Powerites, not just for participants. "It lasts all of the day—twenty-four hours." Whatever happened within the triumvirate had to be analyzed to death. "What does it mean? Where is it going? Why is it happening? What does it imply should happen in the future? How is everybody in the group, as part of the group, feeling? Doing? What they represent? What they mean?" This was how Edward had spent the last dozen years of his life. The continual encounter group stew that surrounded him gave the inspiration for his writings. But beyond that, he believed this living process of personal therapy was the engine of all human history. Magically, this intimate process influenced all events in the outside world. "Edward feels that his destiny *is* The Power. And The Power is his destiny. So whatever he's doing—that's The Power."

Edward's major creative activity during the three months he lived near Boston was the writing of several short scriptures that never went beyond manuscript stage, and the invention of an extremely complex therapeutic board game called *Contact*. Few members of the house were ever permitted to play the game. Edward changed the rules in mid-play when I was his partner at the board.

Osiris' major creative activity was the invention of a new symbol for the cult. It was unveiled at the Sabbath Assembly, December 14, and was in use only for the duration of the Waltham house. Shown in Figure 16, this emblem is a complex structural transformation of the older Unity Cross. The dragon represents Satan. Edward remarked that the Unity Cross dragon had no wings, while this new dragon possessed both wings and feet, "an Unfallen Serpent, no less!" Inside the coils of the dragon is a cross, dominated yet protected, showing a new relationship between Satan and Christ. Satan now plays the dominant role, yet works with Christ to achieve first Separation, then Unity: first Death, then Rebirth. The cross in the cen-

Figure 16. The New Dragon Symbol Designed by Osiris

ter is actually a cutout area, a hole. In the large wooden emblem made by Mark Lembert, the hole was large enough to put your hand through. Osiris explained that the dragon is *around* the cross, acting as a wall. A wall with an opening like a door. The cross, the door, is a way through. He says this symbolizes The Power itself. "What are we offering? A way out. *Exit*. It's a door that is opened for anybody who wants to go through that door."

The outline of the emblem is rectangular with two notches, one on each side. Osiris explained that these notches were the arms of another cross. The outline of the symbol is a cross turned inside out, as though the whole world outside the emblem were one great topologically tranformed Christian symbol. Thus the symbol contains one cross but is contained by another. Rank-and-file Walthamites found Osiris' creation inscrutable and unappealing. The Omega did not bother to explain its symbolism to them.

For a while they planned to produce pendants following this design, to be worn by all Powerites. Higher-ranked members would wear emblems with little outlines of the Power Sign and the Sign of Union in the upper corners. Middle-ranked members would have only the Power Sign, while low-ranked folk would have plain emblems. Money for this project was never raised, and only a few cardboard mock-ups of the pendant were ever made. Ranks were not introduced, either.

DEVIANCE AND DISINTEGRATION

The house was in desperate need of government. Edward gave no leadership at all. Ariel recalls there was "a lot of personality conflict" living at such close quarters. "Isolde took it upon herself to see that things got done." Mel Potts says, "We asked Edward to put someone as his mediator with him. And after a few days of debate, Edward gave the position to Isolde, making her Head of House." Ariel says, "It's an old Power concept that a house needs a head." As Roger comments, "She's tremendously strong." But as soon as Isolde began exercising authority, the pressure on her became tremendous. Roger was not enthusiastic about the house inspections Isolde held for a while. "You would be docked fifty cents from your allowance every time you screwed up." The allowance, which Isolde dispensed, was only four dollars a week to cover all personal needs.

According to Ariel, "Isolde became unpopular because she was in charge, used to bitch at them to clean their rooms, get a job. Mark stirred up trouble by badmouthing." Mark Lembert, styling himself the Marquis de Lombardia, flashed a marvelous homemade purple cape, and said, "I don't see eye to eye with the leaders in this house." One evening the Marquis demanded to see the group's financial records, which Woody was keeping at Isolde's orders. She refused to hand them over. Isolde played the Head of House role in the traditional Power fashion: secretively, dogmatically, and inconsistently. When it became apparent that opposition to her was reaching revolutionary proportions, The Omega installed Bob Stone and Ariel as co-heads of House, and gave the wholly honorary posts of Apartment Heads to Marsha and Maude. "It was total competition in Waltham," Ariel says. "You tried to be manipulating things into the direction you wanted them to go, 'cause we still thought we were creating The Power. I was trying to make damn sure that I was going to have a good position, that we were going to go in the direction I wanted to go in, that I never made a wrong move. So it was like everybody existing in paranoia."

From the very beginning, people were constantly being expelled from the house or made so uncomfortable that they left voluntarily. Unfortunately, this ostracism process never succeeded in pruning the group down to an efficient, cohesive core. There was none. Rico Sorbo and Ron Forbes lived at Waltham only briefly. Rico lost his job in November, just before moving into the house, tried to keep the fact secret, then was embarrassed into leaving when the truth came out. He had been a security guard. Kids threw rocks at him. He called the real cops. His boss said, "If you can't handle things like this yourself, you shouldn't be a guard. You're fired." Ron Forbes also left because he couldn't hold a job. Isolde reprimanded him for doing very little work around the house and sleeping much of the time.

The most dynamic person expelled from the house was Al Capone. He claimed to be the great-nephew of the infamous gangster of the same name, and acted the part. Ariel says, "Al has two very distinct sides. On one side, he's a really fantastic guy who has charisma, enthusiasm, energy, dedication, anything you'd want. And on the other side, he's quite mad and violent. He drinks very heavily." The group told Al he could not drink in the house, but he did anyway. "He couldn't just *drink*, he'd get *wasted*. And when he gets wasted, he gets violent." If someone got in his way, he'd shout, "I'll kill you!" They knew he was capable of it. According to one story, he became angry with The Omega and threw Osiris over a table. Sam Rhodes says Al was often drunk, and "very destructive, very Satanic, ripping things asunder. Ungoverned fury. He'd go around doing great physical damage to other people." A year earlier, when Marsha was visibly pregnant, Al Capone had punched her quite hard in the stomach. Typical Capone behavior. Roger Bergman calls Al "powerful" and "mercurial." At the Thanksgiving party, Al sang some crooner songs of the 1950s, "in his bright yellow sweater with tears in his eyes, terribly sentimental. And everybody thought: This is marvelous! But later he got drunk and went around yelling, 'Bullshit! It's fucking bullshit! Bullshit! Bullshit!' Stomping around in the middle of the Alpha, scaring the daylights out of everybody. Nobody dared say a word."

Al contributed good work managing the kitchens but refused to go out and look for a job. An ex-convict, he did not believe he could find one. On top of all the other problems, Sam says, Al "was going through a very heavy emotional conflict with a girl who was outside The Power. He wanted her, but she thought The Power was a bunch of freaks." Roger says the girl was "a tough bitch of a stripper. She was the only woman who would stand up to him and fight." Sam says the "girl was two-timing him." Roger explains that Al's rival was "a Chinese guy who was paying her off to be his semi-mistress." Al would call her on the phone and come away "teary-eyed," saying "he had to become a man of steel and keep his feelings inside. He had to be tough. He had to be like a rock. She came over a couple of times, and she was amazingly prudish about The Power, called us a Devil Cult. Brought her kids over, and there was an incident where the kids wouldn't stop crying. They were supposed to be sleeping in the next room, and he *smacked* one of the kids, and the kid was bleeding from the nose." Sam Rhodes reports Al's Chinese rival was a Kung Fu expert. This presented a problem. Al was a tough guy, but not very brave. Not wanting to lose a fight with his rival, he prepared a surprise. "Al took a hammer to the guy's knee before he could do anything to him. Pow! And the guy was wiped out." The Walthamites were so terrified of Al Capone they could not tell him to leave, but withdrew from him and created an uncomfortable atmosphere. Al left to live with his stripper friend. At last word, he had moved to New York, saying he was going to be a hit man for the Mafia.

A creeping problem that poisoned social life progressively at Waltham was a crime wave of petty thefts. The members never pooled their private property. They were extremely possessive about their rooms, and complained that their privacy was often violated. Mel Potts, who slept in a hallway, used to throw open doors and burst into rooms without knocking. The identity of the house thieves was never determined, although there was much evidence against several people. Mark ran up hundred-dollar phone bills without any intention of paying for them. When Isolde accused him, he denied any guilt, then accused her of using church money to buy special food for herself. In January, someone stole Isolde's copies of the doctrinal Missal from her room. Marsha's radio disappeared. Money vanished from several rooms. Mail was intercepted, opened, and deprived of any checks and cash it contained. One of the two electric typewriters was stolen. D. Lord said that he had hidden three dollars in the handle of a screwdriver. Only Ron Forbes knew about it. The money was gone. D. Lord said he suspected Ron had run off with Marsha's radio, but Marsha said that was impossible. The mood of the house was ill feeling and suspicion. Some suspected Quincy. Some suspected D. Lord. Some suspected Mark. Some suspected various guests. D. Lord said many of his best woodworking tools had been vanishing from the basement. I happen to know that D. Lord himself secretly sold some of these tools for booze money. The thefts continued as long as anyone was living at Waltham. Perhaps everybody was the thief.

One big step toward disintegration was the affair of Quincy, Wendy, and Julio. All three were useless, miserable people. Wendy came from a completely uncommunicative family. I met her father and brother. Neither chose to speak with me during the half hour I visited with them. Wendy said her father never let her mother leave the house until the day she died. Wendy herself was extremely dispirited and withdrawn. Quincy was an infantile fellow. He claimed his troubles had begun when he was sixteen.

His mother seduced him and began having sex with her son on a regular basis. His father gave silent acceptance. After a long time, Quincy ran away from home. He and Wendy met, she got pregnant, and they married in The Power. Quincy's level of maturity is indicated by the fact that he once dragged me into a toy store and begged me to buy him a two-dollar set of plastic toy soldiers.

Julio Famagusta, an unwashed, lazy character, was just barely human enough to get sexually hungry. He leched after a street teenybopper named Georgia, but she rebuffed him. He made a pass at Mark's girl, Blanche, but Mark scared him off. He went after Wendy and cleverly began to develop a sexual relationship that included Quincy. Wendy's husband had been in particularly bad emotional shape for several days. He cried on Vita Cordova's shoulder about the terribly heavy demands Isolde was making on him to get a job. He convinced Wendy, Blanche, and Roger to have a hugging festival while they were standing in the Alpha. Onlookers called it "spiritual masturbation" and "group sex." Quincy was open to Julio's advances. The three of them began a session of group sex, but Quincy was unable to get adequately aroused. He fled the scene in disgrace, leaving Julio to have intercourse with Wendy. Quincy told me his self-confidence had been shattered. He felt he was a complete failure as a husband.

The secret was kept for only a few hours. Quincy told Isolde, seeking help, but she reacted badly. Afraid the affair would ruin Edward's faith in her ability to run the house, she made Quincy swear not to tell The Omega. He unburdened himself to me, because there was no one in the house with whom he could share his feelings. They all despised him, just as many despised each other. At midnight, when everybody was gathered for Evening Assembly, Edward, Osiris, and Lilith unexpectedly burst in and took over the situation. For two hours they discussed the state of the house. I watched Quincy squirm in the corner, afraid his shame would come into the open. Julio kept dropping hints that he had something to say, each time causing Quincy terrible anguish. Finally Julio boasted he had gotten into "heavy contacts" with Quincy and Wendy. "Shut up, Julio!" Quincy shouted, but it was too late. Edward slowly and gently drew Quincy out. Stammering and ashamed, Quincy told part of the story. Edward remained calm, relaxed, accepting. He toyed with his pipe and smiled. He said adultery was not a sin. There are no sexual rules at all in The Power. He asked Quincy what he thought he had lost. Everything, Quincy replied. Edward disagreed. Either the relationship between Quincy and Wendy had never been worth anything, or it was strong enough to survive current difficulties. There was no reason to blame anyone. There was no justification for prohibiting similar sexual behavior in the future. If Julio and Wendy wanted to carry on an affair, then that was fine. No person could own another. Each person must be completely free to follow the desires of the moment.

D. Lord disagreed strenuously. He was extremely possessive over Rose, his "old lady," and felt that marriage should be sacred. Lilith angrily told him marriage was an abomination. She hated marriage. To hell with it! Edward commented that conventional marriage was part of the Human Game, foolishness. Powerites should not need futile symbols of false security. Nobody gave Quincy help or sympathy. As Ariel put it, "The ideal of The Power was not to be a problem-handling center, but a community that was going to grow and thrive."

Within a few days, Quincy had decided to leave the house and take Wendy with him. She was miserable. "I feel like I'm coming apart," literally torn in two directions at once. They had no money. At first they were afraid to seek assistance from the town of Waltham, because they were already guilty of welfare fraud in three states. After two awkward weeks as "guests" of the house, they moved to a decayed apartment in a wreck of a house near Waltham Center. Quincy announced that his place was the new Boston Chapter of The Power, and said he and Wendy would hold a coffee house, Mondays through Thursdays. Nobody came. Quincy acquired a revolver and left it loaded on his TV table to assert a measure of masculinity. He hung a framed certificate stating his honorable service in the U.S. Air Force. Of course, the document was a cheap forgery.

D. Lord was disillusioned by the affair and by his own failure to achieve anything at Waltham. He began drinking heavily, and was finally expelled from the house by Rose. He moved in with Quincy and pretended to be renovating the building for its owner. Finally, Quincy and the owner got a court restraining order to force D. Lord to stay away from them. Ironically, the last time I spoke with him, months later, he had been hired as the security guard for the apartment building that had been constructed on the site of the old Cambridge Power chapter house. The apartments were not yet finished, and his payment was the right to sleep on the concrete floor.

Not all disruptive cult deviance took place in the house. Judas and Georgia were two street hippies who frequently visited Waltham. Judas had assumed this heavy name because it described his purpose in life: betrayal. Blond, twenty-two, cross-eyed, he picked up little Georgia after she ran away from home. She pretended to be grown up, but was only fourteen. They lived on the streets, or under them. They often slept in side tunnels of the Boston subway system. Sometimes they met up with other street people and made bonfires of rubbish in the tunnels to keep warm. When they were permitted to crash with people who had apartments, they were not good guests. Georgia would take her clothes off, then sit chatting with folks, her legs spread wide apart. One time Judas and Georgia began having sex while their host was entertaining visitors. The only space in the room was under the sink, so that was where they began their athletic copulations. When they were done, Georgia got up suddenly, bumped her head on the sink, and fell unconscious. Soon after her fifteenth birthday, Georgia discovered that she was pregnant. Judas said he'd probably stick with her until her belly got too big for sex, then leave her. God knows what finally happened.

When not diverted by outsiders' antics, the Walthamites fought each other in a never-ending scramble. Mark and Blanche refused to accept house discipline. One evening a doctrinal seminar was in progress, presumably one of the most important house activities. Mark pointedly turned his radio up full, and disgustedly told the scripture students that they were jerks. Then he and Blanche went into the adjacent room and began having thunderously noisy sex. They stood against the wall right by the students' ears and bashed into it with every thrust. Blanche screamed and Mark pounded on the thin wall with his fists.

Another time, Blanche attacked Marsha. The telephone was in Marsha's name, so she was responsible for paying the bills. Blanche enjoyed calling her family in Chicago, and racked up a hundred dollars in long distance charges. She did not plan to reimburse Marsha. Screw the phone company! Marsha argued that Blanche was putting her in a bad position. Blanche went to use the phone. Marsha blocked her way. Blanche clouted Marsha twice with the telephone, then threatened her with a kitchen knife! Rose rushed to The Omega, hoping that Osiris would come with his great spiritual power and settle things. He refused to try. The next day, Marsha filed a complaint at the Waltham City Hall. Blanche received a court summons. She promised the judge she would not hit Marsha again, and planned to leave the house in a few days. When the lovely pair finally drove off very early one morning in their car rebuilt with stolen parts, they left behind an overdrawn bank account and an unpaid phone bill. Marsha's phone was disconnected, and she was told she could not get a new one anywhere until she paid up.

The Omega said it was quite shocked and disgusted by all the problems and conflict in the house. Repeatedly, Edward, Lilith, and Osiris commented that the Walthamites could have solved all their problems by studying Power scriptures. Edward felt his teachings were the heart of the cult, yet few of his followers seemed to care about the doctrines at all. Despite the weekly doctrinal seminars and the twice-daily rituals, the

Walthamites never seemed to absorb the basic tenets of the cult. Bob Stone had his own doctrine, Bobbycraft. Julio Famagusta professed to be an exalted mystic and spent more time dervishing in front of his Rosicrucian altar than working around the house. Ron Forbes was one of the few who understood the doctrines, but he enjoyed profaning the services. For example, he once caused a startling interruption at one of the Sabbath Assemblies. Twenty people were present that evening. Roger was the Sacrifist, and Julio the Evangelist. Julio had just begun his sermon, when Ron pulled out a gun and fired at him. Bang! Bang! Bang! Blanks.

One theory of Functionalist sociological analysis is the idea that the shared ideology and collective ritual provided by a religion work to unify the group that practices it. Both ideology and ritual are supposed to be powerful forces producing social structure and cohesion out of chaos. The Power had a vivid, shared set of symbols. The Walthamites participated in seminars and used many elements of Edward's culture in their everyday speech. They sang rousing hymns and enacted dramatic rituals. The result was failure. Neither the ideology nor the ritual seemed to have much strength to hold the members together. Divisions in the social structure and material conflicts remained. I believe that ideology and ritual may have important consequences, but are primarily epiphenomenal. They are extensions of informal social relations. The Power had to exist as a cohesive social group before its culture could have any meaning. A cohesive social group cannot be created by the mere mechanical recitation of ideology and ritual, the superficial expressions of cohesion.

Edward's response to all the schisms was to promulgate new doctrines. He said the cult was evolving into a new, highly differentiated stage in which several branches, each with its own style, would cooperate. He said The Establishment was really only the Jehovian Order of The Power, although it was not yet ready to admit this fact. The Walthamites were the Luciferian Order. Ultimately, The Omega would be supreme over all of them. He conceptually divided his current followers into two Power groups P1 and P2. The first were the people closest to him, mainly the ex-Messengers, and the second were those individuals continually splitting away. P1 was closest to God; P2 was closest to Humanity. They were integrated in his mind through his habitual conceptualization that all reality was divided into cooperating polar opposites. Jehovians and Luciferians, P1 and P2, would work together for common Power goals. His intellectual structures proved, however, to have absolutely no power to influence reality. His mental images could not hold together a disintegrating house of disorganized people.

ECONOMIC FAILURE

Waltham was an economic as well as a social failure. Only Woody and Bob held jobs throughout the life of the chapter. Woody was an orderly at an institution for the mentally retarded, a difficult, menial job. He sometimes worked double shifts to bring in extra money. Bob Stone kept his computer job. Vita Cordova was a telephone secretary at an electronic supply company for a while, and worked as a go-go dancer in Boston's red-light district after that. Quincy and Marsha briefly held security guard jobs. Ron Forbes helped Rose get a job at The Minuteman Restaurant when she lost a secretarial position, but she did not have reliable transportation and lost this job quickly too. Blanche made a few dollars at Señor Pizza, and her boyfriend Mark earned as much by selling his own blood to the blood bank. Four of the men worked at one time or another for the Alert gas station down the road, and a number got intermittent employment through Handy Andy, a manual labor bureau. Julio Famagusta worked a single day for an antique store. He was hired to restore old furniture, and after a few hours of attacking an aged cabinet with definishing goo and scraper, he was happy to rejoin the ranks of the unemployed.

D. Lord did not feel up to looking for outside work. He said nobody would hire an ex-convict, and he was afraid to show his face in Boston because the police wanted him on an assault charge. Instead, he spent many hours setting up a woodworking shop in the basement, collecting antique tools, including a 500-pound radial arm saw. Sam Rhodes helped by illegally rewiring the cellar electric circuit board to accommodate the equipment. Except for the fancy ritual furniture, the only product that ever emerged from this Power wood factory was an uneven, unfinished prototype nicknack shelf. D. Lord complained that he could not start making money until he had a good table saw. The lack of a saw was his perpetual excuse for doing no work. One time Sam Rhodes donated one hundred dollars toward the purchase of a secondhand saw, but Isolde decided to pay off one of Woody's bills instead.

For months, Bob Stone and Sam Rhodes had planned to start a Power Craft Store. Many inexperienced young people imagine they can earn a living through their favorite childhood hobbies. Bob Stone made a photo enlarger out of an old potato chip can. It worked but never achieved commercial quality prints. He also made and sold a few tiny glass horses, using materials provided by a glass crafts kit. Nobody else was able to master the technique. Undaunted, the Walthamites organized on paper The Power Craft Factory, planning to support themselves through candlemaking, glassblowing, woodworking, astrology charts, aura spins, leather work, terrariums, and silkscreening. The greatest effort went into candle manufacture. Even Edward tried his hand at it. Isolde retrieved a huge tin container, a yard square, from the junkyard. It was placed on cinder blocks in the cellar, given an inside floor of bricks, and nearly filled with water. Several large cans were placed inside, each containing wax of a different color. To heat the water and thereby melt the wax, they immersed an electric fry pan and turned it on. The apparatus took so long to heat up that they left the fry pan connected day and night, for weeks. It is a wonder somebody wasn't electrocuted, and an equal wonder the house didn't burn down. The first step in manufacture was to cast white wax candle cores in star-shaped molds, with a long piece of common string for the wick. Then this core was dunked repeatedly in different colors of wax, building up polychrome layers. Before the wax had completely set, the pointed edges were undercut and peeled back like flower petals. The result was an ornate, splendid, fragile centerpiece. Isolde had seen candles like this on sale for several dollars each. Out of more than thirty produced, only three were ever sold. The wax petals habitually broke off, and it seemed impossible to keep the surface of the wax from clouding over.

A last-ditch attempt by Rose to start a coffee house in her bedroom did not even earn enough money to pay for the tea and sugar. Business was bad all around.

Originally, Edward was opposed to street donating. But shortly before Christmas, the Walthamites decided to give it a try. First they needed a magazine to sell. They pulled material from old Power publications, composed poems, and invented little church announcements. Edward contributed an open letter on the future of the cult. Dim photographs showed house residents at work. They printed five thousand copies of their amateur publication at a cost of two hundred and fifty dollars, and planned to ask fifty cents for each copy on the streets. Groups went into Boston a half-dozen times, and once to New York. Without training or proper uniforms, they hawked this pathetic magazine in the winter cold, making themselves miserable. This last Power magazine was designed to net about two thousand dollars. It brought in only a couple of hundred before the project was abandoned.

Retrieving was a fairly successful source of food, liberating what cash there was for other expenses. Much of the food was purchased before mid-December, and the menu included entrees like: Tuna and Noodle Casserole, Sloppy Joes, Arroz con Pollo, Meat Loaf, Shit on Shingles, Rose's Surprise, and Frankfurts and Beans. The Walthamites were still hoping to save up money for the Survival Center, so the Heads of House decreed that absolutely all food should be retrieved. Several times I went out with house members at five in the morning to beg at Boston's vegetable and meat distribution centers. These places are collections of little transshipping warehouses. Big trucks come in from out of state and unload in the middle of the night, then little trucks come and take the food to local supermarkets. The New England Produce Center in Chelsea, really a part of Boston, has nearly fifty of these establishments, each specializing in a different fruit or vegetable, all arranged in immensely long buildings. We would walk from one to the next, begging. "Hello, we are from The Power Church in Waltham. I'm Brother William, and this is Brother Quincy. We have a community center in Waltham where we feed twenty-five families a week. Could you help us by making a donation of food?" We did not mention that the church had no charter or social function. The "twenty-five families" were actually the twenty-five individuals that lived in the house. I was surprised to find that about a third of the managers we spoke with gave us something each time. We had no competition. It would have been easy for anyone to go there, pretend to represent a church, and come away with a carload of food. But the job was terribly unpleasant, and the one car kept breaking down, so Waltham was pitifully short of decent food. Usually we got vegetables. For an entire week the house subsisted on carrot and onion stew (no meat) augmented by stale Sweetie Pie marshmallow cookies. The diet was not sufficiently nourishing for body or spirit.

Waltham retrieving had two sides: begging and stealing. The Power was like a primitive tribe of hunters and gatherers. Begging was like gathering, taking something from nature with no opposition. Stealing was like hunting, taking despite opposition. Antelopes do not like to be killed by hunters. Shopkeepers do not like to be ripped off by thieves. I remember an argument Wendy had with her husband Quincy. He was driving Bob Stone's car, the only working vehicle except for mine, and began boasting about his skill at shoplifting. Wendy said she was good at it too. Quincy said she was a lousy shoplifter. Wendy said no, she was excellent. Quincy ended the argument by bashing into another car. It was a good thing no damage was done, because the car had no insurance and Quincy had no driver's license. I once watched Mark shoplift the sparkplugs he needed to fix up his car. For a week, Roger Bergman took the train to Boston looking for a job; each day he rode in the men's room because he could not afford a ticket. He was retrieving a ride.

The Walthamites slid into debt. They could not keep even, let alone build up a Survival Center fund. Ariel said things were going along okay until "It doesn't look like we're going to make February's rent. We've got a lot of people in the house that are not making any money." The total rent for the three apartments was $875 monthly, not counting utilities. The Omega conferred with the three Heads of House. "So we decided the only thing we can do is say everybody produces eighty dollars a week." There had been an informal goal of "$750 collectively" a week, but now the responsibility fell on each individual. Woody earned $100 per week, and Bob Stone something over $130. Several other members of the house immediately panicked. Pessimism grew, then turned to anger. Tension built to explosive pressure.

A few days after the stern announcement, Marsha picked up a newspaper and began looking through the real estate ads. She had very little money but was contemplating moving out of The Power. Mel Potts reminded her that their names were on the lease of the third apartment of the house. The Omega could not kick her out! With Mark, Blanche, Rose, and D. Lord, she decided to take over the third apartment. Bob and Maude Stone began talking about leaving. Bob mused about starting a cult of his own. Roger, Julio, Isolde, Woody, Ariel, Vita, and Mel stuck with The Omega. A week after this schism, Roger told me the $80 rule was suspended because not all the people in his group had been able to make it. "It was a kind of test," he said, intended to find the real core of Powerites who were really dedicated. Actually, it was an impulsive demand, only afterward defined as a calculated test. A couple of weeks later, Isolde and Woody threw off their onerous responsibilities. They disappeared to join the fundamentalist Church of the Living God.

TORONTO

On February 14, Edward flew to Toronto to check out the group there. There were eight full-time adult members, five of them living with their four children in a large house on Ontario Street. The Toronto Powerites were decent people, most of them gainfully employed, very different from the average Walthamite. Edward admitted, "Boston, in practical and organizational terms, was a fiasco." He decided to abandon it. Lilith supervised preparations to close down the Waltham house, and joined Edward in Toronto on March 2.

Edward had hoped to find among the Walthamites a few worthy people capable of following him. As early as the beginning of November, he said, "I'm testing like fury in all directions. Well, *I'm* not, but something inside me is. It's as though there's very little time, and I must know who's really with me and who's against me. It's a painful and uncomfortable time for everyone. But those who endure it are mine, and those who don't are not." His principle was: "Many are called, but very very few are chosen." Only five were permitted to follow Edward and Lilith to Toronto: Osiris, Ariel, Vita Cordova, Roger Bergman, and—last and least—Melvin Potts, included more for his loyalty than his potential. For the first two weeks of March, they worked like mad people at several jobs in Boston, earned a great amount of money, then abandoned the Waltham house on the fourteenth. The penniless people in Marsha's apartment left at the end of the month. The ritual equipment was moved to the East Boston apartment of Cher and Spic, where a number of seminars, parties, and rituals were held by the last leftover people.

Osiris left Toronto the day after he got there. The cult no longer promised to satisfy his desires for excitement, power, or spiritual growth. He planned to return to his artistic pottery, write a book on Sufism using Arabic sources, and establish his own spiritual retreat in backcountry New England. When he spoke with Lilith on the phone, she told him that his dragon and cross emblem had been abandoned in favor of a completely new symbol invented by Edward. Lilith refused to tell Osiris how it looked, but toyed with him, making him guess. Edward's emblem, she said, would not contain either a dragon or a cross.

When I saw the new symbol in Toronto, I discovered Lilith had been only half right. As shown in Figure 17, it is a double cross, the upright Christian cross combined with the inverted Satanic cross. The Sign of Union was placed at the center of the Christian cross, where the upper arm intersects the vertical bar. The Power Sign was placed on the lower arm, at the center of the Satanic cross. Thus, the two unifying symbols nailed the two opposing crosses together, as Edward says, "in an unbreakable alliance."

There were several reasons why Osiris' dragon symbol was abandoned. Rank-and-file members had neither understood nor liked it. It was so complex that it did not catch the eye of the outsider the way earlier symbols had. There was also a theological reason for its replacement. The dragon, symbolic of Separation, expressed what had happened at Waltham, and Edward hoped to achieve greater success in Toronto with an optimistic new Unity symbol. Finally, the dragon was very much Osiris' personal emblem. It had been part of Osiris' attempt to seize power and status within the cult. After Osiris abandoned Edward, Edward marked the breach between them by abandoning the symbol of Osiris.

Edward resolved that he would not make the same mistakes in Toronto that he had in Boston. He believed that he had not exercised enough control at Waltham, so he made a vigorous effort to seize control of Toronto. He did not realize until too late that this was an equal mistake. The Canadians had already achieved high cohesiveness among themselves and were in

Figure 17. The New Unity Symbol Designed by Edward

reasonably good control of their own lives. While Edward was at a distance, they loved him as their charismatic teacher. By calling themselves Powerites and claiming to follow him, they achieved the feeling that they were glorious pioneers, building a movement of cosmic significance. But when Edward actually came to live with them, their love faded. He expected them to feed, clothe, and house him. He demanded absolute authority. A bad bargain.

For the first time in the history of the cult, Edward participated fully in the rituals. This had the bad effect of putting every other ritual performer in second-rate status. Edward wrote a new set of church incorporation documents designed to make him dictator. "Edward de Forest is the Teacher. He cannot be removed from office. He sits on the Board of Directors. He is entitled to veto any resolution of the board." Adding injury to insult, the last Walthamites arrived. Ariel says, "We hit that place like a ton of bricks!" Suddenly there were two rival groups in the house, and Edward seemed to prefer others over the five original residents of Ontario Street.

Then the most cataclysmic split of all occurred. Lilith, always unpredictable, always adventuresome, began a lusty sexual relationship with Brother Simon, a good-looking young Englishman. The Canadians were deeply shocked. Both Lilith and Simon were newcomers to the house. Ceres, mother of two of the children in the house, was scandalized. She felt Lilith was "acting like the Whore of Babylon," threatening all the relationships in the house. Brother Pericles, who was the leader of the Canadian faction and wanted no competition for that role, pretended to be shocked as well.

The most stricken of all was Edward. All the rhetoric he had given Quincy when Julio had stolen Wendy away proved to be utterly hollow. Edward could not take his own advice, and try as he might, could not console himself with Power teachings. He and Lilith got into terrible fights and ruined the respect the others had for them. On March 17, Edward said, "Now we face the most intense and the greatest vulnerability of all. I've twisted into it. I've brought the pain on myself again. But this time with no obvious way out. Not even the road of death and rebirth. This time I've trapped myself." All his security, the shreds of his remaining self-respect, were tied up in Lilith. He groped for a doctrinal explanation. It was the anniversary of The Separation, at least of the formal date of Edward's expulsion. He decided that the spiritual issues engaged at the time of the original schism had not been resolved, and this new schism was the great opportunity to resolve them for good. Both Kitty and Lilith were JS personalities. He had been terribly dependent on both of them. Perhaps this time he would conquer the JS pattern, or his dependence upon strong women, and achieve the cure he had struggled to find for so many years.

Edward moved out of the house to live with a former Disciple, Harold Day. This fellow was a true gentleman, reasonably prosperous in business, and very kindly. Day tried to mediate between Edward and Lilith. She of course asserted her Luciferian right to free love. The Canadian and American factions at Ontario Street were at each other's throats. Edward appointed Ariel treasurer of the entire group, but Pericles refused to hand over the cashbox and accounts. Ariel comments, "Charles Manson talks about how the coyote is so paranoid, he's totally in time. By the time I got to Toronto, I was so conditioned to paranoia. Got to watch out for my standing, you know, or I'll slip. It was a power struggle. I felt like I was involved in the French Revolution, you know, Robespierre trying to axe Danton. Really tight intrigue. At times it was medieval, palacelike." Unbeknownst to Edward, Pericles pried the locked door off Edward's office, stole his copy of the secret Teachings, Xeroxed it, and replaced everything as it had been. Pericles planned his own cult, without Edward.

On March 25, 1975, the last Power chapter disintegrated. In the afternoon, Edward despaired: "Again the Valley of the Shadow. No light. No relief. No hope." Everyone came together for a long meeting after supper, and the false unity of The Power was formally dissolved. Over the following days, individuals spun off in different directions. Vita and Ariel ultimately returned to Boston. Melvin Potts and three of the Canadians moved into an apartment. Pericles and his woman Bonnie went to British Columbia to start a new life. Others vanished.

For three days Edward would not eat anything. He sat in a corner of Harold's living room, brooding and trembling. "Where the hell do I go from here?" he asked himself. Several of us sat in a circle with him, casting I Ching fortunes. Edward took each of them very seriously. We threw the three silver coins made for Edward by Brother Mark years before. On one side of each was an ornate cross, on the other the head of a goat. Christ and Satan joined. With great interest, Edward read each fortune from a big book and gave his interpretations. He asked himself, "Why don't we all cut our losses and scrap it?" He looked around at me, Vita, Roger, Ariel, and Harold, all soon to disperse. He thought, "Perhaps they're all quite happy playing their alienating games with one another. Perhaps we should just leave them to it. Perhaps the link is totally compulsive on my side. Perhaps the Unity is a myth, after all." Edward's followers abandoned him, but in the end Lilith returned and they were reconciled.

CONCLUSION

George Oberhofer, my able research assistant at Waltham, wrote an excellent term paper for a Harvard deviance course, analyzing the decay of the group in terms of Rosabeth Kanter's model of commitment.[1] He felt the key to the failure of Edward's second cult was his permissive concept of The New Game. The Establishment succeeded in holding members and making money under the authoritarian rule of Jehovah. The new Power died under the liberal regime of Lucifer. Oberhofer says, "What the New Game actually did was to ban the concept of 'blame' within The Power's social structure; in so doing it inhibited the suppression of behavior which undermined the two most basic goals—and needs—of The Power as a sociocultural system." These goals were "the detachment of its members from all other human institutions, and the attachment of them to a more 'godly' way of life." He cites Kanter's lengthy discussion of a long list of "commitment mechanisms" that ensure longevity for utopian communities, norms that bind members and reduce the likelihood of their defection. He writes,

[1] Rosabeth Moss Kanter, *Commitment and Community* (Cambridge: Harvard University Press, 1972).

"In order to remain distinct and cohesively organized, such groups must detach members from the outside world so as to minimize or eliminate any advantage members might see in returning to the outside; they must also attach members to their own social structure so as to provide them with comparative advantages for remaining within the group." To give a simple example: If members can be made to invest prior wealth and current labor in the community, and are not permitted to withdraw any of their investment upon leaving, they will be more likely to stay in order to receive some benefit from that investment. Oberhofer observes that The Omega utterly failed to achieve these ends. Because of its permissive ideology, it refused to exercise authority and enforce norms that would have served commitment and cohesion. "The hierarchy, under the influence of the New Game, could not blame its subjects; their behavior was simply written off as 'enactments' or 'performances.'"

Kanter's analysis fails to ask what factors make it possible to enforce authoritarian norms. She also neglects the question of how successful utopian communities are formed in the first place. As Oberhofer says, the analysis concentrates on commitment mechanisms that maintain cohesion in a group already somewhat cohesive. Authoritarian rule is impossible until after members are already strongly committed to a group. We have seen that The Power emerged from a social implosion that transformed a loosely connected network of individuals into a tight unit. Only after the implosion did its members accept authoritarian rule. The Walthamites were never cohesive. When they arrived in Toronto, they smashed the cohesion that had developed there. Had Edward been a more decisive leader, he might have been able to cull from the mob that swarmed around him a few stable people who were ready to build good relationships with each other and follow him. But the mere suppression of deviance would not have bound together the disorganized, pathological majority of the latter-day Powerites.

I agree with Oberhofer that anarchism is not a good ideology with which to build an authoritarian movement. But as modern psychotherapy has shown, it is possible to build looser, more liberal movements through a network of gratifying intimate relationships around an ideology of freedom. Edward felt that The Establishment had achieved a false success, a plush prison for its members. Authority means loss of freedom. In The Establishment, Kitty's control perspective won out over Edward's liberation perspective. Flattered by people like the Walthamites into attempting a renewal of the old structures, Edward was seduced into self-betrayal. He almost became the slave of his will to power, and only failure saved him.

The Power was Edward's therapy. He was its patient even before he was its creator. To cure himself he had to conquer guilt. "Blame is the core of strife and discord," says one Power Precept. Another says, "Blame is the detonator of all evil"; blame triggers an explosion of wickedness. In his unpublished manuscript *Blame and Demand*, Edward wrote, "Through blame we perpetuate our own self-punishment. It's the greatest burden of all, because it's the source of all other burdens." While an authoritarian religious commune might successfully hold people, it would not be good for them. In another unpublished book manuscript, Edward wrote, "People don't exist to be sacrificed before the altar of religious doctrine. Religious doctrine exists for the overall benefit of people."

On April 26, 1975, Edward de Forest returned to Boston to bid farewell. He was accompanied by Harold and Lilith. Two dozen Powerites crammed into the living room of Cher's apartment for the last Sabbath Assembly ever held. Edward was Evangelist. When it came time for his revelation, he dissolved the ritual, sat in the Sacrifist's chair so he could see everyone, and explained the meaning of The Power. He said it was a mistake to think of The Power as a church organization. The Power was change, not static authority. An informal group of cooperating Powerites could be fine, increasing each person's awareness while preserving his freedom. "But when that becomes the source of your security, when that becomes what you lean on—whether it's for spiritual security, physical security, the security of giving you an identity or a function, or emotional security—it's unstable. It's unreal. It's not The Power. I can give no one here security, nor can any organization I might ever form or have formed. What I can do is help each Powerite to find that security within himself. That is what Power teachings are about." The Power is not a church, but a path of discovery leading each Powerite individually to God. "God, for each one of us, is inside each one of us. And there's the ultimate in security." Edward's parting words were: "To put it bluntly, you're on your own!"

When Harold Day drove back to Toronto that Sunday, he was alone. The last leftover Toronto Powerites demanded to know what had happened to Edward. Harold told the story. He, Bill Bainbridge, Lilith, and Edward were walking through Harvard Square in Cambridge. Lilith and Edward were a few paces behind, talking in low tones. Suddenly they ran up to Bill and Harold, saying: "Look. We're going to leave. We're not going to tell you where we are. We'll be in touch. Bye-bye!" They disappeared into the crowd and were not seen again. When Roger Bergman heard this story, he exclaimed "Jesus Christ!" When Ariel learned that the story was not true, he said, "It never stops, does it!"

ELEVEN

The Triumph of Satan

Satan rules all the strong!
His hordes ride for the
Victory of God!
Salvation! Salvation!
—Power chant.

In the end, Satan triumphed. Schism after schism, The Power shattered. Powerites dispersed to the four winds, and there was nothing left. Christ is Unification, Satan is Separation. The Unity of Christ and Satan was not fulfilled at the end, but at the beginning. The social implosion that created The Power was radical separation from the social environment coupled with radical unification within the small group. That implosion ran its course and could never be repeated. Without complete understanding, the doctrines of the cult described its social experience but were powerless to influence events.

In the end, the Gods flew apart. The Union of Jehovah and Lucifer was accomplished with the marriage of Kitty and Edward. With their divorce, it was broken. The Establishment begged Jehovah to rule them; the new Power groped for the promise of Lucifer. The cohesive Establishment manifested the Spirit of Christ, although in its rejection of Edward it forswore the name of Christ. The disorganized Power manifested the Spirit of Satan, although in Edward's false hopes it denied the name of Satan. In the beginning, The Power separated from the world. In the end, it separated from itself.

Magic and religion are powerless to influence the physical world. There is no heaven above the sky. No divine hand ever reaches through the clouds to raise up the fallen. But mind and society can be influenced. Magic is radical psychology. Religion is radical sociology. Conventional social science is not a powerful force for change, so a social scientist has no right to scorn The Power for its weakness. Not Freud, not Marx, not any of the pseudo-scientific gurus of modern times has been able to cure mankind of its ills. Several founders of The Power admitted to me that the cult had not given them happiness. It had given them intensity. When times were good, they were ecstatic. When times were bad, they were miserable. There was little between.

The Power may have been folly, but it was not madness. It was amoral, but not wicked. The exceptional men and women who formed the cult bet their lives they could rise above average human existence. To rise above, they also had to sink beneath. That is Satan's principle. Their commitment to complete honesty among themselves was compromised by deceitful behavior toward followers and outsiders. The dishonor of their failings was balanced by the honor of their aspirations.

The cult could not transcend the physical world, so it sought glory in the social world. Soon after the implosion, it play-acted millenarianism, asserting moral superiority through flamboyant, apocalyptic prophecies. In search of glory, in flight from normality, it anathematized grey blandness. But the audience for this theatrical performance was conventional society itself. Powerites wanted to have glorious impact, "to create effects." As time passed, and as the value of comfort grew, the cult transformed itself in hopes of achieving acceptance while remaining astonishing. After The Separation, leading Establishers developed close ties of friendship with their equals outside the cult. The Establishment fell back into the world. The Power fell completely out of the world.

After saying farewell to the Boston Powerites, Edward and Lilith stayed for a week with me, then lived in Toronto with Harold Day until they had raised enough money to escape North America. They flew to London at the beginning of June 1975. For a while they stayed with Edward's parents, then moved into a furnished apartment. They both took common jobs, Edward with a shipping company, and settled into ordinary lives. In a few weeks they were married.

They did not give up all hope for The Power. Several former followers in London made contact. Edward even spoke with the man who had made the original P-Scope so many years before. For months Edward had contemplated spreading his teachings through a mail-order correspondence course. A committee consisting of Osiris, Ariel, and myself had worked on this project at Waltham. In the last days in Toronto, Edward had begun assembling his writing into a series of lessons. Once they were established in London, Edward and Lilith began sending out mimeographed lessons to anyone willing to subscribe.

Throughout this book I have said that The Power was a social phenomenon. Every aspect of it, including the intellectual doctrines, rested on a social base. Edward's teachings were a projection of his own social experience and had no meaning to anyone who did not already share his social universe. I wrote to Edward, giving him my basic analysis and stressing the importance of the intense social relations from which everything else had sprung. He replied, "I like your analysis of that area," but he was not about to follow my advice to repeat the same pattern over again.

For Edward, cultic society had been a failure. The true Power was his own experiences, personal feelings, and their expression through his writings. "If the course is a success, it should bring some real Powerites out of hiding. Then, wherever we are actually located, we could begin to hold meetings and courses, and later give personal therapy sessions to those whom *we* regard as suitable to have them. That—in a sense—is the old Power in reverse. And I think it's the right way around. It puts an understanding and absorption of The Power itself *first*, and *then* progresses into personal therapy." My analysis suggests that this plan will not succeed.

Lilith vigorously supported Edward's work but was not confident. Writing from London, she told me she had been disillusioned by the abject failure of so many Powerites to fulfill the promise of the teachings. "It actually causes me anxieties when I realize how easy it is to give lip service to something without it ever really meaning anything. It gives me cause to examine my own motivations around Power teachings and precisely what I'm 'using' them for. I must say I'm not heartened by the 'Powerites' we've met here. ALL of them (and I mean ALL) are in what I would call 'ropey' states. Yet it has never occurred to them that perhaps they could solve some of their problems by reading the Power literature that they possess. If those who have had prolonged contact with The Power are still oblivious of what is contained in its theology, are we being foolish by thinking we will be able to reach anyone who has had NO previous contact with it?"

Edward says he has "mixed feelings" about The Establishment. As usual, he perceives duality, but now he also sees duplicity. "For me there are two Establishments. There's the group of Powerites at the top, which I still regard somewhat as my own personal Frankenstein's monster, and for which I feel very responsible. And then there's the helpless harmless group of Establishers gathered round them, looking for God and security and approval and love. And the two elements are completely alien to one another. *Their* union isn't based on an awareness of a fundamental unity, but on a total unawareness of a less fundamental but much more intense dichotomy!"

To add drama to an Establishment radio show, Mother Amaranth quoted Henry Kissinger: "Every civilization that has ever existed has ultimately collapsed." She used the words of this arch-establishmentarian to assert once again the tired millenarian theme: "You would now have to predict that our kind of society would very probably not last much longer." Kissinger viewed Western Civilization from the detached perspective of an historian. With naive lack of detachment, Father Paul vaguely commented, "It looks as though things are coming to some sort of a close, but maybe there's something better coming up." Mother Amaranth wished her cult could grow into a Utopia destined to follow the collapse of the Grey World. She did not understand that Kissinger's words told the story of The Power exactly: "History is a tale of efforts that failed, of aspirations that weren't realized, of wishes that were fulfilled and then turned out to be different from what one expected. So as a historian one has to live with a sense of the inevitability of tragedy."

BIBLIOGRAPHY

Abroms, Gene M. "Persuasion in Psychotherapy." *American Journal of Psychiatry* 124:9 (March 1968):1212–1219.

Ackerknecht, Erwin H. "Psychopathology, Primitive Medicine and Primitive Culture." *Bulletin of the History of Medicine* 14 (1943):30–67.

Adelson, Joseph. "Psychology, Ideology, and the Search for Faith." *The Public Interest* 46 (Winter 1977):119–125.

Adler, Alfred. *Individual Psychology.* Totowa, New Jersey: Littlefield, Adams and Co., (1929) 1968.

———. *Understanding Human Nature.* Greenwich, Connecticut: Fawcett, (1927) 1954.

Allison, Joel. "Adaptive Regression and Intense Religious Experiences." *Journal of Nervous and Mental Disease.* 145:6 (1968):452–463.

Anderson, Nels. *The Hobo.* Chicago: University of Chicago Press, 1923.

Aronson, H., and Walter Weintraub. "Social Background of the Patient in Classical Psychoanalysis." *Journal of Nervous and Mental Disease* 146:2 (1968):91–97.

Bainbridge, William S. *The Spaceflight Revolution.* New York: Wiley-Interscience, 1976.

Balswick, Jack. "The Jesus People Movement: A Generational Interpretation." *Journal of Social Issues* 30:3 (1974):23–42.

Bandura, Albert. *Principles of Behavior Modification.* New York: Holt, Rinehart and Winston, 1969.

Bastide, Roger. *The Sociology of Mental Disorder.* New York: McKay, 1972.

Becker, Howard S. *Outsiders.* New York: Free Press, 1963.

———, ed. *The Other Side.* New York: Free Press, 1964.

Benedict, Ruth. "Anthropology and the Abnormal." *Journal of General Psychology* 10 (1934):59–80.

———. *Patterns of Culture.* Boston: Houghton Mifflin, 1959.

Berger, Peter L. *A Rumor of Angels.* Garden City, New York: Doubleday, 1969.

———. *The Sacred Canopy.* Garden City, New York: Doubleday, 1969.

Berger, Peter L., and Thomas Luckmann. *The Social Construction of Reality.* Garden City, New York: Doubleday, 1966.

Berk, Richard A., and Joseph M. Adams. "Establishing Rapport with Deviant Groups." *Social Problems* 18:1 (Summer 1970):102–117.

Berkower, Lary. "The Enduring Effect of the Jewish Tradition upon Freud." *American Journal of Psychiatry* 125:8 (February 1969): 1067–1073.

Blau, Peter M. *Exchange and Power in Social Life.* New York: Wiley, 1964.

Blumenstiel, Alexander. "An Ethos of Intimacy: Constructing and Using a Situated Moral Revolution." In *Deviance and Respectability*, edited by Jack D. Douglas. New York: Basic Books, 1970, pp. 435–453.

Blumer, Herbert. "Social Movements." In *Studies in Social Movements*, edited by Barry McLaughlin. New York: Free Press, (1951) 1969, pp. 8–29.

Boas, Franz. "The Ethnographical Significance of Esoteric Doctrines." In *Race, Language and Culture.* New York: Free Press, 1940, pp. 312–315.

Bott, Elizabeth. "Urban Families: Conjugal Roles and Social Networks." *Human Relations* 8:4 (1955):345–384.

Bradford, Leland P., Jack R. Gibb, and Kenneth D. Benne, eds. *T-Group Theory and Laboratory Manual.* New York: Wiley, 1964.

Breggin, Peter Roger. "Psychotherapy as Applied Ethics." *Psychiatry* 34 (February 1971):59–74.

Brown, J. A. C. *Freud and the Post-Freudians.* Baltimore: Penguin, 1967.

Cameron, Norman. "The Paranoid Pseudo-Community Revisited." *American Journal of Sociology* 65:1 (July 1959):52–58.

Camus, Albert. *The Myth of Sisyphus.* New York: Random House, 1955.

Carden, Maren Lockwood. *Oneida: Utopian Community to Modern Corporation.* Baltimore: Johns Hopkins, 1969.

Castaneda, Carlos. *Journey to Ixtlan.* New York: Simon and Schuster, 1972.

Clark, Shirley M., and John P. Clark, eds. *Youth in Modern Society.* New York: Holt, Rinehart and Winston, 1972.

Cline, Victor B., and James M. Richards. "A Factor-Analytic Study of Religious Belief and Behavior." *Journal of Personality and Social Psychology* 1:6 (1965):569–578.

Cloward, Richard A., and Lloyd E. Ohlin. *Delinquency and Opportunity.* New York: Free Press, 1960.

Cohen, Albert K. *Delinquent Boys.* New York: Free Press, 1955.

Cohen, Yehudi A. *Social Structure and Personality.* New York: Holt, Rinehart and Winston, 1961.

Cohn, Norman. *The Pursuit of the Millennium.* New York: Oxford University Press, 1970.

Collier, John. *Visual Anthropology: Photography as a Research Method.* New York: Holt, Rinehart and Winston, 1967.

Corathiel, Elisabethe. *Oberammergau and Its Passion Play.* Westminster, Maryland: Newman Press, 1960.

Cox, Harvey. *The Feast of Fools.* New York: Harper and Row, 1969.

―――. *The Secular City.* New York: Macmillan, 1966.

Crowley, Aleister. *The Confessions of Aleister Crowley.* Edited by John Symonds and Kenneth Grant. New York: Hill and Wang, 1969.

Darnton, Robert. *Mesmerism and the End of the Enlightenment in France.* New York: Schocken, 1970.

Davis, Rex, and James T. Richardson. "The Organization and Functioning of the Children of God." *Sociological Analysis* 35:4 (1976):321–339.

Dean, Stanley R. "The Role of Self-Conducted Group Therapy in Psycho-rehabilitation: A Look at Recovery, Inc." *American Journal of Psychiatry* 127:7 (January 1971):934–937.

Deikman, Arthur J. "Implications of Experimentally Induced Contemplative Meditation." *Journal of Nervous and Mental Disease* 142:2 (February 1966):101–116.

Dentan, Robert Knox. *The Semai: A Nonviolent People of Malaya.* New York: Holt, Rinehart and Winston, 1968.

Devereux, George. "Normal and Abnormal: The Key Concepts of Ethnopsychiatry." In *Man and His Culture*, edited by Warner Muensterberger. New York: Taplinger, (1956) 1969, pp. 113–136.

―――, ed. *Psychoanalysis and the Occult.* New York: International Universities Press, 1953.

Dohrman, H. T. *California Cult.* Boston: Beacon Press, 1958.

Douglas, Jack D. *Investigative Social Research.* Beverly Hills, California: Sage, 1976.

Douglas, Mary. *Purity and Danger.* Baltimore: Pelican, 1970.

Dudek, S. Z. "Regression and Creativity." *Journal of Nervous and Mental Disease* 147:6 (1968):535–546.

Durkheim, Emile. *The Division of Labor in Society.* New York: Free Press, 1964.

―――. *The Elementary Forms of the Religious Life.* New York: Free Press, (1915) 1965.

―――. *Suicide.* New York: Free Press, 1951.

Durkheim, Emile, and Marcel Mauss. *Primitive Classification.* Chicago: University of Chicago Press, 1963.

Eaton, Joseph W., and Robert J. Weil. *Culture and Mental Disorders.* Glencoe, Illinois: Free Press, 1955.

Edgerton, Robert B. "Conceptions of Psychosis in Four East African Societies." *American Anthropologist* 68 (1966): 408–424.

Eister, Allan W. "An Outline of a Structural Theory of Cults." *Journal for the Scientific Study of Religion* 11 (4): 319–333.

Eliade, Mircea. *The Forge and the Crucible*. New York: Harper and Row, 1962.

———. *Rites and Symbols of Initiation*. New York: Harper and Row, 1958.

Ellwood, Robert S. "Notes on a Neopagan Religious Group in America." *History of Religions* 2:1 (August 1971): 125–139.

Erikson, Erik H. *Childhood and Society*. New York: Norton, 1963.

———. *Identity, Youth and Crisis*. New York: Norton, 1968.

———. *Insight and Responsibility*. New York: Norton, 1964.

———. *Young Man Luther*. New York: Norton, 1962.

———, ed. *The Challenge of Youth*. Garden City, New York: Doubleday, 1965.

Erikson, Kai T. *Wayward Puritans*. New York: Wiley, 1966.

Evans-Pritchard, E. E. *Witchcraft, Oracles, and Magic among the Azande*. New York: Oxford University Press, 1937.

Eysenck, Hans J. "The Effects of Psychotherapy." *International Journal of Psychiatry* 1 (1965): 99–144.

Faris, Robert E. L., and H. Warren Dunham. *Mental Disorders in Urban Areas*. Chicago: University of Chicago Press, 1967.

Felton, David. "The Lyman Family's Holy Siege of America." *Rolling Stone* (December 23, 1971): 40–60; (January 6, 1972): 40–60.

Festinger, Leon, H. W. Riecken, and S. Schachter. *When Prophecy Fails*. New York: Harper and Row, 1956.

Filstead, William J., ed. *Qualitative Methodology*. Chicago: Markham, 1970.

Finkel, Norman J. *Mental Illness and Health*. New York: Macmillan, 1976.

Flammonde, Paris. *The Mystic Healers*. New York: Stein and Day, 1975.

Fodor, Nandor. *Freud, Jung and Occultism*. New Hyde Park, New York: University Books, 1971.

Fogerty, Robert S., ed. *American Utopianism*. Itasca, Illinois: Peacock, 1972.

Fortune, R. F. *Sorcerers of Dobu*. New York: Dutton, 1932.

Foucault, Michel. *Madness and Civilization*. New York: Random House, 1965.

Frank, Jerome D. "The Bewildering World of Psychotherapy." *Journal of Social Issues* 28:4 (1972): 27–43.

———. *Persuasion and Healing*. New York: Schocken, 1961.

Frank, Jerome D., and Earl H. Nash. "Commitment to Peace Work." *American Journal of Orthopsychiatry* 35:106–119.

Frankl, Viktor E. *Man's Search for Meaning.* New York: Washington Square Press, 1963.

———. *Psychotherapy and Existentialism.* New York: Simon and Schuster, 1967.

Freud, Sigmund. "Analysis Terminable and Interminable." In *Therapy and Technique.* New York: Collier, 1963, pp. 233–271.

———. *Civilization and Its Discontents.* New York: Norton, (1930) 1961.

———. *The Future of an Illusion.* Garden City, New York: Doubleday, (1927) 1961.

———. *Studies in Parapsychology.* New York: Collier, 1963.

Freudenberger, Herbert J. "Staff Burn-Out." *Journal of Social Issues* 30:1 (1974):159–165.

Fuller, R. Buckminster. *I Seem to Be a Verb.* New York: Bantam Books, 1970.

———. *Operating Manual for Spaceship Earth.* New York: Pocket Books, 1970.

———. *Utopia or Oblivion.* New York: Bantam, 1969.

Gans, Herbert J. *The Urban Villagers.* New York: Free Press, 1962.

Gardner, Martin. *Fads and Fallacies in the Name of Science.* New York: Dover, 1957.

Giallombardo, Rose. *Society of Women: A Study of a Women's Prison.* New York: John Wiley and Sons, 1966.

Glaser, Barney G., and Anselm L. Strauss. *The Discovery of Grounded Theory.* Chicago: Aldine, 1967.

Glock, Charles Y., and Robert N. Bellah, eds. *The New Religious Consciousness.* Berkeley: University of California Press, 1976.

Glock, Charles Y., and Rodney Stark. *Religion and Society in Tension.* Chicago: Rand McNally, 1965.

Goffman, Erving. *Asylums: Essays on the Social Situation of Mental Patients and Other Inmates.* Garden City, New York: Anchor, 1961.

———. *Behavior in Public Places.* New York: Free Press, 1963.

———. *Encounters.* Indianapolis: Bobbs-Merrill, 1961.

———. *The Presentation of Self in Public Places.* Garden City, New York: Doubleday, 1959.

Goldhamer, Herbert, and Andrew W. Marshall. *Psychosis and Civilization.* Glencoe, Illinois: Free Press, 1953.

Gouldner, Alvin W. *Enter Plato.* New York: Harper and Row, 1971.

Granovetter, Mark. "The Strength of Weak Ties." *American Journal of*

    Sociology 68:6 (1973): 1360–1380; 80:2 (1973): 524–531.

Gritzback, Erich. *Hermann Goering: The Man and His Work*. London: Hurst and Blackett, 1939.

Gurr, Ted Robert. *Why Men Rebel*. Princeton: Princeton University Press, 1970.

Gursslin, Orville R., Raymond G. Hunt, and Jack L. Roach. "Social Class and the Mental Health Movement." *Social Problems* 7:3 (1959): 210–218.

Gusfield, Joseph R. *Symbolic Crusade*. Urbana: University of Illinois Press, 1963.

Habenstein, Robert W., ed. *Pathways to Data*. Chicago: Aldine, 1970.

Haley, Jay. *The Power Tactics of Jesus Christ*. New York: Avon, 1969.

———. *Strategies of Psychotherapy*. New York: Grune and Stratton, 1963.

Hall, Manley Palmer. *An Encyclopedic Outline of Masonic, Hermetic, Qabbalistic and Rosicrucian Symbolic Philosophy*. Los Angeles: Philosophical Research Society, (1928) 1945.

Hammett, Van Buren O. "A Consideration of Psychoanalysis in Relation to Psychiatry Generally, Circa 1965." *American Journal of Psychiatry* 122 (1965): 42–54.

Henry, Jules. *Jungle People*. New York: Vintage, (1941) 1964.

Hes, Jozef Ph. "From Native Healer to Modern Psychiatrist—Afro-Asian Immigrants to Israel and Their Attitudes towards Psychiatric Facilities." *International Journal of Social Psychiatry* 13:1 (Winter 1966–67): 21–27.

Higgins, Paul C., and Gary L. Albrecht. "Hellfire and Delinquency Revisited." *Social Forces* 55:4 (June 1977): 952–958.

Hilgard, Ernest R. "Altered States of Awareness." *Journal of Nervous and Mental Disease* 149:1 (1969): 68–79.

Hirschi, Travis. *Causes of Delinquency*. Berkeley: University of California Press, 1969.

Hirschi, Travis, and Rodney Stark. "Hellfire and Delinquency." *Social Problems* 17:2 (Fall 1969): 202–213.

Hollingshead, August B., and Frederick C. Redlich. *Social Class and Mental Illness*. New York: Wiley, 1958.

Homans, George C. *The Human Group*. New York: Harcourt, Brace and World, 1950.

———. *Social Behavior: Its Elementary Forms*. New York: Harcourt Brace Jovanovich, 1974.

Houriet, Robert. *Getting Back Together*. New York: Avon, 1972.

Howard, John R. *The Cutting Edge*. Philadelphia: Lippincott, 1974.

Huizinga, Johan. *Homo Ludens*. Boston: Beacon Press, 1950.

Iwai, Hiroshi, and David K. Reynolds. "Morita Psychotherapy: The Views from the West." *American Journal of Psychiatry* 126:7 (January 1970):1031–1036.

Johnson, Weldon T. "The Religious Crusade: Revival or Ritual?" *American Journal of Sociology* 76:5 (March 1971):873–890.

Joll, James. *The Anarchists.* Boston: Little, Brown, 1964.

Kane, Francis J., Charles D. Wallace, and Morris A. Lipton. "Emotional Disturbance Related to T-Group Experience." *American Journal of Psychiatry* 127:7 (January 1971):954–957.

Kanter, Rosabeth Moss. *Commitment and Community.* Cambridge: Harvard University Press, 1972.

Kaplan, Bert, ed. *Studying Personality Cross-Culturally.* New York: Harper and Row, 1961.

Karmel, Madeline. "Total Institution and Self-Mortification." *Journal of Health and Social Behavior* 10:2 (June 1969):134–140.

Kato, Masaaki. "Report on Psychotherapy in Japan." *International Journal of Social Psychiatry* 5:1 (Summer 1959):56–60.

Kelly, George A. *A Theory of Personality.* New York: Norton, 1963.

Keniston, Kenneth. *Young Radicals.* New York: Harcourt, Brace and World, 1968.

Kennedy, John G. "Nubian Zar Ceremonies as Psychotherapy." *Human Organization* 26:4 (Winter 1967):185–194.

Kiev, Ari. *Transcultural Psychiatry.* New York: Free Press, 1972.

———, ed. *Magic, Faith, and Healing.* New York: Free Press, 1964.

Kiev, Ari, and John L. Francis. "Sabud and Mental Illness." *American Journal of Psychotherapy* 18:1 (January 1964):66–78.

King, Francis. *Magic—The Western Tradition.* New York: Avon, 1975.

———. *The Rites of Modern Occult Magic.* New York: Macmillan, 1970.

Kornbluth, Jesse. "The Führer over EST." *New Times* (March 19, 1976): 36–52.

La Barre, Weston. *They Shall Take Up Serpents.* New York: Schocken, 1969.

Laing, R. D. *The Politics of Experience.* New York: Ballantine, 1967.

Larson, Richard F. "The Clergyman's Role in the Therapeutic Process: Disagreement between Clergymen and Psychiatrists." *Psychiatry* 31 (1968):250–263.

———. "Clerical and Psychiatric Conceptions of the Clergyman's Role in the Therapeutic Setting." *Social Problems* 11:4 (Spring 1964): 419–428.

Lederer, Wolfgang. "Primitive Psychotherapy." *Psychiatry* 22 (August 1959):255–265.

Lemert, Edwin. "Paranoia and the Dynamics of Exclusion." In *Human*

Deviance, Social Problems and Social Control. Englewood Cliffs, N.J.:
Prentice-Hall, 1967, pp. 246–264.

Lerman, Paul. "Gangs, Networks, and Subcultural Delinquency." *American Journal of Sociology* 73:1 (July 1967):63–72.

Levi, Eliphas. *Transcendental Magic.* New York: Weiser, 1974.

Lévi-Strauss, Claude. *The Elementary Structures of Kinship.* Boston: Beacon
Press, 1969.

————. *The Raw and the Cooked.* New York: Harper, 1970.

————. *The Savage Mind.* Chicago: University of Chicago Press, 1962.

————. *The Scope of Anthropology.* London: Cape, 1967.

————. *Structural Anthropology.* Garden City, New York: Doubleday,
1967.

————. *Totemism.* Boston: Beacon Press, 1962.

Lewis, I. M. *Ecstatic Religion.* Baltimore: Pelican, 1971.

Lifton, Robert Jay. "Protean Man." *Partisan Review* (Winter 1968):13–
27.

Linn, Lawrence S. "Social Identification and the Seeking of Psychiatric
Care." *American Journal of Orthopsychiatry* 38:1 (1968):83–88.

Lipset, Seymour Martin. *Rebellion in the University.* Boston: Little, Brown,
1971.

Lofland, John. *Doomsday Cult.* Englewood Cliffs, N.J.: Prentice-Hall,
1966.

Lofland, John, and Rodney Stark. "Becoming a World-Saver: A Theory of
Conversion to a Deviant Perspective." *American Sociological Review*
39:6 (1965):862–875.

Lubchansky, Isaac, Gladys Egri, and Janet Stokes. "Puerto Rican Spiritualists View Mental Illness: The Faith Healer as a Paraprofessional."
American Journal of Psychiatry 127:3 (September 1970):312–321.

Lyman, Stanford M., and Marvin B. Scott. *A Sociology of the Absurd.* New
York: Appleton-Century-Crofts, 1970.

McCall, George J., and J. L. Simmons, eds. *Issues in Participant Observation.*
Reading, Mass.: Addison-Wesley, 1969.

McIntosh, Christopher. *Eliphas Levi and the French Occult Revival.* New
York: Weiser, 1972.

MacKenzie, Norman, ed. *Secret Societies.* New York: Crescent, 1967.

Maddi, Salvatore R. *Personality Theories: A Comparative Analysis.* Homewood, Illinois: Dorsey, 1968.

Malinowski, Bronislaw. *Argonauts of the Western Pacific.* New York: Dutton, 1961.

————. *Sex and Repression in Savage Society.* New York: Meridian,
(1927) 1970.

————. *The Sexual Life of Savages.* New York: Harcourt, Brace and World, 1929.

Mannheim, Karl. *Ideology and Utopia.* New York: Harcourt, Brace and World, 1936.

Manvell, Roger, and Heinrich Fraenkel. *Goering.* New York: Simon and Schuster, 1962.

Maslow, Abraham H. *Religions, Values, and Peak-Experiences.* New York: Viking, 1970.

Matza, David. *Becoming Deviant.* Englewood Cliffs, N.J.: Prentice-Hall, 1969.

Merton, Robert K. *Social Theory and Social Structure.* New York: Free Press, 1968.

Messing, Simon D. "Group Therapy and Social Status in the Zar Cult of Ethiopia." In *Magic, Witchcraft, and Curing*, edited by John Middleton. Garden City, New York: Natural History Press, 1967, pp. 285–294.

Michael, Stanley T. "Social Class and Psychiatric Treatment." *Journal of Psychiatric Research* 5 (1967):243–254.

Milgram, Stanley. *Obedience to Authority.* New York: Harper and Row, 1974.

Moroto, Aiko. "Conditions for Accepting a New Religious Belief: A Case Study of Myochikai Members in Japan." Unpublished Master's Thesis in Sociology, University of Washington, Seattle, 1976.

Mueller, Claus. "Notes on the Repression of Communicative Behavior." In *Recent Sociology No. 2*, edited by Hans Peter Dreitzel. New York: Macmillan, 1970, pp. 101–114.

Muensterberger, Warner, ed. *Man and His Culture: Psychoanalytic Anthropology after "Totem and Taboo."* New York: Taplinger, 1969.

Natanson, Maurice. *The Journeying Self.* Reading, Mass.: Addison-Wesley, 1970.

Newman, Ernest. *Wagner as Man and Artist.* New York: Knopf, 1924.

Nicholi, Armand M. "Harvard Dropouts: Some Psychiatric Findings." *American Journal of Psychiatry* 124:5 (November 1967):651–658.

Niebuhr, H. Richard. *The Social Sources of Denominationalism.* Cleveland: Meridian Books, 1929 (1957).

Nietzsche, Friedrich. *The Birth of Tragedy.* New York: Random House, (1872) 1967.

Nisbet, Robert A. *The Quest for Community.* London: Oxford University Press, 1953.

Opler, Marvin K., ed. *Culture and Mental Health.* New York: Macmillan, 1959.

Pande, Shashi K. "The Mystique of 'Western' Psychotherapy: An Eastern
        Interpretation." *The Journal of Nervous and Mental Disease* 146:6
        (June 1968): 425–432.

Papanek, Victor. *Design for the Real World*. New York: Bantam, 1972.

Parsons, Talcott. "Mental Illness and 'Spiritual Malaise': The Role of the
        Psychiatrist and of the Minister of Religion." In *Social Structure and
        Personality*. New York: Free Press, 1964, pp. 292–324.

Patrick, Ted, and Tom Dulack. *Let Our Children Go!* New York: Ballan-
        tine, 1976.

Pauwels, Louis, and Jacques Bergier. *The Morning of the Magicians*. New
        York: Avon, 1968.

Payne, Barbara P., and Kirk W. Elifson. "Commitment: A Comment on
        Uses of the Concept." *Review of Religious Research* 17 (3): 209–215.

Perls, Frederick, Ralph F. Hefferline, and Paul Goodman. *Gestalt Therapy*.
        New York: Dell, 1951.

Peters, Victor. *All Things Common*. New York: Harper, 1965.

Peterson, Severin. *A Catalog of the Ways People Grow*. New York: Ballan-
        tine, 1971.

Polsky, Ned. *Hustlers, Beats, and Others*. Garden City, New York: Double-
        day, 1969.

Pratt, William F. "The Anabaptist Explosion." *Natural History* (February
        1969): 6–23.

Procopius. *The Secret History*. Baltimore: Penguin, 1966.

Quarantelli, E. L., and Dennis Wenger. "A Voice from the Thirteenth
        Century: The Characteristics and Conditions for the Emergence of
        a Ouija Board Cult." In *Deviance: Action, Reaction, Interaction*, edit-
        ed by Frank R. Scarpitti and Paul T. McFarlane. Reading, Mass.:
        Addison-Wesley, (1973) 1975, pp. 143–157.

Quitkin, Frederic M., and Donald F. Klein. "Follow-Up of Treatment
        Failure: Psychosis and Character Disorder." *American Journal of Psy-
        chiatry* 124:4 (1967): 499–505.

Rabkin, Richard. *Inner and Outer-Space—Introduction to a Theory of Social
        Psychiatry*. New York: Norton, 1970.

———. "Is the Unconscious Necessary?" *American Journal of Psychiatry*
        125:3 (September 1968): 313–319.

Rachman, Stanley. *The Effects of Psychotherapy*. Oxford: Pergamon, 1971.

Regardie, Israel. *My Rosicrucian Adventure*. St. Paul, Minn.: Llewellyn
        Publications, 1971.

Rieff, Philip. *The Triumph of the Therapeutic*. New York: Harper and Row,
        1966.

Riesman, David. *The Lonely Crowd.* New Haven: Yale University Press, 1961.

Riessman, Frank, Jerome Cohen, and Arthur Pearl, eds. *Mental Health of the Poor.* New York: Free Press, 1964.

Rinder, Irwin D. "New Directions and an Old Problem: The Definition of Normality." *Psychiatry* 27 (1964): 107.

Roberts, Ron E. *The New Communes.* Englewood Cliffs, N.J.: Prentice-Hall, 1971.

Rogler, Lloyd H., and August B. Hollingshead. "The Puerto Rican Spiritualist as a Psychiatrist." *American Journal of Sociology* 67: 1 (July 1961): 17.

Roheim, Geza. *Magic and Schizophrenia.* Bloomington: Indiana University Press, 1955.

Rosen, George. *Madness in Society.* New York: Harper and Row, 1968.

Rosenfeld, Edward. *The Book of Highs.* New York: Quadrangle, 1973.

Roszak, Theodore. *The Making of a Counter Culture.* Garden City, New York: Anchor, 1969.

Rothman, David J. *The Discovery of the Asylum.* Boston: Little, Brown, 1971.

Rousseau, Jean-Jacques. *The Social Contract.* Baltimore: Penguin, 1968.

Rowden, David W., Jerry B. Michel, Ronald C. Dillehay, and Harry W. Martin. "Judgments about Candidates for Psychotherapy: The Influence of Social Class and Insight-Verbal Ability." *Journal of Health and Social Behavior* 11:1 (March 1970): 51–58.

Salter, Andrew. *The Case Against Psychoanalysis.* New York: Harper and Row (1952) 1972.

Sandifer, Myron G., Anthony Horden, Gerald C. Timbury, and Linda M. Green. "Similarities and Differences in Patient Evaluation by U.S. and U.K. Psychiatrists." *American Journal of Psychiatry* 126:2 (August 1969): 206–212.

Sargant, William. *Battle for the Mind.* New York: Harper and Row, 1971.

Scheff, Thomas. *Being Mentally Ill.* Chicago: Aldine, 1966.

Schein, Edgar H., and Warren G. Bennis. *Personal and Organizational Change through Group Methods.* New York: Wiley, 1965.

Schleiermacher, Friedrich. *On Religion.* New York: Harper and Row, (1799) 1958.

Schmeidler, Gertrude, ed. *Extrasensory Perception.* New York: Atherton, 1969.

Schofield, William. *Psychotherapy: The Purchase of Friendship.* Englewood Cliffs, N.J.: Prentice-Hall, 1964.

Schutz, Alfred. "On Multiple Realities." In *Collected Papers.* The Hague: Nijhoff, 1971, Volume I, pp. 207–259.

Seitz, Philip F. D. "ESP-Like Experiences in a Psychoanalyst: A Possible Psychological Mechanism." *Psychoanalysis and Contemporary Science* 4 (1975): 189–209.

Shapiro, David. *Neurotic Styles.* New York: Basic Books, 1965.

Shupe, Anson D. " 'Disembodied Access' and Technological Constraints on Organizational Development: A Study of Mail-Order Religions." *Journal for the Scientific Study of Religion* 15:2 (1976): 177–185.

Silverman, Julian. "Shamans and Acute Schizophrenia." *American Anthropologist* 69 (1967): 21–31.

Simmel, Georg. *Conflict and the Web of Group-Affiliations.* New York: Free Press, 1955.

———. *The Sociology of Georg Simmel.* Edited by Kurt H. Wolff. New York: Free Press, 1950.

Sjoberg, Gideon, ed. *Ethics, Politics, and Social Research.* Cambridge, Mass.: Schenkman, 1967.

Slater, Philip. *The Pursuit of Loneliness.* Boston: Beacon Press, 1970.

Smelser, Neil J. *Theory of Collective Behavior.* New York: Free Press, 1962.

Snell, John E. "Hypnosis in the Treatment of the 'Hexed' Patient." *American Journal of Psychiatry* 124:3 (September 1967): 311–316.

Sobel, B. Z. *Hebrew Christianity: The Thirteenth Tribe.* New York: Wiley, 1974.

Sommer, Robert. "Some Costs and Pitfalls in Field Research." *Social Problems* 19:2 (Fall 1971): 162–166.

Spence, Lewis. *An Encyclopaedia of Occultism.* New Hyde Park, New York: University Books, 1960.

Spraggett, Allen. *Kathryn Kuhlman: The Woman Who Believes in Miracles.* New York: World, 1970.

Sprague, W. D. *Case Histories from the Communes.* New York: Lancer, 1972.

Srole, Leo, Thomas S. Langner, Stanley T. Michael, Marvin K. Opler, and Thomas A. C. Rennie. *Mental Health in the Metropolis.* New York: McGraw-Hill, 1962.

Stark, Rodney. "Psychopathology and Religious Commitment." *Review of Religious Research* 12:3 (1971): 165–176.

Stewart, Kilton. "Dream Theory in Malaya." In *Altered States of Consciousness*, edited by Charles T. Tart. New York: Wiley, 1969, pp. 159–167.

Stone, Walter N., and Murray E. Tieger. "Screening for T-Groups: The

Myth of Healthy Candidates." *American Journal of Psychiatry* 127: 11 (May 1971): 1485–1590.

Strauss, Anselm, Leonard Schatzman, Rue Bucher, Danuta Ehrlich, and Melvin Sabshin. *Psychiatric Ideologies and Institutions.* New York: Free Press, 1964.

Stuart, Richard B. *Trick or Treatment: How and When Psychotherapy Fails.* Champaign, Illinois: Research Press, 1970.

Sutherland, Edwin H. *On Analyzing Crime.* Chicago: University of Chicago Press, (1942–1947) 1973.

Swanson, Guy E. "Monotheism, Materialism, and Collective Purpose: An Analysis of Underhill's Correlation." *American Journal of Sociology* 80:4 (January 1975): 862–869.

Symonds, John. *The Magic of Aleister Crowley.* London: Muller, 1958.

Szasz, Thomas S. *The Manufacture of Madness.* New York: Harper and Row, 1970.

————. *The Myth of Mental Illness.* New York: Delta, 1961.

Tart, Charles T., ed. *Altered States of Consciousness.* New York: Wiley, 1969.

Taselle, Sallie, ed. *The Family, Communes and Utopian Societies.* New York: Harper and Row, 1972.

Thompson, Hunter S. *Hell's Angels.* New York: Ballantine, 1967.

Thrasher, Frederic M. *The Gang.* Chicago: University of Chicago Press, 1927.

Tiryakian, Edward A. "Toward the Sociology of Esoteric Culture." *American Journal of Sociology* 78:3 (November 1972): 491–512.

Toch, Hans. *The Social Psychology of Social Movements.* Indianapolis: Bobbs-Merrill, 1965.

Torrey, E. Fuller. "What Western Psychotherapists Can Learn from Witchdoctors." *American Journal of Orthopsychiatry* 42:1 (January 1972): 69–76.

Underhill, Ralph. "Economic and Political Antecedents of Monotheism: A Cross-cultural Study." *American Journal of Sociology* 80:4 (January 1975): 841–861.

Van Gennep, Arnold. *The Rites of Passage.* Chicago: University of Chicago Press, 1959.

Vogt, Evon Z. *The Zinacantecos of Mexico: A Modern Maya Way of Life.* New York: Holt, Rinehart and Winston, 1970.

Wallace, Anthony F. C. "Dreams and the Wishes of the South: A Type of Psychoanalytic Theory among the Seventeenth-Century Iroquois." In *Magic, Witchcraft, and Curing*, edited by John Middleton. Garden City, New York: Natural History Press, 1967, pp. 171–190.

———. "The Institutionalization of Cathartic and Control Strategies in Iroquois Religious Psychotherapy." In *Culture and Mental Health*, edited by Marvin K. Opler. New York: Macmillan, 1959, pp. 63–96.

———. "Revitalization Movements." *American Anthropologist* 58:2 (1956):264–281.

Walzer, Michael. "Puritanism as a Revolutionary Ideology." In *Studies in Social Movements*, edited by Barry McLaughlin. New York: Free Press, (1963) 1969, pp. 118–154.

Watts, Alan W. *Psychotherapy East and West*. New York: Ballantine, 1961.

Wax, Murray L. "Tenting with Malinowski." *American Sociological Review* 37:1 (February 1972):1–13.

Wax, Rosalie H. *Doing Fieldwork*. Chicago: University of Chicago Press, 1971.

Webb, Eugene J., Donald T. Campbell, Richard D. Schwartz, and Lee Sechrest. *Unobtrusive Measures: Nonreactive Research in the Social Sciences*. Chicago: Rand McNally, 1966.

Weber, Max. *The Protestant Ethic and the Spirit of Capitalism*. New York: Scribner's, 1958.

———. *The Sociology of Religion*. Boston: Beacon Press, (1922) 1963.

Weil, Andrew. *The Natural Mind*. Boston: Houghton Mifflin, 1972.

Weintraub, Walter, and H. Aronson. "A Survey of Patients in Classical Psychoanalysis: Some Vital Statistics." *Journal of Nervous and Mental Disease* 146:2 (1968):98–102.

Whitaker, Dorothy Stock, and Morton A. Lieberman. *Psychotherapy through the Group Process*. New York: Atherton, 1964.

White, Harrison C., Scott A. Boorman, and Ronald L. Breiger. "Social Structure from Multiple Networks." *American Journal of Sociology* 81:4 (1976):730–780.

Whitworth, John McKelvie. *God's Blueprints*. London: Routledge and Kegan Paul, 1975.

Whyte, William Foote. *Street Corner Society*. Chicago: University of Chicago Press, 1943.

Wieder, D. Lawrence, and Don H. Zimmerman. "Generational Experience and the Development of Freak Culture." *Journal of Social Issues* 30:2 (1974):137–161.

Wilson, Robert Ward. "A Social-Psychological Study of Religious Experience with Special Emphasis on Christian Conversion." Unpublished doctoral dissertation, University of Florida, 1976.

Winnicott, D. W. *Playing and Reality*. New York: Basic Books, 1971.

Winter, Gibson. *The Suburban Captivity of the Churches*. New York: Macmillan, 1962.

Wolfe, Tom. *The Electric Kool-Aid Acid Test*. New York: Bantam, 1969.

Wolpe, Joseph, and Stanley Rachman. "Psychoanalytic 'Evidence': A Critique Based on Freud's Case of Little Hans." *Journal of Nervous and Mental Disease* 130 (1960): 135–148.

Wuthnow, Robert. *The Consciousness Reformation*. Berkeley: University of California Press, 1976.

Yablonsky, Lewis. *The Violent Gang*. Baltimore: Penguin, 1970.

Young, Michael, and Peter Willmott. *Family and Kinship in East London*. Baltimore: Penguin, 1957.

Zablocki, Benjamin. *The Joyful Community*. Baltimore: Penguin, 1971.

Zweig, Stefan. *Mental Healers*. New York: Ungar, (1932) 1972.

INDEX